CASES IN CORPORATE FINANCE

Cases in Corporate Finance includes 60 unique case studies that illustrate the application of finance theories, models, and frameworks to real-life business situations. The topics cover a wide range of sectors and different life cycle stages of firms. The book bridges a crucial gap in topical emerging market case coverage by presenting industry-relevant case studies in the Indian context and on themes pertinent to the current business environment.

Through the case studies included in the book, the authors offer insights into the essential areas of corporate finance, including risk and return, working capital management, capital budgeting and structure, dividend decisions, business valuation, and long-term financing. Cases included in the book are decision-focused and provide opportunities to carefully analyse risk-return trade-offs and apply tools to evaluate critical financial decisions.

The book will be helpful for students, researchers, and instructors of business management, commerce, and economics.

Mayank Joshipura is a Professor of Finance, Associate Dean-Research, and Chairperson of the Ph.D. programme at the School of Business Management, NMIMS Deemed to be University, Mumbai. He holds a Ph.D. and an MBA in Finance and a Bachelor of Engineering degree in Power Electronics. He attended and completed a certificate programme on "Creating Value through Financial Management" from the Wharton Business School, USA, and the Glocoll progamme from Harvard Business School, USA. He has two and half decades of experience in management education, research, and consulting.

Sachin Mathur is Associate Professor, Finance, at the School of Business Management, NMIMS Deemed to be University, Mumbai. He holds an MMS degree and a Ph.D. from NMIMS, Mumbai and a Bachelor of Technology degree in Chemical Engineering from Institute of Technology, BHU, Varanasi. He has over 15 years of industry experience including as Head of Research at CRISIL Ltd. He is a CFA charter holder.

CASES IN CORPORATE FINANCE

Mayank Joshipura and Sachin Mathur

LONDON AND NEW YORK

Designed cover image: © Getty Images

First published 2024
by Routledge
4 Park Square, Milton Park, Abingdon, Oxon OX14 4RN

and by Routledge
605 Third Avenue, New York, NY 10158

Routledge is an imprint of the Taylor & Francis Group, an informa business

© 2024 Mayank Joshipura and Sachin Mathur

The right of Mayank Joshipura and Sachin Mathur to be identified as authors of this work has been asserted in accordance with sections 77 and 78 of the Copyright, Designs and Patents Act 1988.

All rights reserved. No part of this book may be reprinted or reproduced or utilised in any form or by any electronic, mechanical, or other means, now known or hereafter invented, including photocopying and recording, or in any information storage or retrieval system, without permission in writing from the publishers.

Trademark notice: Product or corporate names may be trademarks or registered trademarks, and are used only for identification and explanation without intent to infringe.

British Library Cataloguing-in-Publication Data
A catalogue record for this book is available from the British Library

ISBN: 978-1-032-60115-1 (hbk)
ISBN: 978-1-032-72448-5 (pbk)
ISBN: 978-1-032-72447-8 (ebk)

DOI: 10.4324/9781032724478

Typeset in Sabon
by Deanta Global Publishing Services, Chennai, India

CONTENTS

EXHIBITS

ACKNOWLEDGEMENTS

We owe our gratitude to many people for enabling us to write and enrich this book. Indeed, this work would not have been possible without their contribution and support. Many of the cases were developed while teaching our courses along with our colleagues, and we would like to acknowledge the intellectual inputs and feedback received from them. We also thank the NMIMS University for allowing us to use the library and its other resources to complete our work. Several academicians from other institutions and other professionals too helped us with their valuable suggestions.

More specifically, we would like to thank the following persons for their inputs, suggestions, feedback, and support: Dr Ramesh Bhat, Dr Chandan Dasgupta, Dr Smita Mazumdar, Dr Sangeeta Wats, Dr Sudhanshu Pani, Dr Anupam Rastogi, Dr Paritosh Basu, Dr Ranjan Chakravarty, Dr Samveg Patel, Dr Durgesh Tinaikar, Dr Nehal Joshipura, Dr Tanushree Mazumdar, Dr Vasant Sivaraman, Dr Suresh Lalwani, and Prof. Prem Chandrani.

We are thankful to the entire team at Routledge for the timely completion of this project. We take this opportunity to acknowledge the contributions of our students in shaping our thought process over the years and in having inspired us to write this book to share our thoughts with the learners.

Finally, we thank our family members for their unconditional support, constant encouragement, and allowing us spare time to use productively during the challenging Covid-19 lockdowns.

Mayank Joshipura
Sachin Mathur

ABBREVIATIONS

AC	Asbestos cement
ACES	Autonomous vehicles, connected vehicles, electrification, and shared mobility
ACMA	Automobile Component Manufacturers Association
AGM	Annual general body meeting
AGR	Adjusted gross revenue
ARPU	Average revenue per user
ARR	Average revenue per room
ASBA	Application supported by blocked amount
ASL	Avenue Supermarts Ltd
AT1	Additional Tier-1
BAL	Bharti Airtel Ltd
BCBS	Basel Committee on Banking Supervision
BCG	Boston Consulting Group
BEV	Battery-operated vehicle
BRLM	Book running lead managers
C&W	Cables and wires
CAGR	Compounded annual growth rate
CAPM	Capital asset pricing model
CAR	Capital adequacy ratio
CCI	Competition Commission of India
CEO	Chief executive officer
CFO	Chief financial officer
CFROI	Cash flow return on investment
CMO	Chief marketing officer

COCO	Company-owned company-operated
CoCos	Contingent convertible capital instruments
COGS	Cost of goods sold
CR	Conversion ratio
CUF	Capacity utilisation factor
CVA	Cash value added
CY	Calendar year
DCF	Discounted cash flow
DDM	Dividend discount model
DDT	Dividend distribution tax
DMA	Definitive merger agreement
DoT	Department of Telecommunications
E&P	Exploration and production
EBOs	Exclusive brands outlets
ECB	External commercial borrowings
EDLC/EDLP	Everyday low cost/everyday low price
EPS	Earnings per share
ESG	Environment, social, and governance
ETF	Exchange-traded fund
EVA	Economic value added
EVs	Electric vehicles
F&B	Food and beverage
FAME	Faster Adoption and Manufacturing of Electric Vehicles
FCCB	Foreign currency convertible bonds
FMEG	Fast-moving electrical goods
FPO	Follow-on-public offer
FTA	Foreign tourist arrivals
GDP	Gross domestic product
GDRs	Global depository receipts
GESCO	Great Eastern Shipping Company
GFC	Global financial crisis
GFS	Governance-for-Stakeholders
GMP	Grey market premium
GMV	Gross merchandise value
GNP	Gross non-performing assets
GoI	Government of India
GRM	Gross refining margin
GST	Goods and services tax
HPY	Holding period yield
ICEVs	Integral combustion engine vehicles
InvIT	Infrastructure investment trusts
IPL	Indian Premier League
IPO	Initial public offer

IRR	Internal rate of return
IT	Information technology
ITSL	IDBI Trusteeship Services Ltd
KMBL	Kotak Mahindra Bank Ltd
KMFL	Kotak Mahindra Finance Ltd
LCVs	Light commercial vehicles
LIBOR	London Interbank Offer Rate
LIC	Life Insurance Corporation
LTCG	Long-term capital gains
M&M	Mahindra and Mahindra Ltd
MDP	Management development programme
MHCVs	Medium and heavy commercial vehicles
MM	Modigliani and Miller
MMDR	Mines and Minerals (Development and Regulation) Act
MPT	Modern portfolio theory
MTPA	Million tonnes per annum
NAVs	Net asset values
NBFC	Non-banking finance company
NCDs	Non-convertible debentures
NII	Non-institutional investor
NIM	Net interest margin
NPV	Net present value
NSE	National Stock Exchange
NSM	National sales manager
O2C	Oil-to-chemicals
ODI	Overseas direct investments
OEMs	Original equipment manufacturers
OFS	Offer for sale
OTT	Over-the-top
PE	Private equity
PGCIL	Power Grid Corporation Ltd
PIPE	Private equity in public enterprise
PONV	Point of non-viability
PSB	Public sector bank
PUTL	Power Grid Unchahar Transmission Ltd
QARP	Quality at a reasonable price
QIB	Qualified institutional bidder
QIP	Qualified institutional placement
R&D	Research and development
R&M	Refining and marketing
RACs	Room air conditioners
RBI	Reserve Bank of India
RE	Rights entitlements

REVPaR	Revenue-per-available-room
RIA	Registered Investment Advisor
RII	Retail individual investor
RIL	Reliance Industries Ltd
ROCE	Return on capital employed
ROE	Return on equity
ROIC	Return on invested capital
RTA	Registrar and transfer agent
RTO	Regional Transport Office
RWN	Rating watch negative
SC	Supreme Court
SEBI	Securities and Exchange Board of India
SEZs	Special economic zones
SOTP	Sum-of-the-parts
SSSG	Same-store sales growth
TIL	Tata International Limited
UPI	Unified payment interface
VC	Venture capital
WACC	Weighted average cost of capital
WDV	Written-down value
YTC	Yield-to-call
YTM	Yield-to-maturity

INTRODUCTION

Participant-centered learning has emerged as a superior method of teaching–learning over conventional teaching. 360-degree active learning, where participants learn from the instructor and fellow participants, enhances their learning experience. The instructor's role in such a learning approach is that of facilitator. Participant-centered learning emphasises the process of discovery rather than the dissemination of knowledge. It focuses on skill building (How to do?) rather than simply imparting knowledge (What to do?). The use of cases in management education, especially with a decision focus pioneered by Harvard Business School in the early 20th century, has become the focus of management education. A case with a decision focus in which the protagonist faces the dilemma of choosing between alternative courses of action, with limited information and time on hand, is considered a potent learning instrument. The case discussion forces participants into the protagonist's shoes, who can be entrepreneurs, managers, analysts, investors, etc. Case discussion has emerged as a powerful tool for learning concepts, theories, and frameworks and applying them to solve real-life business problems.

Top business schools offering MBA or PGDM in India have adopted case-based teaching over several decades. However, most business schools and undergraduate management and commerce colleges have not adopted a participant-centered learning model and continue to follow the conventional method of lecturing to impart knowledge. This deprives participants of the joy of active learning and participation in discovering and building skills to apply models and frameworks in solving real-life problems.

We have taught in MBA and Executive Education programmes at leading business schools in India and have used various case studies over the years.

DOI: 10.4324/9781032724478-1

We noticed that good case studies written in the Indian context and relevant in the present times are short in supply. Some cases are too long, dated, and not written in the Indian context, while others are mere discussion cases. In addition, management cases from best-case publishing houses are costly and beyond the budget of most colleges offering programmes in management and commerce. This book bridges this gap by providing a wide variety of right-sized, decision-focused finance cases written in the most recent setting. These cases can be used in various courses such as Financial Management, Corporate Finance, Strategic Financial Management, Advanced Financial Management, and Business Valuation.

Since the dawn of the 21st century, the finance function has gained strategic significance and has emerged from the accounting shadow. The role of finance in creating value for stakeholders is well-known. Raising, deploying, and managing funds offers opportunities to create value for stakeholders at each stage. Critical financial decisions, such as working capital management, capital budgeting, capital structure, and dividend payout, require careful analysis of risk-return trade-offs and far-reaching consequences. While decisions are tagged as good or bad with the benefit of hindsight, using the right frameworks and models helps connect the dots between seemingly unrelated pieces of information, facilitating informed and better decision-making. Given the VUCA world and the globalised nature of businesses, financial risk management has become central to the success of any business organisation. To cover all dimensions of financial decision-making, we divided the books' cases into six parts. These cases cover a full spectrum of industries and the life cycle of firms.

The first part illustrates working capital management decisions. Most companies find it essential to manage their working capital well because it affects returns, growth, and risk. Efficient management of stocks and trade receivables can lead to a shorter operating cycle, faster asset turnover, and higher return on capital. However, a lack of working capital funds can affect business growth. An aggressive financing policy may increase the liquidity risk.

A company's working capital need depends on the nature of its business and the business conditions. A high-growth company requires more working capital than a stable-growth company. A company facing seasonal demand requires variable working capital throughout the year. Receivables and stocks may build up rapidly when a company encounters an unexpected slowdown in sales.

Companies use suppliers' credit and other current liabilities to fund their working capital needs. They can bridge the remaining working capital gap with retained profits and external sources such as cash credit, overdraft facilities, working capital demand loans, commercial papers, factoring, and letters of credit. Companies may also fund a part of the working capital gap using long-term sources, such as term loans or equity capital. Companies must also manage the various market and credit risks associated with working capital.

Working capital policy decisions, operating, and financing can affect funding needs. They may also impact the trade-off between returns and growth or between returns and risk. Liberal credit terms, for example, can accelerate sales growth but lengthen operating cycles. Similarly, excessive reliance on short-term loans may temporarily reduce the cost of funds but increase liquidity risk.

Working capital decisions affect a company's financial health. Managers use financial ratios to compare the performance of their companies with past trends and peers. They usually prepare forecasts for financial planning and cash budgets to estimate the required short-term funds. They also use scenarios to assess the impact of policy decisions on operating cycles, returns, financing, and liquidity. The first 11 cases cover the main aspects of working capital management in various business situations. They explain companies' challenges with high growth, cyclical or seasonal demand, and demand shocks. These cases discuss various financing alternatives for working capital and trade finance. They provide opportunities to assess working capital requirements, prepare cash budgets, recommend credit policy decisions, analyse financial ratios, prepare long-term forecasts, and evaluate the creditworthiness of companies.

In the second part, we include cases that address long-term investment decisions. Long-term investment is essential for business growth. Through proper evaluation, managers can select projects that enhance the value of the company. Conversely, poorly selected projects may fail to recover the opportunity costs of investment. Constraints and risks play significant roles in such decisions.

Companies tend to use various investment criteria when choosing projects. Net present value (NPV) is the preferred method for project selection. The NPV method involves discounting relevant cash flows at an appropriate rate, covering the opportunity costs of money and risk. This is also consistent with the maximisation of shareholder wealth. However, despite the known limitations of these techniques, companies often use the internal rate of return, payback period, and even book rates of return.

Cases 12–21 cover a variety of investment situations. The cases allow the application of proper criteria and estimates of cash flows and discount rates. Managers must choose the correct technique and discount rate, evaluate a replacement project considering only incremental cash flows, and choose a suitable evaluation criterion when comparing mutually exclusive projects, particularly for projects that differ in size and duration. Managers often make capital budget decisions under uncertainty. Tools to handle uncertainty include sensitivity analysis, scenario analysis, simulation, decision-tree analysis, and real options. Some cases have covered the application of such tools.

In the third part, we cover risk and return, and cost of capital. The two pillars of corporate finance decisions are the time value of money, risk, and returns. We know that Rs 100 now is not worth the same tomorrow due to inflation; hence, we must make the necessary adjustments to nominal cash flows to account for the time value of money. In addition, there are instances where we need to forecast future cash flows to arrive at a decision, and in the absence of a crystal ball, we need to account for the rise in cash flows. Therefore, the concept of the time value of money and adjusting cash flows to account for inflation and riskiness is central to corporate finance. It is the foundation of stock and bond valuation, the evaluation of capital budgeting proposals, and business valuation. Making personal finance decisions, such as calculating life value and buying a life insurance policy annuity for retirement, is equally important.

While most of us may associate risk with adverse outcomes and tend to avoid them, that is not true. Risk has two dimensions. On the one hand, it offers opportunities; on the other, it may lead to adverse outcomes. Therefore, strategic risk-taking and identifying, measuring, and mitigating undesirable risks are critical for a business's success. We know that all decisions are about risk-return trade-offs, and one would expect a positive reward for assuming greater risk. The relationship between risk and expected returns should be positive to this extent. However, the portion of the total risk is diversifiable, called unsystematic risk; hence, no reward is attached. Therefore, one should expect a reward for assuming a non-diversifiable component and systematic risk.

As they say, do not keep all the eggs in one basket. The identification and measurement of risk is the first step in managing it. Risk is measured using the variance of the standard deviation of cash flows or returns and calculated using the beta that measures the sensitivity of a firm's or its stock's return to a well-diversified benchmark portfolio. The higher the systematic risk, the higher the required return. From the investors' perspective, the required return rate is the capital cost. Why? Because a firm primarily uses two sources of funds, debt and equity (or some hybrid variant), investors providing money to a firm take a risk and hence seek a reward commensurate with the risk they take. The higher the business and financial risks, the higher the return investors require. Most businesses differ in multiple aspects: industry, industry life cycle, capital intensity, competitive position, etc. They are financed differently; hence, investors require different returns from different firms, and each firm has a different cost of capital. Similarly, if a firm has multiple businesses within a given firm, different divisions have different costs, and even different projects may have different degrees of risk. Hence, the cost of capital for such a project will differ from that of the firm itself.

A correct estimate of the cost of capital is crucial for a firm in several ways. For example, choose an appropriate discount rate to evaluate a capital budgeting proposal, evaluate a potential acquisition target, or design a performance measurement and reward system for managers based on measures such as economic value added (EVA). There are several approaches to measuring both the costs of debt and equity. Estimating a firm's cost of capital requires several inputs. While estimating a listed firm's capital cost is relatively easy, it is challenging for a private firm, start-up and division, or specific project. Cases 22–33 are divided into three major buckets: five on the Application of Time Value of Money and Risk and Return. The following five cases are related to the Cost of Capital, and the last two are related to risk management.

In the fourth part, we deal with capital structure and dividend decisions – two topics that are central to financial theory and its implication for financial strategy. Interest interplay between many factors and multiple perspectives drives capital structure decisions. Modigliani and Miller's propositions provide a theoretical foundation when they state that capital structure is irrelevant, given certain assumptions, such as the absence of taxes. As we relax our premises, we add more branches to our understanding. We add taxes, distress costs, agency costs, signalling, financial slack, and equity dilution; the list of factors continues to increase.

Instead of unifying the theory, we obtain multiple explanations. We may expect firms to aim for optimal capital structures that balance their distress costs against interest tax savings, but we observe different behaviours. While some firms target an optimal capital structure, others have zero debt, while others are aggressively debt-laden. We need a layered understanding: we must consider the life cycle, growth pattern, industry environment, and business conditions of each company.

Likewise, our understanding must be grounded in Modigliani and Miller's proposition of homemade dividends for investors' payout decisions, dividends, and share buybacks. Once again, they try to convince us that the dividend decision is irrelevant and to counter them, we must challenge their assumptions. In this process, we grew our list of the many factors determining payouts. An exhaustive list of factors in the standard boilerplate dividend distribution policy of any Indian company can be found in its annual report. However, we encounter different behaviours that need explanation once we observe what management does and does not say.

Managers, investors, and creditors may disagree with the appropriate policies for debt and payouts. Financial strategy is not divorced from business; it is nested within business strategy. Therefore, managers often try to convince investors, creditors, analysts, and credit-rating agencies of their strategic imperatives. On the other hand, creditors emphasise prudence and conservatism. Shareholders press managers to align their interests with those of the investors. We must examine the companies' structure, payouts, and capital allocation from these multiple perspectives.

Where should we look at the gap between theory and practice? A good starting point is a company's financial statement. Interpreting solvency and liquidity ratios from the balance sheet can be achieved through practice. We can compare dividend ratios across periods and among peers. If the balance sheet best depicts the capital structure, income statement, and dividend policy, we must turn the page to the cash flow statement to understand capital allocation. To gain a complete understanding, we must complement financial analysis with an analysis of the business situation and the firm's strategies. Cases 34–40 in this module address the gap between the theory and practice of capital structure and payout decisions. They introduce ideas, demonstrate the many factors at play, and narrate how managers encounter real business challenges beyond the textbook.

In the fifth part, we cover Business Valuation, a critical and complex task in modern finance. One may need to value a business to raise funds and obtain an investor on board for a merger or acquisition transaction. While there are well-laid frameworks and models to value private and public firms, none provides a sure-shot answer. Prof. Aswath Damodaran[1] describes valuation as a craft. He says that valuation is neither science nor art. The principles of science, such as physics and chemistry are precise and universally applicable. However, the same is not valid for valuation models. There are three popular business valuation models: discounted cash flow, relative valuation, and contingent claim valuation (option valuation). None of these approaches is an exception. Exceptions are the rule rather than the exception of valuation models.

On the other hand, valuation is not art; it is not like music or painting. If one is born gifted, it is not easy to excel. Value is not related to creativity. The valuation is more like a craft, like a sculptor making sculptures or statues. Everyone has these tools, but only a few can use them to give meaning to a piece of stone. Purposeful practice is the mantra to hone the craft of business valuations. This involves matching numbers with a story. Inputs about profitability, growth, risk, and reinvestment requirements are crucial to a business's value. One's valuation depends on one's version of the story about the business. Hence, two individuals might value the same business differently if their story about how it would evolve differs. Valuation depends on the industry in which the business operates, the industry life cycle, the industry's competitive landscape, the regulatory environment, the business cycle, and many more. To this end, valuation becomes multidisciplinary. One must understand the business model and industry dynamics to value a business. Cases 41–52 focus on business valuation, ranging from the valuation of public and private companies in different sectors and stages of the life cycle. It also covers cases of economic value-added (EVA) and the analysis and valuation of the employee stock options (ESOPs).

Financial management involves three significant steps: raising, deploying, and managing funds. The sixth part, covers raising long-term funds, which is important because it impacts a firm's capital and capital structure. Private and public firms require long-term funds to fund investment opportunities to seek organic growth or growth through acquisitions. While firms can rely on retained earnings as an internal equity financing source, they are often sufficient to finance available investment opportunities. Firms in financial distress must rely only on external sources of funds. The firm has to make several decisions while raising long-term financing: equity, debt, or hybrid securities; raising funds in domestic markets or tapping global markets; raising funds in domestic currency or foreign currency; and so on. Several factors drive a firm's choice, including the life cycle stage of the firm, industry, size, market conditions, regulatory constraints, creditworthiness, prevailing tax regime, and accounting standards. For instance, in the early stages of its life cycle, a firm relies on Angel Investors, Crowd Funding, Venture Capital Financing, and Private Equity and then goes for an Initial Public Offer (IPO) and looks for Private Equity in Public Enterprise (PIPE), Follow-on-Public Offer (FPO), and Rights Issue as a source of external equity as a listed entity.

The choice of instrument, currency, market, and mode of issuance are critical factors that directly affect firms' cost of capital, capital structure, credit rating, and ability to raise funds in the future. As a result, innovative financing can be a source of competitive advantage for a firm and provide an edge over its competitors. Cases 53–60 facilitate discussions on various sources of long-term funds. It covers IPO and IPO processes, Rights Issues, Foreign Currency Convertible Bonds (FCCB), Hybrid Securities, Start-up Financing, Acquisition Financing, Project Financing, and Infrastructure Investment Trusts (InvIT).

The authors have written the cases in this book to facilitate decision-making perspectives and not to reflect on effective or ineffective decision-making. The cases include a mix of business situations that the authors have created and business situations based on actual companies. The authors have used business situations of actual companies to help illustrate the application of corporate finance concepts in the real world and have used only publicly available information, including management comments or quotes, with sources mentioned. The third-party protagonists, wherever mentioned, have all been created by the authors to bring an external perspective, and do not represent any specific person or organisation.

The bouquet of 60 cases encompassing the entire range of financial decisions and relevant topics will help postgraduate and undergraduate management and commerce college instructors to implement the participant-centred learning model in their classrooms. We offer necessary support to instructors by providing case analysis, Excel spreadsheets, teaching plans, assignment questions, and mapping of cases with relevant book chapters of popular finance textbooks.

The journey of a thousand miles begins with a single step, and we have taken the first step by writing this casebook to facilitate participant-centred learning in financial management. We are sure that instructors and participants will contribute to enriching the learning experience.

Mayank Joshipura
Sachin Mathur

Note

1 Prof. Aswath Damodaran is a Professor of Finance at Stern School of Business, New York University, USA.

PART I

Financial Planning and Working Capital Management

1

MONARK BUILDING MATERIALS

Estimating Working Capital Fund Requirements

In April 2020, Vinita Jagtap, General Manager – Finance, of Monark Building Materials (MBM), was worried about the implications of the credit-rating agency placing the company on a negative watch. The rating action had followed the subdued performance of MBM in the financial year 2019–20 (FY20) and the likely further deterioration in performance due to Covid-19-induced lockdown in the peak season of FY21.

MBM's Business Segments and Performance

Incorporated in 1934, MBM operated in two business segments – building products and steel buildings. The building products' segment earned 66% of the revenues. It catered to rural customers, offering traditional grey corrugated sheets and modern coloured corrugated roofing sheets. MBM was one of the leading manufacturers of asbestos cement (AC) roofing in India but had gradually diversified into non-asbestos building products.

Accounting for 34% of MBM's revenues, the steel buildings segment provided pre-engineered buildings for commercial, industrial, and warehousing applications. The segment offered the much-needed diversification for MBM, primarily because of the regulatory risks related to the production and use of asbestos products in India and the import of asbestos from other countries. India had banned the mining of asbestos. Once the largest asbestos producers in the world, Brazil and Canada had already banned the mining and sale of asbestos, and currently, Russia and Kazakhstan were the largest exporters.

MBM had a well-established position in both the businesses, having built sufficient manufacturing capacities and an extensive dealer network of over

DOI: 10.4324/9781032724478-3

7,000 dealers covering more than 1 lakh villages and 600 cities. However, the intensity of competition was high in both businesses. Apart from other strong players, MBM faced competition from manufacturers of galvanised iron roofing sheets in AC roofing.

Asbestos and steel were the critical raw materials for AC roof sheets and buildings and accounted for more than 50% of the costs. Operating margins were volatile due to fluctuations in raw material prices and limited pricing flexibility due to the competition. The manufacturers could pass on the increase in raw material prices to the end-customers of pre-engineered buildings in those cases where the contracts allowed it.

Sales were affected during 2019–20 due to weaker volumes and prices of building products, particularly towards the end of the fourth-quarter due to the Covid-19-induced lockdowns. Raw material costs increased both due to higher prices of materials and the depreciation of the rupee against USD, thereby adversely affecting the operating margins. Lower sales also reduced the asset turnover, which, together with lower margins, negatively impacted the return on capital employed (see Exhibit 1.1 and 1.2).

Sizing the Working Capital Requirement for 2020–21

The existing bank's decision to reduce the sanctioned cash credit limit from Rs 40 crores to Rs 25 crores due to lower expected volumes and higher perceived risk had strained its relationship with MBM. Vinita was in discussion with a new bank, Sumangal Bank, for working capital facilities. Sumangal Bank was willing to match the previous bank's interest rate and other terms but required a margin of 25% on inventories and 30% on trade receivables.

EXHIBIT 1.1 MBM's Profit and Loss Statement

Rs Crore	*FY 2018*	*FY 2019*	*FY 2020*
Revenues	**1,279**	**1,411**	**1,293**
Operating Expenses	**1,169**	**1,284**	**1,237**
Cost of Goods Sold	936	1,051	1,020
- Materials Consumed	749	870	766
- Other Manufacturing Costs	187	181	254
- Other Operating Expenses	233	233	216
PBDIT	**109**	**126**	**56**
Depreciation	33	32	25
Interest	15	9	10
Tax	10	21	7
Profit after Tax	**51**	**64**	**14**

Source: Prepared by authors.

EXHIBIT 1.2 MBM's Balance Sheet

Rs Crore	*FY 2018*	*FY 2019*	*FY 2020*
Total Assets	947	1,079	1,023
Non-Current Assets	555	549	574
Property, Plant, and Equipment	341	337	359
Other Non-Current Assets	214	212	215
Current Assets	392	531	450
Raw Material Inventories	112	149	150
WIP Inventories	48	40	33
Finished Goods Inventories	88	141	128
Trade Recievables	80	122	93
Cash and Bank Balance	58	59	37
Other Current Assets	6	21	9
Total Liabilities and Equity	947	1,079	1,023
Total Equity	397	453	455
Non-Current Liabilities	617	673	683
Long-Term Borrowings	58	54	55
Other Non-Current Liabilities	559	620	627
Current Liabilities	329	406	341
Short-Term Borrowings	26	36	24
Trade Payables	153	182	145
Other Current Liabilities	150	187	172

Source: Prepared by authors.

Further, the bank was willing to consider raw material inventory only up to 70 days of raw material consumption, finished goods inventory up to 40 days of cost of goods sold, and trade receivables up to 30 days of credit sales for determining the requirement.

As per Vinita's base-case forecasts, MBM's sales would decline by in FY21 by 10% primarily due to volumes, while prices would remain stable (Exhibit 1.3). Total raw material consumption was also likely to decline proportionately, but raw material prices would not change. Other direct manufacturing costs would stay the same.

In the base case, Vinita also expected trade receivables to increase by five days compared with FY20, whereas finished goods inventories would decline by five days. The rest of the working capital components would remain the same in the days terms, as would cash, other current assets, and liabilities as a percent of sales.

The base case had assumed that MBM would increase the credit period and relax the receivables collection policy. Had MBM not planned the same, Vinita had estimated a 15% decline in sales in FY21. The trade off of the credit policy changes would be the five days longer receivables period and

EXHIBIT 1.3 Assumptions for FY21

	Base Scenario	*Alternative Scenario*
Growth in Sales Volume	–10%	–15%
Growth in Sales Realisation	0%	0%
Change in Raw Material Prices	0%	0%
Bad Debts to Sales	2%	0%
Change in Other Manufacturing Costs	0%	0%
Change in Days Trade Receivables	5	0
Change in Days RM Inventory	0	0
Change in Days WIP Inventory	0	0
Change in Days FG Inventory	–5	–5
Change in Cash as % of Sales	0%	0%
Change in Other Current Assets as % of Sales	0%	0%
Change in Days Trade Receivables	0	0
Change in Other Current Liabilties as % of Sales	0%	0%
Marginal Tax Rate	25%	25%
Opportunity Cost of Funds	15.3%	15.3%

Source: Prepared by authors.

bad debts at 2% of sales due to the relaxed collection policy. On the other hand, the bad debts would otherwise be negligible.

Vinita was wondering whether MBM would receive higher credit limits from Sumangal Bank. She also wanted to check if the related credit policy would be a prudent decision. She decided to complete her worksheet calculations to answer these questions.

Questions

1. Estimate MBM's working capital requirement in FY21, assuming the change in credit policy.
2. How much working capital funding can MBM get in FY21 under the above assumptions and Sumangal Bank's margin requirements? Should MBM change its bank relationship based on these estimates?
3. Is the decision to change the credit policy in FY21 prudent? Verify the same, assuming an opportunity cost of fund of 15.3% and a marginal tax rate of 25%.

2

AMBER ENTERPRISES

Working Capital Assessment for Seasonal Business

Vijay Mehta, credit officer at Novella Bank, reviewed the email he had received from the head office in response to a proposal he had forwarded for review. In his submission, Mehta had recommended approaching select prospective clients with an offer to avail credit facilities at preferential terms compared to their existing lenders.

At the top of Mehta's proposed clients' list was Amber Enterprises India Ltd (Amber). It was May 2019, and whenever he stepped out of his air-conditioned office environment into the sweltering summer heat, Mehta's conviction about Amber's business prospects seemed to grow stronger.

Amber was a leading contract manufacturer of room air conditioners (RACs) and its components, other consumer durables, and automobiles in India. It designed and manufactured RACs and supplied RAC components for leading consumer durable brands, including Daikin, Hitachi, LG, Panasonic, Voltas, Godrej, Bluestar, and Whirlpool.

The email from the head office noted that the current economic scenario and liquidity conditions warranted abundant caution while developing new corporate client accounts. Also, since the highly seasonal nature of Amber's business resulted in uneven cash flows, it was necessary to evaluate its credit metrics on a seasonal basis.

Room Air-conditioner Industry

The market size for air-conditioning products in India was estimated at around Rs 175 billion in 2018–19. RACs constituted the larger market share with an estimated value of Rs 110 billion, while central air-conditioning and other ancillary equipment accounted for the remaning.

DOI: 10.4324/9781032724478-4

The market for RACs in India had been witnessing sustained double-digit growth in the past five years. This growth was supported on the demand side by low household penetration of RACs, increasing product awareness, and a large and growing middle-income urban population. The supporting supply-side factors included easy availability of consumer financing, product innovation, brand choice, competitive pricing, marketing schemes, and increasing distribution reach through physical and online channels.

The demand for air conditioners (ACs) would continue to grow at a high rate in 2019–20. The AC makers were optimistic based on predictions of high summer temperatures. The CEO of a leading AC maker stated that "the industry is poised at an inflection penetration of 7–8 per cent" and further added that "I predict the industry growing at 14–15 per cent during FY2019–20."[1]

The share of inverter ACs had risen, from 12% in 2016–17 to 40% in 2018–19.[2] This was due to the introduction of new energy-efficiency standards in 2018. In inverter ACs, adjusting the power supply to compressors can vary the cooling or heating capacity. Companies introduced new energy-efficient products and increasingly priced their inverter ACs competitively, at a lower price differential vis-à-vis the regular ACs.

The top six players accounted for a 65% share of the Indian market, making it moderately concentrated. Leading players included Voltas, LG, Daikin, Blue Star, Lloyd, and Hitachi. The shifts in product mix from regular to inverter ACs, channel mix from physical to online retailing, and the entry of new players led to intensifying competition and churn in market shares.

The increasing scale of operations justified by the increased market size, high import duties, and the Government of India's thrust on "Make in India" would ensure that a large share of the demand would continue to be met by domestic production. Apart from in-house manufacturing, the leading brands outsourced their RACs to contract manufacturers, such as Amber Enterprises and Dixon Technologies.

Amber's Business

Jasbir Singh and Daljit Singh had promoted and incorporated Amber in 1990 with its headquarters in Gurgram. The company had its manufacturing facilities located in Dehradun (Uttarakhand), Rajpura (Punjab), Jhajjar (Haryana), Kala Amb (Himachal Pradesh), Greater Noida (Uttar Pradesh), and Pune (Maharashtra).

Amber had a 55% market share in outsourced RAC manufacturing and 19% in overall RAC manufacturing in India, built on the back of solid customer relationships with Original Equipment Manufacturers (OEMs). The consumer-durable brands it supplied to collectively accounted for around

75% of the RAC market in India. It had moderate client concentration, with the top five clients accounting for about 68% of revenue.[3] Long product approval cycles of clients, which could be as long as two to three years for critical components, constituted a key entry barrier. Though the customer relationships were long-standing, sales were based on purchase orders and not on firm commitments or long-term supply agreements.

Amber had integrated operations along the value chain since it manufactured the RACs and its components, including heat exchangers, multi-flow condensers, sheet metal components, plastic mouldings, printed circuit boards, and electric motors (see Exhibit 2.1). Its manufacturing facilities were close to the customers' production centres to reduce logistics expenses and provide the opportunity to interact frequently and respond quickly to the customer needs. Flexibility in assembly lines and manufacturing scale were its other vital competitive strengths. Its operating profitability had been healthy, with a return on capital employed at 15.5% in 2018–19.

Amber derived more than 70% of its revenues from RACs. The demand for RACs is seasonal, concentrated from January to May. While RAC manufacturing is working capital intensive, the working capital requirement rises sharply during the peak season. The seasonal business resulted in uneven cash flows, causing pressure on liquidity (see Exhibit 2.2).

Following the demand pattern, Amber followed seasonal production, with a lag of around a quarter to demand. The seasonality had implications for production efficiencies and capacity requirements, which had to be built based on peak requirements. Capacity utilisation in the financial year 2019, which was around 60% on average, reached about 80% in the peak production months.

EXHIBIT 2.1 RAC Business Value Chain

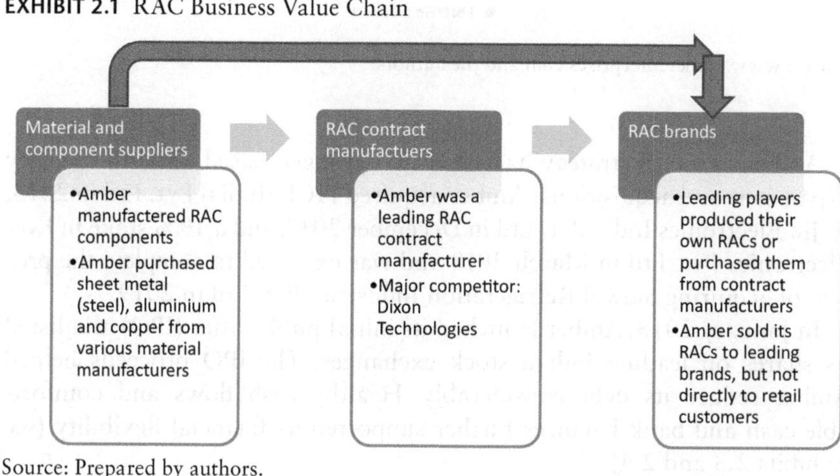

Source: Prepared by authors.

EXHIBIT 2.2 Seasonal Variations in Financial Performance

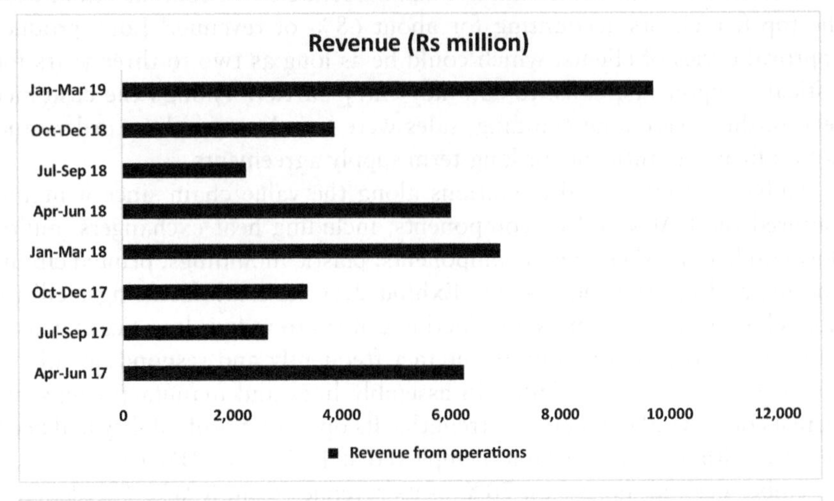

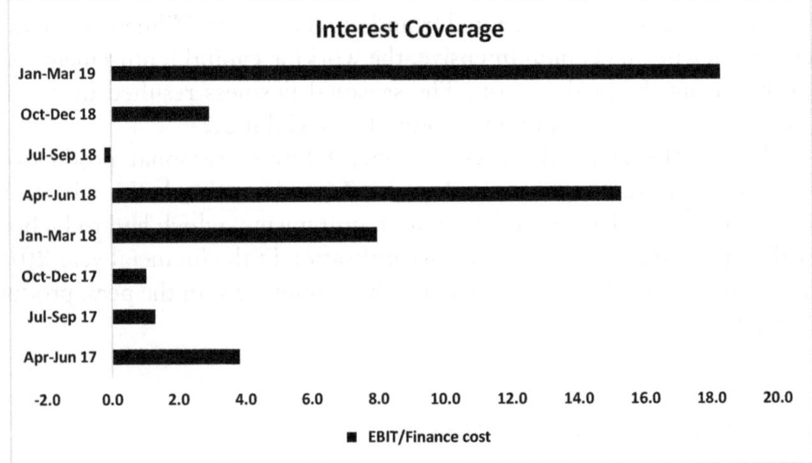

Source: www.amberenterprises.com and the authors.

Amber's growth strategy had been two-pronged based on both capacity expansions and acquisitions. Amber acquired PICL (India) Pvt. Ltd in 2013, IL Jin Electronics India Pvt. Ltd in December 2017, and a 19% stake in Ever Electronics Pvt. Ltd in March 2018 and was expected to complete the process of acquiring Sidwal Refrigeration Industries Pvt. Ltd in 2019.

In January 2018, Amber launched its initial public offer (IPO) and listed its shares on leading Indian stock exchanges. The IPO proceeds helped Amber reduce its debt considerably. Healthy cash flows and comfortable cash and bank balances further supported its financial flexibility (see Exhibits 2.3 and 2.4).

EXHIBIT 2.3 Amber Enterprises: Statement of Profit and Loss

Rs Million	*Quarter-ended*								*Total*	
	30 Jun 2017	*30 Sep 2017*	*31 Dec 2017*	*31Mar-2018*	*30 Jun2018*	*30 Sep2018*	*31 Dec2018*	*31 Mar2019*	*2017–18*	*2018–19*
Income from Operations										
Revenue from Operations	6,241	2,650	3,384	6,920	6,021	2,263	3,888	9,713	19,195	21,884
Other Income	21	18	40	8	11	28	3	49	86	89
Total Income from Operations	**6,262**	**2,667**	**3,424**	**6,928**	**6,031**	**2,290**	**3,890**	**9,761**	**19,281**	**21,973**
Expenses										
Cost of Raw Materials Consumed	4,945	2,350	2,919	5,681	4,997	1,859	3,704	7,970	15,894	18,530
Change in Inventories	366	(185)	(66)	78	24	2	(364)	128	193	(210)
Employee Benefits Expenses	94	99	93	112	115	97	98	111	398	421
Finance Costs	126	102	166	72	29	33	35	52	467	148
Depreciation and Amortisation	104	105	110	113	120	123	122	131	432	496
Other Expenses	272	167	197	370	335	216	228	480	1,006	1,260
Total Expenses	**5,907**	**2,637**	**3,419**	**6,426**	**5,620**	**2,330**	**3,824**	**8,871**	**18,390**	**20,644**
Profit before Tax	355	30	5	502	411	(40)	67	891	892	1,329
Tax	99	7	3	164	123	(22)	28	275	272	404
Net Profit for the Period	**256**	**23**	**1**	**338**	**289**	**(18)**	**38**	**616**	**619**	**925**

Source: www.amberenterprises.com and the authors.

EXHIBIT 2.4 Amber Enterprises: Balance Sheet

Rs Million	*31 Mar 2017*	*31 Mar 2018*	*30 Sep 2018*	*31 Mar 2019*
Assets				
Non-current Assets				
Property, Plant, and Equipment	4,326	4,648	4,640	5,104
Other Non-Current Assets	1,406	2,069	2,308	2,342
Total Non-Current Assets	**5,732**	**6,717**	**6,947**	**7,445**
Current Assets				
Inventories	2,466	3,279	2,715	4,837
Trade Receivables	2,929	3,358	1,761	7,319
Cash and Bank Balances	334	1,205	283	421
Other Current Assets	288	404	662	815
Total Current Assets	**6,017**	**8,246**	**5,421**	**13,392**
Total Assets	**11,748**	**14,963**	**12,369**	**20,838**
Equity and Liabilities				
Equity				
Equity Share Capital	238	315	315	315
Other Equity	3,295	8,515	8,786	9,438
Total Equity	**3,533**	**8,830**	**9,100**	**9,752**
Liabilities				
Non-current Liabilities				
Borrowings	2,195	97	62	1,027
Other Non-current Liabilities	103	264	291	388
Total Non-current Liabilities	**2,298**	**361**	**353**	**1,415**
Current Liabilities				
Borrowings and Other Financial Liabilities	1,712	582	926	933
Trade Payable	4,110	4,785	1,849	8,210
Other Financial Liabilities	388	275	251	393
Other Current Liabilities	96	406	140	528
Total Current Liabilities	**5,917**	**5,773**	**2,915**	**9,671**
Total Equity and Liabilities	**11,748**	**14,963**	**12,369**	**20,838**

Source: www.amberenterprises.com and the authors.

Impact of Business Seasonality

As with other consumer discretionary products, demand for ACs was vulnerable to economic cycles, varying with disposable household incomes. However, the underlying solid demand fundamentals ensured that the adverse conditions, when they arose, were usually temporary and followed by a rebound in revenue growth. While market share churn among players could add to the demand predictability for a contract manufacturer, Amber mitigated this risk by supplying to most leading brands.

More than economic cycles, the primary concern for Amber was the high degree of demand seasonality within the year. The first and fourth quarters of the year accounted for around 70% of the annual revenues. The seasonal variations were not perfectly predictable. The management had noted that the seasonality had been gradually declining over the years.[4] At the same time, unpredictable weather changes had led to unexpected demand patterns. For instance, unseasonal rains in the first quarter of 2019 had affected sales in the peak season, which had caused an inventory pile up for several months during the year.

Mehta knew that the concerns raised by the head office were not misplaced. In a seasonal business, cash flows and credit protection metrics could vary widely across the months. Moreover, utilisation of credit lines would rise sharply as peak season approached and then decline to minimal levels by the end of the peak season. Therefore, he had asked Rahul Juneja, a management trainee, to prepare the quarterly proforma financial forecasts for Amber. He had to review the figures before sending them to the head office. He hoped that he would not have to wait much for the green signal.

Emails Exchanged between Rahul Juneja and Vijay Mehta

Wed 5/15/2019 4:32 PM
To: Vijay Mehta

Sir,

I have been preparing proforma forecasts for Amber Enterprises for 2019–20 as required by you. I am enclosing my assumptions as well as workings for your feedback. For preparing the estimates, I have assumed a 15% growth in revenues, based on industry experts' expectations. The quarterly revenue forecasts follow the historical pattern in seasonality.
However, I am unsure about the adverse effects of slower economic growth and stringent consumer lending in 2019–20. I am also concerned about the sensitivity of my forecasts to a large number of assumptions.
There was another point I wanted to discuss with you. I had recently read an article about an automobile manufacturer who had saved a considerable amount of operating expenses by shifting from seasonal production to level production. Level production entails producing the same quantity of

products every month instead of varying the output based on demand seasonality. The savings could come from an increase in employee productivity, lower over-time, and improved capacity utilization. I am not sure why Amber follows seasonal production instead of level production.

Regards
Rahul Juneja

Thurs 5/16/2019 11:03 AM
To: Rahul Juneja,

Dear Rahul,

I have seen your assumptions, and I think you can go ahead with your forecasts. Ensure that your premises are explicitly stated, have a reasonable basis, and are linked appropriately with your worksheet outputs. To deal with demand uncertainty, prepare the forecasts under alternative growth scenarios.
We need to evaluate the profitability, solvency, and liquidity of seasonal businesses by quarter. Such forecasts are also necessary to estimate the seasonal credit requirements of our clients.
I suggest that you prepare a brief note on the relative pros and cons of level production and its likely impact on fund requirements and credit ratios using Amber as an example. We could discuss the same and use it for future reference.

All the best
Vijay Mehta

Questions

1. Prepare proforma quarterly forecasts of Profit and Loss Statement and Balance Sheet for Amber Enterprises based on assumptions provided in Exhibit 2.5.
2. Prepare quarterly estimates of key profitability and solvency and liquidity indicators, including net profit margin, return on capital employed, debt to equity ratio, interest coverage ratio, and current ratio by quarter.
3. Estimate the impact on profitability, solvency, and liquidity indicators if the company were to use a level production policy instead of a seasonal production policy, assuming that it could save 0.3% in material and 2% in material employee expenses.

EXHIBIT 2.5 Assumptions for Proforma Forecasting

Revenues from Operations	15% growth in annual sales. Distributed in the proportions of 32%, 13%, 18%, and 37% from Q1 to Q4 in that order.
Material Costs	83.5% (combined with change in inventories) of the revenues.
Employee Benefit Expenses	7% annual increase; of the total 80% fixed and evenly distributed, 20% varying with seasonal revenues.
Other Expenses	12% annual increase; of the total 20% fixed and evenly distributed, 80% varying with seasonal revenues.
Depreciation	10% of property, plant, and equipment.
Property, Plant, and Equipment	Increase of 150 million in each quarter.
Other Non-current Assets	An increase of 1000 million each in Q1 and Q2 expected for ongoing acquisition.
Cash and Bank Balance	Minimum level of Rs 400 million, plug to balance on the asset side.
Trade Receivables	2.33 months of sales.
Inventory	2.5 months of total operating expenses.
Other Current Assets	Same as at the end of March 2019.
Equity Share Capital	No change.
Other Equity	Change based only on profits, no dividends.
Non-current Borrowings	Net increase 500 million in each quarter.
Other Non-current Liabilities	Same as at the end of March 2019.
Trade Payables	Estimated as 3 months of cost of materials.
Current Borrowings	Plug to balance on the liability side, minimum level of Rs 500 million.
Other Current Liabilities	Same as at the end of March 2019.
Interest Cost	At 10.5% of average total borrowings.
Other Income	At 8% of average cash and bank balance.
Tax Rate	At 30%.

Source: Prepared by authors.

Notes

1 https://www.livemint.com/industry/retail/ac-makers-expect-a-double-digit-sales-growth-this-summer-1554640433746.html
2 https://www.bloombergquint.com/bq-blue-exclusive/what-helped-air-conditioner-makers-buck-the-trend-amid-a-slowdown
3 https://www.crisil.com/mnt/winshare/Ratings/RatingList/RatingDocs/Amber_Enterprises_India_Limited_September_16_2019_RR.html
4 Amber Enterprises (2018). Earnings Call Transcript Q2 Financial Results FY2019 held on 01.11.2018

3

VALUEBUY RETAIL

Working Capital Requirement for High Growth Business

Avinash Paranjape, Managing Director of ValueBuy Retail Private Ltd, received a phone call from the bank manager of Shivaji Nagar, Pune branch of New Western Bank. The bank had agreed to sanction higher cash credit limits at a lower interest rate than what ValueBuy was currently paying. A formal communication would follow, and based on Avinash's acceptance, the New Western Bank would issue a sanction letter.

For both ValueBuy and New Western Bank, this would be the beginning of a new relationship. Since its incorporation in 2012, ValueBuy Retail had been banking with Sinhagad Bank. The association had run smoothly until recently when it soured since Sinhagad Bank firmly refused to sanction the limits Paranjape had requested. Availability of funds at low cost was critical for a growing retail supermarket business, and Avinash had wasted no time before reaching out to New Western Bank.

Company Evolution and Strategy

The Paranjape family set up ValueBuy Retail in 2012, with the shares privately held through an investment company owned by the family. The family had been running food retailing outlets for several generations, while Avinash Paranjape had been managing a large convenience store in Pune.

Since the past two decades, the organised retailing industry in India had been growing at a high double-digit growth rate due to the benefits of favourable demographics and low penetration of organised formats. Several players had set up organised retail chains to benefit from this growth (see Exhibit 3.1). Not wanting to miss the retailing growth opportunity, Avinash

DOI: 10.4324/9781032724478-5

EXHIBIT 3.1 Growth and Category-wise Penetration of Organised Retailing in India

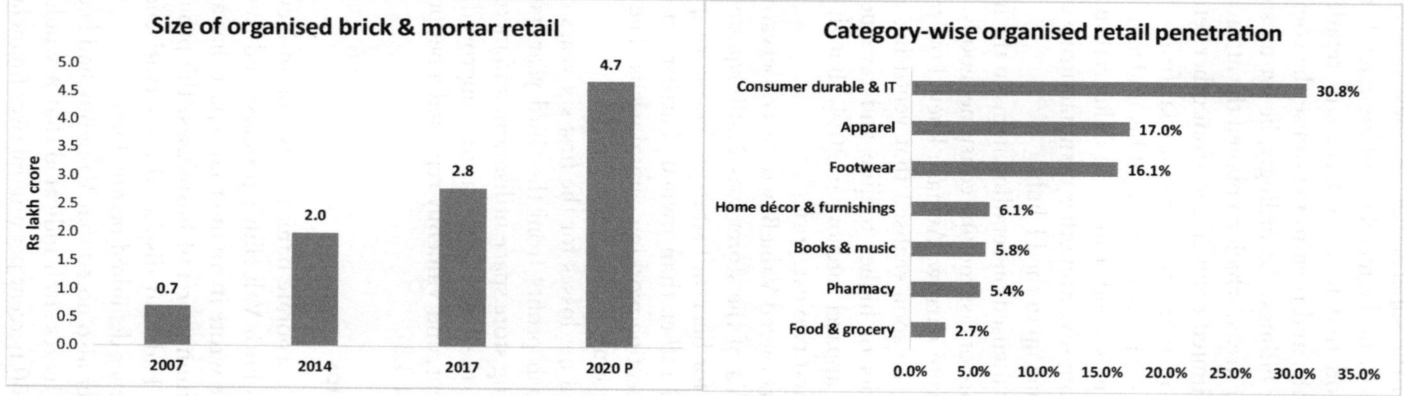

Source: CRISIL Ratings, Economic Times (https://retail.economictimes.indiatimes.com/re-tales/organised-retail-entering-faster-growth-lane/2854).

decided to enter into the supermarket business and brought in the initial capital with the support of the members of his extended family.

Avinash understood that to be a successful retailer, he needed firstly high customer footfalls and then to maximise the conversion rate of those footfalls in customer billings. Accordingly, he set up supermarkets close to residential catchment areas, which combined the attractiveness of high purchasing power and limited competition from other retail chains. ValueBuy established its first store in the city centre not far from Avinash's convenience store to leverage the supply networks and his understanding of the locality. The company set up its second store in an industrial suburb that housed the executives of the automotive and other manufacturing companies. The third and fourth stores came up in the IT hubs.

ValueBuy initially focused on retailing items in the food and grocery category, with some share of fast-moving consumer goods. Though the margins in these categories were narrow, Avinash knew how to run the operations efficiently. However, he soon realised that venturing into other categories could provide benefits of higher topline and revenues. ValueBuy started diversifying into the apparel category in 2014, though the bulk of the sales still came from the first two categories.

Capital constraints forced ValueBuy to be conservative in investment outlays. The average area of the stores was 2,500 square feet, which Avinash felt was appropriate for his retail strategy. The store space, warehouse, and vehicles were rented rather than owned. Further, supplier credit was the preferred mode of meeting working capital needs. The company decided to forego purchase discounts.

ValueBuy reported net losses for the first six years of operations though it started making cash profits from the third year itself. However, as the benefits of scale, rising store space utilisation, and increasing employee productivity kicked in, the operating margins improved. The financial year 2018–19 was excellent, and ValueBuy reported a net profit for the first time (see Exhibits 3.2 and 3.3).

Banking Relationships

The manager at the corporate banking division of New Western Bank had been impressed with both ValueBuy's progress and Avinash's prudence and business acumen. He wrote in an internal report that apart from their valuable experience in running retail businesses, the promoter family and the Managing Director had also displayed conservativeness in their business practices and had never defaulted on any loan.

The bank manager also noted that ValueBuy had been consistently growing at a high rate. His research indicated that it would continue to clock a turnover growth of 30 percent per annum over financial years 2019–20 and

EXHIBIT 3.2 Profit and Loss Statement of ValueBuy Retail

	Year ended March 31		
Rs lakhs	**2017**	**2018**	**2019**
Income			
Sales revenue	998	1,384	1,799
Other income	6	4	6
Total income	***1,004***	***1,388***	***1,805***
Expenses			
Stock of goods purchased	942	1,303	1,692
Decrease (Increase) in Inventory	(65)	(91)	(118)
Stocks Consumed	877	1,212	1,574
Employee Costs	46	60	76
Other expenses	55	76	98
Total Operating expenses	***978***	***1,348***	***1,748***
PBDIT	26	40	57
Depreciation	18	20	23
Profit before interest and tax	8	20	35
Interest	20	23	32
Profit before tax	(12)	(3)	3
Income tax	-	-	-
Profit after tax	**(12)**	**(3)**	**3**

Note: ValueBuy Retail was not expected to pay any income tax on profits till 2020-21 due to unabsorbed losses

Source: Prepared by authors.

2020–21. At the same time, the company was being run efficiently with steady improvement in margins at the gross and operating levels. The improvement in margins could continue with the increasing share of the apparel business.

The credit officer at Sinhagad Bank, in contrast, had viewed the prospects of ValueBuy Retail less favourably. He noted that despite the improvement, the margins and returns of ValueBuy were low, and it was not sure that the company could sustain the gains in performance in 2018–19 in the future. Competition in organised retailing had been intensifying, from both physical stores and e-tailing players.

He had also received reports which suggested that the new stores were not as efficient as the first two stores, and the shift to apparel had contributed to inventory problems, apparently because Avinash and his team did not understand customer requirements in that domain. The bank did not anticipate an early resolution, and inventory days at best would remain at the same levels over the next two years.

Further, ValueBuy had been stretching its suppliers beyond the formal payment terms. A few suppliers were threatening to discontinue their relationship with ValueBuy if the latter continued to pay them beyond a month. In comparison, a strong competitor was availing purchase discounts based on typical terms of 2/10 net 30, making it much more cost-competitive than ValueBuy.

EXHIBIT 3.3 Balance Sheet of ValueBuy Retail

	Year ended March 31			
Rs lakhs	**2016**	**2017**	**2018**	**2019**
Property, plant and equipment, at cost	172	191	213	241
Less: Accumulated depreciation	(30)	(48)	(68)	(91)
Property, plant and equipment, net	***142***	***143***	***145***	***150***
Cash	85	60	49	102
Receivables	9	10	14	19
Inventory	130	195	286	404
Total Current Assets	***224***	***265***	***349***	***525***
Total Assets	**366**	**408**	**494**	**675**
	-	-	-	-
Equity share capital	200	200	200	200
Other equity	(50)	(62)	(66)	(63)
Total Equity	***150***	***138***	***134***	***137***
Long term loan	***80***	***64***	***48***	***132***
Trade payables	52	82	135	199
Short term bank loan	84	124	176	207
Total Current Liabilities	***136***	***206***	***311***	***406***
Total Equity and Liabilities	**366**	**408**	**494**	**675**

Note: ValueBuy Retail had planned a capital expenditure of Rs 30 lakhs in each of the years 2019-20 and 2020-21.

Source: Prepared by authors.

Avinash had been disappointed with Sinhagad Bank, for what he considered was an apparent lack of understanding of the economics of retailing business, as well as for a complete disregard of a long and mutually beneficial relationship. He had provided good business value to Sinhagad in the form of cash credit and term loans. The first term loan of Rs 80 lakhs had been disbursed in March 2016, and the second term loan of Rs 1 crore was disbursed recently, in March 2019. Both the term loans were repayable in five equal annual instalments.

Avinash had been upset when he learned that the second term loan carried the same interest rate of 12% as the first term loan as he had been expecting a rate reduction. However, when Sinhagad Bank informed him that the bank would not raise his cash credit sanction limit beyond Rs 2.20 crores, he began speaking with New Western Bank.

The Loan Terms

A day after the call, ValueBuy received the loan offer terms on mail from the New Western Bank. The bank had agreed to sanction cash credit limits of

Rs 2.86 crores for 2019–20, 30% higher than the company's approved limits in 2018–19. New Western Bank also agreed to offer a rate of 10.5% for the cash credit utilised, as against 11% charged by Sinhagad Bank. It would waive off any charges for unutilised facilities.

The cash credit facility was also subject to some covenants. The renewal terms would depend upon continuous improvement in profitability, solvency, and liquidity ratios over the next two years. Failure to meet these conditions could affect the bank's internal rating of ValueBuy and the future loan terms.

Avinash saw no reason why ValueBuy could not meet the stipulated conditions. Still, he wanted to review the terms before sending an acceptance mail.

Questions

1. Suppose that the Managing Director of ValueBuy Retail states that its debt more than doubled between 2015–16 and 2018–19 due to its capital expenditure. Analyse the information provided in the case to support your arguments for or against this statement.
2. Assess whether the limits sanctioned by New Western Bank would be sufficient to meet the funding requirements of ValueBuy Retail in 2019–20. Make your assumptions where required.
3. If the New Western Bank were to require ValueBuy to finance 25% of its current assets from other long-term sources, estimate the maximum working capital finance it would sanction for 2019–20.

4

ASHOK LEYLAND

Managing Liquidity through the Cycles

Rohan Bakshi, Fixed Income Analyst at Axiom Asset Management Company, saw a news alert on his monitor on the morning of May 14, 2020. Ashok Leyland Ltd (ALL), a leading commercial vehicles manufacturer in India, was planning to issue up to Rs 300 crore of three-year secured non-convertible debentures on a private placement basis, with a green-shoe option of another Rs 200 crore.[1]

Rohan had been forwarded the information memorandum of the issue to his email address. He had to prepare a note with his recommendation considering the likely risks and returns of investing in the issue. Rohan had to assess risks related to default, downgrade, credit spread, and illiquidity.

ICRA, a credit rating agency, had rated the company AA with a negative outlook in March 2020, indicating a high degree of safety, but with the risk of a possible downgrade.[2] Though the issue offered 25 basis points increase in coupon for every notch of downgrade (and an equivalent reduction for upgrade), compared with the 37 basis points gap in spreads between AA and A (difference of two notches), credit spreads had been widening during recent few weeks. Illiquidity was a significant concern, as sudden downgrades in quick succession could result in already shallow trading in any corporate debt paper in India to come to a standstill. Holding illiquid debt paper could be disastrous for open-ended debt mutual funds facing redemption pressure from investors, as had been seen recently in April 2020 when Franklin Templeton India announced the closure of a few of its debt schemes.

DOI: 10.4324/9781032724478-6

Ashok Leyland's Business Profile

Promoted in 1948, Ashok Leyland was the flagship company of the Hinduja group and the second-largest manufacturer of medium and heavy commercial vehicles (MHCVs) in India after Tata Motors. It produced MHCVs and light commercial vehicles (LCVs), special vehicles and engines, and catered to the truck transport, bus transport, and defence segments. The company had manufacturing plants at Ennore (Tamil Nadu), Hosur (Tamil Nadu), Alwar (Rajasthan), Bhandara (Maharashtra), and Pantnagar (Uttarakhand). The company had five subsidiaries, of which the largest was Hinduja Leyland Finance Ltd, originally a captive financier of ALL's vehicles, but which had gradually diversified into other business segments.

A media release by SIAM, the automobile industry association, had reported that the industry had been on a structural slowdown in all segments.[3] Commercial vehicles, for example, had grown at only 3% annually between FY10 and FY20 as compared with 12.7% between FY2000 to FY10 (Exhibit 4.1). The reduced growth was because of slower economic growth, improved efficiencies in the transport sector, and environmental and regulatory reasons.

However, the most noteworthy characteristic of the commercial vehicle industry across decades was its highly cyclical demand. It was typical for MHCVs to witness 3–5 years of consistent high growth, followed by 1–2 years of sharp decline. The cyclical demand pattern was because truck fleet operators needed fewer new vehicles when there was a lower freight transport demand. The fleet operators also tended to postpone the replacement of existing old trucks under adverse economic conditions.

EXHIBIT 4.1 Commercial Vehicle Sales: Industry and Ashok Leyland

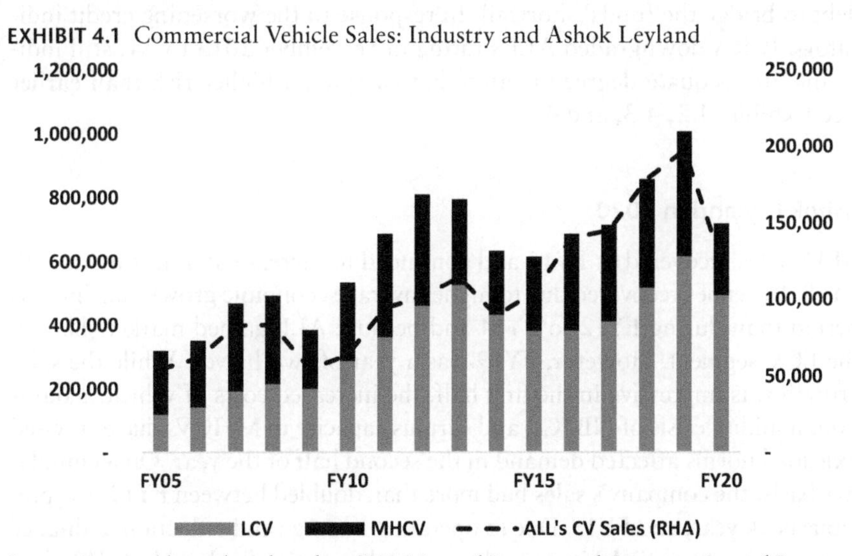

Source: Prepared by authors based on SIAM Annual Reports and Company Annual Reports.

Cyclical revenues had a disproportionate effect on the margins because of operating leverage and financial leverage since manufacturers could not reduce fixed operating and capital costs in response to sharp sales declines. Cash flows would also be stressed if there was a simultaneous build-up of trade receivables and inventories or if the companies were making a huge capital expenditure. Credit rating and fixed income analysts being aware of this problem, tended to rate commercial vehicle companies "through the cycle" to avoid frequent changes in ratings.

Ashok Leyland in 2013

Rohan decided to first analyse the financial trends during the previous downcycle during FY13 and FY14. ALL's sales had declined by 23% cumulatively in those two years. However, price discounts continued to remain high due to intense competition amidst the slowdown. Employee costs and other operating expenses increased in FY13 before being cut in FY14. Consequently, EBITDA margins declined. Fixed capital charges, including depreciation and finance costs, increased. The company reported negligible operating and net profits in FY14.

As dealer stocks remained high, the company tried to manage its working capital requirements by bringing down its inventories drastically in FY14 as well as by stretching its trade creditors. The end of the capital expenditure cycle in FY13 also reduced the cash outflow. Still, the low levels of cash inflow from operations combined with outflows from interest and long-term debt due for repayment meant that ALL had to raise additional long-term debt to bridge the funds' shortfall. In response to the worsening credit indicators, ICRA downgraded ALL's rating in September 2013 to A+, still indicating an adequate degree of safety but carrying a higher risk than earlier (see Exhibits 4.2, 4.3, and 4.4).

Ashok Leyland in 2020

ALL's sales recovered in FY15 and continued to increase at a healthy rate till FY18. Revenues recovered due to higher average economic growth during this period than during FY12 to FY14 and because ALL gained market share in the LCV segment. However, FY19 was a year of two halves. While the sales growth was impressive in the first half, the increased costs of vehicle acquisition, liquidity crisis of NBFCs, and surplus capacity in MHCVs due to revised axle load norms affected demand in the second half of the year. On a cumulative basis, the company's sales had more than doubled between FY12, the previous peak year, and FY19. Due to operating leverage and reduction in finance costs, net profit in FY19 increased to more than thrice the level in FY12.

EXHIBIT 4.2 The Trend in Outside Liabilities

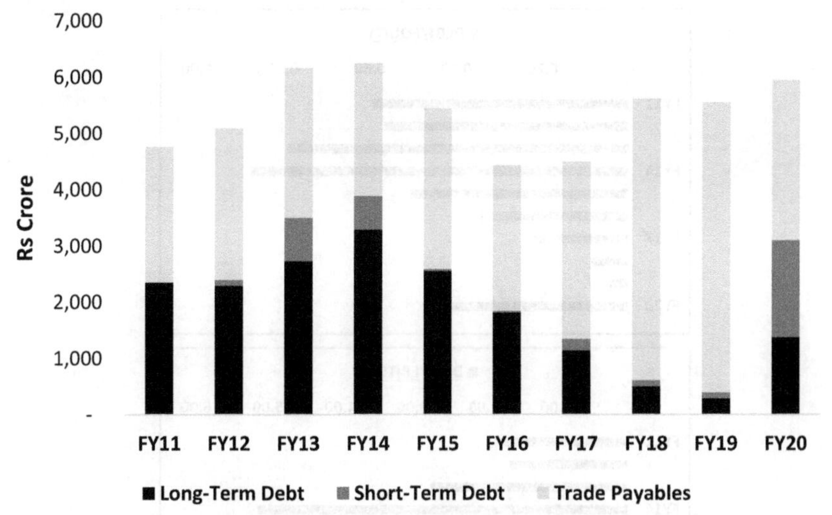

Source: Prepared by authors based on data from CMIE ProwessIQ.

Commercial vehicle sales declined sharply in FY20 due to multiple reasons, including revised axle load norms which allowed each existing truck to carry more load, the liquidity problems of NBFCs, and slowdown in economic growth. Towards the end of FY20, India also announced a nationwide lockdown following the outbreak of the Covid-19 pandemic. Revenues of ALL declined by 39%. However, unlike in FY13 and FY14, the company significantly reduced its total employee expenses by around 23% by lowering bonus and performance-based payments. Further, the company cut other expenses covering delivery charges, production overheads, sales, and administration overheads based on its K54-2 fixed cost reduction programme. The reduction in fixed costs could partly offset the impact of falling revenues on the EBITDA. However, interest and finance expenses increased because the company availed fresh long-term loans to meet its capital expenditure (see Exhibits 4.5 and 4.6).

The outlook for FY21 looked grim, given the uncertainty related to the length of the lockdown. In April, the company had to keep its plant shut, and there was no production. The company also had some capital expenditure plans and was expected to continue to provide working capital support to its subsidiaries. At the end of March 2020, the company had outstanding intercorporate deposits of Rs 500 crore in subsidiaries and group companies. However, liquidity was comfortable since near-term debt repayment obligations were low, and cash and current investments were adequate.

Although ALL remained reliant on the MHCV segment, it had become slightly more diversified by gaining market share in the LCV segment. In

EXHIBIT 4.3 Credit Indicators

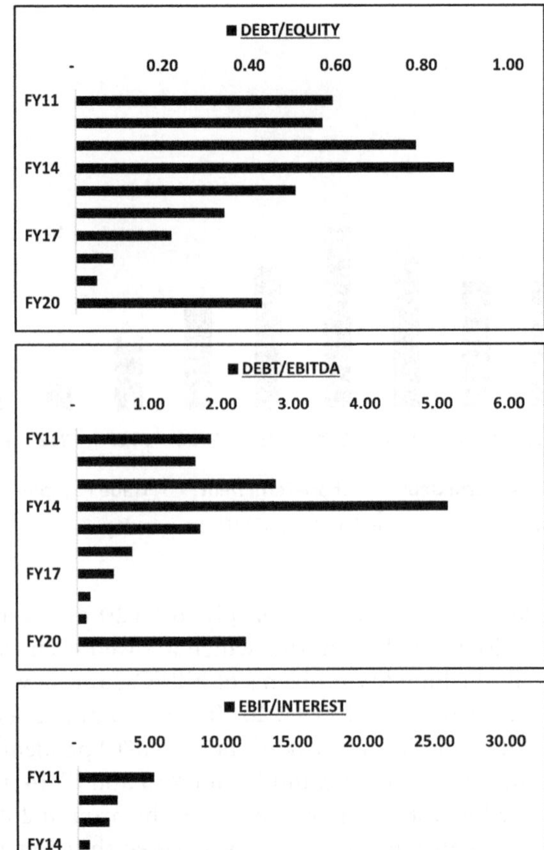

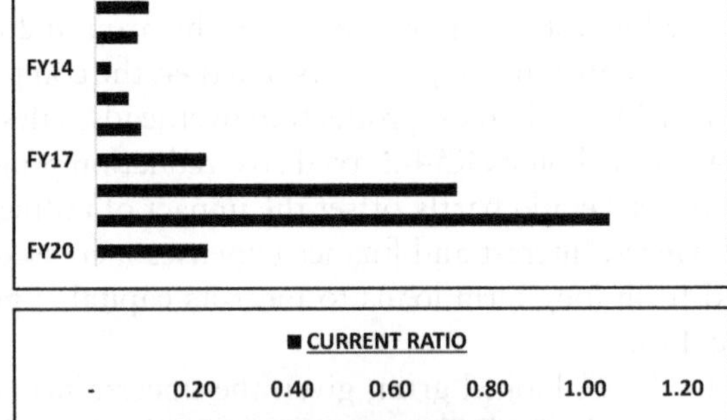

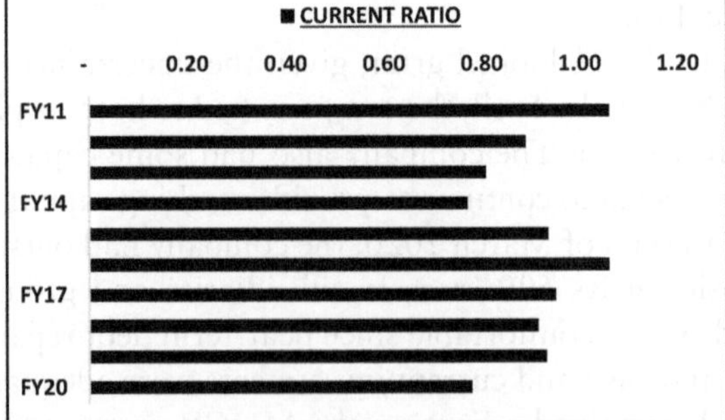

Source: Prepared by authors based on data from CMIE ProwessIQ.

EXHIBIT 4.4 Altman Z-Score and Credit Rating

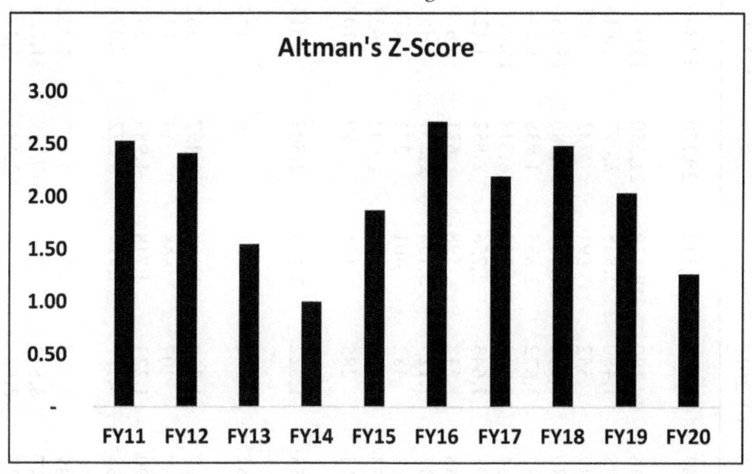

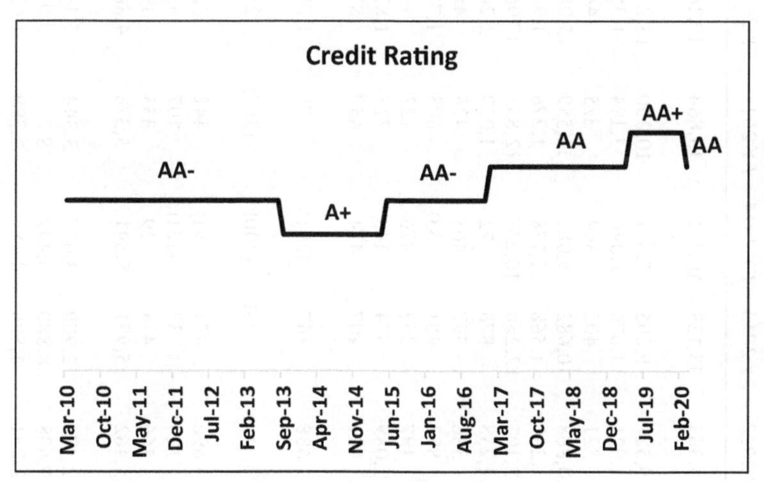

Source: Prepared by authors based on Bloomberg data.

FY20, the company had a market share of 29% in MHCV trucks, 45% in MHCV buses, and over 9% in the LCV segment.

Credit Recommendation

Having completed the analysis, Rohan started writing his credit recommendation and rationale. The critical question he wanted to address was whether ALL in 2020 was better prepared to handle the effects of a cyclical downturn this time than in the previous downcycle.

EXHIBIT 4.5 Trends in Profit and Loss and Balance Sheets of Ashok Leyland

Rs Crore	*FY 2011*	*FY 2012*	*FY 2013*	*FY 2014*	*FY 2015*	*FY 2016*	*FY 2017*	*FY 2018*	*FY 2019*	*FY 2020*
Revenues (net of indirect taxes)	**11,401**	**13,365**	**13,128**	**10,331**	**13,864**	**19,269**	**20,446**	**26,510**	**29,170**	**17,800**
Materials Costs	8,231	9,527	9,205	7,691	10,000	13,246	14,100	18,539	21,550	13,005
Employee Expenses	960	1,021	1,076	1,046	1,184	1,385	1,480	1,838	2,097	1,613
Other Direct Expenses	192	321	402	344	375	449	552	691	732	615
Cost of Goods Sold	9,382	10,868	10,682	9,081	11,559	15,080	16,132	21,068	24,380	15,233
Other Operating Expenses	800	1,239	1,568	1,178	1,276	1,983	2,672	2,685	1,938	1,444
Total Operating Expenses	10,182	12,107	12,250	10,259	12,835	17,064	18,804	23,753	26,318	16,677
Operating EBITDA	**1,220**	**1,258**	**878**	**72**	**1,029**	**2,205**	**1,643**	**2,756**	**2,852**	**1,122**
Depreciation	272	366	397	405	426	488	518	598	621	670
Operating EBIT	948	892	481	(333)	603	1,717	1,125	2,158	2,231	452
Other Income	43	197	393	476	122	156	482	401	371	171
EBIT	991	1,089	874	143	725	1,873	1,607	2,559	2,602	623
Interest and Finance Charges	187	401	407	434	650	815	285	151	99	109
Profit before Extraordinary Items and Tax	803	688	467	(291)	75	1,058	1,322	2,408	2,503	514
Net Prior Period and Extraordinary Items	1	(2)	(3)	(200)	(367)	231	(8)	22	6	152
Profit before Tax	802	690	471	(91)	442	827	1,330	2,386	2,497	362
Tax	171	124	37	(121)	107	437	107	668	514	122
Profit after Tax	**631**	**566**	**434**	**29**	**335**	**390**	**1,223**	**1,718**	**1,983**	**240**
Property, Plant, and Equipment	4,992	5,462	5,971	5,841	5,376	4,868	5,177	5,971	6,272	7,398
Other Non-Current Assets	1,641	2,176	2,909	3,657	3,344	3,149	3,636	3,776	4,487	4,332
Non-Current Assets	6,633	7,638	8,880	9,499	8,719	8,017	8,813	9,747	10,759	11,729
Inventories	2,209	2,231	1,896	1,189	1,399	1,625	2,631	1,758	2,685	1,238
Trade Receivables	1,165	1,231	1,420	1,305	1,248	1,259	1,113	1,008	2,578	1,260

Cash and Bank Balance	180	33	14	12	768	1,593	912	1,049	1,435	1,325
Other Current Assets	431	810	948	1,027	1,283	712	1,554	4,328	1,600	1,705
Current Assets	3,984	4,304	4,277	3,532	4,699	5,189	6,210	8,144	8,298	5,529
Total Assets	**10,617**	**11,942**	**13,157**	**13,031**	**13,418**	**13,206**	**15,023**	**17,891**	**19,057**	**17,258**
Total Equity	3,963	4,212	4,455	4,448	5,119	5,407	6,118	7,246	8,332	7,264
Long-Term Debt	2,348	2,293	2,738	3,297	2,566	1,821	1,146	513	298	1,381
Other Non-Current Liabilities	546	593	668	694	710	1,079	1,227	1,233	1,525	1,509
Non-Current Liabilities	2,894	2,886	3,406	3,991	3,276	2,900	2,373	1,745	1,824	2,890
Short-Term Debt	-	102	767	587	25	25	199	100	100	1,724
Trade Payables	2,411	2,695	2,654	2,361	2,854	2,580	3,153	5,003	5,155	2,838
Other Current Liabilities	1,349	2,047	1,875	1,644	2,144	2,294	3,179	3,797	3,646	2,542
Current Liabilities	3,761	4,844	5,297	4,592	5,023	4,899	6,532	8,900	8,900	7,104
Total Liabilities	6,654	7,730	8,702	8,583	8,299	7,799	8,905	10,645	10,724	9,994
Total Equity and Liabilities	**10,617**	**11,942**	**13,157**	**13,031**	**13,418**	**13,206**	**15,023**	**17,891**	**19,057**	**17,258**
Vehicles Sold	94,106	1,01,990	1,14,611	89,337	1,04,902	1,40,457	1,45,066	1,74,873	1,97,366	1,25,200
Employees	15,812	15,734	14,668	11,552	11,204	10,352	11,906	11,865	12,133	11,463

Source: CMIE Prowess, Company Annual Report, and authors' calculations.

EXHIBIT 4.6 Trends in Cash Flow Statements of Ashok Leyland

Rs Crore	*FY 2011*	*FY 2012*	*FY 2013*	*FY 2014*	*FY 2015*	*FY 2016*	*FY 2017*	*FY 2018*	*FY 2019*	*FY 2020*
Net Profit before Tax and Extraordinary Items	802	690	471	(44)	442	827	1,330	2,386	2,497	362
Add: Net Non-Cash Adjustments	431	585	416	261	680	1,477	995	715	665	849
Operating Cash Flow before Working Cap changes	1,233	1,275	887	216	1,122	2,303	2,325	3,101	3,162	1,211
Decrease/Increase in Trade and Other Receivables	35	(381)	(213)	47	(166)	(25)	320	85	(1,585)	1,317
Decrease/Increase in Inventories	(571)	(22)	335	707	(210)	(349)	(810)	903	(926)	1,447
Increase/Decrease in Trade and Other Payables	366	424	(170)	(338)	1,081	(272)	440	1,578	1,188	(2,600)
Increase/Decrease in Other Current Liabilities	–	–	–	–	–	466	227	403	(1,569)	(415)
Cash Flow Generated from Operations	1,064	1,297	838	633	1,827	2,124	2,502	6,070	269	959
Less: Direct Taxes Paid	150	150	110	32	52	441	348	427	560	94
Cash Flow before Extraordinary Items	914	1,147	728	601	1,774	1,683	2,155	5,643	(291)	865
Less Extraordinary Items	–	–	–	47	-	–	–	–	–	–
Net Cash Flow from Operating Activities	**914**	**1,147**	**728**	**554**	**1,774**	**1,683**	**2,155**	**5,643**	**(291)**	**865**
Net Purchase of Fixed Assets	(350)	(691)	(644)	(110)	94	34	(366)	(534)	(731)	(1,292)
Net Purchase of Investments	(904)	(303)	(514)	(28)	(74)	380	(1,070)	(2,975)	3,003	(430)
Net Income from Investments and Other Items	14	(64)	(7)	30	84	(52)	(40)	80	(31)	(379)
Net Cash Flow from Investing Activities	**(1,240)**	**(1,058)**	**(1,164)**	**(108)**	**104**	**362**	**(1,476)**	**(3,429)**	**2,240**	**(2,102)**

Issue of Shares Net of Issue Expenses	–	–	–	–	667	–	–	5	9	–
Issue of Long-Term Borrowings	460	577	1,171	1,201	157	–	175	–	–	1,215
Repayment of Long-Term Borrowings	87	358	746	859	1,023	728	1,023	1,174	632	240
Issue of Short-Term Borrowings	–	1,178	10,269	13,672	7,600	14,553	6,190	9,240	10,951	12,614
Repayment of Short-Term Borrowings	–	1,083	9,606	13,839	8,175	14,553	6,115	9,339	10,951	11,005
Lease Liability Paid	–	–	–	–	–	–	–	–	–	22
Interest Paid	154	247	363	436	406	268	164	168	103	146
Dividend and Dividend Tax Paid	233	309	309	187	–	154	325	549	860	1,270
Net Cash Inflows from Other Financing Activities	–	–	–	–	–	(60)	(110)	(106)	(30)	2
Net Cash Flow from Financing Activities	**(14)**	**(241)**	**417**	**(449)**	**(1,179)**	**(1,211)**	**(1,372)**	**(2,091)**	**(1,616)**	**1,149**

Source: CMIE Prowess and authors' calculations.

Questions

1. Do a SWOT analysis of ALL in 2020 as a credit from the viewpoint of a debt investor.
2. Analyse the long-term trends in ALL's operating efficiency based on its financial statements.
3. Discuss if ALL was better prepared to handle a cyclical downturn in 2020 than it was in 2013.

Notes

1 Corporate announcement by Ashok Leyland dated May 14, 2020, https://www.bseindia.com/xml-data/corpfiling/AttachHis/98caf715-4db6-4651-847d-b0b272984eba.pdf
2 https://www.icra.in/Rationale/ShowRationaleReport/?Id=93403
3 https://www.siam.in/pressrelease-details.aspx?mpgid=48&pgidtrail=50&pid=475

5

SHOPPERS STOP

The Covid-19 Halt

On August 14, 2020, BS Nagesh, Chairman, Shoppers Stop, addressed the stock analysts at the earnings call for the first quarter of 2020–21. Recounting the challenges faced by the company due to the Covid-19 pandemic, he said:

> Covid regulations continue to hamper opening up the stores, inconsistent, erratic, irregular calls taken by local authorities, sometimes makers open the store, close the store, change the timing. And therefore, there has been inconsistency. Above all, malls and large stores in a few states are closed during the weekend due to government regulations and restrictions. Not only the government restrictions and regulations, but even the consumer behavior has changed. And in the last two months, we have been operating stores, we experienced the following change in behavior: There is significant decline in the footfall, about 92% in June gradually improving to 70% decline as of now.[1]

As the conference call continued, analysts realised that cost reduction could not match the revenue decline, making losses likely for more quarters. Cash losses, as well as outflows on ongoing investment, would lead to cash burn. Could the company withstand the crisis and emerge slowly out of it? Or would it stumble over and fall behind its peers?

Shoppers Stop: Evolution and Outlook

Established in 1991, Shoppers Stop was one of the leading departmental store chains in India. It had 84 department stores and 209 other multi-format

DOI: 10.4324/9781032724478-7

stores operating in a retail space of 4.5 million sq ft as of March 31, 2020. It retailed apparel, cosmetics, household items, food products, books, and home decor. Apparels constituted the largest segment, contributing to more than 61% of sales.

Sales had grown at a relatively sluggish rate of 5.6% per annum during 2015–16 to 2018–19, and the return on capital employed (ROCE) was low, averaging around 9% during the same period. However, since the company had a moderate level of debt, it appeared relatively sound from a credit perspective.

CRISIL Research forecasted the growth in market size of the retail sector in India at 11.5% to 12% per annum from an estimated Rs 66 trillion in 2019–20 to Rs 104 trillion by 2023–24, having grown at an annual rate of 12% during 2013–14 to 2019–20. The retail sector's growth was driven by rising income levels and increased consumer spending. The informal sector dominated due to the prevalence of small stores. However, the share of organised retailing was estimated to increase at 19–21%, reaching Rs 15.5 to Rs 16 trillion by 2023–24.[2]

The organised brick and mortar retail industry faced a significant increase in competition due to rising physical and online retailing investments. The critical competitors for Shoppers Stop included Reliance Retail, Lifestyle Retail, Trent, and Aditya Birla Fashion and Retail.

Fighting the Covid-19 Challenge

In the April–June 2020 quarter, sales were almost washed out due to the lockdowns, falling sequentially by 92% to Rs 56 crore from Rs 724 crore in the previous quarter (see Exhibit 5.1 for share price impact). Purchases

EXHIBIT 5.1 Shoppers Stop: Share Price Trend

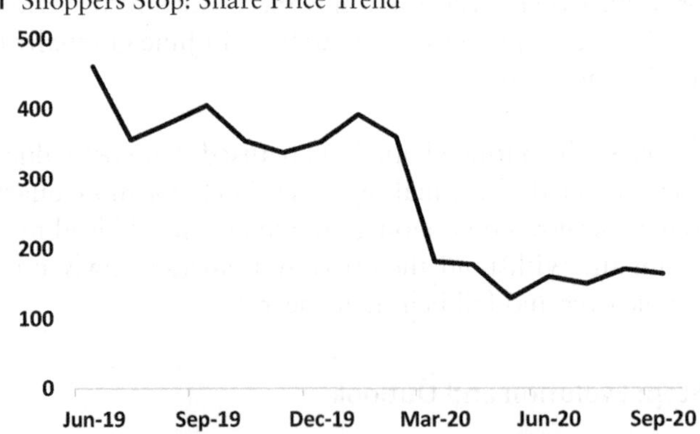

Source: Prepared by authors based on data from www.bseindia.com

of stock-in-trade fell by a proportional 79%, a sharp increase in inventory partly offset that reduction.

Shoppers Stop held aggressive re-negotiations of lease rentals to bring down other expenses. Travel expenses became nil, and other administrative costs were cut by 75%. The company also started bringing down the employee costs in June, but workforce rationalisation initially led to one-time expenses. A change in useful life resulted in a decline in reported depreciation. Despite the cost reductions, the company reported a net loss of Rs 120 crore.

The company had saved Rs 185 crore in costs during the quarter, and the full-year savings were expected to be Rs 450 crore. Shoppers Stop could also increase the share of the higher-margin private-label business to 15%, which was still low compared to peers. The management set a target to increase the percentage of private label in total revenues to 30%. To preserve cash, the company also reduced its planned capital expenditure, focussing on setting up smaller stores in Tier 2 and 3 towns.

Caution or Optimism?

As analysts continued to monitor Shoppers Stop, business volumes gradually returned. Revenues sequentially grew more than fivefold to Rs 297 crore in July–September 2020 quarter, though they were still around one-third of the levels in the same quarter of 2019. Most of the company's stores became operational in August 2020 though they were still operating much below peak levels, and the recovery in demand for apparel was slow. India's north and east regions and the non-metro cities and towns without extended lock-down saw better customer response. The company improved its e-commerce sales by 50% year on year to 7.8% of revenues through significant initiatives and improvements.

The trend in cost reductions in rentals and overheads continued. As sales picked up, the company was able to bring down its inventories. The net loss and operating cash loss declined, though the company had to resort to borrowings to meet the shortfall in cash flows. The trends were similar in the case of peer companies (Exhibit 5.2).

Though the company's management did its best, the analysts had reasons to be cautious. Sales recovery was gradual in the apparel segment, where Shoppers Stop had a high concentration. The competitive intensity was high and increasing, especially in the apparel segment. The company's share of private label business and e-commerce sales, while improving, was still low. Did the management have any more levers left to drive the company out of its problems if the pandemic crisis lingered long rather than ended soon?

EXHIBIT 5.2 Trend in Financial Performance

Rs Crore	*Financial Year Ending*		
	March 2018	*March 2019*	*March 2020*
Revenue from Contracts with Customers	3,697	3,578	3,464
Total Income	**3,713**	**3,597**	**3,498**
Purchase of Stock-in-trade	2,243	2,794	2,174
Decrease/(Increase) in Inventories	25	-716	-167
Employee Benefits Expense	316	330	335
Other Expenses	902	924	571
EBITDA	***228***	***264***	***586***
Depreciation and Amortisation Expenses	115	141	450
Finance Costs	38	14	197
Profit before Exceptional Items and Tax	75	110	-62
Profit for the Year	**214**	**65**	**-142**
Property, Plant, and Equipment	600	545	506
Right to Use Assets#	–	–	1,342
Total Non-Current Assets	1,189	1,067	2,406
Inventories	356	1,072	1,239
Trade Receivables	48	47	34
Cash and Cash Equivalents	5	17	4
Investments	20	42	154
Total Current Assets	598	1,409	1,674
Total Assets	**1,788**	**2,476**	**4,081**
Total Equity[a]	904	915	67
Borrowings	44	2	0
Lease Liability[a]	-	–	2,077
Total Non-Current Liabilities	45	3	2,078
Trade Payables	519	1,277	1,522
Borrowings	38	30	155
Lease Liability[a]	–	–	12
Total Current Liabilities	839	1,558	1,936
Total Equity and Liabilities	**1,788**	**2,476**	**4,081**
Cash Flows from Operating Activities	298	202	576
Cash Flows from Investing Activities	-35	-125	-284
Cash Flows from Financing Activities	-171	-63	-433
Net Increase/(Decrease) in Cash and Equivalents	92	13	-141

Source: Prepared by authors based on Shoppers Stop annual reports.

Note: [a]Changes in 2019–20 due to IND AS 116 transition.

EXHIBIT 5.3 Performance Trend Across Peers

Rs Crore	*Apr to Jun 2019*	*Jul to Sep 2019*	*Oct to Dec 2020*	*Jan to Mar 2020*	*Apr to Jun 2020*	*Jul to Sep 2020*
Shoppers Stop						
Revenues	854	866	1,019	724	56	297
EBITDA	139	138	200	75	–106	–38
Net Profit	0	–8	–7	–127	–120	–98
Inventories	n.a.	1,152	n.a.	1,239	n.a.	1,054
Receivables	n.a.	37	n.a.	34	n.a.	27
Cash and Current Investments	n.a.	58	n.a.	158	n.a.	89
Payables	n.a.	1,413	n.a.	1,522	n.a.	1,416
Total Debt	n.a.	1,919	n.a.	2,245	n.a.	2,275
Total Equity	n.a.	342	n.a.	67	n.a.	–128
Market Cap	4,282	3,763	3,276	1,686	1,485	1,523
Trent Ltd						
Revenues	800	855	988	843	248	585
EBITDA	163	129	168	84	–124	0
Net Profit	36	17	49	13	–184	–79
Inventories	n.a.	552	n.a.	608	n.a.	388
Receivables	n.a.	20	n.a.	17	n.a.	14
Cash and Current Investments	n.a.	1,044	n.a.	835	n.a.	631
Payables	n.a.	269	n.a.	298	n.a.	299
Total Debt	n.a.	n.a.	n.a.	2,619	n.a.	n.a.
Total Equity	n.a.	2,343	n.a.	2,468	n.a.	2,170
Market Cap	14,654	17,202	18,739	17,218	21,873	23,885
Aditya Birla Fashion and Retail						
Revenues	2,065	2,308	2,583	1,832	323	1,028
EBITDA	314	339	408	150	-360	-8
Net Profit	22	–2	-38	-146	-410	-188
Inventories	n.a.	2,356	n.a.	2,367	n.a.	2,105
Receivables	n.a.	1,068	n.a.	840	n.a.	911
Cash and Current Investments	n.a.	165	n.a.	274	n.a.	180
Payables	n.a.	2,738	n.a.	2,290	n.a.	1,730
Total Debt	n.a.	1,919	n.a.	5,285	n.a.	5,267
Total Equity	n.a.	1,358	n.a.	1,088	n.a.	997
Market Cap	16,657	16,351	17,926	11,834	9,698	10,943

Source: Prepared by authors based on data from Bloomberg and Shoppers Stop annual reports.

Questions

1. Analyse the trends in quarterly performance of the company in terms of profitability and working capital efficiency (Exhibit 5.3). Do you find that the company's actions to reduce losses and cash burn produced adequate results?
2. Compare Shoppers Stop with its peers before the pandemic affected the Indian economy (March 2020). Based only on the financial figures, which company would have the higher ability to withstand financial stress?
3. Based on figures provided in Exhibit 5.3, rank the companies in terms of how they fared in relative terms during the pandemic.
4. Describe the financial consequences for Shoppers Stop if the pandemic were to last for a few years?

Notes

1 Shoppers Stop (2020). Shoppers Stop Limited Earning Call Transcript for Q1 FY21.

2 https://www.bseindia.com/downloads/ipo/Letter%20of%20offer_300720201202.pdf

6

CASH BUDGETING AT PARISHKAR CLEANTECH

Riya Poddar, Founder and Director of Parishkar Cleantech finished browsing through the company's unaudited financial statements for 2019–20 mailed to her by Vinita Shroff, her finance manager. April 2021 had brought her a feeling of deja vu, with the surge in Covid-19 cases going well beyond the figures seen in 2020. The pandemic was surely going to disrupt her business and temporarily her plans to take it online. More than the bottom line, Riya was concerned about the cash position of her company.

Parishkar Cleantech provided cleaning equipment and supplies to hospitals, hotels, schools, and offices in Mumbai. The company's product range included janitorial service carts, garbage carts, spray bottles, sponges, scourers, dusters, microfibre cloths, glass polishing cloths, cleaning brushes, mops, buckets, protective gloves, and cleaning chemicals. It was a small-sized operation with 21 employees and around 230 business customers. It had recorded sales of around Rs 17 crore in 2019–20, having declined from around Rs 21 crores in the previous year due to the Covid-19 pandemic.

The management team included the two founders, Riya and her sister Richa. While Riya focused on operations and finance, Richa took care of marketing and promotions. Riya was assisted by a purchase manager and a finance manager, while Richa had a team of salespersons helping her.

The SME segment dominated the cleaning equipment and chemicals business in India. Apart from the growth in the key end-use sectors, the increasing awareness of cleanliness and hygiene standards, partly aided by the government's "Swachh Bharat Abhiyan," was driving the growth in this sector.

DOI: 10.4324/9781032724478-8

Having sold off its equipment assembling facility in 2018, Parishkar did not manufacture but was only involved in branding, distribution, and sales. It had developed capabilities in acquiring bulk orders from large customers and fulfilling the orders to customers' satisfaction. Parishkar found it feasible to manage the stocks at moderate levels through accurate demand forecasts and selection of reliable suppliers.

Taking the Business Online

While B2C e-commerce had been on a high growth path over the past two decades, B2B e-commerce in India got a fillip only in the past five years. The recent growth in B2B e-commerce was due to increasing digital transactions and the rising share of the formal economy triggered by demonetisation and GST. The business models of the established B2B platforms had also matured.

Like several other businesses, the penetration of online demand also increased for cleaning equipment across product categories. The rising online penetration provided Parishkar's suppliers an opportunity to sell their products on B2B online platforms directly. Similarly, the more cost-conscious customers, including some facility management companies, had increasingly placed orders online and used the pricing details to negotiate the prices with Parishkar. Thus, pressed on both sides, Parishkar saw a decline in its margins and stagnation in sales growth.

To rejuvenate the business, the founders decided to transition their business online, develop their website, and promote their products on the established aggregator platforms. They aimed to increase the company's geographical reach through online presence and by increasing their network of suppliers and third-party logistics partners. Additionally, they could enter the B2C segment and tap the growing demand for household cleaning equipment.

The game plan was to rapidly increase the business scale with limited incremental selling, general and administrative expenses to offset the continued pressure on gross margins. The incremental costs in 2021–22 included outsourcing website development and maintenance, dedicated computer terminals, and hiring a trained person to undertake online marketing efforts on an ongoing basis. However, to achieve meaningful scales, they would require setting up multiple fulfilment centers and investing more in technology and logistics in the coming years.

Cash Budgeting

Since Parishkar's business was not seasonal, its financial planning had traditionally consisted of preparing annual forecasts. The credit officer at Parishkar's bank also primarily relied on the projected balance sheet to assess the short-term deficit and propose the working capital funding limits.

He also required the monthly stock statements, bank statements, and personal financial documents of the founder-directors.

The Covid-19 pandemic adversely affected the cash flows of Parishkar starting from April 2020. Business volumes dipped as customers' offices were closed. Additionally, several customers delayed payments, citing operational disruptions or cash flow problems. Several suppliers could also not sustain their operations, further affecting business. The adverse effect of the pandemic on cash flows caused Riya and Richa to check the financial position on a monthly and sometimes even weekly basis. As the first wave subsided, the business revived, and the cash position improved to a comfortable Rs 70 lakh by the end of March 2021. But the founders understood the need to be proactive in handling such disruptions.

In this context, Riya had instructed Vinita to prepare a month-wise cash budget for 2021–22. Since the company had no track record of online revenue streams, forecasting uncertainty would increase. But it was the second wave of the Covid-19 pandemic which made forecasting particularly challenging. Riya had therefore asked Vinita to work with two alternative scenarios of business disruption due to the pandemic. In scenario one, the business would gradually return to normal by August 2021. In scenario two, the company would return to normal only by the end of the financial year (see Exhibits 6.1 and 6.2).

Riya had also spoken with the bank credit officer. He had been sympathetic and praised the company for maintaining a good credit record right

EXHIBIT 6.1 Projected Monthly Sales of Physical and Online Business

Rs Lakh	*Base Scenario*		*Alternative Scenario*	
	Physical	*Online*	*Physical*	*Online*
Jan 21	140	0	140	0
Feb 21	140	0	140	0
Mar 21	140	0	140	0
Apr 21	43	7	43	7
May 21	43	7	43	7
Jun 21	72	7	43	7
Jul 21	72	14	50	10
Aug 21	72	14	60	10
Sep 21	116	14	75	10
Oct 21	159	14	90	10
Nov 21	174	14	100	10
Dec 21	174	14	120	10
Jan 22	174	14	140	14
Feb 22	174	14	160	14
Mar 22	174	14	174	14
Apr 22	174	14	174	14

Source: Prepared by authors.

EXHIBIT 6.2 Business Assumptions for 2021–22

1. Customer collections (physical business): 10% in same month, 70% in 1 month, 20% in 2 months.
2. Customer collections (online) for B2B business: 70% in same month, 30% in 1 month; for B2C business: 100% in same month. Proportion of online business – B2B (80%), B2C (20%).
3. Cost of goods sold to be 85% of sales for the physical business, 90% of sales for online business. Purchases made one month in advance.
4. Supplier payments: 30% in the same month, 60% after one month, 10% after two months.
5. Other expenses (annual): Rs 1.49 crore for employee expenses, Rs 34 lakhs for advertising and promotion, Rs 9 lakh for admin expenses. The online business contributed Rs 7.5 lakh to new employees and Rs 1.5 lakh for administrative costs. The payments for other expenses may be assumed to be made within the month and evenly distributed during the year.
6. Depreciation on building and computers of Rs 6 lakh during the year.
7. Interest payment of Rs 3 lakh each in April, July, October, and January.
8. Income tax payments of Rs 82,000 were due in June, Rs 1.63 lakh each in September and December, and Rs 1.36 lakh in March. The alternative scenario assumes that advance tax payment is made only in June due to expected loss during the year.
9. Planned capital expenditure of Rs 5 lakh in April and Rs 3 lakh in September on account of hardware and software to support online business.
10. Minimum cash balance must be maintained at Rs 50 lakh.

Source: Prepared by authors.

through the pandemic. He informed Riya that the bank would be willing to provide additional short-term loans to a limit of Rs 40 lakh on an ad hoc basis as and when the need arose. The interest rate on the ad hoc loan would be 15% per annum. The interest would be payable quarterly, and the loan and any accrued but unpaid interest would be due for repayment by the end of the year.

Questions

1. How soon could the company run into a cash deficit? Would the ad hoc support of Rs 40 lakh from the bank be sufficient?
2. What levers could the founders use if the cash deficit exceeded the bank's support? Should they delay the investment in online business?

7

SPARK ELECTRICALS

Reviewing FMEG Business Credit Policy

On February 8, 2020, Krish Fernandez, Chief Executive Officer (CEO) of Spark Electrical Enterprise, called her secretary and instructed: "Call Pragati, Pallavi and Prapti for an urgent meeting at 3.00 pm today, in my conference room. Inform them; we will discuss the credit policy changes (Exhibit 7.1) for the rapidly growing, high-margin, Fast Moving Electric Good (FMEG) business." Pragati, Pallavi, and Prapti were Chief Marketing Officer (CMO), Chief Financial Officer (CFO), and National Sales Manager (NSM), respectively, at Spark. Each one of them was associated with Spark for over a decade.

Spark Electricals and Indian Electricals and Home Appliances Market

Krishna Awasthi established Spark Electrical in 1993 to cater to the rapidly growing cables and wires (C&W) Indian market. Post-1991 reforms, there was a significant push towards infrastructure building, which propelled growth in the C&W business. Given the attractiveness of the business, many Indian and multinational firms entered the business, but Spark could establish itself as a "value for money" player with good brand recall. As a result, it dominated the C&W market with an 11.3% market share for the calendar year (CY) 2019. The electricals and home appliances market in India was worth Rs 45,000 crore and Rs 70,000 crore, respectively. The electricals and home appliances market was excepted to grow at 12% and 15% between 2019 and 2025.[1] Spark reported Rs 7,000 crore of revenue in FY19 and earned Rs 840 crore in EBITDA (FMEG contributed to 140 crore to EBITDA[2]) and Rs 490 crore in net income on a balance sheet size of

DOI: 10.4324/9781032724478-9

EXHIBIT 7.1 Pallavi's Email to Krish

February 8, 2020
Dear Krish,
Greetings.

Further to our meeting on February 1, 2020, I prepared the following proposals based on inputs received from Prapti and my analysis.

We have three-stage credit management process. Credit granting decision, credit terms and collection process.

Currently, we divide our dealers and customers into four major categories: Excellent, good, average and sub-standard. We extend full credit to our Excellent and good category customer, whereas we grant limited credit to average customers and sell goods only on open account to sub-standard customers. Our standard credit terms are "2.5/10 net 60." However, only 10 percent of the customers avail discount and those customers who do not avail the benefit of discount take about 75 days to pay their dues. Given business compulsions and competitive pressures, we do not take any action in such cases. Our collection efforts are robust, and the bad debt losses are around 2% of total sales. However, some dealers and customers think that we are too aggressive compared to our competitors. A few dealers have mentioned that while they might be willing to do business with us, they view our prudent collection efforts as arm twisting.

We have come up with four proposals to incentivise our dealers and customers. We can look at implementing any one or a combination after a thorough discussion on underlying assumptions and consequences. Please note that these proposals are for FMEG business only.

Proposal 1:
Offer full credit to dealers and customers with an average rating, and that will boost sales by 10%. However, this incremental sale might come with higher bad debt losses of close to 5%. I hope our sales team can ensure that such high bad debt losses remain confined to incremental sales only.

Proposal 2:
Change credit terms from current "2.5/10 net 60" to "2.5/10 net 75". It will increase sales by 6% and reduce the proportion of customers availing discount to only 5% and those who do not avail discount will pay only after 85 days. I am not sure, but such a decision might increase bad debt losses by 0.2% on entire sales rather than just incremental sales.

Proposal 3:
Change in credit terms from "2.5/10 net 60" to "3/10 net 75". It will encourage those who want to pay early and at the same time, offers flexibility to those who require a more extended credit period. Such a decision will increase sales by 12% and the proportion of customers availing discount from present 10% to 35%. Those who do not avail of discount might pay only after 85 days. The higher proportion of customers availing of discount might reduce the percentage of bad-debt losses by at least 20 basis points, given that some customers having cheap access to bank credit might not want to forgo the benefit of higher trade discount offered.

Proposal 4:
Relaxation in collection efforts will increase sales by 5%. However, such a decision will lead to the average collection period going up to 75 days (proportion of customers availing discount will not change.) It will also increase bad debt losses by 30 basis points on entire FMEG sales.

Our post-tax weighted average cost of capital is 13%, and we pay an effective 25% tax on our income. We can borrow funds from the bank at 8%.

I have done some preliminary cost-benefit analysis for these proposals and will present it during the meeting.

Yours Sincerely
Pallavi

Rs 5,000 crore revenues, EBITDA and net income reported an excellent compounded annual growth rate (CAGR) of 15%, 25% and 35%, respectively, over five years ending FY19. While C&W and other business-to-business grew at 11% CAGR, FMEG[3] business, started just seven-year back, was the real show-stopper. It delivered 45% CAGR over five year, and its contribution in total revenue jumped from 4% to 10% in a five-year time. The trend was likely to continue. Not only did it contributed to growth, but it was also a margin business.[4] Accordingly, Spark focused on building its stronghold in the FMEG business. Out of a total of 4000 odd dealers across India, a little more than 2000 were exclusively for its FMEG business. Spark's products were available at more than 1,50,000 outlets across India.

FMEG Business[5]

Fans, lights, LEDs, switchgears, switches formed the FMEG business. Rising Indian middle class, discretionary income, rural electrification, urbanisation and digital connectivity were driving growth in FMEG market. Fans, switches, switchgears, and lighting dominated the FMEG business with market size of Rs 9,300, Rs 4,300, Rs 21,000, and Rs 22,300 crore, respectively. It was a large market and expanding at a hectic pace. Both organised and unorganised, regional and national players were competing to gain their share of the pie from this fast-growing, profitable business opportunity.

Credit Policy for FMEG Business

Spark, on average, had an average collection period of anywhere close to 80 days, with bad debt losses close to 2%. However, in the last few years, Spark worked closely with its dealers and banks to arrange channel financing for dealers to boost its business and collection efficiency. By 2019, channel financing contributed to dealers funding. However, the collection period was still hovering around 70 days. Recently, Pragati and Prapti pushed for liberalising credit policy followed by Spark given the nature of competition. They both felt that the FMEG business was growing at a healthy rate; there was potential for more. A rigid credit policy followed by Spark, which might be appropriate for C&W business, might prove to be a hurdle in exploiting its full potential of FMEG business. The earlier meeting ended in a stalemate as Pallavi did not agree to such a proposal. She cited plenty of examples to counter such relaxation in credit policy. Doing so might increase in days sales outstanding, increase in working financing requirement, increase bad debt losses, and increased collection efforts. However, Prapti argued that relaxation in credit policy would substantially increase sales and the corresponding increase in operating profit, offset the increase in financing cost, and a potential increase in bad debt losses. Krish asked Pallavi to look into possible changes in levers of credit policy and the impact of such changes on Spark's net income. Pallavi sought inputs from Prapti, prepared her note, and emailed it to Krish, Pragati, and Prapti. On receipt of this email, Krish called for a meeting as they had to roll out a new credit policy for dealers and their customers for the FY21.

Krish wanted to know specific answers before finalising the credit policy for FY21.

1. What would be the change in net income should Spark decide to relax credit standards?
2. What would be the change in net income should Spark decide to offer a longer credit period?
3. What would be the change in net income should Spark decide to offer a higher cash discount?
4. What would be the change in net income should Spark decide to relax its collection efforts?
5. What would be the feasibility of changing multiple levers of credit policy at the same time?

Notes

1 Havells' Investor's presentation, Feb 2020. https://www.havells.com/HavellsProductImages/HavellsIndia/pdf/About-Havells/Investor-Relations/Events/Havells_India_Limited_February_2020.pdf accessed on March 30, 2021.
2 Rs 25 crore of the fixed cost related to FMEG business (other than depreciation) was already subtracted before arriving at FMEG EBITDA.
3 FMEG means Fast Moving Electric Business.
4 B2C means Business to Consumer, and B2B means Business to Business.
5 Adapted from Polycab's corporate presentation. https://polycab.com/wp-content/uploads/2021/01/Polycab-India-Limited_Q3FY21-Corporate-Presentation.pdf accessed on March 30, 2021.

8

BREAK-EVEN ANALYSIS OF SRI KRISHNA RESTAURANT

Sri Krishna was a small restaurant located in suburban Mumbai that provided various traditional Indian cuisines during lunch and dinner hours. During the 1990s to early 2000s, the restaurant used to do good business catering to customers from nearby locality including families, small offices, and students. However, it continued to operate out of rented space, as the landlord did not want to sell, and Murali, the owner, did not want to move to an alternative location. Gradually, as customer preference moved away from traditional cuisines and conventional service to alternative cuisines and quick service, business levels dropped, and the restaurant started making losses.

The Operations

The restaurant was open to diners between 11.30 a.m. and 3.30 p.m. and between 6.30 p.m. and 11.30 p.m. throughout the week. The restaurant was closed only on five weekdays during the year. The restaurant's dining space consisted of ten tables with seating combinations for two, four, or eight people. The average table turnover rate was 1.5 per day on weekdays and 2.5 per day on the weekends. Though occasionally large families, groups of office employees, and students visited Sri Krishna, the most typical customer profile was a couple with an average bill of Rs 600 per group on the weekdays.[1]On weekends, the average group size increased to four, and the average bill rises to Rs 900 per group. Sri Krishna offered an early-hours discount of 25% on weekends for orders placed between 6.30 p.m. and 7.30 p.m., a practice it had started 20 years ago when the place used to get

DOI: 10.4324/9781032724478-10

crowded by 8.00 p.m. Around 10% of the weekend diners continued to avail themselves of the discount.

Murali managed to keep tight control on costs. The main variable costs included food materials comprising nearly 25% of revenues. Cooking gas was an additional, relatively minor, variable expense.

Fixed costs consisted primarily of lease rentals, wages, depreciation on equipment, utilities, professional fees, advertising, and promotion (Exhibits 8.1 and 8.2). Due to old age, Murali occasionally visited the restaurant and appointed a manager to oversee the supervision.

Sri Krishna had leased space of 1600 sq. ft. Of this space, half was dedicated to dining space, 25% to the kitchen area, and the remaining 25% to reception, billing, and manager's desk. The lease rental was Rs 120 per sq ft per month. Depreciation on equipment was Rs 2 lakh.

EXHIBIT 8.1 Staff Details

Designation	*Nos.*	*Annual Salary (Rs)*
Manager	1	4,00,000
Cashier	1	2,40,000
Head Chef	1	2,40,000
Chefs	2	1,80,000
Waiter	3	1,50,000
Security Guard	1	1,20,000
Cleaners	2	90,000
Kitchen Helper	1	90,000

Source: Prepared by authors.

EXHIBIT 8.2 Other Operating Expenses

Expense	*Amount*
Advertising & Promotion (incl. Website)	10,000
Professional Fees	20,000
Utility – Cooking Gas	24,000
Utility – Electricity	1,20,000
Utility – Water Tax	6,000
Utility – Telephone/Internet	24,000
Supplies – Cleaning	12,000
Supplies – Office	6,000
Breakage	6,000
Repairs & Maintenance	12,000
Garbage & Pest Control	12,000
Insurance Premium	30,000
Miscellaneous Expenses	12,000

Source: Prepared by authors.

EXHIBIT 8.3 Fixed Assets

Asset	*Rs*
Deposit	16,00,000
Licences	20,000
Kitchen Equipment & Utensils	20,000
Furniture & Interiors	2,00,000
Cutlery	20,000
Air-conditioning	1,00,000
LCD	30,000

Source: Prepared by authors.

Exhibit 8.3 provides the details of Sri Krishna's fixed assets. The restaurant maintained an average inventory of materials of around five days. The average receivables arising out of credit card account transfers were low, at about two days. The bank balance was maintained at around Rs 3 lakh and petty cash at around Rs 20,000.

Sri Krishna maintained payment terms of 15 days with its suppliers. It had a line of credit from the local bank of Rs 3 lakh but used it based on actual need. Long-term funds included equity of Rs 15 lakh and a term loan of Rs 6 lakh to be repaid over six years. The total interest paid worked out to Rs 1.2 lakh per annum. Being a proprietorship, the effective tax rate borne by Murali on account of profits or losses from Sri Krishna was his marginal income tax rate of 30%.

The SRK Transformation

Murali decided to make Sri Krishna profitable by increasing prices, bringing down the costs to the extent feasible, market research, renovation, and rebranding, including advertising and promotion under the new name "SRK." He estimated that by improving the sourcing of their food supplies, they could bring the material costs down from 25% of revenues to around 22% of revenues at current prices. Excluding the one-time expenses he would incur on the transformation, he reckoned that he would bring down the annual fixed costs other than lease rentals and depreciation by around 10%. Moreover, based on the brand, ambiance, and menu changes, he reckoned that he could increase table turnover by 20%.

He enlisted the help of Rosita, a market research consultant, to decide an optimal change in menu prices. Based on her research, Rosita believed that there was little room to increase the prices of menu items, given the competition. Given Rosita's feedback, Murali decided to focus on the table turns and cost controls instead.

Questions

1. Prepare the revenue and profit model of Sri Krishna restaurant based on existing business data.
2. Explain why the restaurant is making losses by doing a break-even analysis of revenues for the existing restaurant. Next, conduct a sensitivity analysis of the profits with volumes by estimating the degree of operating, financial, and total leverage. Finally, validate your results by comparing them with actual change.
3. Estimate the new break-even and degree of leverage under the proposed plan. Will SRK make profits based on your estimates?

Note

1 Excluding GST of 5%.

9

IKON PAINTS

Long-Term Financial Plan

Harsh Mittal was eagerly awaiting the commercial operation of the new paint units of Ikon Paints from April 2019. As one of the promoters and the person who envisioned the business, Harsh was excited about witnessing the growth of his new venture. The Ikon group was a leading player in the steel business and a fast-growing challenger in India's cement and construction businesses.

Ikon's rationale for entering the paint business was simple. The paints industry in India had an estimated turnover of Rs 42,000 crore. Asian Paints, the market leader, had a market share of close to 39%, enjoyed a net margin of more than 12%, and a return on equity of around 25%. Moreover, because of its dominant position over the past three decades, and highly profitable growth, Asian Paints also enjoyed a high price to earnings multiple of more than 60.

Assuming an annual industry growth of 11% per annum, a target market share by the financial year 2024–25 (FY25) of around 8–10%, net profit margin of 10%, and price to earnings multiple of 60, Harsh estimated that Ikon Paints could reach a value of $4 billion, before launching an initial public offer (IPO) in FY25. These back-of-the-envelope estimates were ambitious given the well-entrenched position of dominant players who accounted for over 70% of the industry revenues (see Exhibit 9.1) and the economies of scale required in manufacturing, sales, and distribution.

To help execute this plan, Harsh had brought in the best team of experienced paints industry professionals led by K Vijayan, Chief Executive Officer of Ikon Paints, and a marketing veteran from the paints industry. The company also leaned extensively on the Ikon group for its brand, captive

DOI: 10.4324/9781032724478-11

EXHIBIT 9.1 Trend in Net Sales of Leading Paint Companies

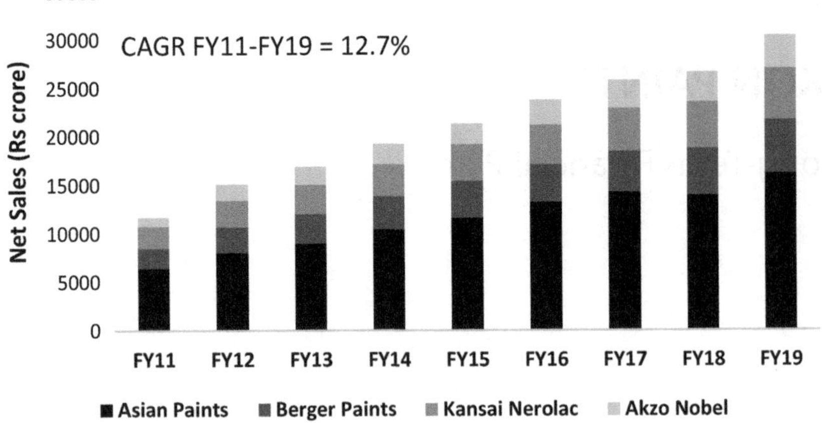

Source: Prepared by authors based on data from CMIE Prowess.

purchase of industrial paints, and most importantly, for financial support. The management developed a more realistic business and financial plan with inputs from the business heads, technical consultants, market surveys, and industry research.

Business Plan

Manufacturing Set Up

Ikon planned to set up one paint manufacturing plant at Vijaynagar in Karnataka (Ikon-K) and one at Vasind in Maharashtra (Ikon-M). Ikon-K would have a capacity of 100,000 KL per annum to produce decorative paints, while Ikon-M would have 25,000 KL per annum to make industrial paints.

The production would start during FY20, and both the plants would reach peak capacity utilisation in three years when the company would double its capacities; 75–80% of the production would be for decorative paints and 20–25% for industrial paints.

Marketing

Ikon, under the leadership of Vijayan, had prepared a detailed marketing plan for its decorative paints. The company planned a soft launch in Bangalore, followed by Hyderabad, Kochi, and Chennai in the south, followed by Mumbai, Pune, Nagpur, Ahmedabad, Surat, Vadodara, and Rajkot in the west. In the second year of operation, the company would try to extend its reach to the north and east of India.

It would set up an extensive dealership network, including exclusive Ikon Paint dealers in tier 1 cities and multi-brand dealers and multi-product dealers in tier 2 and tier 3 cities, capitalising on Ikon group's dealer network of cement and construction materials. The dealerships would be stocked adequately, and Ikon was prepared to absorb the high costs of slow-moving inventory in the initial months.

The advertising campaign would revolve around the lack of price transparency in the industry with such a wide range of prices for products that catered to the same need. In comparison, Ikon's pricing was transparent and straightforward, projected as one price for all the colours.

For industrial paints, the Ikon group would account for nearly half the output in the initial three years. Ikon Paints would approach all the business customers of the group's steel, construction, and cement businesses to increase the share of other customers gradually.

Project Cost and Financing

Initial costs would include capital expenditure for the capacities, preliminary and pre-operative expenses, margin for working capital required in FY20, and initial losses. The company would fund the all-inclusive project cost of Rs 600 crore by a term loan of Rs 400 crore and promoters' equity of Rs 200 crore. The term loan carried a rate of interest of 10% per annum to be paid semi-annually. The loan principal was repayable in ten half-yearly instalments starting from October 2020. Ikon tied up with another bank for a working capital loan to the extent of 75% of the working capital gap at an interest rate of 9% per annum.

The Ikon group would keep investing in the company to fund the losses in the initial few years in the form of equity and short-term unsecured loans. In addition, Ikon Steel had given a corporate guarantee for the loans. Based on the group's financial profile and support, the credit-rating agency had given Ikon Paints an investment grade rating of BBB-/stable.

Assumptions for Long-Term Financial Plan

The management used the following assumptions for preparing long-term financial projections:

Assumptions for revenues and operating expenses (Exhibit 9.2).

1. The paint industry estimated at Rs 42,000 crore in annual revenues in FY19 was forecasted to grow at a yearly rate of 11% until FY25. Ikon Paints was estimated to achieve a market share of 4% by FY25. Exports would be negligible during this period. Production capacities would be set up sufficiently in advance to ensure that there would be no constraints in achieving the expected market shares.

EXHIBIT 9.2 Assumptions for Revenue and Operating Expenses

	FY20	*FY21*	*FY22*	*FY23*	*FY24*	*FY25*
Industry Growth Rate	11%	11%	11%	11%	11%	11%
Ikon Paints' Market Share	0.50%	1.00%	1.50%	2.50%	3.25%	4.00%
Material and Packaging Costs (% of sales)	75%	59%	59%	59%	59%	59%
Employee Benefit Expenses (Rs cr)	39	60	69	110	145	175
Other Manufacturing Costs (% of sales)	1%	1%	1%	1%	1%	1%
Selling and Distribution (Rs cr)	60	130	215	320	460	560
Other Expenses (Rs cr)	20	25	30	45	50	55

Source: Prepared by authors.

2. Raw material and packaging costs: The cost of raw materials and packaging would be 52% and 7% of sales, except in FY20, when the raw material cost would be 68% of sales due to high price discounts.
3. Employee benefit: The employee benefit expenses would be semi-variable. The employee expenses would increase with capacities, production, and inflation.
4. Selling and distribution expenses would initially be high at around 25% of sales and decline below 18% of sales by FY25.
5. Other manufacturing costs would be at 1% of sales.
6. Corporate tax would be at an effective rate of around 29%, including surcharges. The company could carry forward tax losses for up to 8 years. There would be a slight loss of Rs 5 crore in FY19.

Assumptions for capital costs and financing Exhibit 9.3

1. Capex: The initial project cost, including preliminary expenses, preoperative expenses, and capital expenditure, was Rs 500 crore. The company would need to spend an equivalent amount to increase capacities by the end of FY22 and FY25. All the capacities were assumed to be commissioned by the end of the year. The annual maintenance capital expenditure would be roughly the same as the annual depreciation on the books of accounts in the previous year.
2. Depreciation: The company depreciated the assets using the straight-line method based on assumed useful life and residual value for the reported financial statements. The estimated weighted-average useful life was 25

years, and the residual value was 5% of the acquisition cost of assets. For income tax purposes, the company would charge depreciation on written-down value based on the prescribed rate. The weighted average rate given the mix of assets would be 17%.

3. Working capital: At the end of March 2019, Ikon Paints would maintain a beginning inventory (from purchased stock) of Rs 16 crore and a cash balance of Rs 7 crore. Against these current assets, it would have trade payables of Rs 13 crore. Exhibit 9.3 shows the assumptions for working capital for FY20 to FY25.
4. Equity & dividend: The promoters would bring in equity to partly finance the initial investment and losses. The company planned to schedule its IPO in FY25. The company would make no dividend payments till FY25.
5. Term loans and short-term loans: Exhibit 9.3 shows the details of term loans. Working capital loans would fund 75% of the working capital gap. In addition, short-term unsecured loans from promoters would meet short-term funding deficits. The company would raise the loans at the end of the year so that the interest would be applicable for the entire next year. The applicable interest rate was estimated to be 10% on long-term loans and 9% on short-term debt (Exhibit 9.3).

EXHIBIT 9.3 Assumptions for Capital Costs and Financing

	FY19	*FY20F*	*FY21F*	*FY22F*	*FY23F*	*FY24F*	*FY25F*
Capex for Incremental Capacity (Rs cr)	500	–	–	500	–	–	500
Working Capital							
–Inventory (Days COGS)	120	100	90	90	90	90	90
–Trade Receivables (days sales)	90	60	60	60	60	60	60
–Cash (% of sales)	5%	4%	4%	4%	4%	4%	4%
–Trade Payables (days of materials)	150	120	120	120	120	120	120
Equity (Rs cr)	150	50	150	250	–	–	400
Term Loan 1 (Rs cr)	350	50	–	–	–	–	–
- Scheduled Repayments	–	–	–40	–80	–80	–80	–80
Term Loan 2 (Rs cr)	–	–	–	400	–	–	–
–Scheduled Repayments	–	–	–	–	–	–40	–80

Source: Prepared by authors.

Questions

1. Prepare an estimate of the revenues, operating expenses, and profit before depreciation, interest, and tax (PBDIT).
2. Prepare the following estimates related to investments:
   a. Capex schedule.
   b. Depreciation schedule – both for financial reporting and income tax purposes.
   c. Working capital schedule.
3. Use a rough estimate of interest cost based on the term loan schedule and working capital finance requirement. Then, estimate the income tax to be paid based on these estimates.
4. Prepare a table of sources and uses of funds. Hence, estimate the external funding requirement by source. Revise the estimates of interest cost and the income tax paid, if necessary.
5. Prepare a balance sheet and statement of profit and loss.
6. Estimate the following financial ratios:
   a. Profitability: PBDIT margin, net profit margin, return on capital employed, return on equity.
   b. Solvency & liquidity: debt to equity, debt to PBDIT, debt service coverage ratio (DSCR), current ratio.
7. Create a stress scenario with lower sales growth (by 2% every year) and higher material costs (by 2% every year). Then, check the impact on the debt service coverage ratio.

10

CREDIT RATING OF DINESH ORGANICS

Vaibhav Zende, credit officer at Navbharat Bank, Pune, was scrutinising a proposal from an existing client to enhance the credit facility. The client was Dinesh Organics Ltd (DOL), a small specialty chemicals manufacturer with whom the bank had more than five years of relationship. Apart from an increase in cash credit limits for working capital, DOL had also requested a term loan for capacity expansion.

Vaibhav wanted to forward the proposal to the credit committee for approval with a favourable recommendation. But the credit approval process required him to review the internal rating based on updated information. The current rating had been dated, and he would have to check the business, the financials, and the management track record before recommending a rating for the company in his note.

Specialty Chemicals Industry in India

The specialty chemicals industry in India had an estimated size of approximately USD 32 billion (Rs 2.3 lakh crore) in 2019, as per a report by FICCI.[1] It had grown at an annual rate of about 12% in the past five years (Exhibit 10.1) and would grow at a marginally higher rate of 12.4% per annum over the next five years. The industry comprised various segments, the largest two being agrochemicals and dyes and pigments.

Specialty chemicals differed from commodity chemicals in terms of custom products for specific applications, which required extensive research and development (R&D). Players who continuously invested in R&D and product innovation enjoyed higher and more stable margins and higher returns on capital employed than in commodity chemicals. In specific segments such

DOI: 10.4324/9781032724478-12

EXHIBIT 10.1 Specialty Chemicals Industry Median Performance (2018–19)

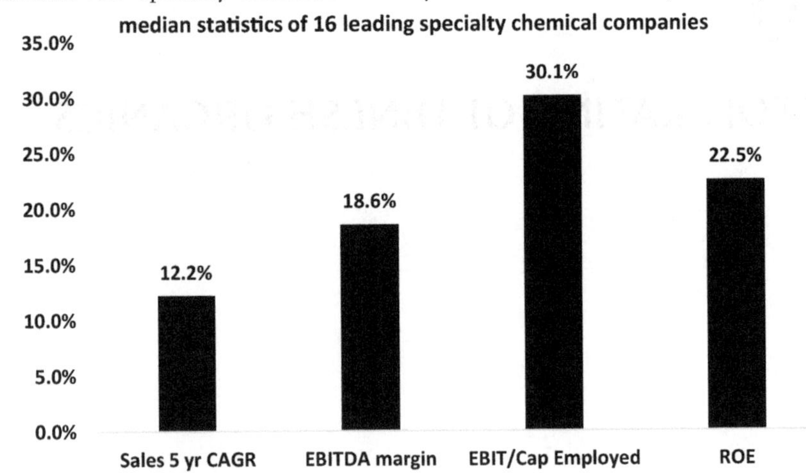

Source: Authors' estimates.

as dyes and pigments, the ban on manufacturing in developed economies and increasingly in China had resulted in increasing growth opportunities for Indian players. Indian companies were consequently operating at healthy capacity utilisation and were making significant investments in new capacities and R&D.

The critical success factors in the industry included production scale, R&D, product development, and diversification of products and customers. In some segments, having diverse raw material sources, distribution and branding also mattered.

Evolution and Growth of Dinesh Organics

Incorporated in 1987, Dinesh Organics Ltd manufactured water-based specialty chemicals (see Exhibits 10.2 and 10.3). It had an installed capacity of 6000 MT per annum, divided between two manufacturing units at Tarapur in Maharashtra. The company also had a modern R&D centre at Chinchwad in Pune. The company had 80 employees on its payroll.

DOL had been founded in 1987 by Dinesh Sawant as a private limited company and was converted into a public limited company in 2017 and had issued shares to the public by an initial public offer on the NSE Emerge platform for small and medium enterprises in 2018. Dinesh held 65% of the shares, 6% was held by his son Ajay, and public shareholders had the rest. Dinesh was the Managing Director of the company, while Ajay was the Director-Operations. Other senior management team members included two directors for textile and chemicals verticals, one director for technology, and one for business development. All the directors had more than two decades of experience in the specialty chemicals industry.

EXHIBIT 10.2 Credit Comparison with Similar Size Specialty Chemical Companies (2018–19)

Rs Crore	*Dinesh Organics*	*Sangita Chemicals*	*Vincent Specialty*	*Amzure Alkali*
Revenues	79.5	187.7	32.4	71.6
EBITDA	6.2	9.2	3.3	7.8
PAT	1.8	3.9	0.1	1.7
Total Equity	15.6	35.3	27.5	52.0
Total Debt	14.1	29.2	18.6	18.0
EBITDA Margin	7.8%	4.9%	10.3%	10.9%
EBIT/Capital Employed	21.8%	14.0%	4.2%	6.4%
Return on Equity	16.8%	11.8%	0.2%	3.3%
Average Asset Turnover	1.45	2.83	0.63	0.80
Avg. Gross Current Asset Days	187	120	223	193
Current Ratio	1.26	1.86	1.58	1.11
EBIT/Interest and Finance Charges	2.16	2.84	1.47	1.62
Debt/Equity	0.91	0.83	0.68	0.35
Debt/EBITDA	2.28	3.19	5.56	2.31
Rating 1–8 Scale (8 is highest)	4 (old rating)	5	3	4

Source: Prepared by authors.

The company aimed to produce high-quality polymers by a low-cost, environment-friendly process. It imported and processed the monomers and other raw materials and supplied the output to the domestic and export markets.

DOL catered to various industries such as paints, adhesives, paper, textiles, and construction. The main products included organic peroxides, paint driers, chemicals used in acrylic emulsions, cello tape adhesive, white paper coating, and textile fibre binders.

In 2018–19, Dinesh Organics had recorded a 22% growth in turnover to Rs 79 crore. Nearly 91% of sales had been from the domestic market, of which top ten customers accounted for 62%. All the customers were reputed and had more than ten years of business relationship with DOL. The remaining 9% were export sales to three customers, of which two were from Africa and one from Vietnam. The sales were on an order basis, and DOL had no long-term contracts with the customers. Though DOL focused primarily on the western region of India, it faced stiff competition from other regional and pan-India competitors.

The average utilisation of the manufacturing capacities had been 60% in 2018–19. The management had plans to expand the production capacity to manufacture two new specialty chemicals with an investment of Rs 4 crore.

EXHIBIT 10.3 Financial Trends of Dinesh Organics

Rs Crore	*2014*	*2015*	*2016*	*2017*	*2018*	*2019*
Revenues	38.3	37.6	32.8	52.4	65.3	79.5
Total Income	**38.3**	**39.4**	**32.9**	**52.9**	**65.5**	**79.8**
Cost of Goods Sold	29.3	34.9	22.4	40.0	46.7	57.9
Other Operating Expenses	6.6	6.2	7.6	9.1	13.9	15.8
EBITDA	2.4	(1.6)	3.0	3.9	5.0	6.2
Depreciation	0.4	0.4	0.3	0.5	0.6	0.8
EBIT	2.0	(2.1)	2.7	3.4	4.4	5.4
Interest and Finance Charges	1.5	1.7	1.9	2.0	2.2	2.6
Profit after Tax	**0.3**	**(2.4)**	**(0.4)**	**0.9**	**1.7**	**1.8**
Total Equity	4.8	3.0	3.4	4.3	6.0	15.6
Long-Term Debt	1.6	0.9	2.3	2.1	2.9	1.9
Short-Term Debt	6.9	6.5	10.1	9.7	12.5	12.3
Trade Payables	10.9	7.3	7.6	15.5	19.4	24.1
Current Liabilities	18.8	15.1	18.9	26.2	32.9	37.5
Total Liabilities	20.5	16.0	26.6	34.0	41.8	46.1
Total Equity and Liabilities	**25.3**	**19.0**	**30.0**	**38.3**	**47.8**	**61.7**
Property, Plant, and Equipment	5.7	3.5	9.5	10.2	10.5	11.0
Inventories	6.7	0.4	3.3	6.3	10.4	17.1
Trade Receivables	10.8	7.7	12.0	16.1	18.2	22.4
Cash and Bank Balance	0.2	0.3	1.1	0.7	0.8	3.4
Current Assets	19.4	14.1	19.4	25.8	33.9	47.3
Total Assets	**25.3**	**19.0**	**30.0**	**38.3**	**47.8**	**61.7**
Cash flow from Operating Activities	3.2	0.4	3.2	3.6	2.7	(1.5)
Cash flow from Investing Activities	(0.6)	1.8	(6.2)	(2.0)	(1.3)	(1.0)
Cash flow from Financing Activities	(2.6)	(2.2)	3.9	(2.1)	1.4	4.4

Source: Prepared by authors.

This initiative was essential to increase the level of product and customer diversification.

Evaluating Creditworthiness

Having collected the information, Vaibhav started his financial analysis. The financial performance of the company had improved significantly in the past three years. The debt-to-equity ratio had improved after the IPO. The bank loan utilisation had been high over the past six months at close to 96%. But the company had never defaulted, and the repayment track record had been good so far.

EXHIBIT 10.4 Navbharat Bank's Internal Rating Framework

Parameters	*Sub-parameters*	*Weight*	*Score (1 to 8)*
			1 lowest to 8 highest
1. Business Evaluation	Industry Prospects	10%	
	Operating Efficiency	10%	
	Market Position	10%	
2. Financial Evaluation	Profitability	15%	
	Solvency	15%	
	Liquidity	15%	
3. Management Evaluation	Track Record	10%	
	Conservatism	5%	
	Account Conduct	10%	
Final Rating (round-off)		100%	

Source: Prepared by authors.

Navbharat Bank required internal ratings to be provided with all proposals on an 8-point scale. Ratings of 5 to 8 increased from moderate to the highest safety, whereas ratings from 4 to 2 moved from moderate to very high risk. Rating of 1 stood for default. Since the bank had been facing high net performing assets, the management had restricted new credit exposures only to companies that received a rating of 5 and above and enhanced credit exposures only to companies with a rating of at least 4 with sufficient justification. The previous credit officer handling the DOL account had given it a rating of 4 nearly eighteen months earlier. Vaibhav had to review and recommend a fresh rating.

Questions

1. Based on the information available in the case, score the company on a 1-to-8-point scale based on the framework provided in Exhibit 10.4.
2. Write a rationale for your recommended rating in not more than 500 words.
3. What will be the consequence for Navbharat Bank if Vaibhav gives DOL (a) Lower rating than justified, (b) A higher rating than justified? What can the bank do to mitigate the risks and implications of errors due to subjectivity in ratings?

Note

1 https://www.avendus.com/crypted_pdf_path/img_5f72fec709f754.34126596_Indian%20Specialty%20Chemical%20Industry.pdf

11

TATA INTERNATIONAL

Ann Philipose, a Mumbai-based research analyst, working with Oliver Rothman Consultants, had just been assigned her next project by her employer in July 2019. It was to study the creditworthiness of Tata International Limited (TIL), a global trading company belonging to the Tata group. Oliver Rothman was recently hired by a large commercial bank interested in offering buyer's credit to a few of TIL's subsidiaries operating in the UAE and Africa.

Ann's brief was limited to assessing the credit risk, incorporating both business and financial risks. The assessment of economic and policy risks, geopolitical risks, and legal risks would be undertaken later by the Dubai office of Oliver Rothman.

Having done similar projects for a few other Tata group companies, Ann had expected the assessment to be straightforward, given the company's long-established business and the Tata group's financial resources. However, she soon discovered that TIL had diverse businesses and a complex business structure. Ann had to study several financing arrangements and a gamut of risks and risk mitigation strategies before reaching her conclusions. Further, she found that the company appeared to have several weaknesses and threats counterbalancing its strengths and opportunities. Finally, she had to understand the implications of the perpetual bond issuances by the company since while they were bonds, the instruments also had equity-like characteristics.

Business Evolution

The Tata group was one of the largest business groups with headquarters in India. It had revenues of USD 110.7 billion, of which 64% were from

DOI: 10.4324/9781032724478-13

EXHIBIT 11.1 Profile of Group Companies

	(Rs Crore)	*Country*	*Holdings and Verticals*	*Net Assets*	*Share in Profit*
	Tata International Ltd (TIL)	India	Parent company, trading of minerals and agro	1,988	80
	Subsidiaries				
1	Tata International Singapore Pte (TISPL)	Singapore	Holding company for all future outbound investments, minerals trading	257	(109)
2	Tata Africa Holdings (TAHPL)	South Africa	Holding company for Africa, distribution	89	(39)
3	TIL Leather Mauritius (TLML)	Mauritius	Holding company for outbound investments	177	(1)
4	Tata International Metals (Americas)	USA	Trading in metals	227	12
5	Tata International Metals (Asia)	Hong Kong	Trading in metals	103	(15)
6	Tata Automobile Corporation (SA)	South Africa	Distribution of auto products	86	10
7	Tata International Metals (UK)	UK	Trading in metals	86	5
8	Tata Africa Services (Nigeria)	Nigeria	Distribution of auto and non-auto products	73	(16)
9	Tata Zambia	Zambia	Distribution of auto and non-auto products	62	(10)
10	Tata Uganda	Uganda	Distribution of auto and non-auto products	61	6
11	Tata Africa Holdings (Kenya)	Kenya	Distribution of auto and non-auto products	47	(41)
12	Tata De Mocambique	Mocambique	Distribution of auto and non-auto products	40	41
13	Tata Africa Holdings (Tanzania)	Tanzania	Distribution of auto and non-auto products	38	(11)
14	Alliance Finance Corporation	Tanzania	Auto and equipment finance	32	5
15	Tata Africa (Senegal)	Senegal	Distribution of auto and non-auto products	30	8
16	Tata International West Asia DMCC	UAE	Trading in metals	30	10
17	Euro Shoe Components	India	Manufacture and sale of footwear components	29	7
18	Monroa Portugal	Portugal	Footwear retail	27	(2)
19	Motor Hub East Africa	Tanzania	Distribution of auto and non-auto products	24	2
20	Pamodzi Hotels	Zambia	Hospitality Services	20	2
21	Calsea Footwear	India	Manufacture and sale of footwear	16	(2)
22	Tata Africa Holdings (Ghana)	Ghana	Distribution of auto and non-auto products	16	(5)

(*Continued*)

EXHIBIT 11.1 Continued

	(Rs Crore)	*Country*	*Holdings and Verticals*	*Net Assets*	*Share in Profit*
23	Alliance Motors Ghana	Ghana	Distribution of auto and non-auto products	15	2
24	Blackwood Hodge Zimbabwe	Zimbabwe	Distribution of auto and non-auto products	15	1
25	Tata West Asia FZE	UAE	Trading in metals	10	(0)
26	Move on Components E Calcado	Portugal	Manufacture and sale of footwear	10	(26)
27	Tata South-East Asia (TSEA)	Hong Kong	Trading of leather products, metals, minerals, and distribution	8	(4)
28	Tata Holdings Mocambique	Mocambique	Holdings in Mocambique	7	1
29	Tata Africa (Cote D'Ivorie)	Ivory Coast	Distribution of auto and non-auto products	7	2
30	Newshelf 1369	South Africa	Distribution of auto products	4	0
31	Move on Retail Spain	Spain	Footwear retail	0	(0)
32	Cometal, S.A.R.L.	Mocambique	Distribution of non-auto products	(3)	(4)
33	Tata International Vietnam	Vietnam	Trading in metals	(5)	(2)
34	Tata International Metals SA	South Africa	Trading in metals	(5)	(12)
35	Tata South-East Asia (Cambodia)	Cambodia	Distribution of auto and non-auto products	(6)	(2)
36	Tata Africa Steel Processors	South Africa	Trading in metals	(7)	(6)
37	TAH Pharmaceuticals	Nigeria	Pharmaceutical distribution	(14)	(11)
38	Tata International Canada	Canada	Trading in agro	–	–
39	M'Pumalanga Mining Investment	Mauritius	Dormant	–	–
40	M'Pumalanga Mining Resources	Madagascar	Dormant	–	–
41	Tata Zimbabwe	Zimbabwe	Dormant	–	–
42	Tata International Trading Brasil	Brazil	Dormant	–	–
	Joint Ventures (50% stake of TIL group)				
1	Tata Precision Industries	India	Manufacturing of high precision parts	2	1
2	Tata International GST AutoLeather	India	Manufacturing and trading automotive leather	1	0
3	Tata International DLT	India	Trailer manufacturing, stake held for sale	–	14

Source: Prepared by authors based on Tata International annual report 2018–19.

businesses outside India. It had 700,000 employees across 30 companies belonging to 10 business clusters with operations in over 100 countries. The Tata group companies were highly reputed, and the Tata brand was among the most valuable brands globally. Tata Sons was the main holding company, and philanthropic trusts held two-thirds of its stake.[1]

Incorporated in 1962, initially as Commercial and Industrial Exports Ltd, TIL evolved as one of the leading export houses in India over the next few decades. In 1968, the company was renamed Tata Exports Ltd. In 1969, the company commenced exports of Tata commercial vehicles. In 1973, the leather division was set up, and the company became one of the largest exporters of leather and leather products in India within the next ten years. In 1994, the company set up a new division to export steel and engineering products of Tata Steel and its associate companies. In 1998, the company was renamed Tata International Ltd.

In 2010, TIL forayed into the domestic footwear retail business under the TASHI brand. It also acquired the Chennai-based Bachi Shoes Ltd. in the same year and merged it with TIL in 2017. However, the company discontinued the retail operations of footwear in India in 2014 due to poor financial performance.

In 2012, TIL decided to renew its focus on trading, emphasising key verticals, including metals, distribution, leather and leather products, and minerals. In 2013, it forayed into agricultural trading in select geographies.

By 2019, Tata International was a premier trading and distribution company with a worldwide network of subsidiaries and offices and over 7,000 employees. It operated in five key business segments. These included metals trading, distribution, leather and leather products, minerals trading, and agri-trading.

The company, along with its subsidiaries, had a business network spanning 39 countries. In the financial year 2019 (FY2019), TIL reported worldwide revenues of USD 2.59 billion (Rs 18,068 crores).

Key Business Segments

Leather and leather products were one of the oldest businesses of TIL. The company had partnered with leading global brands across key product segments, including fashion leather, performance leather, footwear, and garments. Some of the leading brand partners included Clarks, Caleres, Wolverine, Gabor, Deichmann, Zara, H&M, and Marks & Spencers. TIL was also the largest exporter of children's shoes from India.

TIL group conducted its leather and leather products business through TIL, its joint venture, Tata International GST AutoLeather Ltd, and its subsidiaries in Hong Kong, Africa, Portugal, and Spain. The company had established two facilities at Chennai and Dewas in India for manufacturing leather and leather products.

It had development centres in China and Portugal and a design studio in Italy. The company also held a significant stake in Move-on Shoes, a leading Portuguese footwear retailer.

Metals trading was the most significant TIL business, comprising nearly half its revenues and one-third of its allocated assets. The main products traded included steel, metallics and rolls, and customised engineering products for the aluminium industry. Metals trading was conducted principally through several of its subsidiaries in the UK, Hong Kong, US, UAE, South Africa, and Vietnam.

Minerals trading business primarily consisted of thermal coal imports into India, China, and Vietnam, apart from trading of pet coke, base metals, ores, and fluxes and alloys. TIL was amongst the top three imported coal traders in India. The minerals trading business was conducted by TIL and its subsidiary Tata International Singapore Pte Ltd.

The agri-trading business was established in 2013, with a sourcing network in Myanmar, the ASEAN region, Africa, and Canada. Pulses and sugar were the principal commodities traded by the company. Other items included beans, raw cashew nuts, sesame, and rice. The primary market served was India. The agri-trading business was principally conducted by TIL and Tata International Singapore Pte Ltd.

Having started with automobile distribution in Africa in 1977, the distribution business was focused on automobiles and farm machinery. TIL was the leading distributor of Tata Motors vehicles with operations in 12 countries. It had also diversified into the distribution of farm machinery of John Deere and Massey Ferguson, two leading global manufacturers of farm equipment. The distribution business was mainly conducted through TIL's wholly owned subsidiary Tata Africa Holdings (SA) Proprietary Ltd and the latter's subsidiaries in Africa.

In all, TIL had 42 subsidiaries and three joint ventures operating across the world (see Exhibit 11.1). Apart from the five key business segments, these operated in diverse businesses, including luxury hotels, bus body building, vehicle assembly, and bicycles (Exhibit 11.1).

Competitive Position

The company had grown rapidly in the past by expanding into its key businesses and geographies. TIL's vision now was to be globally significant in each of its chosen businesses by 2025.

TIL's competitive strengths included knowledge and strategic positioning in key geographical markets, business diversity, global presence, well-established systems and processes, experienced management team, and the reputation, brand equity, business, and financial strength of the Tata group (see Exhibit 11.2). Most directors and business heads had over 20 years of experience, usually with TIL or Tata group companies.

EXHIBIT 11.2 Profile of Key Tata Group Companies

Rs '00 Crore	*Sector*	*Market Cap as on 31 Mar 2019*	*Book Value as on 31-3-2019*		*Credit Rating (Long Term) at the End of June 2019*
			Equity	*Debt*	
Tata Sons Pvt Ltd	Holding Company	Not Listed	439	314	AAA (ICRA, Aug 2018)
Top 11 Companies by Market Capitalisation (98% of Group Market Cap)					
Tata Consultancy Services Ltd	Software	7,510	848	82	AAA (ICRA, Mar 2019)
Titan Company Ltd	Consumer Goods	1,013	61	24	AAA (ICRA, Feb 2019)
Tata Motors Ltd	Automobile	580	558	1,062	AA (CARE, Feb 2019)
Tata Steel Ltd	Steel	365	713	1,008	AA (CARE, Feb 2019)
Voltas Ltd	Home Appliances	208	42	3	AA+ (ICRA, Mar 2019)
Tata Power Company Ltd	Power	201	204	485	AA- (CRISIL, Jun 2019)
Tata Consumer	Consumer Goods	188	84	11	AA+ (ICRA, Oct 2018)
Indian Hotels	Hotels	183	52	23	AA+ (CARE, Oct 2018)
Tata Communications Ltd	Telecom	175	(2)	100	AA+ (CARE, Dec 2018)
Tata Chemicals Ltd	Chemicals	149	153	61	AA+ (CARE, Jan 2019)
Trent	Retailing	129	16	5	AA+ (CARE, Jul 2018)
Tata International Ltd	Trading	Not listed	14	33	A+ (CARE, Mar 2019)

Source: Prepared by authors based on data from Capitaline database.

The businesses were highly competitive, with key local and global competitors being present in each vertical, for instance, Arcelor Mittal in metals trading, Adani Enterprises and Noble Group in coal trading, and Superhouse and Mirza International in footwear. Price competition was intense in metals, minerals, and agricultural products. Some of the competitors were vertically integrated and had higher economies of scale. The competitive scenario explained why though TIL group had expanded its businesses rapidly, its margins remained under pressure.

Efficient logistics management and network being critical for cost competitiveness, the TIL group used a global chartering desk to customise deliveries according to the needs of its customers and suppliers. The group's logistics function provided support in surveys, and international freights, in-land and over-land logistics, and, where required, stocking and warehousing.

Dedicated logistics personnel were responsible for the execution of individual physical shipments for specific geographical areas or products. As part of their cargo shipment responsibilities, the logistic personnel would determine the physical allocation of matches between sales and purchases or inventory storage and sales to decide the sources and shipment destinations of the commodity units. The logistic personnel would also use freight brokers to identify and charter appropriate ships, determine when the product and port facilities were ready for loading. They would also arrange for bunker fuel for the vessel, deal with port authorities and custom brokers, ensure insurance coverage, and monitor shipments and warehouse storage progress. The logistics personnel would also ensure the issue and operation of appropriate payment and security instruments, ensure prompt issue and handling of shipping documents, and monitor the execution and collection of payments. In completing these tasks, the logistic personnel was aided by the group's experts in chartering and insurance and the finance personnel.

Financial Performance

After witnessing a period of rapid revenue growth during 2009–10 to 2014–15, TIL's consolidated revenues fell in 2015–16 and recovered only marginally in 2016–17. Operating profits remained stagnant over this period, and the company reported net losses during most of the years (see Exhibit 11.3). The reasons for poor profitability included losses incurred in the leather

EXHIBIT 11.3 Trend in Revenues and Operating Profits

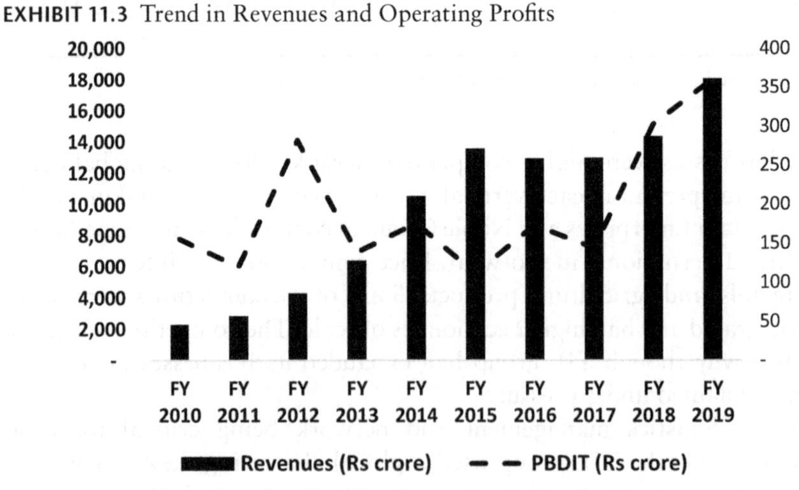

Source: Prepared by authors based on Tata International annual reports.

division and footwear retailing business and foreign currency fluctuations. Significant net losses led to erosion of networth and, together with debt-funded acquisitions, resulted in high gearing (see Exhibit 11.4).

The company's efforts to improve the profitability of its divisions, mainly leather and divestment of unprofitable businesses, resulted in an improvement in operating profits in 2017–18. The leather segment, which had been loss-making, reported earnings at the PBIT level in 2018–19 (see Exhibit 11.5). TIL sold off assets of its solar division in 2018–19 and its trailer manufacturing joint venture in May 2019.

Though leather and distribution segments shrunk, the metals and minerals business segments grew fast, contributing to healthy revenue growth for the past two years. Despite the improvements in revenue growth and operating profitability, the net profits remained minimal, and the gearing remained high.

The company was expected to continue to focus on improving its profitability. As part of the strategy of divesting small or non-core businesses and investments, the company had initiated the process of divesting from solar module mounting structures and bicycles business.

Financing Arrangements

TIL used diverse sources of funding for working capital and trade financing. These included trade payables, export packing credit, buyer's credit, cash credit accounts, debtors bill discounting, working capital demand loans, and commercial paper (see Exhibits 11.6, 11.7, and 11.8).

The pattern of short-term funding varied between the parent, TIL, and the other group companies. The largest source of financing was trade credit for both TIL and the group companies.

The second significant source of funding was export packing credit for the parent company, followed by working capital demand loans, commercial paper, and debtors bill discounting. However, for the rest of the group, the key funding sources other than supplier's credit included buyer's credit, followed by cash credit and working capital demand loans.

Export packing credit in Indian rupees was available against the security of the parent company's entire inventory and trade receivables. It was a form of pre-shipment finance extended for exports for purchase, manufacturing, or processing of goods before shipment against letters of credit, firm export orders, or evidence of an export order. It could generally be liquidated by negotiation of export bills or by receipt of export proceeds. However, banks provided flexibility to clients with a good track record in repayment terms or extending credit under a "running account" facility without insisting on prior letters of credit or evidence of export order.

EXHIBIT 11.4 Tata International: Consolidated Financial Statements (Abridged)

Rs Crore	*2014–15*	*2015–16*	*2016–17*	*2017–18*	*2018–19*
Statement of Profit and Loss					
Total Income	**13,674**	**13,049**	**13,150**	**14,572**	**18,274**
Revenue from Operations	13,602	12,957	13,011	14,372	18,068
Operating Expenses	13,561	12,876	13,006	14,269	17,913
PBDIT	112	173	144	303	361
Depreciation and Amortisation	103	73	71	57	48
PBIT	9	100	73	246	313
Finance Costs	181	204	239	200	246
Share of JV & Associates	(4)	(31)	(4)	8	13
Exceptional Items	107	54	(16)	103	12
Tax	58	100	43	71	21
Profit from Continuing Operations	(128)	(180)	(229)	87	71
Profit from Discontinued Operations		–	–	(76)	(107)
Profit for the Year	**(128)**	**(180)**	**(229)**	**10**	**(36)**
Balance Sheet as on 31st March					
Non-Current Assets	1,406	1,322	1,275	1,416	1,371
Property, Plant, and Equipment	375	410	403	365	341
Investments	507	374	322	333	306
Trade Receivables	–	–	25	27	–
Current Assets	4,711	4,314	4,732	4,883	6,326
Inventories	1,491	1,442	1,660	2,001	2,423
Trade Receivables	2,249	1,892	1,868	1,992	2,786
Cash and Equivalents	371	434	560	363	425
Other Bank Balances and Investments	15	179	155	6	8
Total Assets	**6,117**	**5,636**	**6,007**	**6,299**	**7,697**
Total Equity	1,477	1,193	1,647	1,646	1,418
Unsecured Perpetual Securities	721	713	1,448	1,444	1,448
Non-Current Liabilities	527	679	494	579	333
Borrowings	494	653	458	546	301
Current Liabilities	4,113	3,765	3,866	4,074	5,946
Borrowings	2,060	2,157	2,287	2,365	2,961
Current Maturities of Non-Current Debt	297	73	126	136	78
Trade Payables	1,506	1,231	1,206	1,287	2,540
Total Liablities	4,640	4,444	4,360	4,653	6,279
Total Equity and Liabilities	**6,117**	**5,636**	**6,007**	**6,299**	**7,697**
Cash Flow Statement					
Net Cash Flow from Operating Activities	**(149)**	**99**	**(297)**	**(367)**	**(1)**
Operating Profit before Working Capital Changes	79	116	47	130	166
Net Change in Working Capital	(142)	97	(281)	(476)	(81)
Net Cash Flow from Investing Activities	**32**	**191**	**(21)**	**270**	**51**
Net Cash Flow from Financing Activities	**326**	**(227)**	**444**	**(100)**	**13**
Net Increase in Cash and Equivalents	209	63	126	(197)	62

Source: Prepared by authors based on Tata International annual reports.

EXHIBIT 11.5 Profile of Key Segments

Rs Crore	*Leather*	*Minerals*	*Metals*	*Distribution*	*Agri*	*Others*
EBIT						
2018–19	40	57	225	84	(8)	(56)
2017–18	(77)	44	118	(140)	100	3
2016–17	(13)	14	92	31	(26)	1
2015–16	(8)	19	85	12	24	6
Revenues						
2018–19	1,072	4,560	8,390	1,543	1,472	313
2017–18	1,071	4,234	6,193	14,593	6,845	421
2016–17	1,133	2,044	5,771	2,132	1,701	66
2015–16	1,287	2,290	5,514	2,148	1,474	123
Assets						
2018–19	653	1,204	2,124	1,384	775	226
2017–18	756	1,217	940	1,800	118	170
2016–17	729	993	1,763	1,809	214	75
2015–16	886	635	1,561	1,647	392	432

Source: Prepared by authors based on Tata International annual reports.

EXHIBIT 11.6 Dividends, Finance Costs, and Lease Rentals

Rs Crore	*2016–17*	*2017–18*	*2018–19*
Dividend	8.7	8.8	0.3
Distribution on Perpetual Securities	47.4	90.1	89.9
Interest Expense on Borrowings	174	162.2	216.4
Interest on Bill Discounting	4	11.6	11.9
Other Borrowing Costs	61.4	26.3	17.6
Lease Rentals	51.7	42.7	42.2

Source: Prepared by authors based on Tata International annual reports.

TIL group companies mainly used buyer's credit to finance their purchases and secured against the receivables of the respective subsidiary. Under this arrangement, an overseas bank would extend a loan to the subsidiary by crediting an account of the subsidiary's bank held with it (known as "Nostro account"). The loan would be used to pay the seller immediately. The subsidiary's bank could typically open a letter of credit for the credit period allowed by the supplier. On the expiry of this period, the buyer's credit would be utilised to settle payment under the letter of credit. The lending bank could ask for a letter of comfort to facilitate the granting of buyers' credit. Availing of buyers' credit enabled access to funds in a preferred currency, such as dollars, against a less stable sellers' currency. It also helped the

EXHIBIT 11.7 Sources of Finance for TIL: Standalone and Group

Rs Crore, as on 31 March 2019	*Standalone*	*Consolidated*
Long-Term Sources		
Equity Share Capital	40	40
Reserves	748	(85)
Perpetual Securities	1,200	1,448
Term Loans from Banks	–	379
Short-Term Sources		
Trade Payables	931	2,540
Export Packing Credit	294	294
Buyers Credit	-	1,356
Cash Credit Accounts	0	720
Debtors Bill Discounting	47	47
Working Capital Demand Loan	184	237
Commercial Paper	79	79
Other Bank Loans	–	228
Current Maturities of Term Loans	–	78

Source: Prepared by authors based on Tata International annual report.

subsidiary negotiate a better discount since the seller was assured of receiving proceeds on the due date.

The subsidiaries also used cash credit facilities extensively. Under the cash credit facility, each company could withdraw funds from the bank up to the sanctioned credit limit. A running cash credit account would be maintained to withdraw periodically based on requirements and deposit the surplus funds. The cash credit limits were approved against the first charge on the current assets of each company. Though the advances under cash credit facilities were technically repayable on demand, there was no specific repayment date.

Further, though the limits were sanctioned for a year, they were typically rolled over at the end of the period. The interest was paid on the net amount used and not on the sanctioned limits. These features made cash credit a highly flexible funding arrangement for the subsidiaries.

Working capital demand loan was a temporary accommodation provided beyond sanctioned credit limit and was used both by the parent company and the subsidiaries. The interest rate was higher on such loans than on regular credit.

Such loans were available against hypothecation of inventory and receivables and mortgage of factory land and building and plant and machinery. Unlike hypothecation, in which the possession and ownership remained with the borrower but created only a charge in favour of the lender, the lender got the full legal title in a mortgage.

EXHIBIT 11.8 Details of Financing for TIL Group (Consolidated)

Rs Crore, as on 31–March 2019	*Total*	*Secured*	*Unsecured*	*Maturity*	*Interest Rate*	*Security*
Long–Term Sources						
Equity Share Capital	40					
Reserves	(85)					
Perpetual Securities	1,448	–	1,448			
Issued by TIL	1,200	–	1,200	Callable: 3 yrs	9.30%	–
Issued by Tata Intnl Singapore Pte Ltd	248	–	248	Callable: 5 yrs	6.65%	–
Term Loans from Banks	379	379	–			
State Bank of India	17	17	–	Mar 2020	10%	Charge of fixed properties in S Africa
Exim Bank of India (1)	113	113	–	Dec 2020	USD: LIBOR (6 mth) + 4.5%	Corporate guarantee
Exim Bank of India (2)	199	199	–	Sep 2020	USD: LIBOR (6 mth) + 2.25%	Corporate guarantee
Exim Bank of India (3)	39	39	–	Dec 2020	USD: LIBOR (6 mth) + 2.25%	Corporate guarantee
National Bank of Commerce	11	11	–	Aug 2021	365d T-Bills + 4.5%, Floor: 11.5%	Letter of comfort
Short–Term Sources						
Trade Payables	2,540	-	2,540			
Export Packing Credit	294	164	131			Inventory & trade receivables of TIL
Buyers Credit	1,356	20	1,336			Receivables of respective company

(*Continued*)

EXHIBIT 11.8 Continued

Rs Crore, as on 31–March 2019	*Total*	*Secured*	*Unsecured*	*Maturity*	*Interest Rate*	*Security*
Cash Credit Accounts	720	32	688			1st charge on current assets of each company
Debtors Bill Discounting	47	40	7			Receivables of respective company
Working Capital Demand Loan	237	54	183			Hypothecation & mortgage of assets[a]
Commercial Paper	79	-	79			-
Other Bank Loans	228	20	208			Hypothecation & mortgage of assets[a]
Current Maturities of Term Loans	78	78	–			Same as term loans

Source: Prepared by authors based on Tata International annual report, 2018-19.

[a]Hypothecation of inventory, receivables; mortgage of factory land & building, plant & machinery

Bill discounting of debtors and commercial paper were the sources used by the parent company. In bill discounting, the banks held the debtors' bills as security for the credit. When a bill was discounted, TIL would be paid the discounted amount. The bank would receive the total amount on maturity. TIL also periodically raised funds from the domestic money market using commercial paper, an unsecured promissory note. Banks were again the subscribers to the commercial paper issue.

The TIL group used a mix of equity, perpetual securities, and term loans for long-term financing. At the group level, there was no reliance on internal resources due to losses. There had been two perpetual securities issues, one by TIL and one by Tata International Singapore Pte Ltd. These securities were coupon-bearing bonds but with no maturity. However, they could be redeemed by the issuers by exercising the call option after three years and five years, respectively.

The majority of the term loans were raised by the TIL group companies from Exim Bank, as floating-rate loans issued against the corporate guarantee. In addition, one term loan had been taken from the State Bank of India and another one from the National Bank of Commerce.

Financial Risk Management

The TIL group used an enterprise-wide risk management process. The parent company, TIL, had institutionalised an Apex Tender Committee, consisting of domain experts to consider and approve high-value proposals. The committee evaluated due diligence, credibility checks, counterparty credit risks, logistics risks, country risks, legal and regulatory risks.

TIL group was exposed to market risks, including commodity price risk, currency risk, and interest rate risk. Commodity price risk resulted from volatility in prices of metals, minerals, leather, agro-products, and freight costs. Apart from ensuring central management of trading operations and control processes, TIL used derivatives to hedge its commodity and freight exposure. Currency risks arose both from forex trading operations as well as foreign currency borrowings. TIL group used currency derivatives to hedge the currency risks partially. The majority of the currency derivative contracts were on USD, followed by Euro, GBP, and ZAR. TIL group used a mix of floating and fixed interest rate borrowings to manage the interest rate risk. It used interest rate swap and forward interest rate contracts.

Apart from the market risks, the TIL group was also vulnerable to credit risk and liquidity risk. Credit risk arose from a large number of customers across diverse industries and geographies. The group adopted a policy to deal with only creditworthy counterparties and, where appropriate, obtaining collateral from the counterparties or purchasing credit guarantee insurance cover. It also rated its major customers based on publicly available financial information and its trading records and conducted ongoing credit evaluations. Customer diversity ensured that credit risk exposure to any single counterparty was not significant, being limited to a maximum of 20% of gross monetary assets in group companies and 5% in the case of other counterparties. Active management of credit risk entailed using letters of credit, bank guarantees, parent group guarantees, advance payments, and factors and forfaiting with recourse to the group. The group also started selling receivables to banks and other parties on without recourse basis.

TIL group relied on multiple banks for both fund and non-fund-based working capital facilities for managing its liquidity risk. It also used debt instruments, including commercial paper, to access funds from the debt market. Around 95% of the financial liabilities at the end of March 2019 were due to mature within one year. The group invested its surplus funds in highly liquid and low-risk avenues, including bank fixed deposits and liquid schemes of mutual funds.

The Rating Decision

Ann had to analyse all the business and financial information that she had compiled. She considered first estimating all the relevant financial ratios and interpreting the financial performance and position of the TIL group. She also wanted to understand the appropriateness of the short-term and long-term financing choices made by TIL.

As part of her report, Ann had to recommend the rating of TIL on a 10-point scale, where 1 was the worst and 10 was the best. She had to factor into her rating TIL's market position and operating efficiency in its business segments, the management's track record in terms of business performance and use of credit, the solvency and liquidity position of the company, its risk management practices, its financial flexibility and the ability to mobilise financial resources. Finally, she also had to consider the Tata group support.

Questions

1. Assess the financial performance and financial position of Tata International Ltd group.
2. Analyse the various sources of trade and working capital financing used by Tata International and its subsidiaries. Comment on the relative merits, features, and application of each short-term source of funding.
3. Build a rating framework to analyse the credit risk of Tata International, defining some relevant risk parameters and giving scores and weights to those parameters. Write a brief rationale to explain your rating.

Note

1 Based on information from https://www.tata.com/about-us, https://www.tata.com/business/overview, https://www.tata.com/business/tata-sons, https://www.tata.com/brands-showcase

PART II

Capital Budgeting Decisions

12

RANJIT'S DELIVERY VANS

Making the Replacement Decision

Ranjit Grewal decided to upgrade his fleet of delivery vans for the first time in February 2020. Ranjit owned an automobile service centre in Ludhiana. Operating delivery vans was a side-business that he had started five years earlier by buying five used Mahindra and Mahindra light commercial vehicles (LCVs). His younger brothers are managing it now.

The delivery vans had gotten old, resulting in frequent breakdowns which in turn resulted in the loss of business. On the other hand, the ability of the brothers to create business had increased with experience and personal networks, and they wanted to operate larger vans to cater to the increased business. Given the funds available to him and requests from his brothers, Ranjit decided that it was time to replace the delivery vans.

Investment Alternatives

Ranjit discussed four different proposals with his brothers. The first and second proposals pertained to upgrading the van's body, and the third and fourth proposals were regarding replacing the vans themselves.

The first proposal was to get a new van body fabricated for the existing vans by an LCV body-building company. On average, the bodybuilder would charge Rs 1.5 lakh for each van. The new body would increase the cargo-carrying capacity of the van and make it more suitable to carry a broader range of goods. The cheaper second proposal was to get the body of the vans repaired and refurbished. Ranjit thought this alternative was a low hanging fruit, given its attractive economics, though it would increase the business only marginally.

DOI: 10.4324/9781032724478-15

The third proposal was to sell the old vehicles and buy new larger LCVs. This proposal could increase the business twofold, both due to the increased reliability of new vehicles and their size, but required significant investment. The fourth proposal was a cheaper alternative to the third one. It consisted of replacing the existing fleet with larger used vehicles. While this resulted in both lower investments and inflows than buying new LCVs, the impact was much greater than working only on the bodies of the vans.

Ranjit got the detailed estimates of the upfront investments, annual business revenues and costs and sale value on disposal (net of capital gains tax) assumed after five years from his brothers. He estimated the incremental cash flows of each proposal compared with the cash flows from the existing fleet (Exhibit 12.1).

He compared the four alternative proposals using two yardsticks. First, he calculated the number of years it would take for each alternative to pay back the upfront investment. Second, he estimated the average accounting rate of return that he could earn on each investment. He decided to compare the return on investment with 18%, which he reckoned that he could make on marginal investment in his automobile servicing business, which carried a risk similar to the delivery vans.

Ranjit found all the proposals attractive using his criteria, though he did not favour buying new larger vans as they were expensive. To him, the economics seemed to support the decision to repair the van bodies.

Revisiting the Decision

As the Covid-19 pandemic hit India, the Central Government declared a nationwide lockdown followed by extended lockdowns in various states in different phases, including Punjab. The lockdown reduced the volumes of both the businesses of Ranjit, and he had to postpone any investment decision.

EXHIBIT 12.1 Estimates of Cash Flows by Proposal (February 2020)

	Incremental Cash Flows (Rs)					
Proposal	*Investment*	*Year 1*	*Year 2*	*Year 3*	*Year 4*	*Year 5*
Buy New Van Body	(7,50,000)	3,30,000	3,30,000	3,30,000	3,30,000	4,80,000
Repair Existing Van Body	(1,50,000)	1,50,000	1,50,000	1,50,000	1,50,000	1,50,000
Upgrade to a Larger New Van	(45,00,000)	13,50,000	13,50,000	13,50,000	13,50,000	33,50,000
Upgrade to a Larger Used Van	(15,00,000)	5,40,000	5,40,000	5,40,000	5,40,000	10,40,000

Source: Prepared by authors.

EXHIBIT 12.2 Estimates of Cash Flows by Proposal (November 2020)

	Incremental Cash Flows (Rs)					
Proposal	*Investment*	*Year 1*	*Year 2*	*Year 3*	*Year 4*	*Year 5*
Buy New Van Body	(7,00,000)	2,10,000	2,70,000	3,30,000	3,30,000	4,70,000
Repair Existing Van Body	(1,45,000)	1,25,000	1,50,000	1,50,000	1,50,000	1,50,000
Upgrade to a Larger New Van	(37,50,000)	6,00,000	9,00,000	13,50,000	13,50,000	31,00,000
Upgrade to a Larger Used Van	(12,50,000)	3,75,000	4,80,000	5,40,000	5,40,000	9,90,000

Source: Prepared by authors.

As the lockdown started to ease, Ranjit became more optimistic about the prospects of his businesses. In early November 2020, he decided to revisit the plan to invest in the delivery vans business. But he found that there were more significant discounts available on new vans in the weaker economic scenario, and the prices of used vans and body-building services had declined. On the other hand, he had to consider a reduced level of incremental business in all the proposals. Finally, he lowered his hurdle rate for comparing the returns of the four alternatives to 16.5%, based on the prospects of reduced returns for his automobile service business.

As Ranjit started to compare the four proposals (Exhibit 12.2), he was sure that under an adverse economic scenario, the proposal that required the least investment held even greater merit.

Questions

1. Rank the four proposals based on NPV, IRR, payback period, and accounting rate of return in February 2020.
2. Rank the four proposals based on NPV, IRR, payback period, and accounting rate of return in November 2020.
3. Which proposal was the best according to you in February 2020 and in November 2020?

13

MOODY SINGH'S FOOD TRUCK

Scaling up the Business

Mudita Singh (Moody) was considering whether to buy a food mini-truck. Her mobile food business, currently carried out of a minivan, had been flourishing. However, the size of her van placed a limit on the kitchen equipment, serving-counter space and hence the range of menu choices. For the same reason, she was also not able to take catering orders for small parties.

Moody realised that a light truck with larger body dimensions would help to increase her business but would also cost more. She intended to scale up her business but was acutely aware of the high failure rate in the food-retailing business, and therefore wanted to make a financially prudent decision.

Business Evolution

The mobile food business, prevalent in several other countries, had started to develop in India only in recent years. Its prevalence varied across cities, depending upon demographics, outdoor eating preferences, and local regulations. The food minivans and food trucks were initially customised by small operators who fabricated the body and did the necessary fitments of stoves, storage shelves and washbasins in the vehicles. Subsequently, larger and more professionally run firms started customising the trucks. As business developed, the automobile Original Equipment Manufacturers (OEMs) began selling their van and light truck variants pre-fitted with kitchen equipment to food entrepreneurs.

Moody Singh started her mobile food business in April 2018 in New Delhi, one of the cities that had seen mobile eateries sprung up in several locations. She purchased a food van converted from a five-year-old vehicle

DOI: 10.4324/9781032724478-16

by a small fabricator and a point of sale system for Rs 3 lakh. The vehicle was old, which Moody estimated would last her for six years, but enough to ensure payback on her initial investment. She took a loan of Rs 2.23 lakh, which covered two-thirds of her initial fixed and working capital requirement, carried an annual interest rate of 15%, and was repayable in five equal yearly instalments. The working capital included one week of raw materials and two weeks of other operating expenses. As she made cash purchases, payables were negligible.

An agent helped her get the necessary licence from the food safety and standards authority, a no-objection certificate from the fire department, and a permission letter from the municipal body. She hired two assistants to help her cook, serve, and manage the customer orders. She designed the menu carefully, preferring a standard fare of sandwiches, burgers, chaats, and juices which could be prepared and served efficiently in limited space. She also got some pamphlets inserted into newspapers and used social media to promote her business.

It took some months for her to get a fixed parking space on rent and attract customers by presence, promotion, and word-of-mouth referrals. For 2018–19, the first year of operations, the business reported a net loss but reasonable cash profit.

As the business grew further, 2019–20 was turning out to be an even better year. Average monthly revenues were 50% higher than the previous year, and the business had turned profitable. However, revenue growth had started to slow down on a month-on-month basis since November 2019. She was also seeing larger rivals getting catering orders for small parties and occasionally even for weddings.

Growth was critical for the scalability of Moody's mobile food business. Her long-term business strategy involved a hub-and-spoke model where several food trucks would retail food at various city locations and catered by a centralised kitchen. Building such a business model would require onboarding investors, who would want to see evidence of high growth before investing.

The Food Truck Alternative

Moody Singh evaluated her choices. Her existing food van was already profitable, and she estimated that she could run it profitably for another five years before selling the vehicle due to its age. She found the current resale value of her food van, net of taxes, would be around Rs 1.4 lakh.

The alternative she considered was buying a new food mini-truck by the end of March 2020. The size of the mini-truck would allow her to increase the revenues significantly, by 30%, as compared to the food-van, particularly from catering orders across the city. The fixed capital cost of the mini-truck

EXHIBIT 13.1 Forecasted Financial Performance of Food Van

Rs Lakhs	*Financial Year Ending March 31*						
	2019	*2020 E*	*2021 F*	*2022 F*	*2023 F*	*2024 F*	*2025 F*
Revenues	12.00	18.00	19.80	21.78	23.96	26.35	28.99
Raw Materials	6.00	9.00	9.90	10.89	11.98	13.18	14.49
Employee Costs	5.28	6.62	6.96	7.45	7.97	8.53	9.12
Other Operating Expenses	0.50	0.55	0.58	0.61	0.64	0.67	0.70
Total Operating Expenses	11.78	16.17	17.44	18.94	20.58	22.37	24.32
PBDIT	0.22	1.83	2.36	2.84	3.37	3.98	4.67
Depreciation	0.90	0.63	0.44	0.31	0.22	0.15	0.11
PBIT	(0.68)	1.20	1.92	2.53	3.16	3.83	4.56

Source: Prepared by authors.
Note: The estimated resale value of the food van at the end of FY 2025 is estimated at Rs 20,000.

EXHIBIT 13.2 Forecasted Financial Performance of Food Truck

Rs Lakhs	*Financial Year Ending March 31*				
	2021 F	*2022 F*	*2023 F*	*2024 F*	*2025 F*
Revenues	25.74	28.31	31.15	34.26	37.69
Raw Materials	12.87	14.16	15.57	17.13	18.84
Employee Costs	6.96	7.45	7.97	8.53	9.12
Other Operating Expenses	0.80	0.90	0.95	0.99	1.04
Total Operating Expenses	20.63	22.50	24.49	26.65	29.01
PBDIT	5.11	5.81	6.66	7.61	8.68
Depreciation	3.00	2.10	1.47	1.03	0.72
PBIT	2.11	3.71	5.19	6.58	7.96

Source: Prepared by authors.
Note: The estimated resale value of the food truck at the end of FY 2025 is Rs 1.6 lakh.

with pre-fitted kitchen equipment and other accessories would be Rs 10 lakh. The working capital requirements would increase proportionately based on the size of the business. Though this would be a new vehicle, she anticipated shorter working life of about five years, considering greater use for mobility (see Exhibits 13.1 and 13.2).

The Replacement Decision

Moody consulted her friends who had recently graduated from business schools for helping her make a financial decision. They provided her with an estimate of the cost of capital and advised her to use the net present value criteria. They estimated the cost of capital of her business as 18%. Since her business was a sole proprietorship, the business income would get clubbed with her income and would incur a marginal tax rate of 30%, as applicable in her case. Moody also approached her uncle, who was a general manager in the finance department of a company. Based on his experience in handling capital budgeting, her uncle advised her to use the internal rate of return (IRR) as the primary criteria and the payback period as the secondary criteria.

Because of the conflicting advice, Moody was unsure of the decision criteria to use. She was also not sure as to how to implement the criteria for the replacement decision. Should she compare the NPV, IRR, or payback periods of the new and existing alternatives, or was there a better approach?

Finally, Moody was worried about making a wrong decision due to forecasting errors and uncertainties. For example, if the truck could achieve a business increase of 50% instead of 30%, how would that change her decision? Further, she was also worried that the coronavirus epidemic could spread in India as it had in China and some other countries. As of date, six confirmed cases of infection had been reported in India. She wanted to know which decision would be appropriate in the worst case if she could not do any business after March 2020 for one full year.

Questions

1. Based on the forecasts provided in the exhibits, estimate NPV, IRR, and payback period of both the alternatives.
2. Estimate the incremental cash flows of the replacement decision. Hence, check if the replacement decision would be correct if the truck could achieve a business increase of (a) 30% over minivan, (b) 50% over minivan, (c) no business after March 2020.

14

DBS AUTO'S ELECTRIC TWO-WHEELERS

Cash Flow Projections

On June 1, 2021, Meher Bulsara – Senior Manager (Finance) at DBS Auto Company, called a meeting with two of her team members, Danish Merchant and Lakshmi Nadar. She wanted to discuss the preparation of estimates to support an investment decision regarding the company's proposed electric two-wheelers project (EL-2). DBS Auto was a mid-sized auto component player producing aluminium die-cast engine components for two-wheeler companies.

Electric Two-Wheelers' Market in India

The electric two-wheelers' market in India had been a small but fast-growing market, with estimated sales of 144,000 vehicles in 2020–21, constituting a little over 1% share of the total two-wheeler sales in the country.[1] The main challenges had been low customer adoption due to concerns related to battery costs, driving range, and the availability of charging stations. Limited availability of after-sales and parts businesses and battery recycling and re-usage capabilities were other constraints. Six players accounted for 90% of the sales led by Hero Electric, Okinawa Autotech, and Ampere Vehicles. Despite their leadership, the electric two-wheeler operations of these players were not profitable due to high cost of components and low sales volumes.

Experts expected to see an explosive growth in the demand for electric two-wheeler over the next ten years, especially in entry-level two-wheelers driven by the reduced total cost of ownership, improved charging infrastructure, lower battery prices, government incentives, and increased customer readiness. According to McKinsey, the electric two-wheelers demand in India could grow explosively to about 9 million units by 2029–30, accounting for 35–40% of all two-wheelers sold.[2] As they achieved economies of

DOI: 10.4324/9781032724478-17

EXHIBIT 14.1 DBS Auto's Financial Summary

Rs Crore	*March 2019*	*March 2020*	*March 2021*
Total Income	2,322	2,717	2,487
EBITDA	295	363	389
Profit after Tax	136	179	214
Non-Current Assets	793	937	1,017
Current Assets	578	551	480
Total Assets	1,371	1,488	1,498
Equity	896	1,040	1,158
Non-Current Liabilities	12	23	25
Current Liabilities	463	425	314
Total Debt	448	312	290
Market Capitalisation	4,481	5,200	5,792

Source: Prepared by authors.

scale and as the cost of battery components reduced with increasing localisation, the electric two-wheeler players could achieve break-even levels of sales followed by a period of high profitable growth.

DBS Auto's EL-2 Project

Meher briefed Danish and Lakshmi about DBS Auto's plans. The initial plan was to set up a capacity of 50,000 electric two-wheelers and then scale up with a target to achieve a market share of 4–5% by 2025. The positives of the project were that DBS Auto had access to the most cost-effective battery technology from its US-based collaborator and was financially stronger than many of the existing players. The negatives of the project included uncertainty regarding scaling up, high initial capital intensity, and a long payback period. She also believed that the management would not consider the project significant enough to allocate organisational resources if the project's net present value (NPV) were less than Rs 1000 crores.

Meher shared the estimates prepared earlier by a former colleague based on ballpark estimates. She assigned the task of preparing the revised cash flow forecasts to Danish and the cost of capital to Lakshmi. Danish immediately started gathering all the required information to prepare the cash flow estimates (see Exhibits 14.1 and 14.2). After three days, he submitted his forecasts and a note explaining his assumptions to Meher (Exhibit 14.3).

Questions

1. Provide your opinion regarding each point in Danish's analysis (Exhibit 14.4).
2. Prepare your estimate of NPV for the EL-2 Project, explaining your assumptions.

EXHIBIT 14.2 Previous Workings of Net Present Value of EL-2 Project

Rs Crore	*FY 2023*	*FY 2024*	*FY 2025*	*FY 2026*	*FY 2027*	*FY 2028*	*FY 2029*	*FY 2030*	*FY 2031*	*FY 2032*
Revenues	–	–	78	238	484	958	1,559	2,292	2,874	3,210
Cost of Goods Sold	–	–	47	143	291	575	935	1,375	1,724	1,926
Other Operating Expenses	25	50	100	150	206	268	324	382	436	493
EBITDA	(25)	(50)	(69)	(55)	(13)	115	300	535	714	791
Depreciation	–	15	28	54	76	98	121	136	151	160
EBIT	(25)	(65)	(97)	(109)	(89)	17	179	399	563	631
Capex	100	100	200	200	226	248	221	236	216	225
Net Working Capital (NWC)	-	7	15	5	–	–	–	–	–	–
Tax Rate	28%									
Terminal Growth Rate	6.5%									
Cost of Capital	12%									
EBIT(1-t)+Depreciation	(18)	(32)	(42)	(24)	12	110	250	423	556	614
Less: Capex	100	100	200	200	226	248	221	236	216	225
Less: Change in NWC	–	7	8	(10)	(5)	–	–	–	–	–
Net Cash Flows	(118)	(139)	(250)	(214)	(209)	(138)	29	187	340	389
Terminal Value										7,539
Total Cash Flows	(118)	(139)	(250)	(214)	(209)	(138)	29	187	340	7,928
Net Present Value	**2,045**									
NPV under Alternative Discount Rates										
10%	4,200									
11%	2,869									
12%	2,045									
13%	1,492									
14%	1,101									
15%	813									
16%	595									

Source: Prepared by authors

EXHIBIT 14.3 EL-2 Project's NPV Estimate by Danish Merchant

Rs Crore	*FY 2023*	*FY 2024*	*FY 2025*	*FY 2026*	*FY 2027*	*FY 2028*	*FY 2029*	*FY 2030*	*FY 2031*	*FY 2032*
Revenues	–	–	39	159	363	794	1,364	2,037	2,443	2,626
Cost of Goods Sold	–	–	23	95	218	476	818	1,222	1,466	1,576
Other Operating Expenses	25	50	100	150	206	268	324	382	436	493
EBITDA	(25)	(50)	(84)	(86)	(61)	50	222	433	541	557
Depreciation	–	15	28	54	76	98	121	136	151	160
EBIT	(25)	(65)	(112)	(140)	(137)	(48)	101	297	390	397
Interest	3	3	6	6	7	7	7	7	6	7
Profit before Tax	(28)	(68)	(118)	(146)	(144)	(55)	94	290	384	390
Capex	100	100	200	200	226	248	221	236	216	225
Net Working Capital (NWC)	–	7	13	6	2	–	–	–	–	–
Tax Rate	19.7%									
Terminal Growth Rate	10.0%									
Cost of Capital	12%									
Method 1: Terminal Value Using Perpetuity after 10 Years										
EBITDA	(25)	(50)	(84)	(86)	(61)	50	222	433	541	557
Less: Interest (1-t)	2	2	5	5	6	6	6	6	5	6
Less: Tax	(6)	(13)	(23)	(29)	(28)	(11)	19	57	76	77
Less: Capex	100	100	200	200	226	248	221	236	216	225
Less: NWC	–	7	13	6	2	–	–	–	–	–
Net Cash Flows	(122)	(146)	(279)	(268)	(266)	(193)	(23)	134	245	250
Terminal Value										13,725
Total Cash Flows	(122)	(146)	(279)	(268)	(266)	(193)	(23)	134	245	13,975
Net Present Value	**3,789**									

(Continued)

EXHIBIT 14.3 Continued

Rs Crore	*FY 2023*	*FY 2024*	*FY 2025*	*FY 2026*	*FY 2027*	*FY 2028*	*FY 2029*	*FY 2030*	*FY 2031*	*FY 2032*
Method 2: Terminal Value Using Valuation Multiple after 5 Years										
EBITDA	(25)	(50)	(84)	(86)	(61)	50				
Less: Interest (1-t)	2	2	5	5	6	6				
Less: Tax	(6)	(13)	(23)	(29)	(28)	(11)				
Less: Capex	100	100	200	200	226	248				
Less: NWC	–	7	13	6	2	–				
Net Cash Flows	(122)	(146)	(279)	(268)	(266)	(193)				
Terminal Value						750				
Total Cash Flows	(122)	(146)	(279)	(268)	(266)	557				
Net Present Value	(463)									

Source: Prepared by authors.

EXHIBIT 14.4 Danish Merchant's Analysis of EL-2 Project's Cash Flows

To: Meher Bulsara
From: Danish Merchant
Date: June 4, 2021
Subject: Cash Flow Forecasts for EL-2 Project

I have estimated the cash flows for the EL-2 project based on the following assumptions:

1. Methodology for estimating project cash flows: Net cash flows based on continuing value

I have relied on net cash flows instead of net income. I have excluded the impact of non-cash expenses such as depreciation but have considered the effect of taxes. I have also assumed that since this is a high growth business, it will have continuing value beyond the period of my explicit forecasts. I have therefore estimated a terminal value of the project by two methods, growing perpetuity and valuation multiples.

2. Estimates of net cash flows

I had to change the revenue and operating profit forecasts due to the short-term impact of the Covid-19 pandemic and the revised long-term outlook for the industry growth. To estimate the net cash flows, I started with EBITDA to completely exclude the effect of depreciation. However, I did subtract the interest expense net of the tax shield on interest and taxes. I further deducted the estimated capital expenditure and net working capital to estimate annual net cash flows.

3. Estimates of continuing value

I used two methods to estimate the continuing value. In the first method, I used the growing perpetuity formula. I applied the formula after ten years of explicit cash flow projections and assumed a terminal growth rate of 10%. I believe this a conservative estimate of growth, considering that electric two-wheelers will continue to gain share from conventional vehicles for a long time.

In the second method, I considered detailed cash flow projections only till FY 2028. Given the uncertainty regarding the growth rate of electric two-wheelers, I have lesser confidence in projections beyond 5 to 6 years. I applied the company's recent year's EV/EBITDA multiple of around 15 to the EBITDA of FY 2028.

Source: Prepared by authors.

Notes

1 https://www.business-standard.com/article/electric-vehicle/sales-of-electric-vehicles-in-india-fell-20-to-236-802-units-in-fy21-smev-121042200514_1.html
2 Mckinsey & Company (2020). The unexpected trip: The future of mobility in India beyond COVID-19.

15

EVALUATING INVESTMENT CHOICES FOR "THE ORIENTAL" RESTAURANT

Jayatirtha Singh (Jay) entered his office after spending one hour of late afternoon in his favourite pastime – looking after the antiques he had collected. It was time to get down to business, evaluating some decision alternatives for The Oriental, a fine-dining restaurant that Jay had been running for the past ten years. What had started as a stellar restaurant, getting both high star ratings and full occupancy in the first few years, gradually became the favourite dine-out only of the old loyal customers. The financials had followed the business down the elevator, and the restaurant reported losses in 2017–18 and marginal profits in 2018–19.

Over the past month, Jay had been considering a proposal from Delikos, a partnership firm run by two young restaurateurs, to lease part of his space to open a café. The partners had been introduced to Jay by Mithuna Sen, a consultant whom Jay had hired to find a solution to the financial problems of The Oriental. After initial discussions, the partners and Jay had agreed to the specifics of the proposal. The partnership firm would lease space from The Oriental to run the café for four years.

Mithuna had suggested that Jay should also think alternatively about The Oriental running a café itself. Though Jay had not initially given this proposal much thought, he had lately come around to provide more serious consideration to that alternative.

The Retail Food Service Industry

The Indian food service industry had total revenues of Rs 3.7 trillion as of 2018, according to CARE Ratings, having recorded a growth of 8.4% per annum during 2013–2018. According to a report prepared by FICCI and

DOI: 10.4324/9781032724478-18

PWC, the industry trends were driven by robust economic growth, a favourable demographic profile, increasing internet penetration, increasing focus on health and wellness, and technological innovations.

Organised formats constituted 30–35% of the business, but most of the revenues comprised unorganised outlets. Casual dining was the largest market segment, accounting for 55% of revenues, followed by quick-service restaurants and fast food with 20%.

While many food service outlets started every year due to low entry barriers, the failure rate was also high. Several outlets could not achieve adequate table turnover and operating efficiency for profitable operations.

The Oriental

Jay started The Oriental as a fine-dining restaurant in suburban Mumbai in 2010 near a growing cluster of offices that came to be known as "Technology Street." He decided to buy rather than lease a 4,000 sq ft space for a total value of Rs 40 million since he was confident of demand growth and had recently sold an equivalent value residential property in the main city. He spent another Rs 30 million on interiors, equipment, and working capital to start the business, mainly funded by a bank loan.

Jay had planned the layout, keeping in mind future business growth. After providing for the kitchen and reception area, there were 2000 sq ft of space left. However, based on current demand estimates, Jay decided to use only 1500 square feet as dining space, partitioning away nearly 500 sq ft as a lounge area labelled Jay's Gallery. While conceiving the lounge space's idea, Jay believed that in around three years of operations, the business would grow enough to justify closing it to expand the dining space. The dining space had 20 tables with different seating configurations. Jay personally supervised the interior decoration, the choice of furniture, furnishings, and cutlery, and The Oriental received high praises from initial visitors and critics.

After trying to work with several Asian cuisines, Jay settled on the Chinese. He brought in an expert head chef, who then trained other junior chefs. The Oriental limited the range of cuisine and emphasised consistency of quality, hygiene, and service. Jay paid the staff above industry salaries, paid personal attention to their grooming, but he was a tough taskmaster. As the business grew, Jay appointed a manager to oversee the day-to-day operations, but the work culture remained ingrained in the employees, and employee attrition levels were low.

Jay's Gallery was positioned on one side closer to the restaurant entrance. It housed a few comfortable sofa chairs, a small library of various books, a series of wall paintings and photographs, and a shelf of Jay's collectibles. On several evenings, Jay himself landed up and regaled the guests sitting in the lounge with many stories about his experiences and collections. While limiting the dining space provided the restaurant a busy look, Jay's Gallery became an attraction for several guests, helping stagger demand during peak hours and cultivating the restaurant's image as a warm and charming place, as described by a celebrity who had visited the place.

However, demographic changes were not in favour of The Oriental. The millennials joining offices on Technology Street increasingly preferred the quick service formats, cafes, and pubs. As some of the older customers were transferred or left their organisations, revenues shrank for a few years before The Oriental made some smart changes in the menu and improved some processes to reduce customer waiting time. While revenues did grow in 2019, it was clear to Jay that he no longer held any realistic option to expand the restaurant's dining area.

The Mutually Exclusive Alternatives

Jay looked at the two alternatives Mithuna had laid out for building a small café adjoining The Orientale with a common main entrance.

Fun Café

The Oriental had to set up a partition and provide 500 sq ft of space currently occupied by the lounge on lease to Delikos to operate the Fun Café for four years. The lease rentals would be Rs 42.500 per month in the first year and escalate by 4% every subsequent year. As per the agreement, The Oriental was to undertake the basic renovation, which would entail a spend of around Rs 250,000 to Rs 350,000. The Orientale would also spend Rs 20,000 per annum on essential repairs and maintenance.

Delikos would bear the rest of the capital investment and pay for the utilities and relevant operating expenses. The Orientale would depreciate the renovation costs over the project's life using the straight-line method, assuming zero salvage value.

Jay's Art Café

In this alternative, The Oriental was to set up its café. The upfront capital investment would be in the range of Rs 2.2 to Rs 2.4 million. Estimated revenues would be around Rs 3.65 million in the first year based on 50 covers per day and an average billing of Rs 200 per cover. The main costs would include food and beverage costs, employee costs, and other operating expenses. The life of the equipment and other project investments would be six years. The capital investment would be depreciated over the project's life using the straight-line method with zero salvage value. Annual capital expenditure would be equal to the depreciation expense.

Mithuna had prepared four Exhibits for Jay's benefit. Exhibit 15.1 provided a summarised version of the income statement of The Oriental.

Exhibit 15.2 included forecasts of revenues and contribution margins of The Oriental over the next six years. Exhibit 15.3 provided the basis of projected expenses for Jay's Art Café. Exhibit 15.4 summarised responses to three customer survey questions which probed the likely impact of closing down Jay's Gallery on The Oriental's revenues.

Mithuna had also prepared a few points in response to Jay's queries. These were as follows:

- Value recovered by the closure of the lounge: The estimated net salvage value of the furniture in the lounge area would be Rs 50,000.
- Allocable common facilities: In addition to the incremental costs, the allocable overheads for the café based on sharing common facilities, including washrooms, would be around Rs 50,000 per annum.
- Transfer of employees: The Oriental had extra employees who could be redeployed in Jay's Art Café. The redeployment would bring down the employee headcount to be recruited for the café by around one-third with a proportionate impact on employee costs.
- Capital structure: The Oriental's existing capital structure consisted of 70% equity and remaining debt. The cost of equity was estimated as 18%, while the average cost of debt was 12%. The applicable tax rate was 25%.

EXHIBIT 15.1 Profit and Loss Statement of The Oriental

(Rs '000)	*2017–18*	*2018–19*
Revenue	13,021	13,672
Raw Materials	3,971	4,102
Employee Costs	2,604	2,700
Depreciation	3,600	3,600
Other Expenses	1,302	1,350
Total Operating Expenses	11,478	11,752
EBIT	1,543	1,920
Interest	2,000	1,700
Profit before Tax	(457)	220
Tax	–	55
Profit after Tax	(457)	165

Source: Prepared by authors.

EXHIBIT 15.2 Forecasts for The Oriental

(Rs '000)	*2019–20*	*2020–21*	*2021–22*	*2022–23*	*2023–24*	*2024–25*
Revenues	13,945	14,224	14,509	14,799	15,095	15,397
Contribution Margins	9,762	9,957	10,156	10,359	10,566	10,778

Source: Prepared by authors.

EXHIBIT 15.3 Basis of Expenses for Jay's Art Café

Cost Head	*Basis*
Food and Beverage Costs	40% of revenues
Employee Costs	12% of revenues
Other Operating Expenses	15% of revenues
Depreciation	Straight-line for six years with nil salvage value

Source: Prepared by authors.

EXHIBIT 15.4 Customer Response to Questions Related to the Lounge

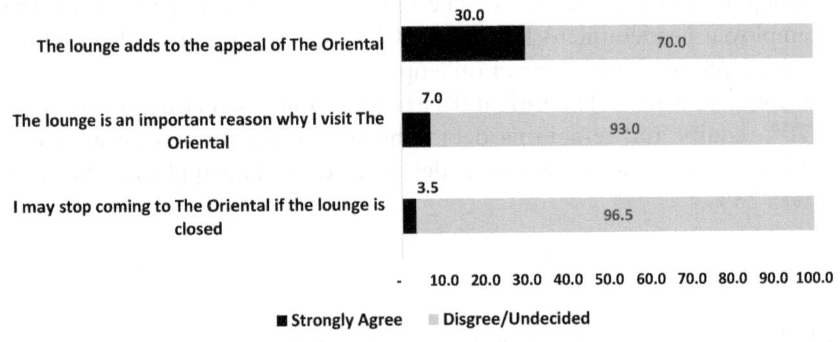

Source: Prepared by authors.

Questions

1. As the restaurant had turned around and reported positive cash flows, was there any merit in evaluating either alternative? Under what conditions could Jay reject both the alternatives?
2. Estimate the NPV, IRR, profitability index and payback period for both the alternatives.
3. How should Jay compare the two alternatives given different investment outlays and different project lives? Explain with detailed calculations.

4. How could Jay make a sound decision considering the uncertainty regarding the estimates, including capital investment, cost of capital, and potential loss of patrons due to closure of lounge? Illustrate with estimates, based on your assumptions.
5. Which alternative would you recommend to Jay, based on your answers to the above questions?

16

BREATHFRESH

Evaluating Launch of Ayurvedic Toothpaste

In early December 2020, Rajeshwari Kamath, Chief Financial Officer (CFO) at BreathFresh Products Ltd, had just returned from an intense meeting with the Chief Executive Officer (CEO), Rajneesh Krishna, and the Senior Management Team from the Marketing and Sales Department. The meeting was about launching a new category of toothpaste following the grand success of Patanjali's DantKranti, which allowed them to gain double-digit market share in the Indian toothpaste market from absolute zero in just about five years by the end of the year 2018. Colgate's response in the form of its toothpaste brand VedShakti allowed them to consolidate its leadership position. Colgate was building an entire platform around VedShakti to offer multiple product offerings under the same brand.

With Rs 180 crore of EBITDA on the total sales of Rs 600 crore and an asset base of Rs 500 crore, BreathFresh was a three-decade-old personal care products firm headquartered in Kochi. It had a strong presence in the Oral care category, and it enjoyed a double-digit market share. Despite being there in the Ayurveda Capital State of India, it had never thought of capitalising on the Naturals and Ayurveda pitch. It was now thinking of launching its new toothpaste brand "Ayurshakti" and building a brand platform to launch other products under the "nature and ayurvedic" sub-segment.

The launch of Ayurshakti required substantial upfront investments in a manufacturing facility, sourcing capabilities and significant investments towards advertising and sales promotion. Given the intense competition from toothpaste brands build on Natural and Ayurveda appeal from Patanjali, Colgate, and Dabur, it would not be easy for BreathFresh to gain substantial market share even in southern India. The bone of contention between Rajeshwari and the marketing team was the potential cannibalisation of its

DOI: 10.4324/9781032724478-19

EXHIBIT 16.1 Ayurshakti' Sales and EBITDA Margin Forecasts

Year	*Early Jan 2021*	*2021*	*2022*	*2023*	*2024*	*2025*	*2026*	*2027*	*2028*
Sales (Rs crore)		30	60	90	120	150	125	100	50
EBITDA Margin (%)		30%	32%	34%	36%	38%	33%	30%	27%
Initial Investments (Rs crore)	150								
Product Launch Expenses (Rs crore)	10								

Source: Prepared by authors.

toothpaste brands, especially, Gumpure, which was launched two years ago and was a big hit in the market. It promoted Gumpure as a complete toothpaste, and now the launch of Ayurshakti might adversely impact the sales of Gumpure and other toothpaste brands. The sales team presented forecasts for Sales and EBITDA margins for Ayurshakti from 2021 to 2028 and initial investments in manufacturing facilities and upfront product launch expense (see Exhibit 16.1). Building from there, Rajeshwari started working on other financial numbers to evaluate the financial feasibility of launching Ayurshakti.

Indian Oral Care Market

The segment oral care as part of the personal care market covered all products used for daily mouth care routines such as toothpaste, mouthwashes, manual toothbrush, and floss. According to Statista, the Indian oral care market, Rs 10,535 crore in 2020 would grow to Rs 15,997 crore by 2025, which would grow at Compounded Annual Growth Rate (CAGR) of little under 9%. India would be the fifth-largest oral care market by the end of 2021, with a market size of nearly Rs 11,500 crore, with the USA leading the pack with a market size of 57,088 crore. China (Rs 37,365 crore), Japan (Rs 18,628 crore), and Brazil (Rs 14,453 cores) would be at the second, third, and fourth spot.[1]

Colgate Palmolive (India) led the charts with more than half of the Indian oral care market in 2018. However, in a five-year stellar run since launch, Patanjali captured more than 10% of the market share in the Indian oral care market. It built its "Natural and Ayurveda" niche, inspired many to jump into the top-heavy market and gave BreathFresh and others the confidence that they could challenge market leaders and succeed.

Evaluating Financial Feasibility of Ayurshakti

Rajeshwari noted that BreathFresh had already spent Rs 5 crore on Research and Development (R&D), marketing research and test marketing to evaluate the technical feasibility and Ayushakti's market potential.

In addition, Rajeshwari noted down the following related to Ayurshakti's launch.

- The net working capital of 20% of sales will be required at the beginning of every year.
- Cumulative bad debt losses of Rs 10 crore related to Ayrshakti will be by the end of 2028. For the convenience of calculation, it is expected to occur only in 2028. EBITDA margin forecast does not capture potential bad debt losses.
- Ayurshakti would not be relevant beyond 2028 (the other products launched under the same brand platform might be but not the toothpaste); BreathFresh will sell off manufacturing facility dedicated to Ayurshakti's production. It would earn the salvage value of Rs 5 crore more than the residual book value of the plant and machinery, and the entire working capital will be released except for the loss on account of bad debt.
- The launch of Ayurshakti might affect the sales of other popular toothpaste brands of BreathFresh; such loss will be 10% of Ayurshakti sales in any given year. The blended EBITDA margin for other products would be 30% for the 2021–2028 period.
- The sales team did not allocate overheads in their EBITDA margin forecasts. The overheads will be 10% of total sales. However, only half of the overheads would be specific to the Ayurshakti project.
- The effective corporate income tax rate for BreathFresh for the forecast period will be 25%. The applicable depreciation rate will be 25% on written down value (WDV) basis.
- BreathFresh cost of capital is 10% at the end of the year 2020. However, given the relatively risky nature of the project, it might want to use a higher discount rate. However, she was not sure what should be the exact discount rate?

Questions

1. How do you prepare unlevered free cash flow projections for the Ayurshakti project?
2. How do you treat upfront marketing research and test marketing cost?

3. Do you club initial investments and upfront product launch expenses? Why? Why not?
4. What is the payback period of the project? What is the NPV of the project @ 10% discount rate? What is the IRR?
5. What is an appropriate discount rate for the project? How does the choice of discount rate impact the financial feasibility of the project?

Note

1 Source: Statista

17

AMEX

Evaluating New Business Opportunity

At 8.00 a.m. on January 2, 2020, Kevin Sharma, the CFO of AMEX Engines enterprise, reached the office an hour before time. He had to give his reasoned recommendation on the new investment proposal discussed during the strategic meet held on December 15, 2019.

Established in 1980, AMEX was a significant player in manufacturing the engine parts for the integral combustion engine (ICE) vehicles. AMEX had its head office and the largest plants in Chennai in India's southern region. With Rs 20 billion in revenue and Rs 2 billion of net income for FY2019, AMEX was one of the reputed players in Indian auto components markets. It had a decent presence in both original equipment manufacturers (OEMs) and the replacement market.

While the firm had been doing well, the primary concern raised during the strategic meet was how AMEX could sustain its profitable operations over the next decade and beyond. Governments at the centre and states pushed for faster electric vehicle adaptation (EVs) over the next decade. Niti Aayog, a policy advisory body of the Indian Government, set an ambitious target of selling only EVs beyond 2030. While it was too ambitious, such a policy shift towards EVs and away from ICEV would disrupt the auto and auto component industry. The engine parts manufacturers would face an existential threat.

It was time to make a strategic shift and look for investment opportunities to capitalise on the government's push for electric vehicles. The long-term shift from manufacturing EV parts was one of the strategic alternatives; it would not be easy. It would need significant investments in new plants and machinery. In the interim, AMEX management evaluated the feasibility to invest in EV charging stations in Chennai and Delhi. They looked to

DOI: 10.4324/9781032724478-20

capitalise on the current incentives and subsidies announcements made by various states in their EV policies.

Indian Auto Components Industry

Indian auto components industry contributed 2.3% of India's Gross Domestic Product (GDP) and one-fourth of its manufacturing in 2020. It employed 5 million people and hence was one of the biggest employment generators. The industry had grown at the compounded annual growth rate (CAGR) of 6.5% to reach the $50 billion mark over the last five years. Export grew at a faster rate of 7.6% during the same period and reached near USD 15 billion. According to Automobile Component Manufacturers Association (ACMA), the industry aimed to achieve USD 200 billion in total revenue with USD 80 billion in export revenue by 2026.[1] Growth in domestic demand, export opportunities, policy support, and cost advantage were critical drivers for rapid growth.

One could classify auto components in six broad categories: engine components, transmission and steering components, suspension and braking components, electrical parts, and others (see Exhibit 17.1 for more details). The expected disruption because of autonomous vehicles, connected vehicles, electrification and shared mobility (ACES) would create challenges for some while opportunities for other auto components manufacturers. For instance, electrification would reduce demand for ICE components and demand increase for electric motors, battery systems and battery cells. The value-add composition of a vehicle would completely change; e.g., cost of powertrain in a passenger vehicle was engine – 30%, transmission – 25%,

EXHIBIT 17.1 Auto Components: Major Segments and Sub-segments

Segment	*Sub-segment*
Engine Components	Engine valves, fuel injection systems, piston, cooling systems, powertrain components
Transmission and Steering Components	Gears, wheels, steering systems, axels, clutches
Suspension and Braking Components	Brake and brake assemblies, brake linings, shock absorbers
Equipment	Headlights, halogen bulbs, wiper motors, dashboard instruments
Electrical Parts	Starter motors, spark plugs, electric ignition systems, flywheel magnetos
Others	Body and chassis, sheet metal parts, fan belts

Source: Prepared by authors based on IBEF Auto components report (https://www.ibef.org/industry/autocomponents-india).

control/injection – 20%, auxiliaries – 10%, and exhaust – 15%. The battery-operated vehicle (BEV) in 2030 would have a very different cost of power-train: battery pack and battery management system – 70%, e-motor – 20%, power electronics – 5%, and transmission – 5%.[2] Such change would force many auto-component manufacturers to re-look at their business model entirely, especially those in engine components manufacturing.

Investment Proposal

India's government approved Rs 100 billion under the second phase of FAME India (Faster Adoption and Manufacturing of Electric Vehicles in India) in its bid to promote manufacturing and faster adoption of EVs. The setting up of charging stations had been de-licensed. Any individual or entity could set up public charging stations by complying with necessary technical and performance standards. Kevin's team had come up with essential details of all the capital expenditure and operating expenses and estimates of charging demand for the next seven years (see Exhibits 17.2 and 17.3). The following assumptions were used to make demand and revenue projections.

- Public charging station (PCS) would operate for 20 hours a day for 360 days a year.

EXHIBIT 17.2 One-time Investments and Running Cost Estimates for a Public Charging Station in Delhi

Initial Investment/Recurring Expense	*In INR*
New electricity connection (250 KVA) with transformers, caballing, and other items	7,50.000
Civil works (Flooring, boards, painting, shed etc.)	2,00,000
EVSE management software – integration with chargers and payment gateway	40,000
CCTV and surveillance setup	30,000
Site maintenance staff (2 persons)	@ 15,000/person/month (increase 5% annually)
Network service provider fees	6000/month
Lease rental fees (subsidised)	50,000/month
Advertising and promotion	4,000/month
EVSE management software recurring fees	10% of the net margin on electricity charge

Source: Prepared by authors based on Niti Aayog's Handbook on Electronic Vehicle Charging Infrastructure Implementation.

EXHIBIT 17.3 Minimum Charger Requirement and Cost Estimates for a Public Charging Station

Charger Type	*Charger Connectors*	*Rated Voltage (V)*	*Number of Charges in PCS*	*Cost of Charger/ Charger Block (in INR)*	*Number of Simultaneous Vehicles that can Be Charged*
Fast	CCS (min 50 kW)	200–1000	1	7,00,000	1
Fast	CHAdeMO (min 50 kW)	200–1000	1	7,00,000	1
Fast	Type-2 AC (Min22 kW)	380–480	1	1,20,000	1
Slow	Bharat DC-001 (15kW)	72–200	1	2,25,000	1
Slow	Bharat AC-001 (10kW)	230	1	70,000	3
Slow	Battery Swapping Station (15kW)	230	-	Cost to be borne by swap station technology proprietor	-

Source: Prepared by authors based on Niti Aayog's Handbook on Electronic Vehicle Charging Infrastructure Implementation.

- Capacity utilisation factor (CUF) would be 50% for the first year and grow at 10% every year to reach 90% by the end of the fifth year.
- The electricity charges would be passed on to customers, and the PCS would earn a margin of Rs 2 per kWh.
- The terminal value for chargers would be the residual book value at the end of seven years. Chargers' economic life would be ten years, and they would be depreciated at a 10% annual rate throughout their entire life. The effective income tax rate for AMEX was 33%.
- Other investments would be fully depreciated over seven years using the straight-line method and fetch zero scarp value.

Cost of Capital

AMEX could borrow funds from the market at 8% per annum and had a beta of 1.1. The expected market risk premium was 7%. The target debt/equity ratio for AMEX was one. AMEX would use its weighted average cost of capital (WACC) for a moderate risk project. However, it followed a policy of using WACC-2% and WACC+2% for low-risk and high-risk projects.

AMEX preferred projects with a payback period of fewer than four years. The prevailing risk-free rate was 6%

Decision Time

With all numbers inserted in the excel sheet, Kevin had to decide whether he should recommend management and the board of AMEX to go ahead with setting up 200 charging stations. Would this proposal clear the four-year payback period criteria of AMEX? Should it be treated as a low-risk, moderate-risk or high-risk project? Why? What would be the NPV of the project? How would his decision change if the centre or state government offer a 25% subsidy on charger costs?

Notes

1 https://www.ibef.org/industry/auto-components-presentation
2 https://www.mckinsey.com/~/media/McKinsey/Featured%20Insights/Asia%20Pacific/The%20auto%20component%20industry%20in%20India%20preparing%20for%20the%20future/ACMA%20Vertical_Onscreen_Final.ashx

18

SAFEWHEELS

Evaluating Investment in Electric Vehicles (EV) Fleet

In early January 2021, Tapan Das, Chief Financial Officer (CFO) at Safewheels Cab Services, was busy evaluating a proposal to replace diesel vehicles with electric vehicles. Safewheels Cab Services was established in 2007 as one of the early radio cabs with operations in Mumbai, Delhi, Kolkata, and Bangalore. By the end of 2019, it had its operations in 25 Indian cities. It was planning to add 20 more cities under its coverage by 2025. Delhi government's announcement of its new Electric Vehicles (EV) policy came just about at the right time for Safewheels. It had to replace its ageing fleet of 100 cars plying in Delhi, immediately. Since Safewheels had moved to the aggregator-based business model, it wanted fewer vehicles in its fleet.

Safewheels earned an excellent reputation with a fleet of Maruti-Esteem sedan cars, well-trained drivers, and android app-enabled award-winning services. Safewheels soon became the preferred option for business travellers for airport transfer and beyond. In 2014, Safewheels decided to switch from an inventory-based model to an asset-light aggregator model.[1]And the results were visible. It reported a profit for the first time in 2014, and it continued with its hybrid business model. They maintained a fleet of about 400 cars and operated on the aggregator model beyond that. It allowed them to expand rapidly and had a presence in more than 20 cities by 2020.

However, by 2020, the business-to-consumer (B2C) segment of the on-demand-taxi market was becoming extraordinarily competitive, and margins were evaporating. With FY20 revenue of Rs 2000 million and net income of Rs 10 million,[2] Safewheels was finding it difficult to keep its head

DOI: 10.4324/9781032724478-21

above the water. Fading profitability and intense competition in the B2C segment made it difficult for Safewheels to sustain profitable operations.

Safewheels decided to renew its focus on the business-to-business (B2B) segment of the business and targeted doubling its fleet of premium sedans/SUVs to 800 in the next year. Premium cars and well-trained chauffeurs in uniform would ensure a superior customer experience. Given the capital-intensive nature of the inventory-based business model, it initiated the process of fundraising to ensure the availability of funds. Management at Safewheels believed that its inventory-based model in metro cities would earn higher margins and faster topline growth. The idea was to focus on niche areas such as employee transportation, airport contracts, and car rentals.

Future of Shared Mobility and On-Demand Taxi Market in India

India's on-demand taxi market gained traction with the launch of taxi-forsure in Bangalore, and Uber entered India around the same time. However, the on-demand taxi market picked up only when Ola launched its app with better coverage. Initially, bookings were desktops and laptops, and there were issues with weak internet connectivity. However, things changed when Reliance Jio launched its services in 2016, resulting in data explosion and rapid smartphone penetration in India. Decreasing smartphones costs, cheaper data, and better internet speed and coverage increase in traffic in metro cities and high fuel prices resulted in the popularity of car-hailing services in India. Ola and Uber enjoyed the dominant market share with a combined presence in more than 50 Indian cities.

According to a Morgan Stanley report,[3] India would be the shared mobility leader by 2030. In 2017, shared miles were only 10% of 257 billion miles driven; however, by 2030, that number would jump to 35%, which implies an 18% CAGR. The number might touch 50% by 2040.

Rising fuel costs, heavy import reliance of India for fuel requirements, and increased pollution levels required immediate attention.

> To confront the ongoing challenges of pollution and urbanisation, India will need to transition to electric vehicles (EVs), shared mobility and autonomous driving. We believe government policy could play an important role in driving the auto industry to embrace these changes.
>
> *(Ridham Desai, Head of India Research at Morgan Stanley)*

Further, Morgan Stanley expected 50% of vehicles sold in 2040 in India would be EV.[4]

SWITCH: Does it Make Sense?

While there were no two views on EVs' bright future in India, there were several challenges when Safewheels first thought of building a fleet of EV sedans. Up to 30%, higher initial cost, lack of charging infrastructure, long charging time, and lower range of EVs neutralised benefits of lower operating and maintenance costs and made such switch unviable. However, a lot had changed since then. The Government of India rolled out Faster Adoption and Manufacturing of Electric Vehicles (FAME) in India (I and II). It announced several incentives for switching to EV, setting up charging infrastructure, and manufacturing EVs in India.

State governments announced policies to incentivise switch to EVs. The Delhi government had notified its EV policy in August 2020 (see Exhibit 18.1). It announced further incentives during the "switch Delhi" campaign in early 2021. The incentive for passenger cars would be in the form of a subsidy of Rs 5,000 per kWh of battery capacity. The Delhi government further announced an exemption from RTO tax for both EVs for private and commercial use. The government set an ambitious target of having at least 25% of new vehicles sold by 2024 to be EVs.[5] Under the "switch Delhi" campaign, passenger vehicles, both personal and commercial, were exempted from RTO[6] tax and registration charges (see Exhibit 18.2).

The Proposal

It was high time for Safewheels to replace its fully depreciated 100-car fleet (8-year-old) in Delhi. Market sources suggested that they could sell them for Rs 30,000 apiece for now. While it could continue with its existing fleet of cars for the next two years, it would not fetch zero salvage value after two years. There was a risk that the Delhi government would roll back some of the incentives on EVs by then. Given that, Tapan decided to compare Tata Nexon diesel and Tata Nexon EV's top variants before taking a plunge in the world of EV (see Exhibit 18.3).

EXHIBIT 18.1 Incentives under Delhi Government EV Policy 2020 (in INR)

Electric Two-Wheelers	Up to 30,000
Electric Passenger Vehicles	Up to 1,50,000
Auto Rickshaws	Up to Rs 30,000
E-Rickshaws	Up to Rs 30,000
E-Good Carriers	Up to Rs 30,000

Source: AutocarsIndia (https://www.autocarindia.com/industry/delhi-cm-arvind-kejriwal-urges-faster-adoption-of-evs-with-switch-delhi-campaign-419852)

EXHIBIT 18.2 RTO Tax and Vehicle Registration Charges in Delhi as of Jan 2021

	Petrol Car	*Diesel Car*	*Electric Car*
Road Tax (cars >INR 10L) for Vehicles in the Company's Name	12.5%	12% (15.625%	Nil
Registration Charges	Rs 600	Rs 600	Nil
All diesel cars (except for private registrations) more than 10 years old were already banned in Delhi.			

Source: https://www.mycarhelpline.com/index.php?option=com_easyblog&view=entry&id=155&Itemid=91

EXHIBIT 18.3 Nexon XZA Plus DT Roof (O) Diesel AMT vs Nexon EV XZ Plus LUX

	Nexon XZA Plus DT Roof (O) Diesel AMT	*Nexon EV XZ Plus LUX*
Ex-Showroom Price in Delhi	INR 1.279 million	INR 1.64 million
Fuel Type	Diesel	Electric/battery
Battery		30.2kWh
Mileage	21 km/l	312 km on a full charge
Estimated Diesel/Power Rates in Delhi for the Next Eight Years (Tapan's Estimates)	INR 84/l	INR 10/unit
Insurance Cost (approx. 5.4% of residual book value every year on ex-showroom price)		
Average Maintenance Cost Per Year	1.5% of Ex-showroom price	0.75% of Ex-showroom price
Salvage Value at the End of 8 Years	100,000	150,000
Average Daily Usage (320 days/year)	125 km	125 km
Life of Vehicle/Battery	200,000 km	200,000 km
Depreciation (Straight-line Method)	Five years	Five years
Salvage Value	Nil	Nil

Source: https://www.zigwheels.com/compare-cars/tata-nexon-vs-tata-nexon-ev and authors' estimates

Decision time

Tapan was ready with his excel sheet. It was time to put all available information into an excel sheet and choose between Nexon XZA Plus DT Roof (O) Diesel AMT vs Nexon EV XZ Plus LUX. Safewheels had to decide soon and order 100 premier SUVs before Tata Motors announced potential price hikes. Safewheels was confident of charging Rs 1/km more with ESG (Environment, Social and Governance) sensitive corporate clients on EV SUVs than diesel SUVs. However, Tapan did not include the same in his base case estimates. What would be the base case NPV for EV over diesel modes, given that the cost of capital Safewheels was 15%? Should Tapan use the Safewheels cost of capital for comparison or use a higher discount rate given the riskier nature of EV investment? What would be the internal rate of return (IRR) of the proposal? What should he recommend to the board of the company? Diesel variant or EV variant?

Notes

1 Inventory-based model requires a fleet of firm-owned cars. In contrast, the aggregator (app-based) model matches the passenger and driver in the shortest time and earn a 20/25% commission from the driver. Drivers own cars, and it does not require the firm to own a fleet of vehicles, hence asset-light, and therefore easily scalable.
2 The effective income tax rate applicable for Safewheels was 25%.
3 https://www.financialexpress.com/economy/india-to-be-shared-mobility-leader-by-2030-says-morgan-stanley-report/1191572/
4 https://www.morganstanley.com/ideas/india-mobility-transformation
5 https://www.aninews.in/news/national/general-news/kejriwal-launches-switch-delhi-campaign-plans-electric-vehicle-adoption-to-fight-air-pollution20210204152214/
6 RTO is a Regional Transport Office that maintains a database of vehicles, drivers, and issues licence in various states of India.

19

PVR CINEMA

Should it Take OTT Plunge?

On April 30, 2020, Snigdha Mathur, Head Transaction advisory group at Elixir Capital Partners, addressed its team over a Zoom call. The entire world was in the stranglehold of the Covid-19 pandemic. Most countries, including India, announced nationwide lockdowns to break the virus chain and to avoid the collapse of the National Health Infrastructure (NHS), resulting in the loss of many lives. Most countries accepted a trade-off of saving human lives over facing adverse economic consequences, but that also had its challenges. It would result in large-scale unemployment and the closure of many small- and medium-scale industries. Tours and Travel, Hospitality and Entertainment, and Airline were some of the worst-hit sectors. Governments across the world were announcing the economic packages to blunt the adverse consequences. However, adversity for one might bring an opportunity for the other. So while movie exhibitors found themselves between a rock and a hard place, April 2020 tuned out to be one of the best months for over-the-top (OTT) platforms offering online video streaming services.

Snigdha asked its team to prepare a pitchbook for PVR Cinemas, the market leader in the Indian movie exhibition business. On several occasions, whenever asked about emerging competition from OTT platforms, PVR always downplayed it. It maintained that the movie exhibition business through multiplex chain was a unique experience, and movie-going habits of Indians had not changed. The advent of television, DVDs, and the Indian Premier League were all considered a substantial threat to the multiplex business, but none had posed a severe challenge to the movie exhibition industry. However, Snigdha believed that history had taught us that underplaying emerging competition might pose an existential threat to the

DOI: 10.4324/9781032724478-22

business. Blockbuster, the king of videocassettes and DVD rental business, downplayed the challenge posed by Netflix in the late 1990s and the next five years, Blockbuster was out of the business. However, April 2020 might be the point of inflexion in history given that the cinemas were closed and people locked in their homes powered by cheap, high-speed internet and smartphones consumed online contents.

PVR Cinema

From the launch of its first screen in 1997, PVR had come a long way. With 800 plus screens, PVR had its presence in 64 cities and 21 Indian states. PVR registered an impressive CAGR of 25% from 2012 to 2018 in the number of screens. It was a market leader with more than 25% market share, followed by its closest rival, Inox leisure (close to 20% market share). PVR had grown using a mix of organic and inorganic growth opportunities. PVR acquired Cinemax in 2012 and DT Cinema in 2015, and SPI Cinema in 2018. It was racing towards its ambitious target of 1,000 screens by the end of 2020 (see Exhibit 19.1 for world's top multiplex chains).

PVR reported an operating profit (EBITDA) of Rs 619 crore on Rs 3,118 crore of revenue from operations for FY19. The assets on the balance sheet at the end of FY19 were worth Rs. 3061 crore. It earned nearly 55% of revenues from the sale of tickets, 28% from the sale of F&B, and 10% from advertising. Convenience fees and movie production and distribution were other sources of revenue. While the operating margin was hovering around 18–19% for the past three years, PVR expected it to stabilise at about 20% due to favourable GST rates. While FY18 turned out to be a sluggish year, FY19 looked like it would be one of the best years (See Exhibit 19.2 for five-year financial highlights).

EXHIBIT 19.1 World's Top Multiplex Chains

Sr. No.	*Cinema*	*Country*	*Screens*	*Admit (IN MN)*	*Admit Per Screen*
1	AMC	USA	11,247	347	30,852
2	Cinepolis	Mexico	5,313	338	63,617
3	Cinemark	USA	5,959	277	46,484
4	Wanda	China	4,648	210	45,180
5	Regal Cinemas	USA	7,322	197	26,905
6	CGV Korea	South Korea	3,442	146	42,417
7	PVR	India	800	105	1,31,250
8	Cineworld	UK	2,217	104	46,910
9	Vue Int'l	Uk	1,904	81	42,542
10	Cineplex	Canada	1,676	70	41,766

Source: https://static1.pvrcinemas.com/pvrcms/pvrinvestorDeck_SPI_Cinema_Acquisition.pdf

EXHIBIT 19.2 PVR Cinemas: 5-Year Financial Highlights

Operating Parameters	*FY 2016*	*FY 2017*	*FY 2018*	*FY 2019*	*FY 2020*
Properties	112	126	134	164	176
Screens	516	579	625	763	845
Seats	1,18,124	1,32,026	1,39,509	1,69,976	1,81,917
Cities	46	50	51	65	71
Admits (In Lakh)	696	752	761	993	1,017
Occupancy %	34.30%	32.90%	31.30%	36.20%	34.90%
ATP (Rs)	188	196	210	207	204
SPH (Rs)	72	81	89	91	99
P&L Account (Rs in Lakh)	**FY 2016**	**FY 2017**	**FY 2018**	**FY 2019**	**FY 2020**
Income from Sale of Movie Tickets	99,480	1,12,488	1,24,707	1,63,543	1,73,115
Sales of Food and Beverages	49,774	57,942	62,495	85,839	96,046
Advertisement Income	21,454	25,176	29,693	35,352	37,588
Convenience Fees	3,329	5,816	5,971	13,035	17,193
Other Operating Income	10,919	10,521	10,545	10,787	17,502
Other Income	6,348	6,225	3,134	3,314	3,779
Total Revenues	1,91,304	2,18,168	2,36,545	3,11,870	3,45,223
Film Exhibition Cost	41,975	46,516	53,766	70,193	73,345
Consumption of Food and Beverages	12,483	14,010	15,907	23,874	26,369
Employee Benefit Expense	18,594	22,051	25,407	33,726	39,381
Rent and CAM	41,989	50,220	52,373	63,607	73,220
Other Operating Expenses	40,671	47,784	45,775	58,523	71,514
Total Expenses	1,55,712	1,80,581	1,93,228	2,49,923	2,83,829
EBITDA	35,592	37,587	43,317	61,947	61,394
EBITDA Margin	18.60%	17.23%	18.31%	19.86%	17.78%
Depreciation	11,511	13,838	15,369	19,128	23,244
EBIT	24,081	23,749	27,948	42,819	38,150
Finance Cost	8,395	8,058	8,371	12,801	15,214
PBT Before Exceptional Item	15,686	15,691	19,577	30,018	22,936
Exceptional Item	-1,156	-407	-59	0	0
Share of Net Profit/(Loss) of Joint Venture	–	–	-72	-115	-54
PBT After Exceptional Item	14,530	15,284	19,446	29,903	22,882
Tax	4,668	5,700	7,044	10,963	9,779
PAT	9,862	9,584	12,402	18,940	13,104
PAT Margin	5.15%	4.39%	5.24%	6.07%	3.80%
EPS – Basic	21.05	20.5	26.68	39.77	26.86
EPS – Diluted	21.03	20.5	26.57	39.52	26.72
Balance Sheet (Rs in Lakh)	**FY 2016**	**FY 2017**	**FY 2018**	**FY 2019**	**FY 2-20**
Shareholder Funds	92,132	1,00,551	1,07,617	1,49,615	1,48,051
Total Debt	66,002	81,958	83,052	1,28,240	1,29,468
Other Non-Current Liabilities	672	801	1,060	28,272	3,94,713
Total Sources of Funds	1,58,806	1,83,310	1,91,729	3,06,127	6,72,232
Non-Current Assets	1,44,127	1,94,530	2,05,109	3,45,750	6,67,559

(Continued)

EXHIBIT 19.2 Continued

Operating Parameters	*FY 2016*	*FY 2017*	*FY 2018*	*FY 2019*	*FY 2020*
Net Fixed Assets (Including CWIP)	1,07,557	1,15,030	1,22,864	1,90,998	1,98,397
Goodwill	8,579	43,365	43,447	1,05,330	1,05,204
Right of Use	0	0	0	0	3,00,473
Others	36,135	38,798	69,322	49,422	63,485
Current Assets	45,595	28,039	29,775	39,336	75,361
Less: Current Liabilities	30,916	39,259	43,155	78,959	70,688
Net Current Assets	14,679	−11,220	−13,380	−39,623	4,673
Total Assets	1,58,806	1,83,310	1,91,729	3,06,127	6,72,232

Source: https://static1.pvrcinemas.com/pvrcms/pvrinvestorDeck_SPI_Cinema_Acquisition.pdf

PVR Utsav

In August 2019, PVR launched its new brand, "PVR Utsav," to penetrate non-metro Tier-2 and Tier-3 cities in India. It intended to expand the PVR Utsav screen network to 200 over the next four to five years. The cost per screen for PVR Utsav would be Rs 1.5 crore vs Rs 3 crore for regular PVR screens. The average ticket price would also be lower to Rs 100. However, by April 2020, nationwide lockdown changed the picture entirely.

Rise of OTT Platforms and Emergence of AltBalaji

The global OTT market generated USD 110 billion in revenue in 2018 and expected to grow to USD 438 billion by 2025, at a CAGR of 19%. Before the Covid-19 outbreak, the OTT market was expected to grow at 16.7% by 2020. The estimated market size at the end of 2020 before the Covid-19 pandemic was USD 151.5 billion, whereas the actual market size at the end of 2020 was USD 155.6 billion. Covid-19 accelerated the growth in OTT markets.[1] The story was no different in India. India's digital media industry clocked 31% growth and was worth Rs 220.7 billion at the end of 2019. Advertising remained as the dominant source of income with Rs 191.5 billion coming from advertising while subscription contributed the rest.[2]

Rise of AltBalaj

Since its launch in 2017, AltBalaji was a multi-device subscription video-on-demand platform. It had grown leaps and bounds in three years. AltBalaji was a wholly owned subsidiary of Balaji Telefilms, which had more than two decades of experience in the Indian movie and television industry. Launched by Ekta Kapoor, the daughter of yesteryears Indian filmstar Jitendra Kapoor, Balaji telefilms produced more than 100 TV serials and movies. Its soap opera "Kyu ki Saas Bhi Kabhi Bahu Thi" aired between 2000 and 2008 remained the most successful TV serials in the history of Indian television.

Knowing the pulse of the consumers of Tier-2 and Tier-3 Indian cities gave it an edge over 26 homegrown Indian OTT players. Despite competing with giants like Amazon Prime, Hotstar, Netflix, and Voot, AltBalaji doubled its revenue in one year between FY19 and FY20. It added 12,300 subscribers/day in Q42020 compared to the run rate of 10,000 subscribers/day in previous quarters. It claimed to have 8.4 million monthly active (engaged) uses and a smaller number of profitable customers.

AltBalaji's revenue mix includes subscription revenue, licencing digital content rights, and advertisements on free content service. It reported Rs 77.7 crore in revenue for FY20, growing by 85.5% from FY19. The expenses stood at Rs 19.2.5 crore, grew 17% YoY, the losses shrunk by 3% YoY at Rs 111.5 crore. Significant expenditures for FY20 included the cost of production (Rs 105 crore), Marketing and Distribution (Rs 30 crore), and staff cost (Rs 10 crore). The real boost to the OTT market came from the nationwide lockdown announcement in the third week of March 2020. According to Redseer, online content consumption saw a 35% growth in April 2020 than in January 2020.

Should PVR Take OTT Plunge?

While PVR was facing the brunt of the nationwide lockdown in April 2020, it gave them time to reflect and realign their business strategy for the future. While its OTT looked like it directly competed with the movie exhibition business through multiplex, the annual report of Balaji telefilms for FY20 reported:

> *Aided by a 20% growth in broadband subscriptions and over 4 million connected smart television sets, the OTT segment saw its subscription revenue soar by more than 100% in 2019. However, in 2019, Indian cinema witnessed its best-ever revenues and footfalls in theatres. While some see OTT as a threat to the theatre, it is equally valid that OTT also drives people to theatres, particularly fans of older sequels of franchise movies who wait for new releases.*[3]

Nearly 65% of AltBalaji's subscribers came from Tier-2 and Tier-3 non-metro cities; on the other hand, more than 70% of PVR's revenues came from Tier-1 metro cities. PVR was planning to penetrate the non-metro market with the launch of "PVR Utsav," launch of the OTT platform might turn out to be a better strategy. PVR, too, like Balaji, had more than two and a half decades of experience in the movie exhibition business in the Indian market.

EXHIBIT 19.3 Cash Flow Projections for Proposed OTT Platform (In Rs crore)

	2020	2021	2022	2023	2024	2025	2026	2027	2028	2029	2030
Revenue		20	50	100	210	300	400	500	600	720	750
Expenses (other than Depreciation, interest and tax)		100	140	180	215	230	280	325	390	468	513.5
EBITDA		−80	−90	−80	−5	70	120	175	210	252	276.5
Depreciation		30	34	39	45	51	50	28.5	34.2	41.04	45.03
Tax Expense/Credit (@25%)		27.5	31	29.75	12.5	−4.75	−17.5	−36.625	−43.9	−52.7	−57.87
Net Operating Profit after Tax		−52.5	−59	−50.25	7.5	65.25	102.5	138.38	166.05	199.26	218.63
Capex	−400	40	50	60	60	50	50	30	36	43.2	47.4
Working Capital Requirement (1% of Sales in the beginning of the year)	2	5	10	21	30	40	50	60	72	75	79.5
Unlevered Free Cash Flow		−65.5	−80	−82.25	−16.5	56.25	92.5	126.88	152.25	194.1	211.76

Notes:
1. The terminal growth rate would be between the steady-state inflation rate and the country's nominal GDP growth rate.
2. Capex requirement from 2031 onwards would be 6% of sales, and depreciation would be 95% of Capex.

Source: Prepared by authors.

EXHIBIT 19.4 Additional Assumptions for PVR's OTT Business

Risk-Free Rate	6%
PVR Credit Rating	AA
Yield Spread for AA-Rated Borrower in April 2020	250 Basis Points
Expected Market Risk Premium	8%
OTT Business Debt Beta	0.15
Asset Beta for OTT Businesses Globally and in India	1.2

Source: Prepared by authors.

Financial feasibility of OTT platform for PVR:

On May 15, 2020, Snigdha's team shared its cash flow forecast for PVR's potential OTT venture and other relevant information for her to see the feasibility for such business before preparing a more formal pitch book to present it to PVR's senior management (See Exhibits 19.3 and 19.4). She looked at the balance sheet of PVR and considered evaluating OTT platform business using two alternative financing plans.

a) Fixed amount of debt for OTT business that could be repaid over next ten years or carried on in perpetuity
b) Using a fixed target debt-to-value ratio of 0.4 and maintain it on an ongoing basis.

She noted down the following questions for her to answer:

1. What is the value of OTT business, assuming PVR was entirely equity funded? What are the annual projected free cash flows? What should be the appropriate discount rate?
2. What is the value of OTT business using the Adjusted Present Value (APV) approach if PVR chose to fund the business with 50% of total initial investments using debt and maintain that debt in perpetuity?
3. Value the OTT business assuming PVR maintained OTT business level debt-to-value ratio of 0.4 continuously? What would be the end of the year implied debt levels in such a scenario?
4. Use debt balances in question 3, value OTT business using capital cash flow (CCF) approach.
5. How does the value of OTT business differ using WACC, APV, and CCP approaches? What are the assumptions related to the financial policy of the firm? Which method do you think is easier to implement and appropriate?

Notes

1 https://www.researchdive.com/covid-19-insights/310/over-the-top-market accessed on April 18, 2021.
2 Balaji Telefilms Annual report 2019-20, p. 56. https:.//www.balajielefilms.com/pdf/annualreports/balajiannualreports/Balaji%20Telefilms%20APR%202019-20.pdf
accessed on April 18, 2021.
3 https:.//www.balajielefilms.com/pdf/annualreports/balajiannualreports/Balaji%20Telefilms%20APR%202019-20.pdf
accessed on April 18, 2021.

20

NEOGENE TYRES

Capital Budgeting Under Uncertainty

Neogene Tyres had a meeting of the capital budgeting committee scheduled for June 2021. The proposals to be discussed included a new radial truck and bus tyres' unit near Ajmer, Rajasthan. Radha Suryavanshi, Manager – New Projects, was working on the financial model after taking inputs from the business unit.

The new project appeared to be acceptable based on the investment criteria defined by the capital budgeting committee. But the committee had in the past rejected proposals that failed to consider the impact of various risks and uncertainties. Radha was determined to avoid making that mistake.

Neogene's New Project

The Indian tyre industry had a turnover of Rs 60,000 crore in 2019–20.[1] Sales could be divided into original equipment, replacement, and exports, of which replacement segment was the largest, accounting for 67% of the tonnage. A significant share of the tyres sold comprised cross-ply, but the proportion of radial truck and bus tyres steadily rose to around 50%.

Neogene Tyres was a mid-sized tyre manufacturer which produced radial car and light commercial vehicle tyres mainly for the replacement segment. With the new project, Neogene could enter the radial truck and bus tyres segment, which would provide an opportunity to scale up the size of its business significantly.

The new projects division had prepared the business plan for the truck and bus radial project. The team had assumed an investment of Rs 750 crore in setting up the capacity over the next two years. Output growth would be high

DOI: 10.4324/9781032724478-23

in the initial years, and the plan provided for further expansions before the capacity utilisation hit peak levels. Neogene already had established suppliers for raw materials, including natural rubber, crude oil-based materials such as synthetic rubber and carbon black, and other materials such as steel tyre cord. The business plan ended with financial projections for the next ten years.

Radha revised the financial model of the project. She separated the critical assumptions from the financial projections. Whereas the original model had varied all the assumptions from year to year, Radha decided to smoothen the assumptions related to prices and costs. Commodity prices were tough to forecast on a year-by-year basis (Exhibit 20.1). She also chose to smoothen the capital expenditure such that it changed with the sales, although actual capacity additions would be in steps rather than in small increments. Radha wanted to create an interactive model, which allowed the output to change based on a few assumptions. She ensured that the smoothening had a negligible impact on the key results.

She also added assumptions relating to terminal growth and applied a discount rate her division used for such projects. The NPV of the project was positive and significant, and the internal rate of return was much above the internally set hurdle rate. Though the payback period was extremely long, Radha noted that the project would become cash-flow positive within a few years. She also decided to prepare a detailed analysis and presentation of the new project's viability under uncertainty.

EXHIBIT 20.1 Trend in Crude Oil and Natural Rubber Prices

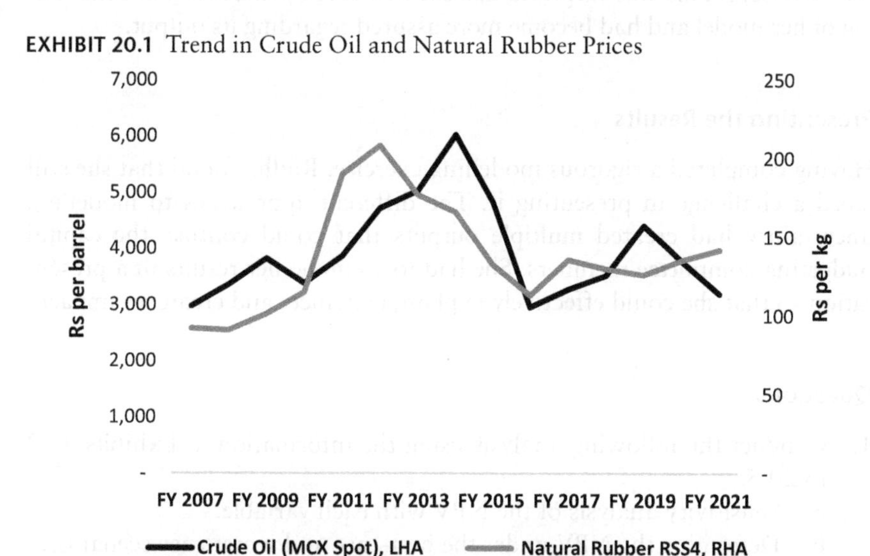

Source: Prepared by authors based on crude oil (MCX Spot) prices data from Bloomberg; Natural Rubber (RSS4) prices from www.rubberboard.gov.in

Handling Uncertainty

Sensitivity analysis allowed Radha to determine how a key input variable changed, say natural rubber prices affected a key output variable, say NPV of the project. Radha found it easy to implement the data-table feature of the spreadsheet once she had a reasonable range for input values. The limitation was that she could see the impact of one variable at a time. Although it was possible to create two-way analysis tables, she had to assume that each input changed independently.

Radha learned that Monte Carlo simulation was not "sensitivity analysis on steroids," as she had imagined, considering the ability to run numerous trials. She had to determine the distribution characteristics of the input variables she wanted to change and the correlations between the variables. For example, it was likely that tyre price realisations were positively correlated with raw material prices and tyre demand. She was reasonably sure of the distribution and correlation assumptions in tyre prices, natural rubber, and crude oil-based on the historical price data. She downloaded and used a free trial version of popular simulation software to run the trials.

In comparison to sensitivity analysis and Monte Carlo simulation, Radha found scenario analysis relatively staid. Radha had to think hard to determine plausible scenarios and choose only those assumptions which were mutually consistent. This constraint limited the number of scenarios, and Radha considered only one best-case and one worst-case scenario. However, at the end of the exercise, Radha was surprised that she had developed a better understanding of her model and had become more assured regarding its output.

Presenting the Results

Having completed a rigorous modelling exercise, Radha found that she still faced a challenge in presenting it. The different approaches to modelling uncertainty had created multiple outputs that could confuse the capital budgeting committee members. She had to combine her results in a presentation so that she could effectively explain, convince, and create an impact.

Questions

1. Conduct the following analysis using the information in Exhibits 20.2 to 20.5.
   a. Sensitivity analysis of the NPV with each variable.
   b. Determine the NPV under the best-case and worst-case scenarios.
   c. Conduct 10,000 Monte Carlo trials and determine the proportion of trials with positive NPV.
2 Summarise the results of your analysis using the three approaches in an integrated manner.

EXHIBIT 20.2 Assumptions for the New Project

Rs Crore		*FY 2024*	*FY 2025*	*FY 2026*	*FY 2027*	*FY 2028*	*FY 2029*	*FY 2030*	*FY 2031*	*FY 2032*	*FY 2033*
Sales in FY24		500									
% Increase in Sales Volumes			100%	40%	27%	18%	13%	9%	8%	6%	6%
% Increase in Net Realisation			3.0%	3.0%	3.0%	3.0%	3.0%	3.0%	3.0%	3.0%	3.0%
Raw Material Cost in FY24		320									
Natural Rubber		160									
Crude-Oil Based Chemicals		110									
Other Raw Materials		50									
% Increase in Natural Rubber Price			1%	1%	1%	1%	1%	1%	1%	1%	1%
% Increase in Crude Oil Price			5%	5%	5%	5%	5%	5%	5%	5%	5%
-Elasticity with Crude-Based Materials	0.5										
% Increase in Other Raw Material Price			3.0%	3.0%	3.0%	3.0%	3.0%	3.0%	3.0%	3.0%	3.0%
Direct Labour and Manufacturing Costs in FY24		150									
Direct Labour and Manufacturing Costs – % Variable	50%										

(Continued)

EXHIBIT 20.2 Continued

Rs Crore		*FY 2024*	*FY 2025*	*FY 2026*	*FY 2027*	*FY 2028*	*FY 2029*	*FY 2030*	*FY 2031*	*FY 2032*	*FY 2033*
Inflation in Direct Labour and Manufacturing Costs	5%										
Other Operating Expenses in FY24		75									
% Increase in Other Operating Expenses			15%	15%	12%	10%	10%	10%	8%	6%	4%
Depreciation Rate (WDV)	15%										
Corporate Tax Rate	25%										
Initial Capex in FY22 and in FY23	375										
Sales/Net PPE		0.70	1.60	2.30	3.00	3.50	3.50	3.50	3.50	3.50	3.50
Net Working Capital at the End of FY23	25										
Net Working Capital as % of Sales	8.33%										
Terminal Growth Rate	5.50%										
Discount Rate	10.50%										

Source: Prepared by authors.

EXHIBIT 20.3 Financial Projections for the New Project

Rs Crore	*FY 2022*	*FY 2023*	*FY 2024*	*FY 2025*	*FY 2026*	*FY 2027*	*FY 2028*	*FY 2029*	*FY 2030*	*FY 2031*	*FY 2032*	*FY 2033*
Total Sales			500	1,030	1,485	1,943	2,361	2,748	3,086	3,432	3,748	4,092
Natural Rubber Costs			160	323	457	586	699	797	878	958	1,025	1,097
Crude-Based Material Costs			110	226	324	421	509	590	659	730	793	862
Other Material Costs			50	103	149	194	236	275	309	343	375	409
Total Material Costs			320	652	929	1,202	1,444	1,662	1,846	2,031	2,193	2,368
Direct Labour and Manufacturing Costs			150	236	298	355	406	454	498	544	588	636
Other Operating Expenses			75	86	99	111	122	134	148	160	169	176
Total Operating Expenses			545	974	1,326	1,668	1,972	2,251	2,492	2,734	2,950	3,181
PBDIT			(45)	56	159	275	389	498	594	698	797	911
Net PPE	375	750	714	644	646	648	675	785	882	981	1,071	1,169
Depreciation			113	107	97	97	97	101	118	132	147	161
PBIT			(158)	(51)	63	178	292	396	476	566	650	750
Net Working Capital		25	42	86	124	162	197	229	257	286	312	341
PBIT (1-t) + Depreciation	-	-	(6)	69	144	231	316	399	475	557	635	723
Capex	375	375	77	37	99	99	124	212	214	231	237	259
Change in Net Working Capital	-	25	17	44	38	38	35	32	28	29	26	29
Net Cash Flow	(375)	(400)	(99)	(12)	7	94	157	155	233	296	371	436
Terminal Value												9,196
Net Cash Flow Incl. Term. Val.	(375)	(400)	(99)	(12)	7	94	157	155	233	296	371	9,632
NPV	2,689											
IRR	29.2%											

Source: Prepared by authors.

Note: All cash flows were assumed to occur at the end of the year.

EXHIBIT 20.4 Range of Assumptions for Scenario Analysis

Rs Crore		*FY 2024*	*FY 2025*	*FY 2026*	*FY 2027*	*FY 2028*	*FY 2029*	*FY 2030*	*FY 2031*	*FY 2032*	*FY 2033*
Base Case											
% Increase in Sales Volumes			100%	40%	27%	18%	13%	9%	8%	6%	6%
% Increase in Net Realisation			3.0%	3.0%	3.0%	3.0%	3.0%	3.0%	3.0%	3.0%	3.0%
% Increase in Natural Rubber Price			1.0%	1.0%	1.0%	1.0%	1.0%	1.0%	1.0%	1.0%	1.0%
% Increase in Crude Oil Price			5.0%	5.0%	5.0%	5.0%	5.0%	5.0%	5.0%	5.0%	5.0%
Sales/Net PPE		0.70	1.60	2.30	3.00	3.50	3.50	3.50	3.50	3.50	3.50
Net Working Capital as % of Sales	8.33%										
Terminal Growth Rate	5.50%										
Discount Rate	10.50%										
Best Case											
% Increase in Sales Volumes			100%	40%	30%	20%	15%	10%	9%	7%	5%
% Increase in Net Realisation			3.5%	3.5%	3.5%	3.5%	3.5%	3.5%	3.5%	3.5%	3.5%
% Increase in Natural Rubber Price			0.0%	0.0%	0.0%	0.0%	0.0%	0.0%	0.0%	0.0%	0.0%
% Increase in Crude Oil Price			3.0%	3.0%	3.0%	3.0%	3.0%	3.0%	3.0%	3.0%	3.0%
Sales/Net PPE		0.70	1.60	2.30	3.00	3.50	3.75	3.75	3.75	3.75	3.75
Net Working Capital as % of Sales	6.67%										
Terminal Growth Rate	6.50%										
Discount Rate	10.00%										
Worst Case											
% Increase in Sales Volumes			100%	40%	25%	16%	13%	9%	7%	5.5%	4.5%
% Increase in Net Realisation			3.0%	3.0%	3.0%	3.0%	3.0%	3.0%	3.0%	3.0%	3.0%
% Increase in Natural Rubber Price			1.0%	1.0%	1.0%	1.0%	1.0%	1.0%	1.0%	1.0%	1.0%

Rs Crore		*FY 2024*	*FY 2025*	*FY 2026*	*FY 2027*	*FY 2028*	*FY 2029*	*FY 2030*	*FY 2031*	*FY 2032*	*FY 2033*
% Increase in Crude Oil Price			7.0%	7.0%	7.0%	7.0%	7.0%	7.0%	7.0%	7.0%	7.0%
Sales/Net PPE		0.70	1.60	2.30	3.00	3.30	3.30	3.30	3.30	3.30	3.30
Net Working Capital as % of Sales	9.00%										
Terminal Growth Rate	4.50%										
Discount Rate	12.00%										

Source: Prepared by authors.

EXHIBIT 20.5 Range of Assumptions for Sensitivity Analysis and Monte Carlo Simulations

Sensivity Analysis	*Low*	*Base*	*High*			
Incremental Volume Growth Rate[a]	–5.0%	0.0%	5.0%			
Tyre Realisation Change	1.0%	3.0%	5.0%			
Natural Rubber Price Change	–2.0%	1.0%	4.0%			
Crude Oil Price Change	0.0%	5.0%	9.0%			
Terminal Growth Rate	4.0%	5.5%	6.5%			
Discount Rate	9.0%	10.5%	13.5%			
Monte Carlo Analysis						
	Normal Distribution			Correlation Matrix		
	Mean	Std. Dev.		Tyre Realn	NR Price	Oil Price
Tyre Realisation Change	3.0%	1.0%		1.00		
Natural Rubber Price Change	1.0%	3.0%		0.70	1.00	
Crude Oil Price Change	5.0%	3.0%		0.50	0.30	1.00

Source: Prepared by authors.

Note: [a]Volume growth rate each year as well as in terminal period, subject to maximum of 6.5%.

Note

1 https://atmaindia.org.in/an-overview/

21

ASHIAN BIOTECH

The AntiCov Vaccine Project

On April 3, 2020, Rishi Bhargav, Chief Executive Officer of Ashian Biotech, held a videoconference with his senior management team regarding the company's future. Lately, he had been under fire from the company's board since Ashian was not pursuing new opportunities aggressively, unlike other biotech firms.

Established in 2007, Ashian Biotech Ltd focussed on drug discovery, drug development, and the manufacture of vaccines. In India, the biotech industry had grown at a rate of around 14% per annum to approximately USD 51 billion by 2018. The Department of Biotechnology, Government of India, had set an ambitious target of increasing the industry size to more than USD 100 billion by 2025.[1]

Ashian Biotech had grown much faster than the industry from a small base during 2011–2016. However, growth had slowed down considerably during 2017–2020. Earnings had not only stagnated but had even begun to decline in recent years.

It was in this context that Rishi had called for the videoconference with the senior management team, including Anshuman Mittal (President – New Projects), Bibek Singh (Chief Operating Officer), and George Cherian (Chief Financial Officer).

Rishi started the meeting by reiterating the key concerns for Ashian Biotech and reminding them about the discussion they had towards the end of February 2020.

Rishi: Good afternoon to all of you. As you may remember, we had discussed our critical problems in February – the growth slowdown, modest

DOI: 10.4324/9781032724478-24

return on equity, and the pressure from the board and shareholders to increase returns. We had given ourselves six weeks to work out plans to address the same. I have been exchanging emails with each of you and believe that we have made significant progress. It is a good time for us to take stock of each proposal and see where we go. Anshuman, would you like to start your presentation?

Investment Proposal 1. AntiCov Vaccine

Anshuman: I am happy that we could quickly identify the opportunity of developing our vaccine for Covid-19. It seemed like such an outrageously ambitious idea in February. Since we could not attract foreign collaborators given our modest business profile, we decided to develop the vaccine indigenously. We put select members of our exploratory research lab under the guidance of one of our top scientists. Now they are confident of achieving a breakthrough soon.

Rishi: What are the next steps?

Anshuman: We are about to complete the development of the vaccine. We will have to do preclinical studies of dosing and toxicity levels. After a review, we will seek approval to start our phase-wise trials. Phase-I and Phase-II trials will be relatively inexpensive, each involving only a few hundred volunteers at select locations. However, Phase-III trials will involve over 20,000 volunteers at multiple locations.

Rishi: How fast can we complete this? Vaccine developments take nothing less than two years at best.

Anshuman: We will have to do this pretty fast. It looks impossible, but the need for speedy rollouts will result in accelerated approvals and acceptance. If we can roll out the vaccine, we expect demand to outstrip supply. Although there could be pricing control, offtake should be remunerative. There can be a possibility of export orders as well. However, there will be competing vaccine candidates. Early mover advantage should be our foremost concern.

George: Do we have some idea of investments and returns?

Anshuman: I have used the services of a business consultant who has provided me with some workings (Exhibits 21.1 and 21.2). These are ballpark estimates. We do not know how things will ultimately pan out. But if all works out well, this project can pay back very quickly.

EXHIBIT 21.1 AntiCov Vaccine R&D Phase Outcomes

Stage	*Timeline*	*Investment*	*P (success)*	*Decision if Success*	*P (Failure)*	*Decision if Failure*
Preclinical Tests	T0+3 months	Rs 10 crore	0.6	Conduct Phase-1 trial	0.4	Abandon the project
Phase-1 Trials	T0+5 months	Rs 20 crore	0.7	Conduct Phase-2 trial	0.3	Abandon the project
Phase-2 Trials	T0+7 months	Rs 30 crore	0.7	Conduct Phase-3 trial	0.3	Abandon the project
Phase-3 Trials	T0+9 months	Rs 200 crore	0.8	Manufacture vaccine	0.2	Abandon the project

Source: Prepared by authors.

Rishi: How do we analyse these figures? Can you please explain?

Anshuman: This requires decision tree analysis, wherein you weigh the cash flows in each phase by the probability and then calculate the net present value. We have assumed that this is a 2–3-year opportunity and have decided to use a discount rate of 15%, but of course, I will run this by George.

Rishi: The calculations are beyond my comprehension. I understand, though, that if this works for us, it will enhance our visibility and reputation not only in India but also across the globe.

George: I agree that the Covid vaccine opportunity could be enormous. But everything depends so much on probabilities. I am a bit concerned about so many assumptions and so much uncertainty. Our worst nightmare could be unexpected side-effects halting production after having invested in manufacturing capacity. Also, the funding requirement for third-phase trials and manufacturing appears to be significant.

Anshuman: We will approach the government for grants to fund the R&D spend wholly or partly, given the likely thrust on indigenous vaccine development.

Rishi: I am sure the two of you can review the funding arrangements. Anshuman and George, please explain to me the workings later tomorrow.

The management team took a break before resuming to discuss other proposals and financing. To Rishi, the AntiCov project looked like a good opportunity. But he wanted to understand from Anshuman whether the probabilities and cash flows justified the investment.

EXHIBIT 21.2 Vaccine Manufacturing Phase Outcomes

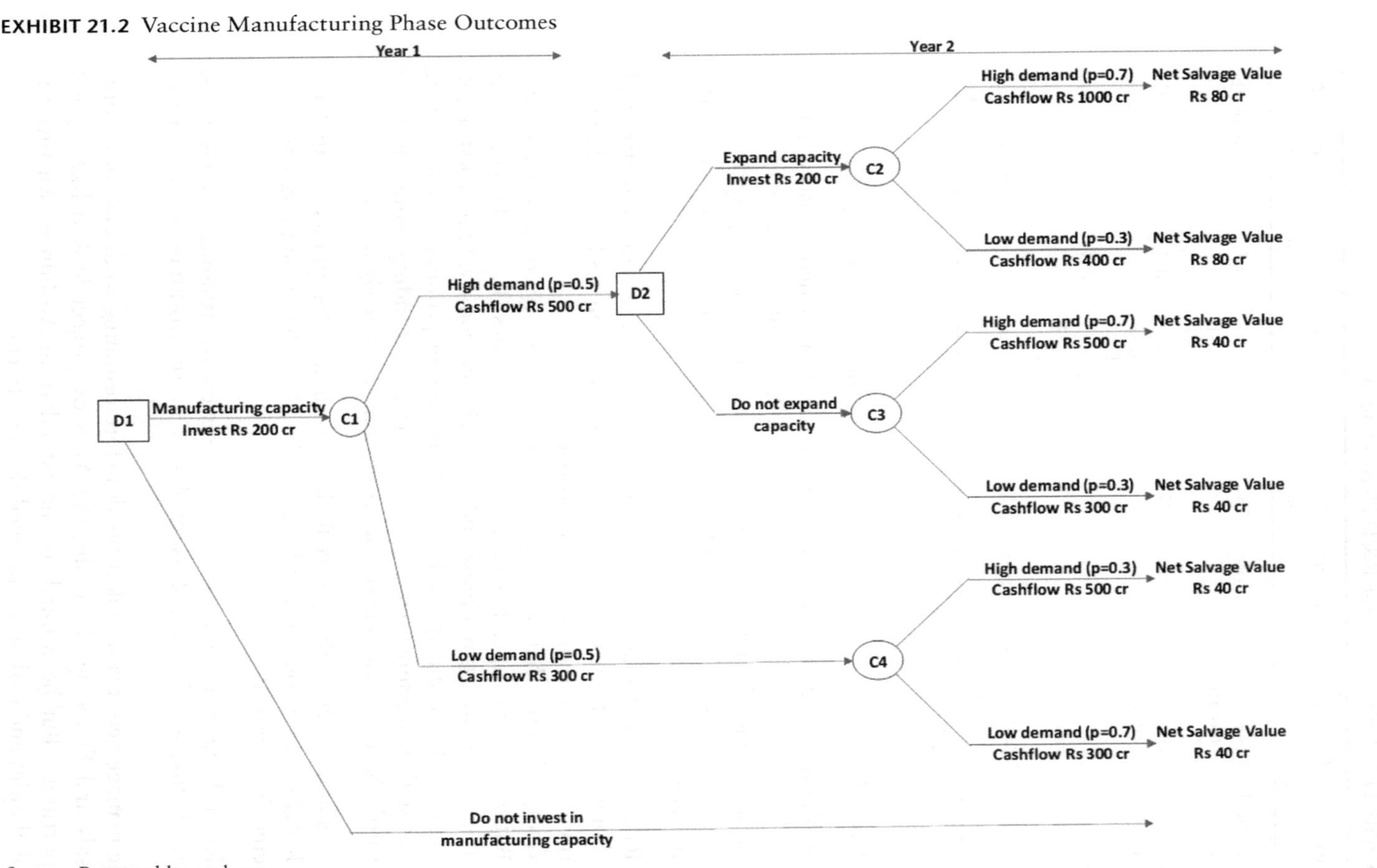

Source: Prepared by authors.

Note: All manufacturing capacity investments are at the beginning of the year. Other cash flows may be assumed to occur near the end of the year.

Assignment Questions

1. Evaluate the project proposal to invest in the development of the AntiCov vaccine. Account for the uncertainty in discount rate assumption.
2. What is the value of the option to expand the manufacturing capacity after one year?
3. How will the attractiveness of the project change if a government grant is available to finance the Phase 3 trials?

Note

1 https://www.birac.nic.in/webcontent/1574377200_Bio_Technology_Report.pdf

PART III

Risk and Return, and Cost of Capital

22

INVESTMENTWAVES (A)

Assessing Client's Life Insurance Requirement

At 11.00 a.m., on January 4, 2021, Monark Vora, Financial Advisor at InvestmentWaves, was preparing for his Zoom meeting with Mehul Shah. Established in 2016, InvestmentWaves was a SEBI[1] Registered Investment Advisor (RIA) with a mission to offer high-quality, low-cost, objective financial advice.

Mehul, a 40-year-old business consultant working with a reputed consulting firm, earned more than Rs 5 million in post-tax annual income. He lived in the city of Pune with his wife Priyanka (39 years) and his two children, Dwait (8 years) and Prisha (4 years).

Mehul approached InvestmentWaves in January 2020 with his "bruised" equity portfolio of Rs 5 million, and he was happy with the performance of his "healed" portfolio during the March 2020 equity market crash and subsequent recovery since then. Mehul was impressed with the way Monark helped calm down his nerves and encouraged him to stay invested during a market crash when he was panicking as many of his friends were exiting equity entirely.

During ongoing conversations with Monark during the pandemic hit 2020, he realised the need for life and health insurance before investment planning. He wanted to understand how much life insurance he needed to support his family expenses, financial goals, and existing liabilities in his absence and which life insurance product he should buy.

Indian Insurance Industry

The Indian Insurance Industry had 57 players in 2020, with 24 players in the life insurance space and 34 players in the general insurance space. Life Insurance Company of India (LIC), a sole public sector insurer in the Life

DOI: 10.4324/9781032724478-26

Insurance space, was the market leader. However, private players had steadily gained market share and collectively accounted for 31.2% market share by the end of FY20 compared to just 2% in FY03. Although the general insurance has six public sector players, the shift there was more significant, and the market share of private players jumped to 56.8% from 15% between FY04 and FY20.[2]

The insurance sector in India touched $280 billion in 2020. The gross premium collected by the insurance industry increased from $ 72 billion in FY16 to $ 108 billion in FY20. The premium from new business in life insurance grew at a steady rate of close to 15% annually, higher than India's nominal GDP growth and hence the insurance penetration[3] had gone up to 4% in 2020 from about 2% in 2000.

Life Insurance Products and Mehul's Insurance Requirement

Indian life insurance companies offered pure life cover, insurance plus investment, and annuity products. Monark advised Mehul to go for only a term insurance plan, which offered protection against the policyholder's premature death. However, it would earn nothing should the policyholder survive the entire policy term.

> life insurance cover should be big enough to generate income that can take care of the expenses, unfunded financial goals and any outstanding liabilities of the family if something untoward happens policyholder. Said Monark

Mehul was unimpressed with the idea. He wanted to understand why he should not go for a plan that offered insurance and investment bundled in one product.

Monark prepared a table of sum-assured vs premium for different life insurance policies along with his calculation of Mehul's life insurance requirement (see Exhibit 22.1 for life insurance products). He made the following explicit assumptions to come up with base case insurance calculations based on information provided by Mehul (see Exhibits 22.2 and 22.3).

- All expenses and funds required for financial goals would grow at an average expected long-term inflation rate of 5%.
- Should there be an insurance claim, the sum assured in the hands of Priyanka would be tax-exempt and, she could deploy it to earn 10% post-tax expected return without taking much risk.
- In the absence of Mehul, annual family expenses would come down by 25% (other than children's school fees).
- Mehul's family would need financial support for the next 20 years.

EXHIBIT 22.1 Types of Life Insurance Policies

Policy Type	*Feature*	*Policy Term (no of years)*	*Premium per Annum*	*Approximated Sum Assured (INR million)*	*Benefit at Maturity*
Term Plan	Pure risk cover	25	Rs 35,000 (40-year-old non-smoker)	10	NA
ULIP	Insurance + Investment opportunity	20	35,000	0.7	Fund value based on investment returns
Endowment Plan	Insurance + Savings	30	35,000	1.5	Guaranteed Sum Assured + non-guaranteed bonus (if any) + non-guaranteed terminal bonus (if any)
Whole Life Policy	Life coverage for whole life	20 (premium paying term)	35,000	0.5	Sum assured at the end of the life or to the policyholder on attaining 100-year age
Moneyback Policy	Periodic returns with insurance cover	20	35,000	0.8	Guaranteed benefits + coverage

Source: Prepared by authors.

EXHIBIT 22.2 Mehul's Personal Balance Sheet (INR 000s)

Liabilities	*Assets (current market value)*	
Housing Loan 8,000	**Investment assets**	
Car Loan 1,500	Direct Equity Portfolio	6,000
	Employees Provided Fund	3,500
	The Public Provided Fund	1,000
	Consumption assets	
	Car	1,300
	Jewellery	1,500
	Other assets	1,000

Source: Prepared by authors.

EXHIBIT 22.3 Mehul's Summary Income-Expense Statement for the Calendar Year 2021 (INR 000s)

Post-tax annual income (for the coming year)	5,000
Annual household expenses	1,000
Annual children school fees	1,000
Discretionary expenses (including replacement of electronic gadgets etc.)	500
Discretionary expenses (family vacations, birthday celebrations, etc.)	1,000

Source: Prepared by authors.

EXHIBIT 22.4 Funds Requirement for Mehul's Financial Goals at Jan 2021 Price (INR 000s)

Dwait's college education (Annual fees for four years, 10 years from now, at the beginning of every year.)	1,000
Prisha's college education (Annual fees for four years, 14 years from now, at the beginning of every year)	1,000
Dwait's marriage (after 17 years)	2,000
Prisha's marriage (after 20 years)	2,500
30th marriage anniversary celebration with Priyanka (world tour)	2,000
Retirement celebration party	1,000

Source: Prepared by authors.

Monark followed a systematic approach to present his insurance requirement calculation for Mehul to decide how much insurance cover he needed.

1. What should be the appropriate level of base case insurance cover required for Mehul to support his family's household expenses for 20 years?
2. How would Monark's calculation change accounting for Mehul's existing assets and liabilities?

3. Mehul might not want his family to compromise on lifestyle, children's education, or marriage celebration in his absence; how should Monark incorporate the same in his calculations? (see Exhibit 22.4 for Mehul's financial goals)
4. While Mehul's family needed financial support to meet household expenses for 20 years, Priyanka would need financial support till the end of her life. She might need 6,00,000 in annual expense (based on 2021 cost of living). How should Monark factor in this additional requirement? The life expectancy in India was generally on the rise due to better healthcare facilities and advances in the medical field.
5. Which life insurance product/s would be the most appropriate for Mehul?

Notes

1 Securities and Exchange Board of India (SEBI) was an Indian capital and commodity markets regulator.
2 https://www.ibef.org/industry/insurance-sector-india.aspx accessed on January 1, 2021.
3 Premium as a percentage of gross domestic product (GDP).

23

INVESTMENTWAVES (B)

Assessing LIC's New Jeevan Shanti

Nisarg Khelurkar (age 35 years) was over the moon as his wife Anjali (age 30 years) delivered a baby girl on February 14, 2021. Their son, Dhruv, was four years, and he was super excited about the arrival of his younger sister. However, he was slightly concerned about the financial responsibilities over the next few decades. Children's education, marriages, family vacations, and much more. While he had been doing reasonably well in his career and started his systematic financial planning five years back, his worry was retirement. He just bought term life insurance to protect his family against any adverse economic consequences in the event of his premature death; he was concerned about how many years of retirement he should provide. While life expectancy in India in 2021 was about 69–70 years, it factors in high infant mortality rates. Besides, advancements in medical sciences, increased awareness about a healthy lifestyle, and the realisation of maintaining good hygiene and minimising the risk of avoidable morbidities had set in society. All these might lead to an increase in life expectancy, in line with developed countries. For example, the life expectancy in Japan and Switzerland was close to 85 years.[1] The challenge facing Nisarg was deciding his withdrawal rate from his retirement nest egg that he would accumulate by turning 60 years. If he used a high withdrawal rate and lived very long, he might run out of funds later in his retirement. On the other hand, if he spent too little and did not live too long, he might live a compromised lifestyle. He was worried about longevity and its financial consequences. So, he called his financial advisor, Monark Vora, Chief Financial Planner at InvestmentWaves, a SEBI-registered investment advisory firm. Nisarg shared his concern with

DOI: 10.4324/9781032724478-27

Monark. Monark shared basic details about LIC's new Jeevan Shanti Plan (see Exhibits 23.1 and 23.2) and requested him to refer to it before the meeting on Sunday, March 7, 2021.

Indian Insurance Industry

The Indian Insurance Industry had two major segments: Life Insurance and General Insurance. Both segments offered various products (see Exhibit 23.3) and catered to individuals' and corporations' diverse needs. According to the EY-ASSCHOM report, by the end of FY18, India was the 11th largest insurance industry globally and 10th in the life insurance segment based on collected premiums. The insurance industry grew at 12% CAGR for the five years ending in FY19 and was expected to grow at 15% for the next few years. According to the India Brand Equity Foundation (IBEF) report, the size of the Indian Insurance Industry was about $280 billion in 2020. There were 57 players, 24 operating in the Life Insurance space and 33 in the General Insurance space. The Life Insurance segment of the industry reported significant growth from 2016 to 2019 (see Exhibit 23.4). The gross premium received had grown from Rs 3669 billion in 2016 to Rs 5084 billion in 2019. The only public sector life insurer, Life Insurance Corporation (LIC) of India, continued to enjoy more than 50% with a new market share of nearly 53% for FY19 (see Exhibit 23.5).

EXHIBIT 23.1 [2]Illustration New Jeevan Shanti Plan

Purchase Price: 10L
Age of Annuitant at entry: 45 years
Deferment Period: 12 years
Age of Secondary Annuitant: 35 years
LIC would pay the nominee 105% of the purchase price on the annuitant's death (or the death of the last surviving annuitant in case of the joint annuity).

Annuity Option	*Annuity Amount Payable for Various Options*			
	Annual	*Semi-annual*	*Quarterly*	*Monthly*
Option 1: Deferred Annuity Single Life	99,400	48,706	24,105	7,952
Option 2: Deferred Annuity for Joint Life	94,100	46,109	22,819	7,528

Notes:
1. 1.8% GST applied to the purchase price.
2. 2% higher annuity (In INR terms) was applicable for the policy purchased online.
Source: Prepared by authors.

EXHIBIT 23.2 [3] Further Incentives Are Available under this Plan – the Incentive for Higher Purchase Prices by Increasing the Annuity Rate as Below

For Rs. 1,000 (purchase price in INR)		
5,00,000 to 9,99,999	10,00,000 to 24,99,999	25,00,000 to 49,99,999
1.5	2.1	2.45

Source: Prepared by authors.

EXHIBIT 23.3 Products Offerings by Life and General Insurance Companies in India

Life Insurance Products	*General Insurance Products*
Term Insurance	Fire Insurance
Whole Life Insurance	Marine Insurance
Endowment Plans	Personal Accident Insurance
Money-back Plans	Health Insurance
Unit Linked Insurance Plans	Personal Liability Insurance
Annuity Plans	Property/burglary Insurance, etc.

Source: Authors' compilation.

EXHIBIT 23.4 Life Insurance Growth in India

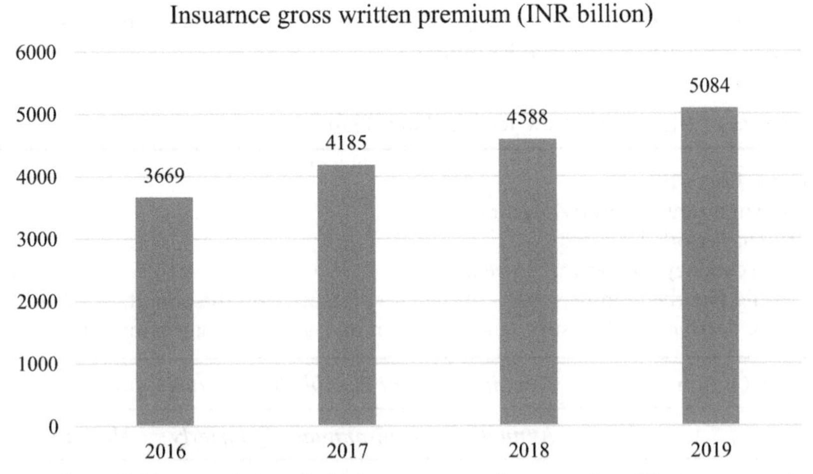

Source: https://bfsi.economictimes.indiatimes.com/news/insurance/how-life-insurers-are-looking-at-2020/72978494 Accessed on March 2, 2021.

EXHIBIT 23.5 Life Insurance Companies Market Share in India (new business in FY2019)

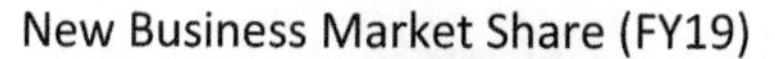

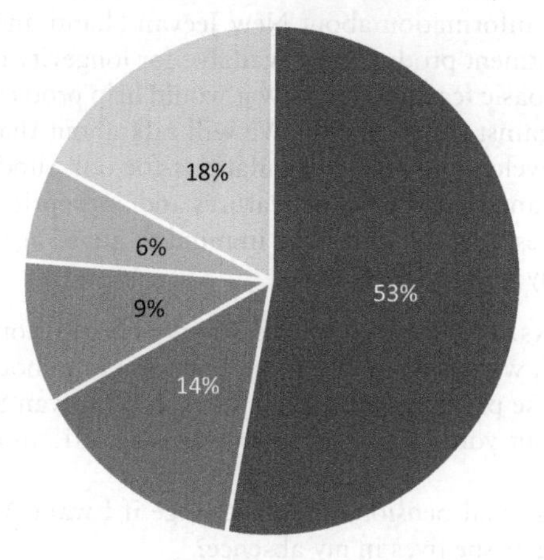

Source: Authors' compilation based on newspaper articles and IBEF industry report.

LIC of India-New Jeevan Shanti

LIC of India launched Jeevan Shanti, an immediate and deferred annuity plan with a minimum return of 110% of the purchase price, guaranteed additions during the deferment period, and benefits on death. Subsequently, it launched Jeevan Akshay-VII, with multiple immediate annuity options, and New Jeevan Shanti, with multiple deferred annuity options.[4]

Nisarg's Mail

10.00 p.m. March 5, 2021, Friday, Monark received a call from Nisarg. He thanked Monark for sharing information about annuity plans and said he had sent an email (see Exhibit 23.6 for email content) with some specific questions. If Monark could come up with some workings before their meeting, it would help him decide. Monark had a series of client meetings scheduled for March 6, 2021; he chose to work on the questions shared by Nisarg on the night of March 5, 2021. He had to burn the midnight oil.

EXHIBIT 23.6 Nisarg's Email Content

Dear Monark,

Thanks for sharing information about New Jeevan Shanti and Jeevan Akshay. I am happy that investment products are available for longevity risk. I could understand the product's basic features and how it would help protect against longevity; it cannot protect against inflation risk. We will talk about that during the meeting. Meanwhile, developing sample calculations for our Sunday meeting would be great for understanding the product features and appropriateness. Please share any other alternatives that you may have in mind to guard against longevity risk. Please find below my questions/doubts.

1. If one invests Rs. 10,00,000 now and wants annual income from the end of next year itself, what will be the annual pension one should expect in terms of % of purchase price/investment ?(I know New Jeevan Shanti is a deferred annuity plan, but you mentioned Jeevan Akshay VII, an immediate annuity plan.)
2. How will the annual pension amount change if I want Anjali to receive the annuity as long as she lives in my absence?
3. There is a monthly annuity option as well. Is it advisable to go for it? Why? Why not?
4. Is there any additional (hidden) cost involved in buying this product? How will it affect my returns?
5. What approximate effective rate of return should I expect (IRR) on such investments (including payment to the nominee on death)?
6. Are there any incentives for buying the product online and for a large sum? How will it affect return in IRR terms? e.g., if I invest Rs. 400,000, Rs. 7,50,000, Rs. 10,00,000, and Rs. 30,00,000.
7. Fill this for a single-life annuity plan. Please calculate an annual Pension as a percentage of the purchase price for my understanding. i.e., 45000 is 4.5% of 10,00,000.

Deferment period	Entry age (30)	40	45	50
Immediate				
One Year				
Five Years				
Twelve Years				

See you on Sunday.

Best,

Nisarg.

Source: Prepared by authors.

Notes

1 https://data.worldbank.org/indicator/SP.DYN.LE00.IN?most_recent_value_desc=true&view=map accessed on March 2, 2021.
2 https://licindia.in/Products/Pension-Plans/LIC-s-New-Jeevan-Shanti-(Plan-No-858)-(UIN-512N338
3 Ibid
4 Immediate annuity plan, where the annuity starts from the end of 1st year itself, whereas in the deferred annuity plan, the annuity begins after the deferment period. Hence, the annuity amount is usually higher than the exact purchase price.

24

WEALTHFROG

Risk-Return Trade-off of Individual Assets vs Portfolio of Assets

Gold ... has two significant shortcomings, being neither of much use nor procreative. True, gold has some industrial and decorative utility, but the demand for these purposes is limited and incapable of soaking up new production. Meanwhile, if you own one ounce of gold for an eternity, you will still own one ounce at its end. — Buffett, letter to shareholders, 2011
Gold may be "lifeless" and "uncivilised," but it can still deliver extraordinary gains, Eric Fry, Editor, Fry's Investment Report, June 2020.

On April 2, 2021, Serena Griffith, Chief Investment Advisor, NRI[1] Clients at WealthFrog Investment Partners was preparing her asset allocation plan for one of her wealthier clients, Amar Kalro, a management graduate from a top school in the USA, working in Pittsburg with a leading consulting firm. After trying several investments avenues, Amar decided to follow a relatively simple approach. He approached a fee-only investment advisory firm to invest in low-cost passive investment vehicles. Serena evaluated US Equity, Gold, Crude Oil, and Indian Equity as potential investment assets for Amar. She prepared a note with a simple example to show the benefit of scientific asset allocation and mathematics behind it.

Portfolio Risk and Return

As they say, "Don't keep all your eggs into one basket," Harry Markowitz, through his Modern Portfolio Theory (MPT), could quantify the benefit of diversification. He showed that the portfolio return would be the weighted average returns of its constituent assets returns. Thus, portfolio risk was a

DOI: 10.4324/9781032724478-28

function of risks of individual assets, weights of assets in a portfolio, and the correlation between the returns of the asset classes.

If two asset classes return had a perfect inverse correlation (–1), one could create a risk-free portfolio by combining two risk assets. However, two asset returns had an ideal direct correlation (+1) between them; one might not benefit from diversification.

Serena prepared a simple stylised example before getting into more complex portfolio mathematics. There were two companies (Exhibit 24.1): one in the business of making sunglass, and another was in the business of making raincoats. The fortunes of both companies were dependent on monsoon, only on monsoon in this case. A bad monsoon, a long spell of sunny, dry days, would do wonders for the sunglass company, and its stock would deliver a 30% return next year. However, it means bad news for raincoat company, and its stock would lose 15% in that case.

On the other hand, if monsoon turned out to be good, raincoat company stock would benefit and deliver a 30% return, whereas sunglass company stock would lose 15%. Thus, investing in raincoat company stock or sunglass company stock essentially becomes a bet on monsoon. Given the probabilities, there was no way to ascertain how the next monsoon season would pen out and, for an investor, no way escapes it if he invested in either sunglass or raincoat company. Essentially such investment would become a bet on monsoon rather than anything else. The stocks expected returns would be 15% for both, but such returns would come with high volatility, measured by the standard deviation of returns. It would be 18.7%.

However, if an investor chose to create an equal-weight portfolio of sunglass and raincoat companies' stocks; notwithstanding what happens to the monsoon, the portfolio return would be 15%, and the riskiness of returns or volatility disappears entirely. It means, by investing in two risky stocks,

EXHIBIT 24.1 Stylised Example of Portfolio Effect in Stocks with a Perfect Inverse Correlation

Monsoon	*Probability*	*Return on Sunglass Company*	*Return on Raincoat Company*	*50:50 Portfolio*
Good	1/3	–15%	30%	15%
Normal	1/3	15%	15%	15%
Bad	1/3	30%	–15%	15%
	E(Ri)	15%	15%	15%
	Standard Deviation	18.71%	18.71%	0

Source: Prepared by authors.

EXHIBIT 24.2 Portfolio Mathematics for Two Assets and n Assets

Portfolio Return:

Two Security Case: $R_P = w_1R_1 + w_2R_2$

N-Security Case: $\dot{R}p = \sum_{i=1}^{n} w_iR_i$

Portfolio Variance:

Two Security Case: $\sigma_p^2 = w_1^2\sigma_1^2 + w_2^2\sigma_2^2 + 2w_1w_2r_{12}\sigma_1\sigma_2$

N- Security Case: $\sigma_p^2 = \sum_{i=1}^{n}\sum_{j=1}^{n} WiWjCo\,\mathrm{var}(Ri, Rj)$

Source: Prepared by authors.

utterly dependent on monsoon, one could create a risk-free portfolio with expected return same as of those individual stocks. How was that possible? Because, returns of the stocks were perfectly inversely correlated (see Exhibit 24.2 for mathematical expressions for return and variance for two assets and n assets portfolios).

In real life, though, it would not be possible to find securities or assets with perfect inverse correlation. However, that does not mean that benefit of diversification would not be available. On the contrary, carefully chosen asset classes often offer a significant improvement in returns per unit of volatility.

Serena's Analysis

Serena realised that relying on a single asset class would not serve the purpose even if one had a long investment horizon. For instance, Berkshire Hathaway's stock, one of the most admired partnerships run by none other than Warren Buffett and Charlie Munger, failed to beat gold returns for the first two decades of the twenty-first century. The underperformance of Berkshire Hathaway could not be discarded as the case of data mining because it was based on 20 years of performance. (Exhibit 24.3). It even surprised Serena. However, she knew the merits of carefully thought-out asset allocation and its benefits. She short-listed four asset classes and studies the historical risk-return profile of each asset classes and the correlation between the return amongst asset classes. She short-listed four asset classes for Amar and came up with her estimates of expected annual returns, the

EXHIBIT 24.3 Berkshire Hathaway vs Gold: Performance Comparison over 1st Two Decades of Twenty-First Century

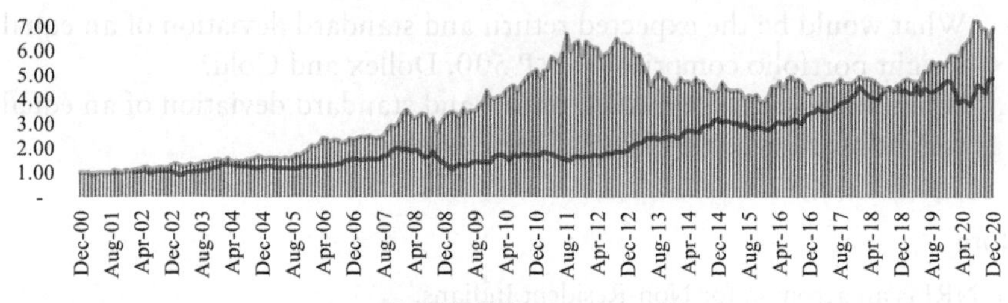

Source: Bloomberg, World Gold Council, and authors' analysis.

EXHIBIT 24.4 Correlation Matrix of Short-Listed Asset Classes Returns

	Brent Crude	*Gold*	*S&P 500 TRI*	*Dollex 30*
Brent Crude	1.00			
Gold	0.19	1.00		
S&P 500 TRI[a]	-0.07	-0.06	1.00	
Dollex 30[b]	0.28	0.10	-0.02	1.00

Source: Authors' analysis and estimates.

[a] TRI means Total Return Index with dividends reinvested.

[b] Dollex 30 means Dollar Sensex.

EXHIBIT 24.5 Expected returns and variability of short-listed asset classes

	Expected Returns	*Standard Deviation*
Brent Crude	7%	30%
Gold	7.5%	18%
S&P 500 TRI	9%	16%
Dollex 30	10.5%	28%

Source: Authors' analysis and estimates.

standard deviation of returns and the correlation matrix. She started evaluating what combination could offer the best return-to-variability trade-off (Exhibits 24.4 and 24.5).

Questions

1. Rank assets based on return-to-variability ratios.
2. Which pair of assets are ideally suited to offer the highest benefit of diversification? Why?

3. What would be the expected return and standard deviation for equal portfolios of each pair of asset classes? Which pair offers the highest reward-to-variability trade-off?
4. What would be the expected return and standard deviation of an equal weight portfolio comprising S&P 500, Dollex and Gold?
5. What would be the expected return and standard deviation of an equal weight portfolio comprising all four assets?

Note

1 NRI is an acronym for Non-Resident Indians.

25

KIRTAN'S DILEMMA

How to Use Risk-Return Analysis to Build a Superior Portfolio?

On February 28, 2021, Kirtan Pradhan returned from his routine jogging at the famous Juhu beach in the heart of Mumbai city, the finance capital of India. While coming back, he reflected upon his five years of career and investment journey and the conversation with his professor and investment mentor a day before. Kirtan had completed his MBA from one of the top business schools in India in 2016 with a major in Marketing. While he had a keen interest in finance and marketing in his first year, he opted for a major in marketing after his summer training. However, in his final term, he opted for an elective in wealth management. He was fascinated by the fact that while several actively managed equity mutual funds with different styles and strategies tried to beat the benchmark indices, most failed to do so. Those who succeeded in a given period found it extremely difficult to sustain their outperformance. He remembered his professor who once said, "While it is possible to outperform the broad market on a gross basis, adjusting for fees and expenses, it is tough to beat a well-diversified portfolio."

He followed his professor's advice and started investing in a low-cost Exchange-Traded Fund (ETF), Niftybees, tracking Nifty50 Index. Nifty50 was one of the most popular benchmark indices tracking Indian markets. Nifty was a market-cap-weighted Index comprising 50 largest and inequity stocks in India, occasionally rebalanced to represent the entire market. Index funds and ETFs were the low-cost investment vehicles allowing investors to invest into passively managed portfolio replicating a particular index. Since the fund manager's role was to replicate the benchmark index, such funds would not require a large team of analysts, resulting in minimal transaction costs and a low fee structure. As a result, indexing had become a prominent

DOI: 10.4324/9781032724478-29

investment option to invest in equity and invest in various asset classes with a small amount and low fees.

Time for a Change

Kirtan remembered the panic call he made to his professor on March 23, 2020. The global equity markets had gone into a tailspin caused by the potential economic standstill caused by lockdowns; his professor just advised him to stay invested and not panic. He was pleased that he could overcome his fear and stayed invested. Since then, global markets turned around and scaled new highs. His Index fund showed a five-year CAGR of 17%+, which was a fantastic return and was worth the volatility that one had to face while investing in equity.

He had settled in his career and understood the value of long-term investing and patience; he thought he could take a little more risk. So he decided to spend some time analysing and doing some active stock-picking. He wanted to invest in stocks of a few good quality businesses that had sustained outperformance for long periods. So he shortlisted three stocks: Info Edge, Bajaj Finance, and Shree Cement.

Info Edge owned a robust business called Naukri.com, the job search platform; it had substantial investments in Indian unicorns such as Zomato, Policybazaar, 99acres.com, and jeevensathi.com and a few other investments in start-ups with the potential to become unicorns. Zomato had already filed for a prospectus with SEBI to come out with an IPO, and others were ready to go public. In Kirtan's view, Info Edge was the retail investors' venture capital/private equity fund.

Bajaj Finance was one of the top NBFCs in the country, and it had proven its mettle in the 2008 global financial crisis, 2018–19 NBFC crisis of India (IL& FS and DHFL saga) and massive turbulence caused by the Covid-19 pandemic. Every time it came out stronger and consolidated its leadership position in the industry.

Shree Cement, one of the lowest-cost cement manufacturers globally, had maintained high margins and return ratios. In the otherwise quasi-cyclical cement industry, it had delivered Steller returns to its investors over the last decade and more (see Exhibit 25.1 for returns of Info Edge, Bajaj Finance, Shree Cement, and Nifty).

Risk-Return Analysis

He remembered lessons learnt in Finance 101 course during his MBA programme. He remembered that there were two components of total risk: diversifiable and non-diversifiable. Investing in a single stock, the total variability

EXHIBIT 25.1 Performance of Shortlisted Stocks and Nifty Index

	Info Edge	*Bajaj Finance*	*Shree Cement*	*Nifty TRI*
1-year return	89.34%	17.89%	16.90%	31.27%
3-year CAGR	56.46%	47.51%	16.82%	12.87%
5-year CAGR	47.64%	54.75%	21.51%	17.28%
10-year CAGR	32.79%	56.50%	31.39%	11.92%

Source: Prepared by authors based on CMIE prowess data.

matters; however, a well-diversified portfolio helps in minimising/eliminating the diversifiable risk (firm/sector-specific risk). Hence, investors should look at non-diversifiable risk before adding stock to a well-diversified portfolio. For example, a market portfolio such as Nifty was a well-diversified portfolio and had near-zero diversifiable risk.

Kiran knew that adding any of the three stock to his market index fund would add an element of diversifiable risk back to his portfolio. The prospect of earning a much greater reward in the form of higher returns might compensate for such higher risk. While he was yet to perform a formal risk-return assessment of the three stocks vis-à-vis market, he knew that the stocks he had chosen were much more volatile than the market portfolio. However, he thought a small allocation and potential diversification benefit would not add much risk to his portfolio. He remembered that while the total risk could be measured by the standard deviation of return, beta[1] was the measure for systematic risk, the component of risk that could not be diversified away using diversification.

Kirtan collected the last five years monthly-return[2] data for Info Edge, Bajaj Finance, Shree Cement and Nifty Total Return Index (Nifty TRI) (Exhibit 25.2). He wanted to ensure that the expected return on his new portfolio would compensate for taking additional risk.

Questions

1. Estimate and compare returns and variability (volatility based on past five years monthly returns) of Info Edge, Bajaj Finance, Shree Cement, and Nifty TRI.
2. Perform the regression of each stock's monthly returns on the Index returns to compute the beta for each stock.
3. How might the return on each stock relate to its riskiness?
4. How would you decompose the total variability of each stock into its diversifiable and not-diversifiable components? How would it help to decide which stock to be added to Nifty ETF?

EXHIBIT 25.2 Monthly Total Returns for Shortlisted Stocks and Nifty TRI

Monthly returns	*Info Edge*	*Bajaj Finance*	*Shree Cement*	*Nifty TRI*
Mar-16	9.5%	16.7%	24%	10.98%
Apr-16	-2.0%	-1.4%	2%	1.44%
May-16	7.4%	11.1%	3%	4.14%
Jun-16	2.3%	5.4%	11%	1.96%
Jul-16	-1.0%	29.7%	11%	4.44%
Aug-16	0.7%	6.2%	7%	1.82%
Sep-16	3.2%	-4.1%	-1%	-1.93%
Oct-16	6.1%	2.3%	-1%	0.26%
Nov-16	-0.5%	-14.9%	-8%	-4.61%
Dec-16	-0.2%	-8.4%	-5%	-0.47%
Jan-17	-8.0%	23.1%	5%	4.60%
Feb-17	4.0%	6.9%	4%	3.83%
Mar-17	-6.5%	5.7%	6%	3.47%
Apr-17	4.3%	9.0%	12%	1.42%
May-17	9.4%	4.0%	-6%	3.46%
Jun-17	13.1%	3.5%	-6%	-0.66%
Jul-17	-3.9%	24.0%	10%	6.12%
Aug-17	-3.2%	4.6%	-5%	-1.48%
Sep-17	14.9%	3.2%	6%	-1.25%
Oct-17	2.8%	-2.0%	2%	5.67%
Nov-17	11.7%	-4.1%	-9%	-1.01%
Dec-17	9.5%	1.7%	5%	2.97%
Jan-18	--2.8%	-4.5%	-5%	4.76%
Feb-18	-5.1%	-2.2%	-3%	-4.69%
Mar-18	-8.3%	7.8%	-3%	-3.43%
Apr-18	5.6%	7.9%	5%	6.19%
May-18	2.3%	10.6%	0%	0.18%
Jun-18	-6.6%	8.8%	-8%	0.02%
Jul-18	15.2%	17.5%	9%	6.23%
Aug-18	19.8%	5.9%	11%	3.01%
Sep-18	-13.1%	-24.1%	-11%	-6.38%
Oct-18	10.9%	9.9%	-18%	-4.87%
Nov-18	-2.1%	6.5%	18%	4.74%
Dec-18	-6.8%	4.2%	5%	-0.07%
Jan-19	21.3%	-2.7%	-9%	-0.24%
Feb-19	2.4%	2.9%	6%	-0.22%
Mar-19	3.0%	14.2%	13%	7.79%
Apr-19	4.9%	2.3%	6%	1.07%
May-19	6.2%	12.0%	9%	1.62%
Jun-19	9.4%	6.2%	1%	-0.90%
Jul-19	-0.1%	-11.7%	-8%	-5.44%
Aug-19	-9.7%	2.5%	-8%	-0.64%
Sep-19	-0.3%	21.4%	2%	4.09%
Oct-19	27.1%	-0.5%	5%	3.70%
Nov-19	2.5%	1.2%	5%	1.50%

(*Continued*)

EXHIBIT 25.2 Continued

Monthly returns	*Info Edge*	*Bajaj Finance*	*Shree Cement*	*Nifty TRI*
Dec-19	–3.9%	3.9%	–3%	0.94%
Jan-20	12.6%	3.1%	13%	–1.68%
Feb-20	–8.9%	2.3%	–1%	–6.33%
Mar-20	–21.5%	–50.4%	–23%	–23.03%
Apr-20	25.2%	4.6%	13%	14.69%
May-20	5.3%	–15.7%	6%	–2.74%
Jun-20	2.9%	44.9%	11%	7.58%
Jul-20	15.7%	14.8%	–6%	7.70%
Aug-20	2.2%	7.3%	–7%	2.97%
Sep-20	11.4%	-6.0%	0%	–1.20%
Oct-20	–2.4%	0.9%	7%	3.69%
Nov-20	21.3%	48.3%	12%	11.44%
Dec-20	10.5%	7.9%	–1%	7.83%
Jan-21	–8.3%	–10.6%	–5%	–2.46%
Feb-21	12.5%	11.2%	16%	6.71%

Source: Prepared by authors based on CMIE prowess data.

Notes

1 Beta is the slope of stock excess returns with respect to excess market returns. Alternatively, it could be calculated as covariance of stock returns with market returns divided by variance of market returns.
2 Total return adjusted for dividends and other corporate actions.

26

BLUESTAR AMC

Assessing Impact of New Valuation Norms on Debt Funds

On March 26, 2021, Priya Tendulkar, CEO of BlueStar Asset Management Company Ltd. (BlueStar-AMC), called for an early morning meeting of fund managers of its debt and hybrid schemes. Most of its debt and hybrid schemes had investments in Additional Tier-1 (AT1) Perpetual Bonds and Tier-2 bonds issued by Indian Banks. Security Exchange Board of India (SEBI) circular on March 15, 2021, on capping mutual funds exposure to AT-1 and Tier-2 bonds and valuing AT-1 bonds at 100-year maturity bonds came as a rude shock for the mutual fund industry. The fear of redemptions and panic selling of AT-1 bonds gripped the industry. AT-1 bonds yield of reputed issuers like State Bank of India (SBI) also jumped by as much as 100 basis points on March 16, 2021. Since then, SEBI had issued an amendment to its circular and AMFI had issued guidelines for valuation of AT-1 and Tier-2 bonds on March 25, 2021.

This sudden turn of events had resulted in a hectic week for Bluestar; investors were making panic calls for redemptions, and convincing them to stay invested had been a big challenge. Investors' confidence in debt funds was at historical low after Franklin Templeton wound down six of its debt schemes in March 2020. Investors were yet to recover their entire capital even after one year, leave alone earning returns. While the liquidity in the market was substantially better in March 2021, sudden redemptions might lead to panic sell of securities by debt funds in a relatively illiquid secondary debt market in India.

Priya and her fund managers had to make two decisions. First, what would be the immediate impact of the change on the net asset values (NAVs) and modified duration of the debt funds, and what would be the long-term

DOI: 10.4324/9781032724478-30

EXHIBIT 26.1 AT-1 and Tier-2 Bonds Owned under BlueStar Short-Term Debt Fund

Type of Bonds	*Date of Issue*	*Date of Redemption*	*Rate of Interest % P.A.*	*Call Option Date*	*Maturity Period in Months*	*Rating Assigned to the Bonds*
SBI Non-Convertible, Unsecured, Basel III – AT-1 Perpetual Bonds-2016 Series II	27-09-2016	Perpetual	8.75	27-09-2021	Perpetual	CARE AA+ by CARE and CRISIL AA+/Stable by CRISIL Limited
SBI Non-Convertible, Unsecured, Basel – AT-1 Perpetual Bonds-2017 Series IV						
	02-08-2017	Perpetual	8.15	02-08-2022	Perpetual	CARE AA+; Stable (Double AA+; Outlook: Stable) by CARE Ratings and CRISIL AA+/Stable by CRISIL Limited
SBI Non-Convertible, Unsecured, Basel III AT-1 Bonds 2018–19 Series 3						
	23-03-2019	Perpetual	9.45	22-03-2024	Perpetual	"CRISIL AA+/Stable" by CRISIL Ratings & "[ICRA] AA+(hyb) (stable)" by ICRA Limited

Source: State Bank of India Website.

valuation impact and attractiveness of AT-1 and Tier-2 bonds for debt funds. After consultation with her fund managers, Priya picked Bluestar Short Term Debt Fund as it had nearly 8% of its total AUM locked into AT-1 bonds (see Exhibit 26.1) and a small exposure in Tier-2 bonds. Soon after the meeting, Priya connected to Divya, Head of Fixed Income Research at BlueStar and asked her to work out the valuation and duration impact of new valuation norms by the end of the day.

AT-1 Bonds

Post Global Financial Crisis (GFC) of 2008, to boost banks Common Equity Tier 1(CET 1) without substantial dilution of banks equity due to fresh equity issuances at distressed valuation, Additional Tier-1(AT-1) bonds were introduced in Basel-III framework.[1] AT-1 bonds were quasi-equity in nature with no fixed maturity, but banks could call them back after the No Call period; e.g., NC5 means bonds that could not be called back before five years. Most AT-1 bonds had predefined call date, and the issuer bank had the right to call back the bond or set a new call date.

AT-1 bondholders claim was inferior to depositors and other bondholders and superior to equity shareholders in normal times. However, in a situation where banks Tier-1 capital fell below a certain threshold, AT-1 bonds would first absorb the losses. These bonds would either be converted to equity shares or written off entirely to prevent the bank's liquidation. Given the hybrid/quasi-equity nature of AT-1 bonds, these bonds were rated one to four notches below the bonds of a similar issuer.

Globally, several banks had issued AT-1 bonds and to protect themselves from severe losses. However, each of them had a different method of recognising/absorbing losses. For instance, Deutsche Bank would write off AT-1 bonds if their CET 1 capital ratio fell below 5.13%; South Korea's Kookmin Bank had a discretionary trigger allowing it to write down AT-1 bonds "in times of stress."

There had been many instances of banks writing off their AT-1 bonds. For example, Austrian Bank Erste wrote off billions of euros in AT-1 bonds in 2014 while the Hongkong based Bank of Jinzhou stopped paying coupon on its CoCo bonds in 2019 to protect its financial health.

Yes Bank AT-1 Bonds Write-offs and Global Precedent

Yes Bank had Rs 8,415 crore worth of AT-1 bonds issued as of March 2020. Yes Bank issued these bonds in two tranches: Rs 3,000 crore in December 2016 and Rs 5,415 crore in October 2017. These bonds were subsequently written off by the bank, much to the dismay of investors. RBI was clear in its reasoning. It said, under Section 45 of the Banking Regulation Act, the PONV[2] was triggered, and the bonds were written off in line with the contract between Yes Bank and AT-1 bondholders and hence there was no merit in any argument against writing off the bonds. Higher returns come with higher risks, and AT-1 bondholders had enjoyed higher yields in the past. In the 2017 issue memorandum, there was no provision for conversion of such bonds to equity, thus paving the way for Yes Bank to write off the liability completely. Thus, AT-1 bondholders lost their entire capital in the process.

Equity shares were not written off first since the company was not under liquidation. Therefore, there was no provision under the AT-1 bonds issue for the write-off of equity shares first. Since seniority of bonds over equity matters only in liquidation, the bonds would be written off while the equity shareholders would continue to hold their shares.

SEBI's March 2021 Circular

One year after the YesBank AT-1 bonds saga, SEBI issued a circular on March 15, 2021 with an intention to safeguard the interest of mutual fund investors. AT-1 bonds must be valued as 100-year maturity bonds from the date of issuance and put a 10% cap to the exposure of mutual funds in AT-1 and Tier-2 bonds. On March 16, 2021, AT-1 bond yields spiked by as much as 100 basis points and their prices fell drastically, The reason was apparent. The bonds that were valued on Yield-to-Call (YTC) basis were suddenly required to be valued at YTM with deemed maturity of 100 years. There might be adverse volatility in NAVs of debt fund with exposure to such bonds once valued using new norms.[3] In addition, there was a severe valuation challenge in finding appropriate yield to value bonds with a 100-year maturity.

In March 2021, Indian banks had outstanding AT-1 bonds over Rs 100,000 crore. Mutual funds owned nearly one-third of such bonds. New valuation norms would result in reduced appetite by debt mutual funds for AT-1 bonds. Banks, especially Public Sector Banks (PSB), relied heavily on AT-1 bonds for their capital requirements. Lack of appetite from one of the largest holders of AT-1 bonds might lead to PSBs asking for the government to provide capital. Also, such a move might destabilise debt funds for the second time in as many years. Given these, Finance Ministry swung into action and urged the regulator to withdraw the 100-year maturity rule to value AT-1 bonds.

A week later, SEBI amended valuation norms for AT-1 and Tier-1 bonds (see Exhibit 26.2) to allow valuation of AT-1 bonds with call date in next two years in a graded manner as 10-, 20-, and 30-year bond, respectively, and retained 100-year valuation requirement for the bonds with call date later than March 31, 2023. AMFI issued guidelines for valuation for AT-1 and Tier-2 bonds on March 25, 2021. According to that, SBI bonds would

EXHIBIT 26.2 SEBI's Amended Circular on Valuation of AT-1 and Tier-2 Bonds (March 22, 2021)

Time Period	*Maturity to Be Considered for AT-1 Bonds (years)*	*Maturity to Be Considered for Tier - 2 bonds (years)*
From April 1, 2021	10	10 years or maturity, whichever is higher
From April 1, 2022	20	Maturity
From October 1, 2022	30	Maturity
From April 1, 2023	100*	Maturity

*100 years from the date of issuance of bond

Source: SEBI Website.

EXHIBIT 26.3 Outstanding AT-1 Bonds of Major Banks with a Call Option in FY22 (Rs. in Crore)

Lender	*Outstanding AT-1 Bonds*	*Call Option Due in FY222*
SBI	33,932	11,210
ICICI Bank	10,120	3,425
Union Bank of India	7,355	4,650
Bank of Baroda	11,307	2,325
Axis Bank	7,000	3,500

Source: ICRA.

serve as benchmark securities and other AT-1 securities as non-benchmark securities. If an issuer failed to call back bonds on the designated call date, all AT-1 bonds of the same issuer, notwithstanding call dates, must be valued as 100-year bonds.

The amendment came as a sigh of relief for Bluestar and the entire mutual fund industry; such graded implementation would allow for a relatively smooth transition. Five banks accounted for nearly Rs 70,000 crore of outstanding AT-1 bonds, and nearly Rs 25,000 crore of them had call options falling in 2022, and given the quality of lenders, most of them would be called back (see Exhibit 26.3).

Bluestar's Dilemma

Bluestar had to assess the impact of new valuation norms on its short duration bond fund and other debt funds. While it might not want to panic sell AT-1 bonds, it had to decide whether and how long to hold on to AT-1

EXHIBIT 26.4 SEBI Debt Fund Classification 2018 (Select Fund Types)

Sr. No.	*Category of Schemes*	*Scheme Characteristics*	*Type of Scheme (uniform description of the scheme)*
3	Ultra-Short Duration Fund	Investment in Debt & Money Market instruments such that the Macaulay Duration of the portfolio is between 3 and 6 months.	An open-ended ultra short-term debt scheme investing in instruments with Macaulay duration between 3 and 6 months.
4	Low Duration Fund	Investment in Debt & Money Market instruments such that the Macaulay duration of the portfolio is between 6 months and 12 months.	An open-ended low duration debt scheme investing in tools with Macaulay duration between 6 months and 12 months.
5	Money Market Fund	Investment in Money Market instruments having maturity up to 1 year.	An open-ended debt scheme investing in money market instruments.
6	**Short Duration Fund**	**Investment in Debt & Money Market instruments such that the Macaulay duration of the portfolio is between 1 year and 3 years.**	**An open-ended short-term debt scheme investing in instruments with Macaulay duration between 1 year and 3 years.**
7	Medium Duration Fund	Investment in Debt & Money Market instruments such that the Macaulay duration of the portfolio is between 3 years and 4 years.	An open-ended medium-term debt scheme investing in instruments with Macaulay duration between 3 years and 4 years.
8	Medium to Long Duration Fund	Investment in Debt & Money Market instruments such that the Macaulay duration of the portfolio is between 4 and 7 years.	An open-ended medium-term debt scheme investing in instruments with Macaulay duration between 4 years and 7 years.
9	Long Duration Fund	Investment in Debt & Money Market Instruments such that the Macaulay duration of the portfolio is greater than 7 years.	An open-ended debt scheme investing in instruments with Macaulay duration greater than 7 years.

Source: SEBI Website.

EXHIBIT 26.5 G-Sec Yields Estimates Based on Traded Bonds and ZCYC Model Rates

Maturity (in years)	*YTM (%) as of March 26, 2021*
< 0.5	3.50
0.5	3.52
1.0	3.80
1.5	4.13
2.0	4.43
2.5	4.71
3.0	4.96
3.5	5.17
4.0	5.37
4.5	5.54
5.0	5.70
5.5	5.84
6.0	5.97
6.5	6.08
7.0	6.19
7.5	6.28
8.0	6.36
8.5	6.44
9.0	6.51
9.5	6.57
10.0	6.62
10.5	6.67
11.0	6.71
11.5	6.75
12.0	6.78
12.5	6.81
13.0	6.84
13.5	6.87
14.0	6.89
14.5	6.90
15.0	6.92
15.5	6.93
16.0	6.94
16.5	6.95
17.0	6.96
17.5	6.97
18.0	6.97
18.5	6.98
19.0	6.98
19.5	6.98
20.0	6.98
20.5	6.98
21.0	6.98
21.5	6.98

(*Continued*)

EXHIBIT 26.5 Continued

Maturity (in years)	*YTM (%) as of March 26, 2021*
22.0	6.98
22.5	6.98
23.0	6.97
23.5	6.97
24.0	6.97
24.5	6.96
25.0	6.96
25.5	6.96
26.0	6.95
26.5	6.95
27.0	6.94
27.5	6.94
28.0	6.93
28.5	6.93
29.0	6.92
29.5	6.92
30.0	6.91

Source: Clearing Corporation of India Limited.

bonds and whether to buy such bonds in future. The other challenge was to see the impact on the modified duration of its short-term bond funds post-implementation of new valuation norms. Would the fund still be able to meet SEBI modified duration criteria for the short-term debt fund category? (see Exhibit 26.4) Divya had already compiled data on the G-Sec Yield curve (Exhibit 26.5), and in her view, an appropriate rate for SBI AT-1 bonds would be 200 basis points higher for all maturities over the G-Sec rate.

Questions

1. What do you understand by AT-1 bonds? Why did SEBI change valuation norms for AT-1 bonds?
2. Why did AT-1 bond respond negatively on March 16, 2021, to SEBI's new valuation norms?
3. Why did Mutual Funds Industry and Finance Ministry urge SEBI to relook at the 100-year valuation norm? What were their concerns?
4. What is your take on an amended version of AT-1 bond valuation norms?
5. What would be the value of AT-1 bonds held by Bluestar short-term bond funds using YTC? What would be the value based on new valuation norms?

6. How would the appropriate discount rate for AT-1 bond cash flows beyond 30-year?
7. What would be the duration of the AT-1 bond under new valuation norms?

Notes

1 AT-1 bonds were also known as Contingent Convertible Capital Instruments (CoCos)
2 PONV was an acronym for Point of Non-Viability.
3 For example, in March 2021, the bond yield for 2024 maturity for AT-1 bonds would be around 6.5%, whereas the bond yield for the 2035 maturity AT-1 bond would be just above 8.5%. Therefore, if the debt fund owned an AT-1 bond with a 7.75% coupon with a call date in March 2024 and March 2035, maturity would trade at a premium if valued using YTC (prevailing practice) but would sell at a discount valued at YTM.

27

APEX FROZEN FOODS

The Cost of Capital

On December 15, 2019, Neha Gupta was deep in her thoughts, staring at a spreadsheet on her laptop screen. Neha was the Senior Partner at Investors' Paradise, a private equity firm based out of Delhi, the capital city of India. Investors' Paradise focused on investment opportunities in unlisted firms with significant growth potential and listed entities with substantial growth runway. Neha was in charge of the Private Investment in Public Equity (PIPE) portfolio at Investors' Paradise. She was evaluating Apex Frozen Food Ltd, a listed firm in the aquaculture business. Apex was about to commission a large production facility that would reduce its dependence on a leased production facility and would allow it to change its product mix, favouring high-margin ready-to-eat shrimps. It would result in substantial improvement in profit margin. The sharp dip in shrimp prices in the USA and Europe and delay in commissioning of the new shrimp facility had resulted in a sharp drop in stock prices of Indian aquaculture stocks (see Exhibit 27.1). However, Neha believed that the stock price dip was an opportunity to invest in Apex as the firm was adding capacity and mitigating risk by investing in backward integration.

Apex Frozen Food: Company Background

Established in 1995, Apex become the leading producer and exporter of processed and ready-to-cook shrimp in India. The company had fully integrated its operations across aquaculture value-chain verticals, including hatchery, farming, processing, and exporting of shrimps. As of December 2019, the company had 15,240 MTPA of processed capacity, close to 1800 acres of farmland and a breeding capacity of 1.2–1.4 billion specific pathogen-free seeds (Exhibit 27.2).

DOI: 10.4324/9781032724478-31

EXHIBIT 27.1 Market Performance of Listed Select Aquaculture Firms in India

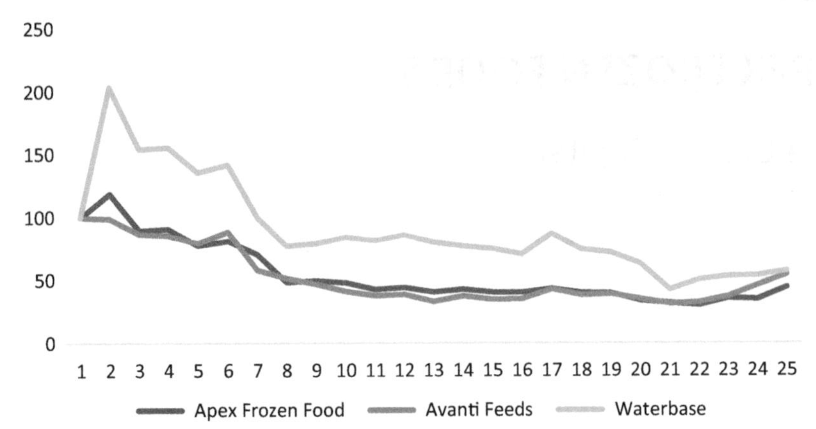

Source: Authors' workings based on data from capitaline.

EXHIBIT 27.2 Value Chain of an Integrated Aquaculture Business

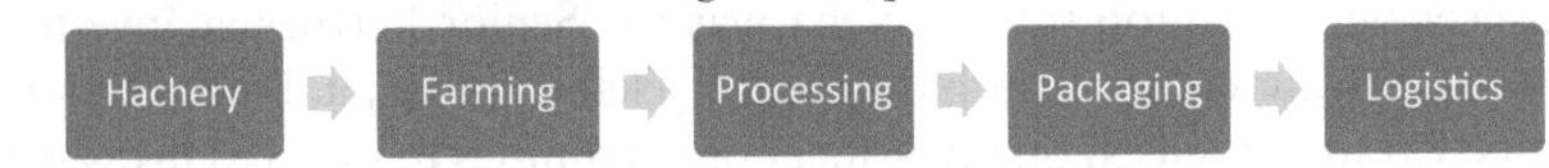

Source: Authors compilation.

The company supplied processed shrimps (mainly while leg and black tiger varieties) in frozen form to the diversified customer base of food companies, retail chains, restaurants, club stores, and distributors across major markets of the USA and European countries. While the business was B2B in nature, and most products were sold under the brands owned by its customers, it sold some of its products under its brand names, such as Bay Fresh, Bay Harvest, and Bay Premium.

Gearing up for the Growth

The company raised close to Rs 1,250 million in August 2017 through Initial Public Offer (IPO). Apex used IPO proceeds to expand shrimp processing capacity by building 20,000 TPA unit at Eastern Godavari District in Andhra Pradesh and gaining more control over the value chain by investing in backward integration.

Fast forward to December 2019; the company was ready with its new Shrimp Processing facility with 20,000 TPA. The new facility would cause an increase in the net shrimp processing capacity to the extent of 14,000 TPA as 6,000 TPA of leased capacity would be released once the owned facility was available. Apex earmarked 5,000 TPA capacity for ready-to-eat shrimp variety, which would result in higher realisation and margin on a per/kg basis. The remaining capacity would meet increased demand from Europe and USA markets and serving new markets such as China and other east Asian countries. The commercialisation of two hatcheries in fiscal 2018 added to the company's breeding capacity, substantially providing them greater control over the supply chain.

Global Seafood Industry

Seafood had remained a key source of nutrition for people across the globe. Seafood products were categorised into two – capture fisheries and aquaculture, based on the type of sourcing. Improved fisheries management and sharp growth in aquaculture over the past several years had resulted in improved per capita consumption from 15kgs in 1995 to 20kgs in 2015. Two decades earlier, the share of capture fisheries was 80%, which declined to 55%, and there was a corresponding increase in the share of aquaculture from 20% to 45% – global seafood consumption was expected to reach 175 million tonnes by 2021. Global seafood consumption had grown at 3% CAGR between 2005 and 2015. While capture fisheries growth remained stagnant, aquaculture volume CAGR was 7%. The trend was likely to continue. The USA, Europe, China, and East Asian countries were major markets and India, Vietnam, and Chile remained large exporters. India's share in aquaculture exports was at 8% in 2015 and expected to grow faster considering favourable government policies. The Indian seafood industry was Rs 1095 billion in 2015–16; 28% of the sales came from exports. While the domestic segment grew at around 12%, exports were growing at about 19% in five years ending 2016. The industry largely remained unorganised, and a few organised players, including Apex, could meet stringent quality standards by significant markets such as USA and Europe.

Apex Frozen Food Financial Performance and the Road Ahead

Apex Frozen Food reported sales of Rs 4,912 million, EBITDA of Rs 587 million and PAT of Rs 302 million. It had total assets worth Rs 5,947 million, more than half in current assets and about 1/5 of that in the CWIP stage (see Exhibits 27.3 and 27.4 for details). However, the stock had seen mixed fortune on the Indian bourses. Apex Frozen Food stock price hit a high of Rs 900 in December 2017 itself but had seen a reversal in fortune, and the price hit a low of sub Rs 200 level in August 2019 before recovering to Rs 295 by December 15, 2019. The sharp price recovery in stock price was partly due to a corporate tax cut announced by the Indian Finance minister in December 2019 that lifted the Indian stocks markets and positive commentary by Apex's management after the 2QFY20 results.

EXHIBIT 27.3 Apex Frozen Foods: Income Statement

	FY 2017	*FY 2018*	*FY 2019*	*1HFY 2020*
Sales & Other Income	7,093	10,185	8,962	5,006
Raw Material	5,317	7,031	5,810	3,465
Employee Expenses	249	389	482	231
Other Expenses	977	1,466	1,599	723
EBITDA	549	1,299	1,111	587
EBITDA Margin (%)	7.70%	12.80%	12.40%	11.70%
Depreciation	63	87	109	61
Finance Cost	112	87	65	57
Profit Before Tax	374	1126	937	469
Tax	123	335	329	166
PAT	251	791	608	302
PAT Margin (%)	3.50%	7.80%	6.80%	6.00%

Source: Prepared by authors based on data from moneycontrol website.

EXHIBIT 27.4 Apex Frozen Foods Balance Sheet (Rs. in Million)

	FY17	*FY18*	*FY19*	*1HFY20*
Assets				
Non-Current Assets	857	1,408	2,456	2,689
Net Block	829	1,111	1,147	1,486
Capital Work-in-Progress	8	209	1,163	1,085
Other Non-Current Assets	21	54	114	81
Deferred Tax Asset	0	35	33	36
Current Assets	1,910	2,902	2,623	3,258
Inventories	638	1,016	1,063	1,454
Trade Receivables	828	674	935	1,260
Cash and Cash Equivalents	46	644	67	122
Other Financial Assets	128	184	218	244
Other Current Assets	270	384	340	179
Total Assets	2,767	4,311	5,079	5,947
Liabilities				
Shareholder's Funds	1,094	3,023	3,551	3,798
Share Capital (Rs 10 face value per share)	240	313	313	313
Reserves and Surplus	854	2,710	3,238	3,485
Non-Current Liabilities	273	101	94	242
Current Liabilities	1,400	1,187	1,434	1,907
Short-term Bank Borrowings	847	722	958	1,072
Trades Payables	309	266	315	442
Other Current Liabilities	44	107	32	54
Current Tax Liabilities	0	0	0	140
Short-term Provisions	199	91	129	199
Total Liabilities	2,767	4,311	5,079	5,947

Source: Prepared by authors based on data from moneycontrol website.

Neha was all set with her cash-flow projections; however, she was unsure about Apex's cost-of-capital. One brokerage house had given a price target of Rs 480/share for December 2020 just two months back using discounted cash-flow valuation approach, but she knew that such valuations were always subject to critical assumptions regarding growth and choice of the discount rate. While she was reasonably sure about her cash-flow projections, there were too many moving parts for her to estimate the correct weighted average cost of capital for Apex. She collected information regarding unlevered beta, risk-free rate, historical market risk premium, and bond-yield spread (see Exhibits 27.5 & 27.6). While she felt she was ready with all necessary information, she was still searching for answers to the following questions:

Questions

1. How would she calculate the cost of debt? Should it be the same or different for long-term and short-term borrowings? What would be the tax rate she should use? The effective tax rate for the firm or marginal tax rate of 33%?
2. What would be the best way of calculating the appropriate cost of equity?

EXHIBIT 27.5 Historical T-Bill and 10-Year G-sec Yields

Date	*10-yr GSEC Yield (%)*	*3-Month T-bill Yield (%)*
Jul-18	7.772	6.71
Aug-18	7.951	6.81
Sep-18	8.024	6.97
Oct-18	7.853	6.95
Nov-18	7.607	6.75
Dec-18	7.37	6.67
Jan-19	7.483	6.58
Feb-19	7.591	6.42
Mar-19	7.346	6.12
Apr-19	7.414	6.4
May-19	7.032	6.12
Jun-19	6.879	6.01
Jul-19	6.369	5.73
Aug-19	6.556	5.42
Sep-19	6.695	5.34
Oct-19	6.643	5.05
Nov-19	6.46	4.91
Dec-19	6.554	5.05

Source: Prepared by authors based on data compiled from Reserve Bank of India and Clearing Corporation of India websites.

EXHIBIT 27.6 Market Risk Premium, Yield Spreads and Unlevered Beta

Historical Market Risk Premium with Different Lookback Periods (India)			
	27-years	10-years	5-years
rm-rf (Arithmetic mean)	11.10%	2.95%	2.62%
rm-rf (Geometric mean)	4.44%	1.23%	1.65%
Long-term USA Market Risk Premium	5%		
Indian Market Annual Volatility	1.5 times USA market volatility		
Yield spread for bank borrowing/corporate bonds			
	Dec-18	Dec-19	
AAA	125 bps	155 bps	
AA	175 bps	225 bps	
A/A-	240 bps	400 bps	
Note: Apex was rated A- in Dec 2019.			
Unlevered beta for Apex Frozen foods based on 1-, 2-, and 3-year data from a brokerage house			
	Unlevered Beta		
1-year	1.51		
2-year	1.46		
3-year	1.35		

Source: Authors compilation.

3. How to decide the weights for debt and equity? Should one use book value-based weights or market value-based weights?
4. Given the challenging market circumstances, what would be the impact of sudden but sticky changes in stock price and short-term borrowing needs in the next quarter? (Price crashes by 25% from Dec 2019 levels, and short-term borrowing doubles.)

28

HUARACHE INDIA LTD

The Cost of Capital

In August 2019, Radha Swaminathan, Chief Financial Officer (CFO) at Huarache India Ltd (HIL), evaluated a significant expansion proposal involving an annual Capex of Rs 200 crore for the next three years. HIL had just raised Rs 175 crore by selling a 24% stake to a private equity (PE) firm. In the deal term sheet, the PE firm insisted that HIL evaluate its investment proposals using Net Present Value (NPV) criteria and accept only those CapEx proposals that could deliver positive NPV.

Radha had been working with HIL for the past ten years, and HIL used the payback period to evaluate Capex proposals. So while she and her team were competent in cash-flow projections to calculate the payback period, she was unsure how critical HIL's weighted average cost of capital (WACC) was in evaluating firms' capital investment proposals. To learn more on the nuances of corporate finance function of professionally managed firms, she attended a week-long management development programme (MDP) on "Financial Decisions and Value Creation" at one of the top business schools in Mumbai. On the third day of the programme, the instructor explained to them many ways to calculate the cost of debt (kd), cost of equity (ke), and WACC for a firm. He gave an assignment to the participants to calculate WACC before the following day's class for a one-to-one feedback session.

Indian Footwear Industry

Indian footwear market was estimated to be Rs 48,000 crore and would grow to Rs 57,500 crore by the end of 2021 and then grow at close to 9% compounded annual growth rate (CAGR) to reach Rs 81,000 crore by 2025 (Volume CAGR would be around 6%). Indian footwear market comprised

DOI: 10.4324/9781032724478-32

leather footwear, athletic footwear, athleisure footwear, and other town footwear. Leather footwear accounted for nearly 45% of the total Indian footwear market. The USA would be the most prominent footwear market with nearly Rs 5,90,000 crore in 2021 sales, and it would be nearly ten times bigger than India. Indian footwear revenue would be Rs 410/person by the end of 2021. The non-luxury segment contributed more than 90% of the footwear sales.[1]

HIL: Company Background

Established in 1975, HIL had become a significant player in the leather footwear market. It earned an FY19 profit of Rs 97 crore in FY19 on the sales of Rs 1,447 crore. The market cap of stock in August 2019 was Rs 670 crore (see Exhibits 28.1 & 28.2 for income statement and balance sheet). HIL had solid brands and a network of more than nearly 160 retail stores and 45 online stores (EBOs – exclusive brands outlets). It had factories in 12 different locations in India. It also operated through franchise stores network and had been following omnichannel distribution model with presence in all major multiband retail outlets and e-commerce platforms. However, the major focus of the firm's expansion drive was ccompany-owned company-operated (COCO) offline stores and online–offline stores where customers can shop footwear online and pick up the delivery by visiting the nearby store. The franchise business had shown de-growth, and HIL had decided to scale it down and focus on offline and mix model (online–offline) COCO stores. The COCO stores expansion route was more capital-intensive, and the expansion had to be measured to ensure that unit economics for each store remained strong. The firm believed that the growth should be contributed by adding new stores and strong same-store sales growth (SSSG).

EXHIBIT 28.1 HIL Income Statements (Rs in million)

Particulars	*FY 2017*	*FY 2018*	*FY 2019*
Revenues	11,319	12,732	14,471
Growth (%)		12.5	13.7
Operating Expenses	9,451	10,457	11,769
EBITDA	1,868	2,275	2,702
Depreciation and Amortisation	359	409	459
EBITDA	1,509	1,866	2,243
Interest Expenses	576	731	773
PBT	933	1,135	1,470
Tax	308	374	500
Adjusted PAT	625	760	970

Source: Prepared by authors.

EXHIBIT 28.2 HIL Balance Sheets (Rs in million)

Particulars	*FY 2017*	*FY 2018*	*FY 2019*
Cash and Cash Equivalents	145	704	263
Sundry Debtors	1,550	2,093	2,777
Inventory	5,520	5,312	6,454
Loans and Advances	76	86	97
Gross Block	7,177	8,177	9,177
Net Block	4,143	4,734	5,275
CWIP	47	70	119
Miscellaneous	1,234	1,323	1,422
Total Assets	12,714	14,321	16,407
Short-Term Bank Borrowings	3,000	3,300	4,200
Long-Term Debt	2,950	3,250	3,200
Creditors and Provisions	488	791	1,112
Total Liabilities	6,438	7,341	8,512
Shareholders Equity (face value of Rs 2)	241	241	241
Reserves and Surplus	6,036	6,740	7,654
Total Networth	6,276	6,981	7,894
Total Networth and Liabilities	12,714	14,321	16,407

Source: Prepared by authors.

Radha's Notes on WACC

Radha referred to her notes from the session on the cost of capital with the following major points highlighted.

The WACC was defined as "long term opportunity cost of funds." The firm typically used two types of funds: owned funds (equity) and borrowed funds (debt).

Cost of Debt (kd)

While HIL used to work out its variant of kd as finance cost (interest payment) divided by all interest-bearing debt, Radha learnt during the programme that such calculation works only if the firm had raised a large chunk of its debt recently. Otherwise, it would not capture the change in interest rate scenario or the firm's credit profile and reflect the firm's historical cost rather than the actual cost.

Instead, if the firm had traded bonds in the market, the yield to maturity (YTM) of the bond would be the correct proxy for the firm's cost of debt. However, HIL had never issued any publicly traded bonds. Moreover, given the poor liquidity in the secondary bond market in India, the market prices or the yields on traded bonds might not reflect the correct cost of debt.

However, another way to calculate the cost of debt was to look at the firm's credit rating and see the credit spread (yield spread) applicable for the given rating. In India's case, the Government of India (GoI) enjoys a sovereign rating and could borrow funds at the lowest possible rate. Any other entity that wants to borrow money in the Indian market in local currency would face higher borrowing costs. The difference between the borrowing cost of any other entity over GoI was called "yield spread." The credit rating of a firm as a proxy for the firm's default risk. Higher the credit rating, lower the default risk and vice versa. It means firms with higher credit rating would have lower cost of debt, and firms with lower credit rating would face higher debt costs.

Cost of Equity (ke)

Measuring the cost of equity had been a challenge, and there were two popular approaches used:

dividend discount model (DDM) and capital asset pricing model (CAPM).

:

DDM could be used with more mature firms with steady or steadily growing dividends, whereas CAPM could be used for any listed entity with historical stock returns and market returns to calculate beta.

Ke using dividend discount model:

$$ke = (D0*(1+g)/P) + g$$

where D0 = just paid dividend, g = dividend growth rate, and P = prevailing stock price.

Ke using CAPM:

$$ke = \text{risk-free rate} + \beta * \text{expected market risk premium}$$

Once the kd and ke were known, WACC could be calculated as

$$WACC = (D/V) *kd* (1-t) + (E/V)*ke$$

where D = value of debt, E = value of equity and V = value of firm. The ideal weights should be based on the firm's target capital structure; in practice, market value-based weight was popular. The book value of debt could be used in the absence of reliable market value of debt/unlisted debt.

WACC Calculation for HIL

Radha compiled sufficient data to calculate WACC for HIL, and she was ready to try her hand at the assignment for tomorrow. The target debt–equity ratio for HIL would be 1:1 given the expected capital intensity of the business. The firm was confident of sustaining the average dividend growth

EXHIBIT 28.3 Historical T-Bill and 10-Year G-sec Yields

Date	*10-Year G-sec Yield (%)*	*3-Month T-Bill Yield (%)*
Aug-18	7.951	6.81
Sep-18	8.024	6.97
Oct-18	7.853	6.95
Nov-18	7.607	6.75
Dec-18	7.37	6.67
Jan-19	7.483	6.58
Feb-19	7.591	6.42
Mar-19	7.346	6.12
Apr-19	7.414	6.4
May-19	7.032	6.12
Jun-19	6.879	6.01
Jul-19	6.369	5.73
Aug-19	6.556	5.42

Source: Bloomberg.

EXHIBIT 28.4 Market Risk Premium, Yield Spreads and Levered Beta in Aug 2019 (Radha's estimates)

Expected Market Risk Premium in India	7.50%	
Yield Spread for Bank Borrowing/Corporate Bonds		
	Aug-18	Aug-19
AAA	125 bps	155 bps
AA	175 bps	225 bps
A/A-	240 bps	400 bps
Levered Beta for HIL Based on 1-, 2-, and 3-Year Weekly Returns		
	Levered beta	
1-year	1.1	
2-year	0.9	
3-year	0.95	

Source: Prepared by authors.

Note: HIL was expected to retain A-rating.

rate of 6% going forward. The recently paid annual dividend was Rs 1 per share (see Exhibits 28.3 and 28.4).

Questions

1. Compare different approaches to calculate cost of debt. Which method is the most appropriate for firms like HIL?
2. Calculate the cost of debt for HIL.
3. Calculate the cost of equity for HIL using the dividend discount model.

4. Calculate the cost of equity using CAPM. Then, how would you adjust levered beta to align with the target debt/equity ratio?
5. How would you decide on the weights of debt and equity in total financing? Would you use market value-based weights or target weights? Why?
6. What is the most appropriate measure of WACC for HIL? How does it help in evaluating capital investment proposals?

Note

1 Source: https://ezproxy.svkm.ac.in:2307/statistics/976367/footwear-market-size-worldwide/Statista, accessed on December 21, 2020

29

BALAJI WAFERS PVT LTD

The Cost of Capital

On a chilly December 2019 evening in Ahmedabad, Aarti Chabarria tried to make sense of the pile of data. She joined as an analyst in a transaction advisory group at Trident Capital last summer. Trident was preparing a pitch for Balaji Wafers Pvt. Ltd, (Balaji) on its fundraising options for its pan-India expansion. Aarti had to prepare a note on valuation and financing options for Balaji and submit it to her immediate boss in the next 24 hours. Trident was preparing a pitchbook including valuation and financing options for Balaji's pan-India expansion. Trident, a Mumbai-based investment bank, was involved in advisory services on M&A, fundraising, IPO management, loan syndication, and more. Aarti had collected information on the industry growth rate, competitive landscape, profit margin, cap-ex, and working capital requirements. However, she got stuck on estimating the cost of capital for Balaji, which is a crucial cog-in-the-wheel for her arriving at Balaji wafer's valuation. Aarti recently completed her MBA (Finance) and knew how to calculate the weighted average cost of capital for firms in different industries. However, the tools she learnt required beta and market-cap of the firm, which is not readily available for unlisted firms. She was wondering, how should she go about calculating the cost of capital for a private firm?

Indian Snacks Market

India had a population of 1.35 billion with a per capita GDP of US$ 2,035, which was expected to grow to 1.4 billion and US$ 2,578 by 2022. Besides, there was a significant increase in affluence and disposable income expected. As a result, population categorised as strugglers would drop significantly between 2016 and 2025. With burgeoning middle class and an increase

DOI: 10.4324/9781032724478-33

in the working population, the organised snacks market for ready-to-eat snacks grew at about 15% CAGR over the past decade. It would continue to grow at a similar rate to touch Rs 43,000 crore by 2021. In 2019, the organised snack market was divided into three major categories: namkeens (36%), extruded snacks (32%), and chips (30%). A definite shift in preference from chips to namkeen and extruded snacks. Extruded snacks was expected to register a CAGR of 19% between 2016 and 2021, followed by 18% for namkeen, and 10% for chips, respectively.

Bajali Wafers: The Company

Virani brothers founded Balaji Wafers in the early 1980s in Rajkot, a fun-loving city of Gujarat, with just Rs. 20,000 of initial capital. Since then, Balaji had grown into a dominant regional player with close to Rs 2,000 crore sales and Rs 1,000 crore in assets by 2018. It enjoyed around 30% market share of Gujarat's organised snacks market, the state with the largest market for savoury snacks in India (13%). Balaji had a 9% market share in the Indian organised snack market, a highly fragmented market dominated by regional players (see Exhibit 29.1). Balaji grew faster than the industry average CAGR between 2013 and 2018 (see Exhibit 29.2). Exhibit 29.3 reports an abridged version of the estimated income statement and balance sheet prepared by Aarti for Balaji at the end of FY20 (not factoring in future fundraising). Balaji was on a sound footing and growing at a healthy pace; the competition intensified as local players such as Gopal foods expanded their reach. In addition, new players were entering the Gujarat market.

EXHIBIT 29.1 Market Share of Significant Players in the Organised Snack Market (at the End of FY 2018)

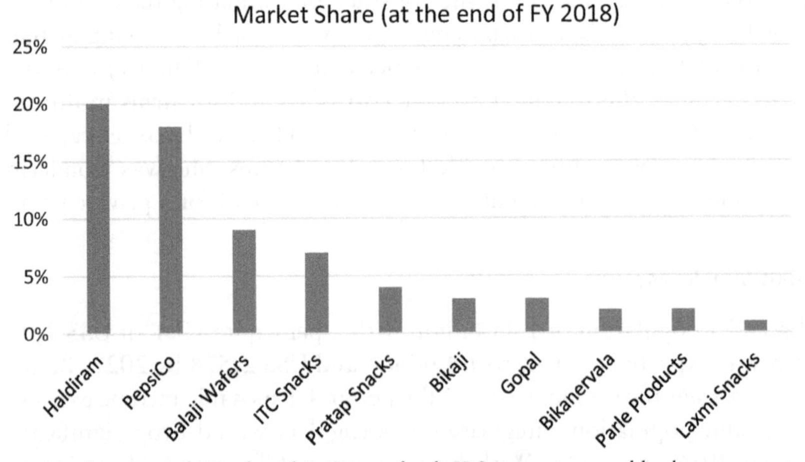

Source: Authors compilation based on Pratap foods IPO prospectus and brokerage reports.

EXHIBIT 29.2 Revenue Growth for Major Players in the Organised Snack Market (2013–18)

	FY 2013 (Rs Crore)	*FY 2018 (Rs Crore)*	*CAGR FY 2013–18 (%)*
Pepsi Co	2,550	3,612	7.2
Haldiram	2,237	5,039	17.6
Balaji Wafers	914	1,840	15.0
Bikanerwala	350	763	16.9
Bkiaji Foods	326	800	19.7
DFM Foods	225	425	13.6
Agro Tech (Foods)	128	195	8.8
Prataap Snacks	344	1037	24.7%

Source: Authors compilation from Prataap Snacks IPO prospectus, company reports and brokerage reports

EXHIBIT 29.3 Balaji's Wafers Estimated Income Statement and Balance Sheet* (Rs Crore)

FY20E Income Statement		*FY20E Balance Sheet*			
Sales	2000	Shareholder' Equity	1000	Fixed assets	1000
EBITDA	160	Long-term Borrowings	200	CWIP	100
Depreciation	60	Short-term Borrowings	10	Current assets	300
EBIT	100	Current liabilities	290		
I	15				
PBT	85				
T	17				
PAT	68				

Source: Prepared by authors based on Pratap Snacks IPO Prospectus and brokerage reports.
Note: Aarti's estimate

"Many new companies from Gujarat are entering the snacks space as the state is one of the biggest markets in India. Apart from growth potential, the transparent regulatory regime, uninterrupted power supply and good governance are key factors.: said H G Kosia, Commissioner, FDCA.[1] There were over 314 Namkeen makers, small and big, in the state.

Growth Financing

The battle had already reached the den of Balaji. After raising Rs 250 crore in 2017 via IPO, Prataap Snacks had ramped up its efforts to expand its capacity and distribution network across the nation. It had acquired Avadh Foods at Rs 148 crore, the fourth largest player in Gujarat. It was investing heavily to ramp up Avadh foods' capacity and had set an ambitious target of doubling sales of Avadh foods in the next three years. Recognising the challenge, Balaji had ramped up its effort to defend the home turf and look for new territories to increase market share. "To crack the North India market, Balaji plans to invest Rs. Seven hundred Crore in a new manufacturing facility in either Chandigarh or Uttar Pradesh," said Mihir Virani, director, Balaji Wafers.[1]

While Balaji had remained a desirable target for several strategic investors and private equity, investors were keen to invest in Balaji. The company, too, was eager to raise growth capital. "We are looking for growth capital investment and are in talks. I cannot give further details or a time frame." Chandu Virani told Reuters that Balaji intends to raise US$ 100–125 million through PE investments by Blackstone Group and Actis in 2013.[2] Pepsico and Kellogg pursued Balaji, but nothing came out. Balaji planned for an IPO in 2017 – around the same time Prataap Snacks launched its IPO, but they dropped the idea by the middle of 2017. "As long as banks are willing to lend, there is no need to go public. There is no IPO this year, although we have been thinking about it in the past," said Chandu Virani, Founder of Balaji Wafers. He further added (talking about Balaji's three plants in Rajkot, Valsad, and Indore), "We have already invested Rs.700 Crore in these three plants and have survived on bank loans to fund them. Once the Indore plant starts running to its full capacity in the next two years, we may look at an IPO."[3]

Fast forward to 2019, and Balaji wafers needed capital: Rs. 750 crore for a new manufacturing facility in north India and further funds to support marketing and distribution activities. They hired movie star Ayushmann Khurrana for the brand endorsement and launched TV commercials in 2019. It needed capital. Balaji's business was profitable with a high EBITDA to operating cash-flow conversion ratio (close to 100%), sales of just below Rs 2,000 crore and EBITDA margin of around 9%, all these were not sufficient to meet its capital requirement.

According to Trident's estimate, Balaji required Rs 1,000 crore of external funds to meet its growth capital for the next five years. Aarti was working towards a combination of Rs 300–400 crore by equity investments from private equity players and arranging remaining funds via term loan from banks. Considering the business's growth trajectory and intensified competition, she felt that debt would be an integral part of the financing mix. The debt-to-equity would remain between 0.4 and 0.6 in book value terms. Aarti gathered information on private equity transactions in the Indian snacks market (see Exhibit 29.4). She compiled information on listed snacks players (see Exhibit 29.5). She concluded that Balaji would get A– rating from rating agencies considering its dependence on debt financing to fund aggressive expansion plans. She hoped that her information should be helpful to estimate the market value of equity and cost of equity for Balaji.[4]

EXHIBIT 29.4 PE Investments in Indian Snacks Market (2014–2019)

Year	*Company*	*Private Equity*	*Stake Sale*	*Valuation (Rs. Cr)*	*Map/Sales*	*Presence*
2014	Bikaji Foods	Light House	13%	720	2x	Regional
2014	DFM Foods	West Bridge	25%	260	1.5x	Regional
2017	Apricot goods	CESC group-Sanjeev Goenka	70%	440	2.2x	Regional

Source: Authors compilation from Prataap Snacks IPO prospectus, company reports and brokerage reports.

EXHIBIT 29.5 Listed Peers' Data as of December 2019*

Company Name	*M-cap (Rs Crore)*	*Levered Beta*	*Net Worth (Rs Crore)*	*Interest-Bearing Debt*	*Sales (Rs Crore)*	*Credit Rating*	*Yield-Spread (basis points)*
Nestle	150,000	0.75	2000	0	12,000	AAA	155
ADF Foods	500	0.78	240	70	260	A–	400
DFM Foods	1050	0.95	150	100	525	BBB+	450
Prataap Snacks	1900	0.55	700	120	1300	A+	300
Agrotech Foods	1400	0.81	450	225	800	AA–	270

Source: Authors compilation based on capitaline data.

*Annual numbers are on the trailing-twelve-months basis (TTM)

Notes

1 Source: TOI, Ahmedabad edition, December 8, 2019. https://timesofindia.indiatimes.com/city/ahmedabad/snack-makers-find-secret-sauce-for-growth/articleshow/72420971.cms
2 https://www.reuters.com/article/balaji-funds-idINL4N0GH1VU20130816
3 https://www.thehindubusinessline.com/companies/balaji-wafers-to-stay-away-from-ipo-this-year/article64304443.ece#:~:text=The%20company%20had%20earlier%20indicated,Virani%2C%20Founder%2C%20Balaji%20Wafers.
4 The prevailing risk-free rate was around 6.5%, and practitioners used a market risk premium of 7% to 8% in 2019.

30

ITC LTD

The Divisional Cost of Capital

Monark Vora, an analyst at InvestmentWaves, loved his experience of staying at hotel ITC Rajputana during his recent Christmas holidays. However, he was unsure of the prospects of the ITC's stocks and its hotel business in specific. On February 1, 2020, he was busy preparing for an important meeting with a prospective institutional client scheduled early next week. The client asked him to come out with a stock idea that fits into the "quality at a reasonable price" bucket. Indian markets were trading at lifetime highs, and It was not easy to find quality at a reasonable price (QARP) investment ideas. However, ITC, a significant wealth creator of the past several years, had failed to participate in the entire rally (Exhibit 30.1a). It had delivered low-single-digit CAGR in the last five years.

Monark was unsure whether ITC was a "value buy" or "value trap"? He decided to use discounted cash flow (DCF) valuation approach to value ITC. He realised that valuing ITC was not a simple task because ITC was a large conglomerate with significant interests in FMCG (including cigarettes), hotels, paperboard and packaging and agribusiness. He looked for sum-of-the-parts (SOTP) valuation – an approach that values each segment separately using segment cash-flow projections, growth rates, and appropriate discount rates. He could easily collect data for cash flows and historical growth rates for each business segment from company filings; estimating an appropriate discount rate for each segment was a challenge. He followed a step-by-step approach and started with the hotel business, as that was the pain point for ITC. By the end of FY19, the hotel business had a low-single-digit return of capital employed (ROCE) with the maximum capital employed in the hotel business.

DOI: 10.4324/9781032724478-34

EXHIBIT 30.1(A) ITC vs Nifty – One-Year Price Movement

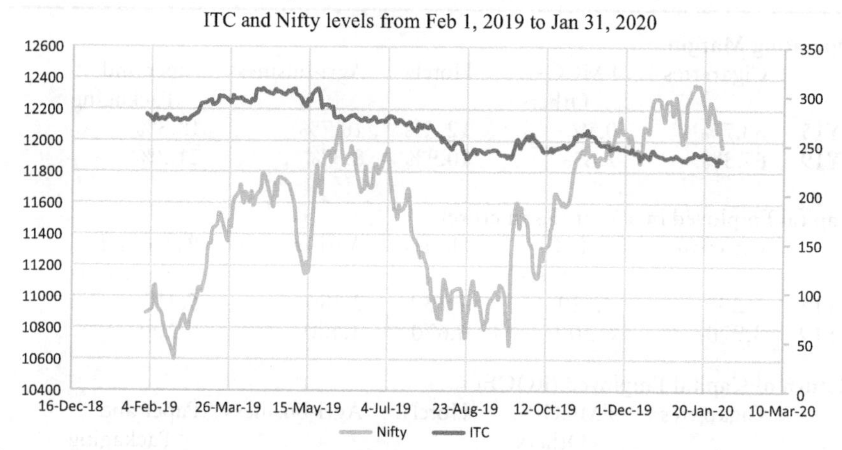

Source: Prepared by authors based on the ITC investor presentations from ITC website.

EXHIBIT 30.1(B) ITC Ltd: Performance Scorecard

			(Rs Crore)
	2008–09	*2018–19*	*10-Year CAGR 08–09 to 18–19*
Net Revenue	15,612	44,415	11.00%
PBT	4,826	18,444	14.30%
PAT	3,264	12,464	14.30%
Capital Employed	14,780	60,005	15.00%
Segment RoCE	39.70%	70.30%	
Market Capitalization	69,751	3,63,714	18.00%
Total Shareholder Returns			20.30%
Sensex (CAGR 08–09 to 18–19)	14.80%		

Source: https://www.itcportal.com/investor/index.aspx

ITC Ltd: The Company

ITC had been a large Indian conglomerate with business interests spread across FMCG (including cigarettes), hotels, paperboard and packaging and agribusiness. ITC had delivered double-digit CAGR in the last ten years on all metrics – top-line growth, bottom-line growth, and growth in market capitalisation (Exhibit 30.1b). At the end of FY19, ITC's revenue, profit after tax and market capitalisation were Rs 44,415 crore, Rs 12,464 crore, and Rs 3,63,714 crore, respectively. It had created significant wealth for its shareholders over the last decade despite lack-lustre performance in recent years. While ITC had done well over the years, its stock price had taken a

EXHIBIT 30.2 ITC Ltd: Major Business Segments Data

Operating Margin

	Cigarettes	FMCG-Others	Hotels	Agri-business	Paper and Packaging
FY15	63.7%	0.1%	12.6%	10.7%	18.3%
FY19	67.3%	2.6%	10.9%	8.3%	21.2%

Capital Employed in a Year (Rs in crore)

	Cigarettes	FMCG-Others	Hotels	Agri-business	Paper and Packaging
FY15	6,230	3,420	4,230	2,180	5,310
FY19	3,970	6,200	6,670	3,400	6,200

Return of Capital Employed (ROCE)

	Cigarettes	FMCG-Others	Hotels	Agri-business	Paper and Packaging
FY15	33.30%	0.8%	1.1%	42.2%	17.1%
FY19	26.70%	5.3%	3.0%	25.2%	20.4%

Source: Prepared by authors based on the ITC investor presentations from ITC website. https://www.itcportal.com/investor/index.aspx

beating in the last two years. It was facing a three-way problem. First, some foreign institutional investors with a new mandate of following environment, social and governance (ESG) norms started selling out of companies in "sin good" business like cigarettes. Second, it struggled due to increased tax on cigarettes, low volume growth, and loss of market share to its peers. Third, its large capital investments in other FMCG and hotel businesses were yet to deliver significant returns. While there was a visible ray of light at the end of the tunnel by the end of FY19, both FMCG and hotel businesses reported their highest ROCE in the last five years; the ROCE for FMCG and hotel businesses were 5.3% and 3.0%, respectively. The total capital employed by ITC at the end of FY19 was about Rs 26,500 crore spread across five major business segments; FMCG and hotels accounted for near half of the total capital employed. ITC could slowly diversify its revenue stream, and FMCG-other, paper, and agri-business contributed meaningfully to the revenue mix. It largely remained a cigarette company with cigarettes business that contributed 85% of FY19 net profit (Exhibit 30.2). FMCG-others and hotels combined contributed to just 2.8% of the company's profits.

Indian Hotel Industry and ITC's Hotel Business

The Indian Hotel Industry had come out of slumber and clocked 6% growth in Revenue-per-available-room (REVPaR) in FY19. The Indian hotel industry had a total capacity of 2,90,000 rooms capacity, with 69,000 in the luxury segment. Foreign tourist arrivals (FTA) was at 10.5 million in 2018 and expected to grow further with improvement in infrastructure and the government's efforts to push the Indian tourism industry. It would cause a greater demand for luxury hotel rooms and higher average revenue per room (ARR). While things were looking up, the hotel industry had failed to earn double-digit ROCE in the last ten years.

ITC had an excellent hotel network with 110 properties spread across 70 locations in India by the end of December 2019. It had four hotels—ITC Hotels, Welcome Hotels, Fortune, and Welcome Heritage in luxury, upper upscale, mid-market and leisure, and heritage segments. ITC had 10,400 rooms with 6,200 rooms under the five-star luxury segment, 3,300 rooms under the fortune brand, and 900 rooms under the heritage brand. The company was scaling up following the "asset-light" strategy. Managed properties contributed over 50% of room inventory by the end of FY19. Besides, the share of food and beverage (F&B) revenue increased with more walk-in guests visiting their best-in-class hotel restaurants. ITC ended FY19 with hotel segment sales and EBIT of Rs 1,665 crore and Rs 178 crore, respectively – sales was up 17.5% whereas EBIT was up 27% from FY18 levels. FY20 was shaping up even better with nine months sales, and EBIT for the period ending December 31, 2019, were Rs 1,372 crore and Rs 115 Ccrore, respectively. Sales was up 18.4%, whereas EBIT was up 29.3% YoY. Despite such impressive performance in the last two years, the hotel business ROCE was a meagre 3%. The hotel business share in ITC's total revenue and profit was less than 4% and 1%, respectively.

Monark collected financial information on a few listed hotel firms in India (Exhibit 30.3) and wondered how to use such information? In addition he compiled other information required to estimate cost of debt and equity (Exhibit 30.4). After compiling the necessary information, he still had to take a call on what should be the appropriate capital structure and credit rating for the hotel business.

1. Should I even calculate the divisional cost of capital for different business segments, given that cigarettes contributed to 85% of ITC's FY19 profits?
2. Should I use all listed hotel firms for comparison or narrow down the list of peers? How should I decide?
3. Most hotel businesses had a beta greater than 1, but ITC had a beta of 0.5 only. Should I use the beta of relevant listed hotel stocks? Should I use ITC's beta? What are the possible consequences?
4. How should I compute WACC for ITC and its hotel business in specific? How will it help in evaluating ITC's capital allocation policy?

EXHIBIT 30.3 Financial Data for ITC Ltd and Selected Listed Hotel Companies in India at the End of September 2019 (Rs Crore)

Company Name	*EBITDA*	*EBIT*	*PAT*	*Total Debt*	*Net worth*	*Net sales*	*ROCE (%)*	*RONW (%)*	*levered beta*	*M-Cap*	*P/E*	*P/B*	*EV*	*Credit rating*
Chalet Hotels Ltd.	388.83	247	-9	1411.03	1,473	987	8.86%	-0.53%	1.1	6925.71	-	4.87	8892.5421	BBB
Country Club Hospitality & Holidays Ltd.	48.46	3.85	-53.67	350	946.96	264.57	0.27%	--5.58%	1.4	106.74	-	0.11	546.6288	NA
E I H Ltd.	474.71	342.15	136.66	499.78	2993.39	1,810.82	7.77%	4.65%	1.42	11577.15	88.01	3.87	11886.7384	AA
Indian Hotels Co. Ltd.	916.71	588.86	244.59	1723.2	4348	4,512.00	8.97%	5.74%	1.1	18356.85	64	4.22	20442.633	AA
Kamat Hotels (India) Ltd.	74.1	55.76	16.6	260.17	-147.84	236.09	13.09%	NA	1.7	116.39	6.89	-0.78	614.289	NA
Lemon Tree Hotels Ltd.	183.28	129.17	55.58	1135.95	875.02	549.51	7.33%	8.45%	1.1	6349.88	112.63	9.13	7514.48	A-
Mahindra Holidays & Resorts India Ltd.	239.43	138.09	59.49	584.86	281.57	2,238.99	14.96%	65.31%	1.15	3190.26	52.8	-6.16	3941.0178	AA
Royal Orchid Hotels Ltd.	49.48	35.16	13.11	91.35	177.48	203.83	12.99%	7.92%	1.6	323.67	27.1	1.91	383.9648	BBB
Taj G V K Hotels & Resorts Ltd.	76.41	59.71	24.31	160.11	391.86	316.87	10.08%	6.39%	1.3	1488.85	54.75	3.8	1684.0764	A+
ITC	20606.13	19209.52	12824.2	NA	59140.87	48352.68	34%	23.80%	0.5	363712.7	28.88	6.36	359576.969	AAA
ITC-Hotels	374	178	122.82	?	?	1,665.00	?	?	?	NA	NA	NA	NA	?

Source: Prowess IQ

EXHIBIT 30.4 Yield Spread, Risk-free Rate, and Market Risk Premium Estimates

Credit Rating	*The Yield Spread in Dec 2019 (basis points))*
AAA	125
AA	175
A	250
BBB	330
BB	420
B	520
Prevailing 10-Year GSEC Yield	7%
Additional Information	
91 days T-bill Yield	5.50%
Expected Market Risk Premium	8%
Applicable Marginal Income Tax Rate	25%

Source: Monark's estimates based on market information

31

DBS AUTO'S ELECTRIC TWO-WHEELERS

Cost of Capital

On June 1, 2021, Meher Bulsara – Senior Manager (Finance) at DBS Auto Company, called a meeting with two of her team members, Danish Merchant and Lakshmi Nadar. She wanted to discuss the preparation of estimates to support an investment decision regarding the company's proposed electric two-wheelers project (EL-2). DBS Auto was a mid-sized auto component player producing aluminium die-cast engine components for two-wheeler companies.

Electric Two-Wheelers' Market in India

The electric two-wheelers market in India had been small but fast-growing, with estimated sales of 144,000 vehicles in 2020–21, constituting a little over 1% share of the total two-wheeler sales in the country.[1] The main challenges had been low customer adoption due to concerns related to battery costs, driving range, and the availability of charging stations. Limited availability of after-sales and parts businesses and battery recycling and re-usage capabilities were other constraints. Six players accounted for 90% of the sales led by Hero Electric, Okinawa Autotech, and Ampere Vehicles. Despite their leadership, the electric two-wheeler operations of these players were not profitable due to high cost of components and low sales volume.

Experts expected electric two-wheeler demand to see explosive growth over the next ten years, especially in entry-level two-wheelers driven by the reduced total cost of ownership, improved charging infrastructure, lower battery prices, government incentives, and increased customer readiness. According to McKinsey, the electric two-wheelers' demand in India could

DOI: 10.4324/9781032724478-35

grow explosively to about 9 million units by 2029–30, accounting for 35–40% of all two-wheelers sold.[2] As they achieved economies of scale and as the cost of battery components reduced with increasing localisation, the electric two-wheeler players could achieve break-even levels of sales followed by a period of high profitable growth.

DBS Auto's EL-2 Project

Meher briefed Danish and Lakshmi about DBS Auto's plans. The initial plan was to set up a capacity of 50,000 electric two-wheelers and then scale up with a target to achieve a market share of 4–5% by 2025. The positives of the project were that DBS Auto had access to the most cost-effective battery technology from its US-based collaborator and was financially stronger than many of the existing players. The negatives of the project included uncertainty regarding scaling up, high initial capital intensity, and a long payback period. She also believed that the management would not consider the project significant enough to allocate organisational resources if the project's net present value (NPV) were less than Rs 1,000 crores.

Meher shared the estimates prepared earlier by a former colleague based on ballpark estimates. She assigned the task of preparing the revised cash-flow forecasts to Danish and the cost of capital to Lakshmi. Lakshmi immediately started gathering all the required information to prepare the cost of capital estimate (see Exhibits 31.1, 31.2, and 31.3). The following afternoon she submitted her estimate and a note explaining her assumptions to Meher (Exhibit 31.4).

EXHIBIT 31.1 DBS Auto's Financial Summary

Rs Crore	*March 2019*	*March 2020*	*March 2021*
Total Income	2,322	2,717	2,487
EBITDA	295	363	389
Profit After Tax	136	179	214
Non-Current Assets	793	937	1,017
Current Assets	578	551	480
Total Assets	1,371	1,488	1,498
Equity	896	1,040	1,158
Non-Current Liabilities	12	23	25
Current Liabilities	463	425	314
Total Debt	448	312	290
Market Capitalisation	4,481	5,200	5,792

Source: Prepared by authors.

EXHIBIT 31.2 Previous Workings of Net Present Value of EL-2 Project

Rs Crore	*FY 2023*	*FY 2024*	*FY 2025*	*FY 2026*	*FY 2027*	*FY 2028*	*FY 2029*	*FY 2030*	*FY 2031*	*FY 2032*
Revenues	–	–	78	238	484	958	1,559	2,292	2,874	3,210
Cost of Goods Sold	–	–	47	143	291	575	935	1,375	1,724	1,926
Other Operating Expenses	25	50	100	150	206	268	324	382	436	493
EBITDA	(25)	(50)	(69)	(55)	(13)	115	300	534	713	791
Depreciation	–	15	28	54	76	98	121	136	151	160
EBIT	(25)	(65)	(97)	(108)	(88)	17	179	399	563	631
Capex	100	100	200	200	226	248	221	236	216	225
Net Working Capital (NWC)	–	7	15	5	–	–	–	–	–	–
Tax rate	28%									
Terminal Growth Rate	6.5%									
Cost of Capital	12%									
EBIT(1-t)+Depreciation	(18)	(32)	(42)	(24)	12	110	250	423	556	615
Less: Capex	100	100	200	200	226	248	221	236	216	225
Less: Change in NWC	-	7	8	(10)	(5)	-	-	-	-	-
Net Cash Flows	(118)	(139)	(250)	(214)	(209)	(138)	29	187	340	389
Terminal Value										7,537
Total Cash Flows	(118)	(139)	(250)	(214)	(209)	(138)	29	187	340	7,926
Net Present Value	**2,045**									
NPV under Alternative Discount Rates										
10%	4,200									
11%	2,869									
12%	2,045									
13%	1,492									
14%	1,101									
15%	813									
16%	595									

Source: Prepared by authors.

EXHIBIT 31.3 Data to Estimate Cost of Capital

Risk-free rate

G-Sec 1 year	3.77%
G-Sec 3 year	4.70%
G-Sec 5 year	5.59%
G-Sec 10 year	6.02%

Equity Market Risk Premium

Method	EMRP	Basis/Source
Historical (5 years)	8.48%	S&P BSE 500 Total Returns Index – 10 Year G-Sec
Historical (10 years)	4.99%	S&P BSE Total Returns Index – 10 Year G-Sec
Implied (forward looking)	4.53%	Bloomberg Estimate
Survey-based	7.00%	Research by Fernandez et al. (2020)*

**Fernandez, P., de Apellániz, E., & F Acín, J. (2020). Survey: Market Risk Premium and Risk-Free Rate used for 81 countries in 2020.*

Unlevered Beta of DBS Auto and Global Electric Vehicle Peers

DBS Auto	0.83	(Levered beta = 1.00)
NIU Technologies*	1.62	
Yadea Group Holdings Ltd.*	0.99	
Jiangsu Xinri E-Vehicle*	1.29	
TESLA Ind.	1.34	
BYD Co. Ltd.	0.90	

* These manufacture electric two-wheelers

Credit Rating of DBS Auto and Electric Two-Wheeler Manufacturers in India

Rs Crore	**Revenue**	**EBITDA**	**PAT**	**Group Support**	**Credit Rating**
DBS Auto	2487 (FY21)	389	214	No	AA
Hero Electric Vehicles	240 (FY20)	n.a.	-3	Yes (1)	BBB
Oknawa Autotech	31 (FY18)	-2.13	-2.37	No	BB
Ampere Vehicles	54 (FY19)	-6.9	n.a.	Yes (2)	A

(1) Hero Eco Group, (2) Greaves Cotton Ltd

Credit Spreads

Basis Points	**1 Year**	**3 Year**	**5 Year**	**10 Year**
AAA	38	52	35	88
AA	129	143	119	162
A	319	319	295	322
BBB	465	465	441	468

Effective Interest Rate Paid

DBS Auto's Interest Rate	5.8%	Estimated as Interest Expense Divided by Average Debt

Tax Rate

Effective	19.7%
Marginal	28%

Debt to Equity

Based on	**D/E**
Existing Book Value	0.25
Existing Market Value	0.05
Target Book Value	0.50
Target Market Value	0.10

Source: Prepared by authors.

EXHIBIT 31.4 Lakshmi Nadar's Estimate of EL-2 Project's Cost of Capital

To: Meher Bulsara
From: Lakshmi Nadar
Date: June 2, 2021
Subject: Cost of Capital for EL-2 Project

I have estimated the cost of capital for the EL-2 project as 10.71% based on the following assumptions:

1. Methodology for estimating the cost of capital: Weighted Average Cost of Capital (WACC)

I used the WACC methodology, which I thought would be the most appropriate since DBS Auto plans to maintain a stable debt to equity ratio in the future. To calculate the WACC, I have first estimated the proportion of equity (E/V) and debt (D/V) in the company's book value in 2020–21 as 0.80 and 0.20, respectively. I have then estimated the cost of equity (Ke) and post-tax cost of debt (Kd[1-t]) and used the following formula to calculate WACC:

WACC = E/V x Ke + D/V x Kd x [1-t]

2. Estimating cost of equity

I used the capital asset pricing model (CAPM) to estimate the cost of equity, Ke using the following formula:

Ke = Risk-free Rate (Rf) + Beta x Equity Market Risk Premium (EMRP)

To estimate the risk-free rate, I considered the yield on a one-year Government of India Security. To calculate my equity market risk premium, I used the difference in the past five year's geometric mean returns between the S&P BSE 500 index and 10-year Government of India security. I estimated the historical beta of DBS Auto as 1.00 by regressing the past two years' weekly returns of the stock against the market returns and used that in the CAPM equation to estimate the cost of equity for the EL-2 project as 12.2%.

3. Estimating cost of debt

I divided the interest paid by DBS Auto last year by the average interest-bearing debt during the year. This ratio provided me with an estimate of pre-tax debt Kd as 5.8%. I multiplied this by (1-t) using the effective rate of tax paid by the company as t. My post-tax cost of debt was therefore 4.66%.

4. Computing WACC

Putting together all my assumptions, I arrived at my figure of WACC as
0.8 x 12.2% + 0.2 x 4.66% = 10.71%

Source: Prepared by authors.

Question

1. Provide your opinion regarding each point in Lakshmi's analysis.
2. Prepare your estimate of the cost of capital for the EL-2 Project, explaining your assumptions.

Notes

1 https://www.business-standard.com/article/electric-vehicle/sales-of-electric-vehicles-in-india-fell-20-to-236-802-units-in-fy21-smev-121042200514_1.html
2 Mckinsey & Company (2020). *The unexpected trip: The future of mobility in India beyond COVID-19.* https://www.mckinsey.com/industries/automotive-and-assembly/our-insights/the-unexpected-trip-the-future-of-mobility-in-india-beyond-covid-19

32

BHAGYODYA STAMPINGS PVT LTD

Hedge or not to Hedge?

On the early evening of December 5, 2018, Vimal Shah, Managing Director and Chairman of Bhagyodya Stampings Limited, was standing in front of the glass window in the chamber of his newly bought office on the 10th floor of a business park SG Highway, Ahmedabad. He reflected upon his business performance over the past two years; it was a relatively low forex volatility period, with moderate appreciation in the Indian rupee vis-a-vis the US dollar. However, exporters like Bhagyodya Stampings would benefit from the weakening of the rupee rather than its strengthening.

Bhagyodya Stampings was manufacturing transformer plates from iron scrap purchased from the domestic market and exporting them mainly to the US. It had reported Rs 150 million and Rs 10 million of sales and net income, respectively, in FY18. Bhagyodya had total assets of Rs 70 million at the end of November 2018.

Rapid depreciation in rupee until mid-October 2018 to nearly Rs. 75/dollar had raised hopes of a possible windfall gain on Bhagyodya's large unhedged positions on dollar receivables. It was expecting $1 million receipts in Jan 2019, for which Vimal had earlier pencilled in USD/INR rate of Rs 67 in his pricing. The possibility of forex gains had partially driven his decision to purchase and move to the new office.

One of the primary reasons behind the sudden fall in the rupee was the sharp spike in crude oil prices. Crude oil (Brent grade) had started trading at US$86/barrel by the end of September 2018. Experts had been forecasting a further increase to about US$ 100/barrel. The spike in crude price was terrible for the Indian economy as increasing import costs contributed to the widening current account deficit. Moreover, with further drying up

DOI: 10.4324/9781032724478-36

of foreign capital flows, the rupee was threatening to hit Rs. 80 per dollar mark. Besides, this was the precise reason Vimal had not hedged his dollar receivables. He reasoned that if the currency was moving in his favour, why kill the prospect of earning windfall gain by hedging.

However, Vimal's expectation of windfall gain started fading as the rupee reversed its direction and appreciated to a level of below Rs. 70 per dollar by the end of November 2018. Unexpectedly, crude had lost over 30% in just about a month and started trading around $60/barrel levels. For a long time, foreign investors, who had deserted Indian markets, finally returned and started pumping money into the Indian markets in November. Now Vimal was staring at a scenario where he may not earn any windfall profit if the rupee were to appreciate back the levels of 67–67.5. The good news for him was that dollar had marginally recovered to above Rs. 70, and it was trading at Rs. 70.6 in the spot market as of December 5, 2018 (see Exhibit 32.1).

Vimal was too concerned about the outcomes of two significant events: the OPEC (Organisation of Petroleum Exporting Countries) meeting on December 6, 2018 and state-election results due on December 11, 2018. If OPEC agreed on significant supply cuts, the crude would start inching higher, leading to a weaker rupee. Similarly, if state election results disappointed the market, global investors would be worried about the unstable government post general election in the middle of 2019. That would result in a sharp depreciation of the rupee. It would work in favour of Bhagyodya.

EXHIBIT 32.1 USD/INR Spot Price Movement from Aug 2018 to Dec 2018

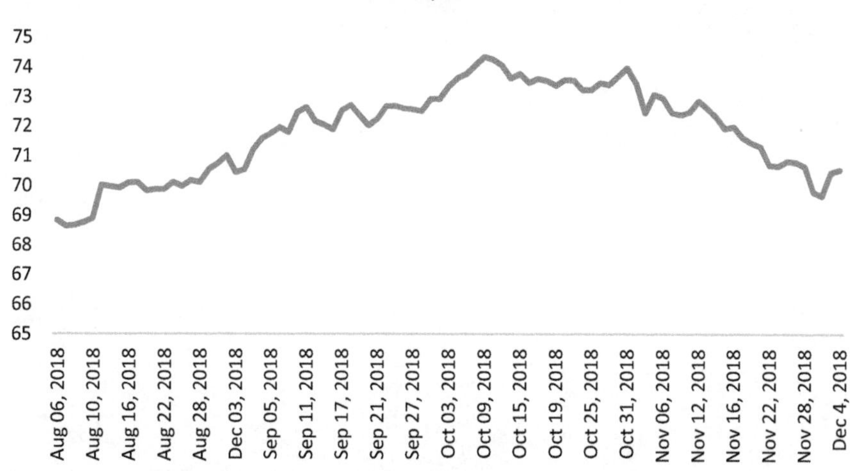

Source: Prepared by authors based on Bloomberg data.

EXHIBIT 32.2 Forward, Future, and Options Rate as of December 5, 2018

USD/INR	*Rates (Rs.)*	*Premium (Rs.)*
Spot	70.51	
29/1/2019 Future Contract	71.05	
29/1/2019, Put @ Rs 71		1.05
29/1/2019 Put @ Rs. 70.5		0.8
29/1/2019 Put @ Rs.69.5		0.45
29/1/2019 Call @ 72.5		0.45
29/9/2019 Call @ 71.5		0.8
USD/INR 29/1/2019 Forward rate by MCB Bank	70.9	

Source: National Stocks Exchange website, authors compilation.

Nevertheless, what if the unfolding of events led to rupee appreciation. Vimal would be cursing himself for not hedging the considerable receivable exposure when the rupee was just about Rs 75/dollar.

What should he do now? Should he leave the position unhedged? Is this still the right time to hedge his exposure – partially or fully? Which instrument should he use? Forward, future or option? Why? Is there a way to retain the upside while protecting the downside without incurring any outflow because of paying options premium? What would be the trade-off? What should be his long-term hedging strategy? (see Exhibit 32.2).

33

GREAT EASTERN SHIPPING: RISK MANAGEMENT

"A ship in harbor is safe, but that is not what ships are built for."
– John A. Shedd[1]

In early May 2021, investors were eagerly awaiting the investor presentation of The Great Eastern Shipping Company (GESCO) based on the financial performance of the January–March 2021 quarter and the financial year 2020–21 (FY21). An earnings conference call with analysts was also scheduled in a few days.

The latest figures had shown significant improvement in earnings, and GESCO's share price had seen a consistent increase over the past six months. Still, a difficult task lay ahead for GESCO's management to explain their strategies in managing the significant risks inherent in GESCO's business to investors and analysts who did not understand the shipping business.

GESCO's Business

Established in 1948, GESCO was India's largest non-government shipping company, owning 46 shipping vessels, 19 offshore vessels, and 4 jack-up rigs. It operated in four shipping segments – dry bulk, crude oil petroleum product and gas, and offshore support services for oil exploration and production (Exhibit 33.1). At the end of March 2021, the promoters held 29% of the shareholding, institutional investors 41%, corporates 6%, and retail investors around 23%.

India's seaborne trade had grown at a moderate annual rate of 4.7% between FY14 and FY19. Cargo carried by Indian ships had grown at an even slower rate of 2.9% in the same period. Indian ships carried less than

DOI: 10.4324/9781032724478-37

10% of Indian seaborne trade, and even this share was slowly reducing. While FY20 continued to be sluggish, the Covid-19 pandemic resulted in declining seaborne trade in FY21. Freight rates continued to remain highly volatile across segments, resulting in significant variation in profit margins.

GESCO's peers in India included Shipping Corporation of India, the largest government-owned shipping company and several smaller players, including Essar Shipping. There were several global competitors in each of GESCO's business segments.

Financial Performance

GESCO had reported a sharp deterioration in its EBITDA margins in FY18, which remained low till FY20 (Exhibit 33.2). It also reported net losses in FY18 and FY19 before reporting a moderate net profit in FY20. As freight rates in the dry bulk segment rose sharply, the company reported a significant increase in EBITDA margin and net profit in FY21. The average return on equity earned by GESCO had been lower than its cost of equity. The low returns affected its share price, which remained below the book value during the past five-year period (Exhibit 33.3).

The challenge in shareholder value creation was not unique to GESCO. During the past two decades, barring the FY05 to FY08 period, the shipping industry worldwide had failed to earn returns more than the cost of capital and maintain firm value above the asset value. Freight earnings were often inadequate to cover both operating and capital costs, except when occasionally events led to unexpected tightness in ships' supply, resulting in a short-lived spike in freight rates. The risks and volatility of the shipping industry were as significant challenges as were its slow growth and low profitability.

Despite its fluctuating profits, GESCO had been able to maintain a good credit profile (Exhibit 33.4). Crucially with adequate liquidity and unutilised borrowing capacity, it retained high flexibility to raise funds for investing in ships when required.

Risks and Risk Management

GESCO faced a wide range of risks in its business. The significant risks included currency risk, commodity price and interest rate risk, freight rate risks, liquidity risk, credit risk, environmental risk. In addition, it faced geopolitical risks, tightness in the availability of skilled personnel, and cybersecurity risks.

Currency risk: GESCO's currency risk arose because it earned revenues predominantly in US dollars. While most of its operating expenses were also denominated in US dollars, providing a natural currency hedge, it was

EXHIBIT 33.1 Fleet Profile of Shipping Business (7 May 2021)

Fleet	*Dead-weight Tonnes*	*Number of Ships*	*Average Age (Years)*
Crude Oil Tankers	1,164,215	9	13.64
Petroleum Product Tankers	1,092,465	18	13.11
Gas Carriers	250,687	6	17.85
Dry Bulk Ships	1,154,702	13	8.07
Total	**3,662,069**	**46**	**12.02**

Source: https://www.greatship.com/upload/investors/presentations/Quarterly_Updates_-_7May21_V1_16_to_9_Uploading_version_final.pdf
Note: The above excludes support vessels and equipment used by the offshore business.

EXHIBIT 33.2 Financial Trends

	Year Ended					
Rs Crore	*March 2016*	*March 2017*	*March 2018*	*March 2019*	*March 2020*	*March 2021*
Revenue (including other income)	**3,926**	**3,623**	**3,141**	**3,830**	**3,948**	**3,568**
EBITDA	2,103	1,937	1,303	1,336	1,428	1,840
EBIT	1,495	1,259	534	563	685	1,598
Net Profit	**1,097**	**755**	**(210)**	**(21)**	**207**	**919**
Total Assets	13,933	15,402	14,664	14,370	13,833	14,146
Total Equity	6,563	7,223	6,928	6,810	6,796	7,704
Total Debt	4,908	5,941	5,532	5,999	5,295	4,431
Cash and Current Investments	3,857	4,338	3,742	3,413	3,436	4,099
Net Debt	1,051	1,602	1,790	2,586	1,859	332
EBITDA Margin	53.6%	53.5%	41.5%	34.9%	36.2%	51.6%
Return on Capital Employed		10.2%	4.2%	4.5%	5.5%	13.2%
Return on Equity		**11.0%**	**−3.0%**	**−0.3%**	**3.0%**	**12.7%**
Net Debt/Equity		0.22	0.26	0.38	0.27	0.04
Credit Rating	CARE AAA BWR AAA	CARE AAA BWR AAA	CARE AAA BWR AAA	CARE AA+ BWR AAA	CARE AA+ BWR AAA	CARE AA+ BWR AAA
Market Capitalisation	4,701	6,288	4,979	4,296	3,025	4,596
Price/Book Value	**0.7**	**0.9**	**0.7**	**0.6**	**0.4**	**0.6**

Source: Capitaline database and authors' calculations.

EXHIBIT 33.3 Share Price Trend

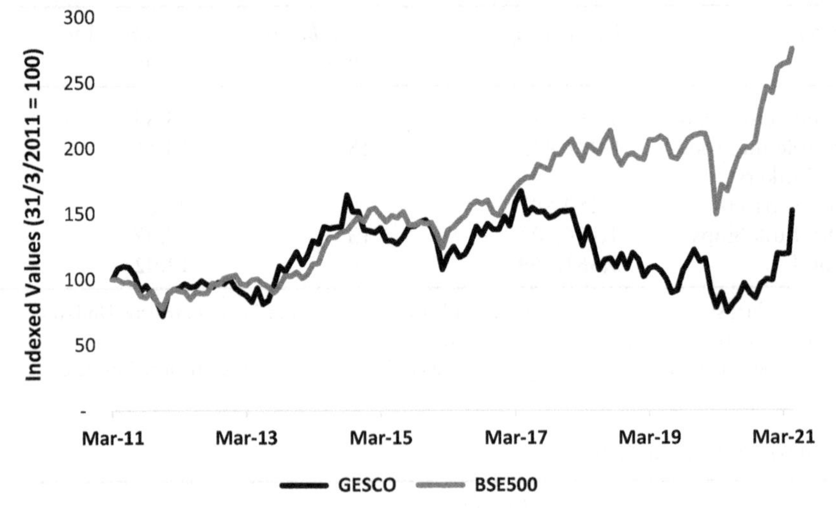

Source: Prepared by authors based on Bloomberg data.

EXHIBIT 33.4 Risk Comparison

	GESCO	*SCI*	*Shreyas*	*S&P BSE 500*
Beta	0.68	1.08	1.22	1.00
Net Debt/Equity	0.04	0.25	0.68	
Credit Rating	AA+	AA	BBB+ (Rating Watch)	
Standard deviation	0.44	0.56	0.68	0.22
Systematic Risk	0.02	0.06	0.07	0.05
Diversifiable Risk	0.17	0.26	0.39	–
Total Risk	0.19	0.32	0.46	0.05

Source: Authors' calculations.
Note: SCI: Shipping Corporation of India; Shreyas: Shreyas Shipping.

a foreign exchange earner on a net basis. The company hedged its currency risk by the sale of plain forward contracts and range forwards.

A range forward could be created by buying a put option with a lower strike price and writing a call with a higher strike price. The put option being a right to sell and writing the call option being an obligation to sell was consistent as GESCO needed to sell foreign currency. Effectively, as shown in Exhibit 33.5, below the lower strike price, the put provided protection. Between the two strike prices, the market price prevailed. Above the higher strike price, GESCO would have to forego the benefits of increased realisation. The range forward could be set at or near zero cost by adjusting the two strike prices. Compared with forward contracts, range forwards was more cost-effective since they allowed GESCO to assume some risk within an acceptable range.

The company had its shipping assets, receivables, and part of its cash and equivalents denominated in US dollars. To reduce the mismatch between foreign currency assets and liabilities, the company borrowed partly in US dollars in the form of amortising loans from ship financiers. For the same reason, the company also used swaps to convert its rupee liabilities on non-convertible debentures (NCDs) into synthetic US dollar debt (Exhibit 33.6). Compared to dollar loans, the synthetic dollar NCDs being non-amortising reduced the pressure on cash flows in the short term and were usually unsecured.

Commodity price risk: Commodity price risk arose due to volatility in bunker fuel prices (Exhibit 33.7), which formed a significant portion of the operating costs. Bunker prices were highly correlated with crude oil prices and had a low correlation with shipping freight rates. The company partially hedged its exposure to the fluctuating bunker costs by using swaps, call options, and fixed price forward contracts.

Interest rate risk: While 85% of the debt was at a fixed interest rate, the company had exposure to floating interest rate debt on USD loans from banks. To hedge its exposure to interest rate movements, GESCO used interest rate swaps, which enabled the company to convert its floating rate interest payments on borrowings to a fixed rate.

Liquidity risk: The company could potentially face liquidity risk either in terms of not being able to repay the loans or make payments for acquiring the ships. It handled the risk by keeping its leverage low. It also maintained sufficient balances of cash and liquid investments to enable the company to capitalise on any opportunities to buy ships when prices were attractive.

Credit risk: The company faced some credit risk due to a moderate level of trade receivables. The credit risk was low due to the high credit quality of customers. The historical collection experience of receivables was good with low levels of bad debts.

Environmental regulations: The International Maritime Organisation (IMO) mandated the IMO 2020 sulphur cap (at 0.5%), with effect from January 1, 2020. This regulation required companies to either make more fixed investments in scrubbers or convert their ships to use liquified natural gas, or buy more expensive low sulphur bunker fuel. GESCO had installed scrubbers on 5 out of its 46 ships and planned to install a scrubber on one more ship and use low sulphur fuel for the remaining vessels to deal with the regulation. Going ahead, sufficient availability of 0.5% sulphur fuel from refiners and the spread between low sulphur and high sulphur fuel prices were crucial factors for bunker costs.

Further, IMO also required ships entering international waters to install ballast water treatment systems (BWTS) to protect aquatic species. GESCO

EXHIBIT 33.5 Illustration of Range Forward to Hedge Currency Risk

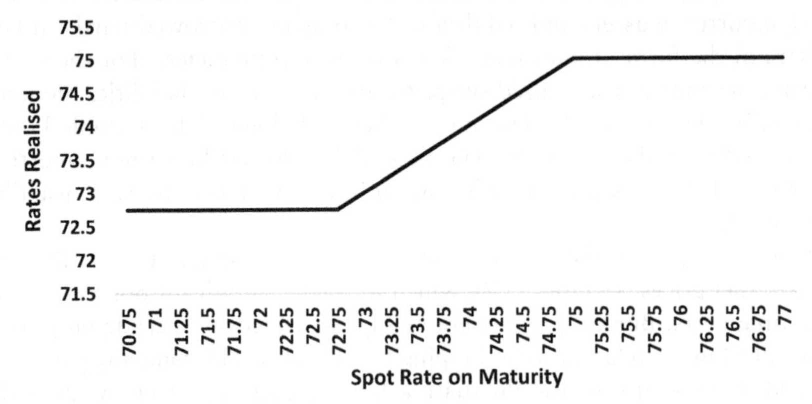

Source: Illustration prepared by authors.

EXHIBIT 33.6 Illustration of Currency Swap to Convert INR Liability to USD

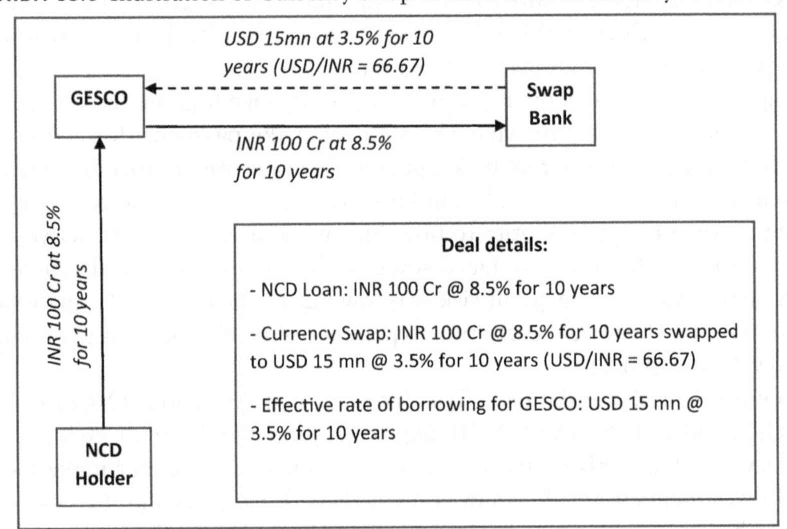

Source: Prepared by authors.

had installed BWTS in 9 vessels and planned to install BWTS in 35 additional ships at the time of their next dry dock over the next five years.

Freight rate volatility: Shipping freight rates tended to be highly volatile (Exhibit 33.8). For comparison, the annualised volatility of changes in the Baltic dry index (which tracked spot freights rates of dry bulk cargo) was

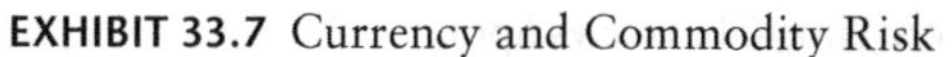

EXHIBIT 33.7 Currency and Commodity Risk

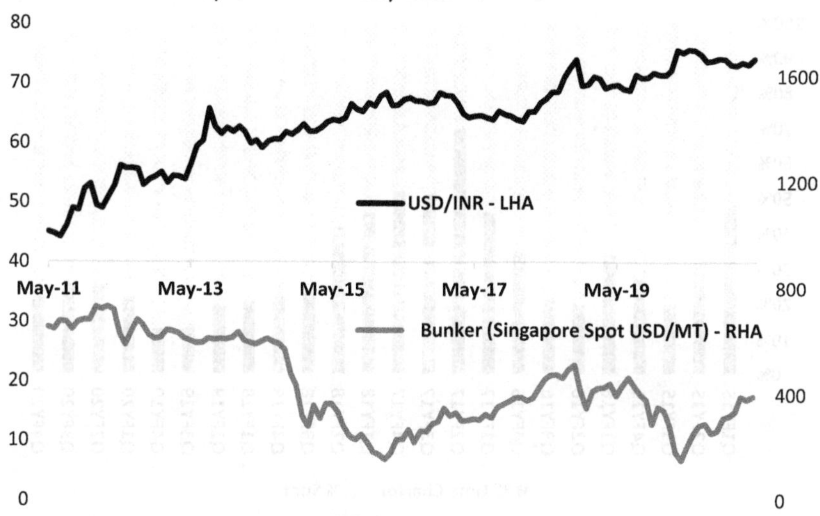

Source: Prepared by authors based on Bloomberg data.

EXHIBIT 33.8 Volatility in Freight Rates

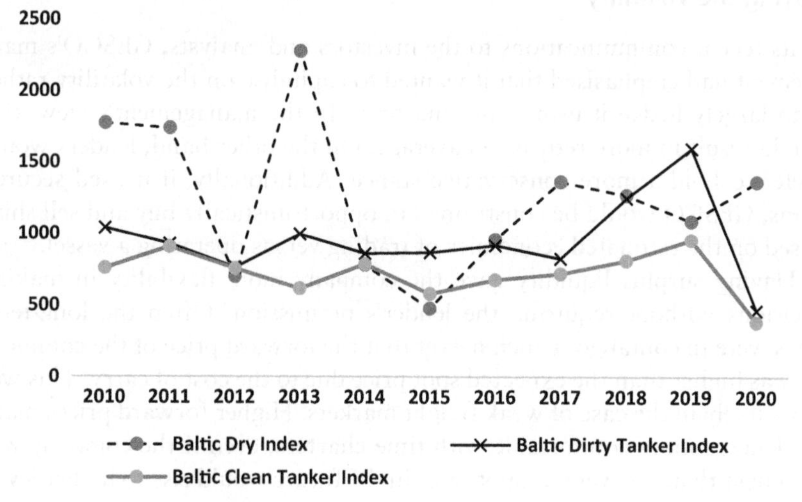

Source: Prepared by authors based on Bloomberg data.

around three times that of crude oil and five times that of the Nifty 50 index. While the company had earlier been fixing the freight rates using time charter contracts, the company had consciously increased its exposure to spot freight rates over the past three years (Exhibit 33.9). This change exposed it to a high risk of loss if the spot freight rates were inadequate to cover the costs but allowed it to take advantage of opportunities to gain from sharp increases in freight rates.

EXHIBIT 33.9 Share of Tonnage Days on Time Charter vs Spot

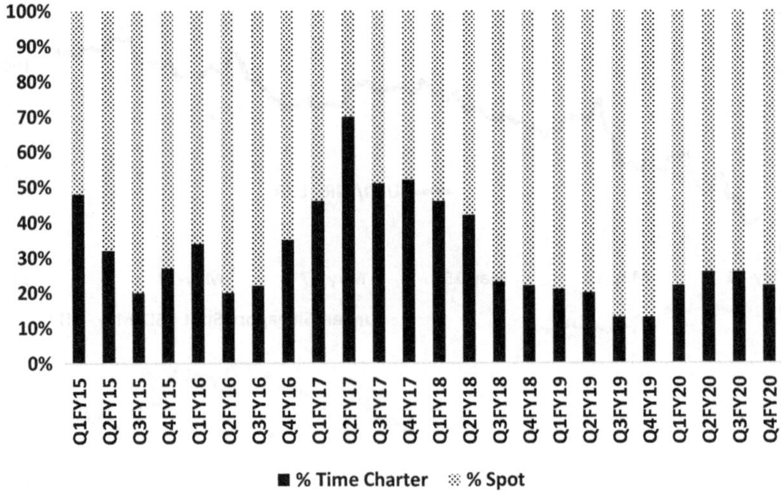

Source: Prepared by authors based on Great Eastern Shipping's investor presentations.

Playing the Volatility

In its recent communications to the investors and analysts, GESCO's management had emphasised that it wanted to capitalise on the volatility rather than largely hedge it using time charters.[2] In the management's view, this would result in more returns on average. On the other hand, lenders would prefer to hold a more conservative stance. Additionally, if it used secured loans, GESCO would be constrained to opportunistically buy and sell ships based on the estimated economics of trading versus operating a vessel.

Having surplus liquidity gave the company more flexibility in making decisions without requiring the lender's permission. Often the long-term rates were in contango, which meant that the forward price of the commodity was higher than the expected spot price due to the cost of carry. This was more likely in the case of weak freight markets. Higher forward prices made the lenders more comfortable with time charters, even if the company was confident that, on average, spot rates in the future would rise to higher levels than the time charter rates.

For instance, in April 2016, Capesize dry bulk ships earned around US$ 2,000 per day in the spot market, which was below the operating expenses. At that time, the 3-year time charter rates were around US$ 8,000 per day, which would have resulted in positive EBITDA. However, average spot rates in the subsequent three years were around US$ 13,500 per day. If the company could anticipate the increase, it would have the freedom to act on its judgement and keep its exposure open to spot freight rates, whereas the lender would have preferred locking in at the time charter rates.

It was plausible for shipping industry experts to predict the long-term direction of freight rates for each segment by forecasting the freight demand and shipping tonnage supply. For instance, it was evident that long-term demand for product tankers would plateau and even decline with the falling consumption of auto fuels due to the shift towards electric vehicles. Further, using the data of new ships being built, the rate at which ships were being demolished, and prices for second-hand vessels, experienced and skilled managements and analysts could make calculated assessments regarding the future.

Short-term predictions were more complex. There were geopolitical factors to consider, such as OPEC's behaviour or the trade war between China and the US. Unexpected events such as the outbreak of the Covid-19 pandemic in early 2020 or the blockage of the Suez Canal in March–April 2020–21 often made short-term forecasts worthless, given the high sensitivity of freight rates to changes in demand or supply.

Therefore, different shipping companies adopted varying stances in taking exposure to freight rate volatility, with varied financial consequences in different periods. For instance, a dry bulk shipping company that tended to follow a chartering strategy with the entire fleet on time charters would have fared better in the first half of 2020 when the Covid-19 pandemic resulted in a sharp decline in freight rates. However, it would miss out on the ten-year peak in freight rates in early 2021 due to the strong revival in Chinese demand for commodities.

GESCO's management had to read the markets right and make its choices carefully. To play with volatility it had to navigate turbulent waters.

Questions

1. What is the difference between hedging risks and managing risks? Categorise GESCO's approach to dealing with its various risks as hedging or managing.
2. Does either hedging risks or taking risk exposures add value to GESCO's shareholders? Use the discounted cash flow valuation framework and capital asset pricing model to frame your answer.

Notes

1 Shedd, J. A. (1928). Salt from my attic. Mosher Press.
2 Investor Presentation, August 2020.

PART IV

Capital Structure and Dividend Decisions

34

THE HOTEL INDUSTRY'S LEVERAGE AT PLAY

Fast-Mover Midcap Fund follows an active investing strategy where it trades stocks based on expected performance in six to twelve months. The fund's research team has selected two stocks from the hotel industry, Oaktree Hotels and Serenity Hotels (Exhibit 34.1). As a research analyst working with the fund, your task is to recommend only one hotel stock to the fund manager.

You have assumed that the revenues of both the hotels will rise in the next year by five per cent only because of the increase in occupancy rates and no planned addition to capacity. You expect changes in average room rates and costs to be negligible. You reckon that both the hotels' price to earnings ratios would not change, and their dividend yields are too small to make a difference to the investment decision. Which hotel stock do you think will provide a higher investment return?

The above is an example of the effects of operating leverage and financial leverage. Operating leverage is prominent in sectors that have high fixed costs, such as hotels, hospitals, airlines, and information technology. The most common fixed cost heads include fixed employee expenses, depreciation, and fixed overheads. Since fixed costs do not increase with the level of business activity, operating profits grow much more than the revenue growth in the presence of operating leverage.

Just like operating leverage, financial leverage works with interest as the fixed cost. Since interest expenses do not change with the level of business activity, the net profits and earnings per share can increase much more than the rise in operating profits in the presence of financial leverage. The combined effect of operating and financial leverage is multiplicative; that is, for

DOI: 10.4324/9781032724478-39

EXHIBIT 34.1 Comparative Profit and Loss Statements of Two Hotel Companies

Rs Crore	*Oaktree Hotels*	*Serenity Hotels*
Revenues	**200.0**	**46.0**
Food and Beverage Expenses	20.0	5.0
Employee Benefit Expenses	50.0	8.0
Depreciation and Amortisation	25.0	7.0
Other Expenses	75.0	11.0
Total Operating Expenses	**170.0**	**31.0**
EBIT	**30.0**	**15.0**
Interest	15.0	-
EBT	**15.0**	**15.0**
Tax (25%)	3.8	3.8
Profit after Tax	11.3	11.3
Number of Shares	2.4	2.8
Earnings per Share	4.7	4.0
P/E	19.2	19.6
Share Price	90.0	78.8

Source: Prepared by authors.
Note: Assume that variable costs include only food and beverage expenses.

a 1% increase in the business level, the percentage increase in net profit and EPS of the company is the product of its operating leverage and financial leverage. Exhibit 34.2 provides the estimation formulas for the degree of leverage.

EXHIBIT 34.2 Degree of Leverage Estimation Formulas

	Formula by Definition	*Formula Based on Cost Structure*
Degree of Operating Leverage (DOL)	$\frac{\%\text{Change in EBIT}}{\%\text{Change in Sales}}$	$\frac{\text{Sales-Variable Costs}}{\text{Sales-Variable Costs-Fixed Costs}}$
Degree of Financial Leverage (DFL)	$\frac{\%\text{Change in EBT}}{\%\text{Change in EBIT}}$	$\frac{\text{EBIT}}{\text{EBIT} - \text{Interest}}$
Degree of Total Leverage (DTL) = DOL × DFL	$\frac{\%\text{Change in EBIT}}{\%\text{Change in Sales}}$	$\frac{\text{Sales-Variable Costs}}{\text{Sales-Variable Costs-Fixed Costs-Interest}}$

Source: Prepared by authors.

Leverage is a double-edged sword. The multiplicative effect of leverage works in a company's favour when volumes increase but can become adverse when business levels fall. In this way, the presence of leverage magnifies both the opportunity and the risk for the company.

The Shift to Asset-Light Models

In the past three decades, many hotel chains across the world have shifted their business strategies to become asset-light. Starting with Marriott International and Hilton Hotels in the 1980s, major hotel companies have reduced the property assets on their balance sheets and have increased the focus on the less-capital-intensive business of operating the hotels for fees.

By splitting the hotel management from real estate, hotel companies can lower their operational risks and exposure to real estate sector risks, grow faster, expand their market shares with lesser capital, reduce their debt, and increase business and financial flexibility. Management agreements and franchising are two standard asset-light models. In management agreements, the hotel operator enters a contract with the hotel owner to undertake all the responsibilities of operating and managing the hotel. The hotel operator earns a management fee, including a fixed component and a profit share. The asset owner retains the residual returns and risks.

In franchising, there is a licence agreement between the hotel brand owner and the hotel owner, which gives the hotel owner the right to operate the hotel under the brand. The hotel owner controls the asset and retains the returns and risks but must pay fees for the franchise, marketing, and royalty to use the brand name. While management contracts reduce the asset intensity of the business, franchising reduces both the asset and employment intensity.

Management fee and franchise income are relatively stable and result in lower operating leverage, protecting the firms from adverse shocks. The downside of the asset-light model is the risk that the asset owner may not renew the management agreement or may renegotiate the terms in its favour. Further, the management fee or franchise-based business is suitable only for major players with competitive advantages in adopting this model, like size and brand name.

Though the shift to asset-light strategies is an old idea, the trend accelerated in the US and Europe after the global financial crisis, when the hotel majors saw their profits and market value dwindle. The international hotel majors have used asset-light arrangements, especially franchising, to operate in India.

The Indian hotel companies, on the other hand, started to shift to the asset-light models only in the past decade. The Indian Hotels Company

EXHIBIT 34.3 Comparison of Hotel Companies on Share of Asset-Light Business, Margins, and Leverage

	Year Ending	*Fee-Income Ratio*	*PPE/ Assets*	*EBIT Margin*	*Debt/EBITDA*
Marriott International	Dec 2019	18%	8%	8.6%	3.79
Hilton Worldwide	Dec 2019	24%	3%	17.5%	4.70
InterContinental Hotels	Dec 2019	33%	20%	13.6%	2.88
Hyatt Hotels	Dec 2019	12%	47%	18.9%	3.89
Indian Hotels	Mar 2020	5%	59%	12.6%	4.61
EIH Ltd.	Mar 2020	–	55%	9.0%	1.24
Lemon Tree Hotels	Mar 2020	1%	76%	22.6%	7.13
Chalet Hotels	Mar 2020	–	56%	23.4%	5.09

Source: Company annual reports and authors' calculations.

(which owns the Taj Group of Hotels) primarily operated, owned or leased hotel properties in 2010. By March 2020, 42% of its hotel rooms were under management contracts. It earned around 5% of its revenues in 2019–20 as fees from managing hotels. A few other major hotel players, including EIH Ltd, which owns the Oberoi and Trident hotels, ITC Hotels (a division of ITC Ltd) and Lemon Tree Hotels, also operated hotels under a management contract. However, the share of fee income in revenues of Indian hotel companies had been much smaller compared to the global majors (Exhibit 34.3). Further, the use of the franchising model had been somewhat limited, compared with the global majors who mainly preferred the franchise model for increasing their global footprint.

Hotel companies in India decided to pursue productivity enhancement measures during the 2016–17 to 2019–20 period to offset the adverse effect of slower economic growth. For Indian hotels, the shift to asset-light strategies and increasing productivity significantly improved the EBIT margin and financial leverage (Exhibit 34.4). Lemon Tree Hotels and Chalet Hotels, having relatively newer properties, did not have legacy high employee costs, unlike the older chains. However, they required significant capital investment to support growth resulting in the build-up of financial leverage (Exhibits 34.5 and 34.6).

The Pandemic's Magnified Effect

The onset of the Covid-19 pandemic in early 2020 tested the preparedness of hotels for a negative shock. The combination of lockdowns and high fixed costs

EXHIBIT 34.4 Financial Trends of The Indian Hotels Company

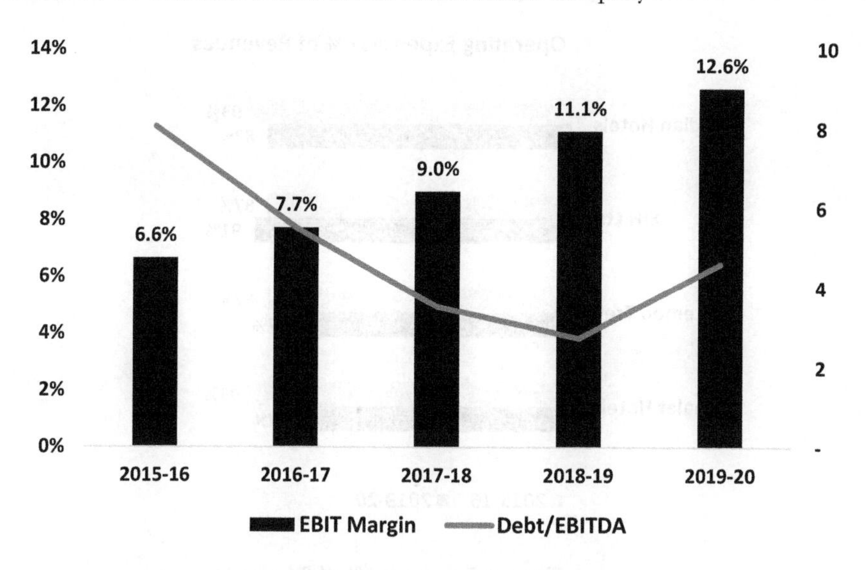

Source: Company annual reports and authors' calculations.

caused considerable losses to the hotels. The degree of leverage was apparent in the transmission from revenue decline to operating profit and further to the bottom-line (Exhibit 34.7). Regardless of their business models, cost structure and productivity, almost all the hotels made operating and net losses.

EXHIBIT 34.5 Cost Structure of Select Hotel Companies in India (2019–20)

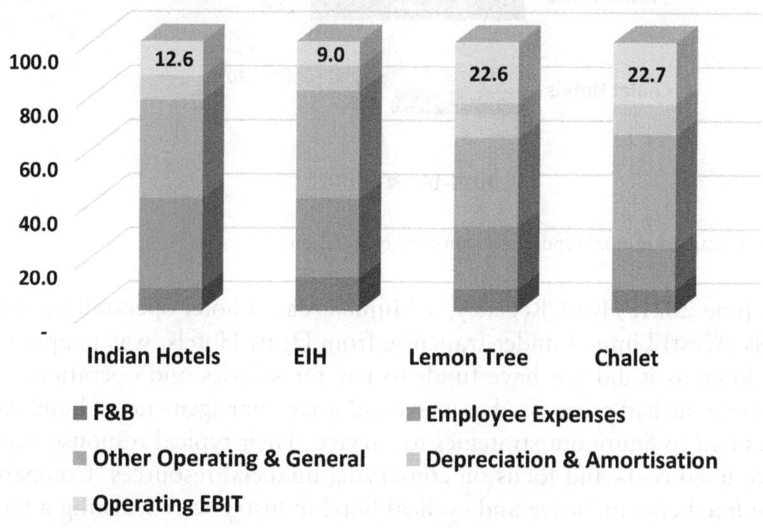

Source: Company annual reports and authors' calculations.

EXHIBIT 34.6 Change in Operating and Finance Costs of Indian Hotel Companies

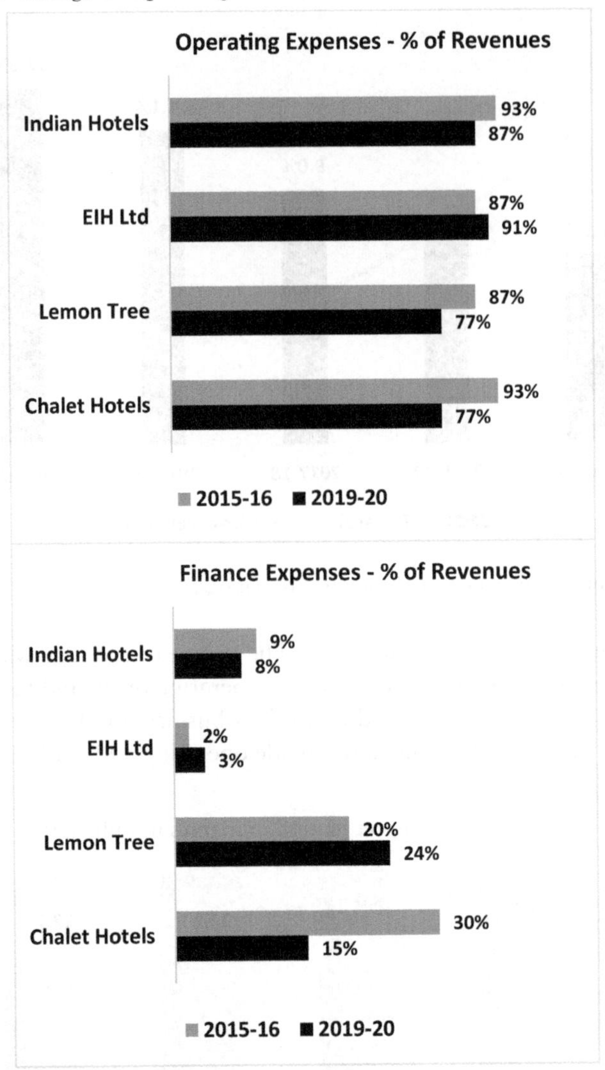

Source: Company annual reports and authors' calculations.

In June 2021, Hyatt Regency, a Mumbai-based hotel operated by Asian Hotels (West) Limited under franchise from Hyatt Hotels, was temporarily shut down as it did not have funds to pay for salaries and operations.[1] As the pandemic had progressed to its second wave, managements of hotel companies had to figure out strategies to survive. Their typical response was to reduce fixed costs and focus on conserving financial resources. Companies in the fixed cost-intensive and cyclical hotel industry were learning a harsh lesson the hard way.

EXHIBIT 34.7 Effect of Leverage on Hotel Bottom-lines during Covid-19 Pandemic

	FY 2020	*FY 2021*	*% Change*
Marriott (USD million)	Dec 2019	Dec 2020	
Revenue	20,972	10,571	-50%
EBIT	1,800	84	-95%
EBT	1,599	(466)	-129%
Hilton Worldwide (USD million)	Dec 2019	Dec 2020	
Revenue	9,452	4,307	-54%
EBIT	1,657	(466)	-128%
EBT	1,244	(924)	-174%
InterContinental Hotels Group (USD million)	Dec 2019	Dec 2020	
Revenue	4,627	2,394	-48%
EBIT	630	(155)	-125%
EBT	542	(282)	-152%
Hyatt Hotels (USD million)	Dec 2019	Dec 2020	
Revenue	5,020	2,066	-59%
EBIT	947	(831)	-188%
EBT	1,006	(960)	-195%
Indian Hotels (Rs crore)	Mar 2020	Mar 2021	
Revenue	4,463	1,575	-65%
EBIT	563	(771)	-237%
EBT	355	(1,009)	-385%
EIH Ltd (Rs crore)	Mar 2020	Mar 2021	
Revenue	1,596	497	-69%
EBIT	144	(425)	-395%
EBT	167	(412)	-347%
Lemon Tree Hotels (Rs crore)	Mar 2020	Mar 2021	
Revenues	669	252	-62%
EBIT	151	(46)	-131%
EBT	0	(215)	n.m.
Chalet Hotels (Rs crore)	Mar 2020	Mar 2021	
Revenues	955	274	-71%
EBIT	223	(110)	-149%
EBT	105	(240)	-329%

Source: Company annual reports and authors' calculations.

Questions

1. Estimate the degree of operating leverage, degree of financial leverage, and total leverage for both hotel companies. Use the formulas provided in Exhibit 34.2.
2. Predict the change in EBIT and EPS of both the companies if revenues increase by 5% only due to demand increase and unit costs remain the same.

3. Was it a good strategy to select among the two hotel stocks based upon the predicted EPS? Explain.
4. Explain how shifting to asset-light models would affect the degree of leverage.
5. Explain the effect of the pandemic on the profits of hotel players (Exhibit 34.7) using the degree of leverage.

Note

1 https://www.livemint.com/companies/news/hyatt-regency-mumbai-closed-until-further-notice-due-to-fund-crunch-11623079650136.html

35

AVENUE SUPERMARTS' CAPITAL STRUCTURE

Nikhil Adalja had moved to the last valuation lever for Avenue Supermarts Ltd (ASL) – its cost of capital. He wondered why ASL's management had been so conservative in terms of its capital structure. He reasoned that using some more debt in the capital structure would reduce the cost of capital and consequently increase the company's value.

As a sell-side equity research analyst, Nikhil had a set template and process for the valuation of companies, primarily using discounted cash flows (DCF). After completing his draft spreadsheet workings, Nikhil used to compare his valuation with the current market price. Though Nikhil believed that stocks were often mispriced, he had learnt to respect the market's view. He would try to consider alternative scenarios on critical variables driving the valuation to try and understand which set of assumptions had been priced in by the market. Nikhil felt confident while issuing either a buy or a sell recommendation for a stock once he had strong reasons to differ from the back-fitted assumptions that would justify the market price.

He had already gone over and changed the operating margin and revenue growth assumptions but still found that his DCF value fell short of the market value as of October 30, 2020. He, therefore, wanted to check the cost of capital estimate and test a range of values using a sensitivity analysis data table in his spreadsheet. While he was reasonably sure of other determinants of the cost of capital, he realised that assuming a nearly debt-free capital structure had been a constraining factor.

Nikhil had seen that ASL's management had not explicitly provided any direction or rationale for its debt policy from the past filings and analyst conference call transcripts. He, therefore, planned to list down all the relevant factors that ASL's management may have considered while deciding its

DOI: 10.4324/9781032724478-40

capital structure and financing choices. He would then go over each aspect and make his final call about what debt to equity ratio he would expect the management to maintain over its various phases of future growth.

Avenue Supermarts' Business

Incorporated in May 2002, Avenue Supermarts operated supermarket chains in India under the brand name D-Mart. It retailed products in the foods, fast-moving consumer goods, general merchandise, and apparel categories. As of the end of March 2020, 214 D-Mart stores operated across India with an aggregate area of 7.8 million sq. ft.

According to CRISIL Research, the retail sector in India would grow at 11.5–12% per annum from about Rs 66 trillion in 2019–20 to Rs 104 trillion by Rs 2023–24, compared with an annual rate of 12% during 2013–14 to 2019–20. Rising income levels and increased consumer spending were driving the retail sector's growth. However, small stores in the informal sector dominated the industry. The share of organised retailing would increase at 19–21%, reaching Rs 15.5 to Rs 16 trillion by 2023–24.[1]

The organised brick and mortar retail industry faced a significant increase in the intensity of competition due to rising investments, including from multinational players in both physical and online retailing. The key competitors for ASL included Reliance Retail, Future Retail, and Aditya Birla Retail among physical retailers and Flipkart and Amazon India among online retailers. In addition, several smaller competitors specialised in verticals such as foods or apparels.

Avenue Supermarts offered low prices to its customers across product subcategories and on all days, rather than the usual practice followed by some competitors offering discounts selectively on some products or specific days of the week. It called this strategy the Everyday Low Cost/Everyday Low Price (EDLC/EDLP) principle. The EDLC/EDLP strategy entailed maintaining low procurement, supply, and operation costs to enable competitive pricing of its products.

The D-Mart stores stocked products that catered to basic needs rather than discretionary spending. To further support its low-cost strategy, the company owned rather than leased its store space, procured its goods directly from vendors, built an efficient distribution and logistics system, and kept minimal inventories. ASL also paid its suppliers promptly to avail of purchase discounts. It also maintained flexibility in its operational costs by having a large proportion of employees on contracts and procuring its products on a purchase order basis rather than by long-term supply arrangements.

ASL was unique among its peers regarding minimal use of suppliers' credit and in predominantly owning rather than leasing its stores. In response to a query from a stock analyst, Neville Noronha, the Managing Director mentioned that ASL would continue with its ownership-based model in the future:

> *we do lease, but like I said most of the properties are owned; leasing would be 20%–30% if we intend to, we will not cross beyond that.*[2]

From 2015–16 to 2019–20, ASL witnessed a 30% annual growth in revenues, 34% growth in EBITDA, and 44% growth in profit after tax. The yearly growth of 25% in the retail business area and 4% in revenue per square feet explained the revenue increase. Efficiency ratios were maintained, with fixed asset turnover being in the range of 4.0 to 4.4 and inventory turnover in the range of 14.2 to 14.9. As a result, ASL enjoyed a healthy return on equity of about 16% in 2019–20 (see Exhibits 35.1, 35.2, 35.3, and 35.7).

Fund-Raising

ASL raised Rs 1,841 crore through an initial public offer (IPO) in March 2017. The company used the IPO proceeds to repay Rs 1,080 crore of debt, Rs 367 crore for capital expenditure on new stores, and the rest for general corporate purposes. In February 2020, ASL raised equity of Rs 4,098 crore through a qualified institutional placement (QIP). The proceeds were to be used to repay part of the debt and for general corporate purpose. In addition, the sale of equity would enable ASL to meet the minimum norm for public shareholding.

The company also raised long-term borrowings in the form of term loans from banks or non-convertible debentures (NCDs) from the market. For example, it raised NCDs of Rs 250 crore in 2016–17 and Rs 300 crore in 2019–20. The NCDs it issued in September–October 2019 were redeemed early by March 2020. It also issued commercial papers to raise Rs 787 crore in 2018–19 and Rs 789 crore in 2019–20.

Due to the IPO and QIP equity issues, ASL could either repay its debt on or before schedule or not utilise its total borrowing capacity. For example, at the end of March 2020, ASL had undrawn committed borrowing facilities from banks of Rs 941 crore. As a result, the company has comfortable solvency and liquidity. At the end of March 2020, ASL's debt to equity ratio was 0.03 on a gross basis and 0.02 net of cash and current investments. Its current ratio was 3.23 (see Exhibits 35.4 and 35.5).

ASL's credit rating rationale issued by CRISIL in October 2020 noted that due to the added liquidity from the QIP funds, the company would be able to meet its required capital investment for nearly 100 stores over the next three years, mainly from internal accruals. CRISIL had reaffirmed ASL's long-term rating at AA+, noting sustenance of gearing below 0.20 as an upward factor and a weakening of gearing to above 0.50 as a downward factor.

EXHIBIT 35.1 Avenue Supermarts Ltd: Consolidated Balance Sheet

(Rs Crore)	*Mar 2017*	*Mar 2018*	*Mar 2019*	*Mar 2020*
Assets				
Non-Current Assets				
Property, Plant and Equipment	2,544	3,276	4,274	5,107
Capital Work-in-Progress	153	147	377	364
Right to Use Assets	–	–	–	717
Investment Properties	27	16	18	17
Goodwill	–	78	78	78
Intangible Assets	6	29	30	29
Financial Assets	59	42	32	3,123
Other Non-Current Assets	51	87	114	294
Total Non-Current Assets	2,841	3,676	4,923	9,729
Current Assets				
Inventories	948	1,163	1,609	1,947
Trade Receivables	21	34	64	20
Investments	4	68	17	15
Cash and Cash Equivalents	33	67	125	106
Bank Balances Other than Cash and Cash Equivalents	1,851	493	94	2
Other Current Assets	121	147	174	258
Total Current Assets	2,979	1,972	2,083	2,348
Total Assets	**5,819**	**5,648**	**7,006**	**12,076**
Equity and Liabilities				
Equity Share Capital	624	624	624	648
Other Equity	3,218	4,045	4,963	10,432
Non-Controlling Interest	0	1	1	0
Total Equity	3,842	4,670	5,588	11,080
Liabilities				
Non-Current Liabilities				
Borrowings	981	246	126	–
Lease Liability	–	–	–	221
Other Non-Current Liabilities and Provisions	52	47	65	49
Total Non-Current Liabilities	1,033	293	191	270
Current Liabilities				
Borrowings	139	7	304	4
Lease Liability	–	–	–	74
Trade Payables	261	317	463	433
Current Maturities of Long-Term Debt	378	186	270	34
Other Current Financial Liabilities	126	151	127	144
Other Current Liabilities and Provisions	41	25	63	36
Total Current Liabilities	944	686	1,227	726
Total Equity and Liabilities	**5,819**	**5,648**	**7,006**	**12,076**

Source: Prepared by authors based on Avenue Supermarts Ltd annual reports.

EXHIBIT 35.2 Avenue Supermarts Ltd: Statement of Consolidated Cash Flows

(Rs Crore)	*2016–17*	*2017–18*	*2018–19*	*2019–20*
Cash Flow from Pperating Activities				
Profit before Tax	760	1,204	1,422	1,745
Adjustments for:				
Depreciation and Amortisation Expenses	128	159	212	374
Finance Cost	122	60	47	69
Dividend, Interest and Rent Income	(20)	(48)	(27)	(35)
Profit on Sale of Propery, Plant, Equipment, and Investment	(7)	(20)	(12)	(13)
Expense on Employee Stock Option Scheme	1	22	17	8
Operating Profit before Working Capital Changes	984	1,375	1,659	2,149
Adjustments for:				
Decrease (increase) in Inventories	(276)	(212)	(445)	(339)
Decrease (increase) in Trade Receivables	(13)	(13)	(31)	45
Increase (decrease) in Trade Payables	66	55	146	(30)
Other Changes	(48)	(73)	(21)	(52)
Cash Flow from Operating Activities	713	1,133	1,309	1,773
Direct Taxes Paid (net of Refunds)	(258)	(403)	(502)	(492)
Net Cash Flow from Operating Activities	**455**	**730**	**807**	**1,280**
Cash Flow from Investing Activities				
Purchase of PPE/ Intangible Assets/ Investments	(645)	(916)	(1,417)	(1,712)
Proceeds from Disposal of Property, Plant and Equipment	10	7	8	6
Investment in Associate	(13)	(42)	–	-
Gain on Sale of Investments	0	17	11	10
Interest and Rent Incomes Received	17	36	40	15
IPO Proceeds in Bank, Pending Utilisation	(1,850)	–	-	-
Realisation from FDs of IPO Proceeds	–	1,359	399	93
QIP Proceeds Deposited in FD	–	–	–	(3,197)
Realisation from FDs of QIP Proceeds	–	–	–	129
Net Cash Flow (used in)/ from Investing Activities	(2,482)	462	(958)	(4,657)
Cash Flow from Financing Activities				
Proceeds from Issue of Shares (net of IPO expenses)	1,841	–	–	–
Proceeds from Issue of QIP (net of expenses)				4,077

(Continued)

EXHIBIT 35.2 Continued

(Rs Crore)	*2016–17*	*2017–18*	*2018–19*	*2019–20*
Proceeds from Exercise of Share Options				110
Proceeds from Long-Term Borrowings	200	–	150	50
Repayment of Long-Term borrowings	(155)	(542)	(16)	(200)
Proceeds from Non-Convertible Debentures	250	–	–	300
Repayment of Non-Convertible Debentures	–	(384)	(170)	(512)
Proceeds from Short-Term Borrowings	60	–	55	261
Repayment of Short-Term Borrowings	–	(153)	(5)	(315)
Proceeds from Commercial Papers	–	–	787	789
Repayment of Commercial Papers	(50)	–	(541)	(1,035)
Payment of Lease Liability	–	–	–	(100)
Interest Paid	(120)	(80)	(51)	(68)
Cash Flow (used in)/ from Financing Activities	**2,025**	**(1,159)**	**209**	**3,357**
Net Increase/(decrease) in Cash and Cash Equivalent	(1)	33	57	(19)
Cash and Cash Equivalents at the Beginning of the Year	34	33	67	125
Cash Acquired on Acquisition	–	2	–	–
Cash and Cash Equivalents at the End of the Year	33	67	125	106

Source: Prepared by authors based on Avenue Supermarts Ltd annual reports.

Despite healthy and growing profits, ASL did not pay out any dividends to its shareholders. ASL's Annual Report of 2019–20 provided the following reason for not paying any dividend:

> *With a view to conserve resources for expansion of business, your Directors have thought it prudent not to recommend any dividend for the financial year under review.*

Ownership and Management

Radhakishan Damani, a noted investor and one of the wealthiest persons in India,[3] had promoted ASL. Damani held in his portfolio companies including

EXHIBIT 35.3 Avenue Supermarts Ltd: Statement of Consolidated Profit and Loss

(Rs Crore)	*2016–17*	*2017–18*	*2018–19*	*2019–20*
Income				
Revenue from Operations	11,898	15,033	20,005	24,870
Other Income	29	69	48	60
Total Income	11,926	15,103	20,053	24,930
Expenses				
Purchase of Stock-in-Trade	10,357	12,847	17,445	21,442
Changes in Inventories of Stock-in-Trade	(276)	(211)	(445)	(339)
Employees Benefits Expense	193	283	355	456
Finance Costs	122	60	47	69
Depreciation and Amortisation Expense	128	159	212	374
Other Expenses	643	762	1,015	1,183
Total Expenses	11,166	13,899	18,631	23,185
Profit before Share of Loss of Associate	760	1,204	1,422	1,745
Share of Net Loss of Associate	(13)	18	-	-
Profit before Tax	747	1,222	1,422	1,745
Total Tax Expenses	268	416	519	444
Net Profit after Tax	479	806	902	1,301

Source: Prepared by authors based on Avenue Supermarts Ltd annual reports.

VST Industries, India Cements, Blue Dart, etc. However, ASL accounted for more than 80% of his equity portfolio by value.

The promoter family held 82.2% of the ASL's shareholding after the IPO. They had to bring down the shareholding to 75% by March 2020, three years after listing the stock, to meet SEBI's norm for a minimum public shareholding of 25%. At the end of September 2020, the promoters held a 75% stake. The share of institutional investors had increased to 16.4% from 5% at the time of listing. The percentage of non-institutional shareholders had declined to only 8.6% (Exhibit 35.8).

ASL had experienced senior management, with several senior executives, including the Managing Director and the CFO, having spent more than a decade with the company. The promoter family had no executive role in the company.

Weighing the Factors

Nikhil accessed his study notes on factors relevant for capital structure choice (see text box below) and prepared a working plan to check each

EXHIBIT 35.4 Historical Capital Structure

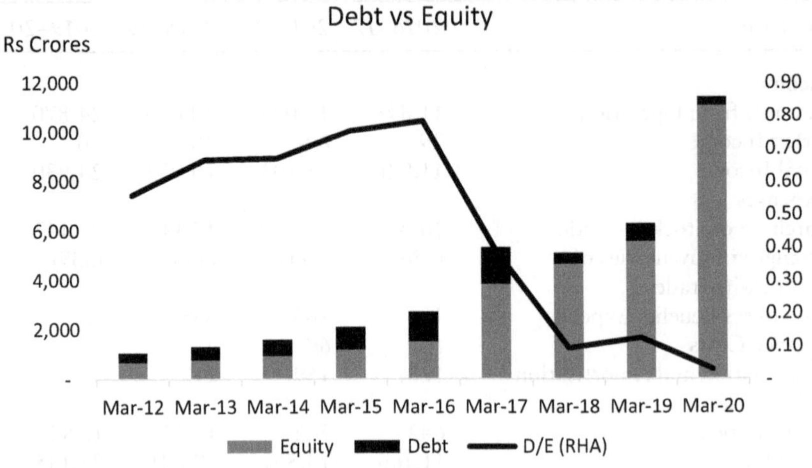

Source: Capitaline database and authors' calculations.

EXHIBIT 35.5 Avenue Supermarts Ltd: Debt Structure

(Rs Crore)	*Mar 2017*	*Mar 2018*	*Mar 2019*	*Mar 2020*
Long-Term Debt				
Term Loans from Banks[1]	382	–	92	–
Non-Convertible Debentures[1,2]	599	246	34	–
Lease Liabilities	–	–	–	221
Total Long-Term Debt	**981**	**246**	**126**	**221**
Short-Term Debt				
Working Capital Loans from Banks[3,4]	139	7	8	4
Term Loans (short term) from banks	-	–	50	–
Current maturities of term loans from banks	177	16	58	–
Current maturities of non-convertible debentures	201	170	212	34
Lease liabilities	-	–	–	74
Commercial paper		–	246	–
Total short term debt	516	193	574	112
Total Debt	1,497	439	700	333

Source: Prepared by authors based on Avenue Supermarts Ltd annual reports.

Notes:

[1] Secured by way to mortgage of specific stores.

[2] Rate of interest on NCD of Rs 34 crore due for redemption in Aug 2020 is 9.4%.

[3] Secured by hypothecation of inventories and trade receivables.

[4] The group had undrawn committed borrowing facilities from banks (Mar 2020: Rs 940.53 crore, Mar 2019: Rs 713.28 crore, Mar 2018: Rs 201.51 crore.

EXHIBIT 35.6 Key Debt and Valuation Metrics of Key Listed Peers

Rs Crores	*Avenue Supermarts*	*Trent Ltd*	*Future Retail*	*Future Lifestyle*	*V-Mart Retail*	*Aditya Birla Fashion*	*Shoppers Stop*
Debt	329	–	10,400	1,186	47	5,267	2,275
Net Debt	249	–	10,335	1,106	43	5,087	2,186
Equity (Book Value)	11,321	2,170	3,126	1,028	408	997	-128
Equity (Market Value)	142,714	23,885	4,886	1,801	3,594	10,943	1,523
Return on Equity (%)	15.6	6.1	0.8	-3.1	11.4	-13.1	-29.0
Dividend Payout (%)	0.0	29.0	–	–	6.3	–	–
Credit Rating	AA+	AA+	BB+	BBB-	AA-	AA	A+
Beta	0.84	1.08	1.50	1.07	1.16	0.96	1.38

Source: Prepared by authors based on Bloomberg data.

Notes:

1. All figures are outstanding as on September 30, 2020, except return on equity and dividend payout which are for the financial year 2019–20.
2. Beta estimated based on regression of three-year weekly returns ending September 2020 with S&P BSE 500.
3. At the end of October 2020, the rates of ten-Year G-Sec, AAA, AA, and A securities were 5.88%, 6.67%, 7.40%, and 8.86%, respectively.
4. The equity market risk premium at the end of October 2020 may be assumed to be 8%.
5. The applicable tax rate may be assumed to be 25.17%.

EXHIBIT 35.7 Avenue Supermarts Ltd: Valuation Ratios

	Mar 17	*Mar 18*	*Mar 19*	*Mar 20*
Share Price	638	1327	1470	2201
Price Earning (P/E)	82.53	105.57	98.01	105.6
Price to Book Value (P/BV)	10.38	17.84	16.4	12.8
Price/Cash EPS (P/CEPS)	65.41	88.16	80.82	84.37
EV/EBIDTA	39.61	58.65	54.46	65.32
Market Cap/Sales	3.12	5.02	4.2	5.27

Source: Capitaline AWS database and authors' calculations.

EXHIBIT 35.8 Shareholding Pattern

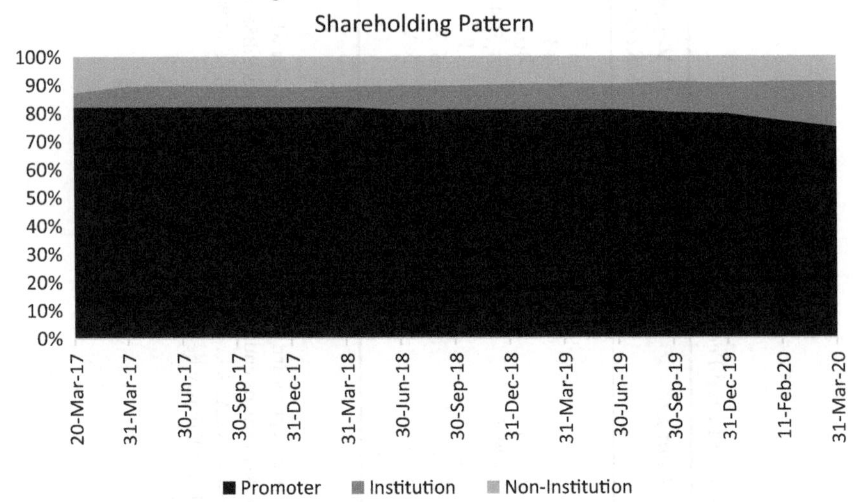

Source: Capitaline AWS database and authors' calculations.

aspect qualitatively and where possible using estimations. For instance, he would estimate the changes in the cost of debt using the likely shift in gearing levels for revision in ratings indicated by CRISIL and the credit spreads data (Exhibit 35.6). He would also estimate the unlevered beta using peer average and then calculate the levered beta and cost of equity at alternative gearing levels. He would use the alternative estimates of the cost of debt and equity at different debt ratios to check if an optimal capital structure would be different from the current one.

Similarly, Nikhil decided to use the data from cash flow statements to check if the operating cash flows could fund investment needs on a sustainable basis. If ASL required external financing, he would then reason out the merits and demerits of using debt to finance the deficit based on pecking order theory. He would similarly assess the relevance and significance of other factors affecting capital structure choice.

In planning this exercise, Nikhil realised that the choice of capital structure was complex, and no single theory or factor would provide a complete explanation. Further, it was likely that the choice could change as the industry entered different phases of growth and competitive intensity. Therefore, he could arrive at different conclusions for the next 3–5 years, 5–10 years, and in the longer term. That could imply using varying costs of capital in his valuation spreadsheet for different time horizons.

Questions

1. Estimate the weighted average cost of capital using different proportions of debt and equity. What is the capital structure the company should target according to the static trade-off theory, and how could it affect the change to the target structure?
2. Determine whether the company will require more external funds during the next three years (2020–21 to 2022–23)? Will the internal cash generation be sufficient to meet financing needs on a sustainable basis? How should the deficit be financed according to the pecking order theory?
3. Analyse the financial flexibility of Avenue Supermarts. Do the actions of the company suggest that financial flexibility is a significant consideration?
4. Is there an industry debt to equity structure considering the data of the listed retailing firms? What could be the reasons for the similarities or divergence of capital structure among players?
5. Based on the factors considered above, what will be a reasonable expectation regarding the company's capital structure over the next three years, ten years, and beyond ten years?

FACTORS RELEVANT FOR CHOICE OF CAPITAL STRUCTURE

1. The trade-off between corporate tax and distress costs: Companies should target an optimal capital structure according to the static trade-off theory. The optimal capital structure is where the rising distress costs of debt offset entirely the present value of taxes saved on interest. At the optimal capital structure, the weighted average cost of capital is the lowest, and consequently, the firm value is the highest.
2. Market timing: Firms are more likely to issue stock when their market values are high relative to book value or past market values.

3. Pecking order: Investors may be aware of the managements' market timing tactics and may infer such issuances to infer that stocks are overpriced. This problem worsens in the presence of significant information difference between management and shareholders. According to the pecking order theory, companies prefer to use those sources of funds that entail the least negative signalling to investors and the lowest cost of security floatation. Hence, the preferred order is internally generated equity, external financing through debt, and external funding through equity.
4. Agency costs: According to the agency costs hypothesis, high debt to equity reduces the agency costs of managers not acting in the interest of shareholders. Managers may have incentives to benefit themselves at the cost of shareholders through higher salaries, perquisites, job security, and use of the firm's assets or cash flows. Higher leverage brings in more control over managers' actions through the threat of liquidation and pressure to generate more cash flows to meet interest expenses.
5. Financial flexibility: Firms tend to preserve debt capacity to make future investments and retain significant unused flexibility even after expanding. Financial flexibility helps firms, in particular high growth firms, avoid costs of underinvestment. Firms may tend to underinvest and pass up positive NPV opportunities in the presence of debt if they perceive that most of the profits will go to pay off the debt holders.
6. Industry effects: Industries with valuable growth opportunities and intangible assets tend to have low debt ratios due to a higher need for financial flexibility and higher vulnerability to distress costs, respectively.

Notes

1 https://www.bseindia.com/downloads/ipo/202052112544Draft%20Letter%20of%20Offer.pdf
2 Avenue Supermarts (2020). Transcript of Q&A at Analyst Investor Call 05.08.2020 https://api.dmartindia.com/corporate/content/file/v1/2/oR9xhnu8jJ9N9iheQzfZzx1g/Transcript%20of%20Q&A%20at%20Analyst%20Investor%20Call%2005.08.2020.pdf
3 https://www.forbes.com/profile/radhakishan-damani-1/?list=rtb/&sh=52c58e3e6c40

36

RELIANCE INDUSTRIES LIMITED

Capital Structure Decision

"Cash is king in good times, but an Emperor in bad times."

– Anonymous.

It was December 20, 2011, and the senior members of Three-star Capital were busy finalising their pitchbook for Reliance Industries Ltd (RIL), one of the largest listed firms in India. The focus of the pitch was to answer the critical question: "How to efficiently use ever-increasing cash in order to serve an ultimate objective of shareholder's wealth maximisation?" The sizeable free cash on RIL's balance sheet led to a constant erosion in its Return on Equity (ROE). The management of RIL could either preserve the cash or choose to deploy this cash in the form of cash dividends or a share buyback. Another way out could have been to use this cash to repay its debt obligations partially or become a debt-free company.

The surplus cash was already creating some stir in the stock market, which could be gauged from the analysts' views on RIL stock.

Kotak Institutional Equities said, "We are not sure of the avenues available for RIL for deploying the large cash flows generating from operations, along with the consideration from BP." Kotak revised its target price with a modest upside of 6% versus a potential upside of 11% in the Sensex.

Ajay Parmar, head of institutional research, Emkay Global Financial Services, told moneycontrol.com

> One of the primary concerns of the markets apart from weak gas production is that RIL is sitting on around USD 16 billion, which is nearly a quarter of its total market cap. Given the quantum of cash, its deployment (or rather lack of it) is a matter of big concern. The company's diversifications

DOI: 10.4324/9781032724478-41

> into unrelated areas like telecom, hotels and financial services have left the markets cold.

He further said that the biggest worry for RIL shareholders could be capital allocation, which had resulted in the company's stock correcting over 20% and underperforming the Sensex by 22% in the past two years as RIL had ventured into unrelated territories.

About RIL

Reliance Industries (RIL) was India's largest private-sector enterprise, with business activities spanning exploration and production (E&P) of oil and gas, petroleum refining and marketing, petrochemicals, textiles, retail, telecom, and special economic zones (SEZ). Backward vertical integration has been the cornerstone of the evolution and growth of RIL. Starting with textiles in the late 1970s, RIL pursued a strategy of backward vertical integration in polyester, fibre intermediates, petrochemicals, refining, and E&P. RIL had global leadership in many of its businesses. It was the largest polyester yarn and fibre producer globally and among the world's top five to ten producers in major petrochemical products. RIL was looking forward to its retail and telecom business to lead the next phase of growth while consolidating its oil and gas business leadership position.

Financial Performance

RIL had been unable to meet the expectations of *Dalal Street*, which was evident from RIL stock price movement in FY 2010–11 (Exhibit 36.1). Existing investors were anxious, and new investors were sceptical. It was time for the company chairman to inform investors about the road ahead. The *Economic Times* elegantly captured the investor sentiment about RIL in its June 2, 2011, edition. It noted:

> Lakhs of investors will eagerly wait for some major announcements from corporate giant Reliance Industries' chief Mr Mukesh Ambani when he addresses the company's annual shareholder meet [in Mumbai] tomorrow. Ambani is expected to announce a slew of initiatives for both existing and new businesses of the energy-to-retail conglomerate, possibly through multiple partnerships and potential acquisitions.

In its 37th annual general meeting on June 3, 2011, Reliance Industries chairman Mukesh Ambani announced a dividend payout of 80%. Declaring that the company will be debt-free this year (FY 2011–12) on a net basis, Ambani said the company's free cash stands at Rs 42,393 crore.

EXHIBIT 36.1 RIL's Stock Price and Sensex Movement During FY11.

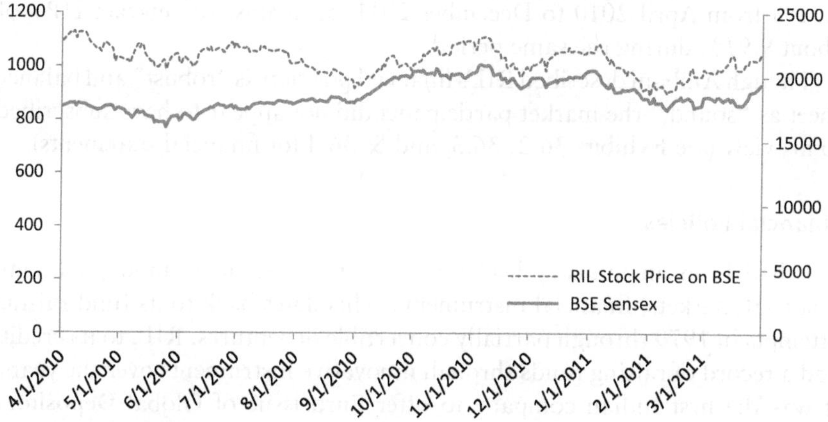

Source: Prepared by authors based on Capitaline database.

While speaking about the strategic perspective for RIL, Ambani said:

> Over the last few years, a recurrent theme of my AGM statements has been the transformational nature of initiatives at Reliance ... In every evolution of the Indian economy, we see seeds of big opportunities for value creation for our shareholders and wealth creation for the nation.

While informing the shareholders about the company's business and financial performance, Ambani proclaimed:

> Reliance has proposed a dividend payout of 80 percent, amounting to 2,385 Crore (US$ 0.53 billion). It is one of the highest dividend payouts in the Indian private sector. With a cash balance of 42,393 Crore (US$ 9.5 billion), our company is in a very strong position financially. Reliance will be completely debt-free, net of cash balances within this year. All these reflect a robust financial position and a sound balance sheet. Reliance envisages the continued pursuit of new opportunities for growth and profitability on the strength of this solid financial foundation.

RIL had outstanding debt of Rs 67,397 crore as of March 31, 2011, against Rs 62,495 crore a year ago. At the same time, RIL had cash and cash equivalents of Rs 42,393 crore as of March 31, 2011, approximately double the level seen a year ago. During the year ended March 31, 2011, RIL had posted a revenue of Rs 2,76,372 crore on assets of Rs 2,21,355 crore. The company posted an adjusted net income of Rs 13,801 crore during the year, representing a Y-o-Y growth of about 8%. The growth in ROE for RIL during this period stood at 15%.

RIL stock generated a modest holding period yield (HPY) of negative *4.11%* from April 2010 to December 2011, as against the market HPY of about *9.91%* during the same period.

Though Ambani described RIL's financial position as "robust" and balance sheet as "sound," the market participants did not appear to have subscribed to his view (see Exhibits 36.2, 36.3, and & 36.4 for financial statements).

Financial Policies

RIL had been an industry leader in adopting first of its kind (in Indian financial markets) financial instruments. This dates back to its fund-raising attempts in 1979 through partially convertible debentures. RIL, to its credit, had a record of raising funds through innovative instruments over the years. It was the first Indian company to offer Euro issue of Global Depository Receipts (GDRs), the first Euro convertible bond issue, the first Indian company to issue 50- and 100-year bonds in the US market.

During the recessionary period of 2008–2010, the company's cash reserves rose from Rs 4,474.16 crore to Rs 13,890.83 rore. While most businesses struggled to remain profitable in the economic downturn, RIL managed to make profits and generate cash from its businesses. The piling up of growing cash reserves at RIL's disposal could mean gains to shareholders in dividends or more growth opportunities in the future.

Mukesh D. Ambani, during the 37th annual general meeting of the company, remarked: "Reliance will be completely debt-free, net of cash balances within this year (FY 2010–11)."

The company used its cash by paying cash dividends to its shareholders. Exhibits 36.5 to 36.7 report RIL's cash balance, loans and advances, dividends and capex history.

The company had made a significant capital expenditure in its upstream Exploration & Production business and the downstream petrochemicals business. The sudden fall in FY 2010–11 could be attributed to deadlock with the Government of India over concerns of cost recovery of capital expenditure in the KG-D6 block, thereby disrupting the company's capital expenditure plans in the E&P vertical. This drop-in capital expenditure was not correlated with RIL's cash assets.

A host of new opportunities were galore in the markets, still to be pursued by RIL. The company attempted to put its substantial cash reserves to good use by overseas expansions through acquisitions. RIL acquired 95% of Infotel Broadband Ltd For Rs 4,800 crore, but it failed in closing any significant acquisitions, including Lyondell Basell (2009, 2011), Value Creation Inc. of Canada (2010), and US Energy Co (2010).

EXHIBIT 36.2 RIL Balance Sheet

(In Rs Crore)	*FY 2008–09*	*FY 2009–10*	*FY 2010–11*
Source of Funds			
Share Capital	1443.93	2978.02	2981
Reserves Total	119814.03	138026.32	151122
Total Shareholders' Funds	121257.96	141004.34	154103
Secured Loans	10747.73	11694.4	10624
Unsecured Loans	65508.87	52911.12	73528
Total Debt	76256.6	64605.52	84152
Other Liabilities	138-9	573.53	1016
Total Liabilities	**197653.46**	**206183.39**	**239271**
Application of Funds			
Gross Block	157182.43	224125.28	238293
Less: Accumulated Depreciation	50138.23	63934.03	80193
Net Block	107044.2	160191.25	158100
Capital Work in Progress	73845.97	17033.68	28174
Investments	6435.54	13112.25	21596
Current Assets, Loans, and Advances			
Inventories	20109.61	34393.32	38520
Sundry Debtors	4844.97	10082.92	15696
Cash and Bank	22742.1	13890.83	30139
Loans and Advances	11049.39	10738.61	8454
Total Current Assets	58746.07	69105.68	92809
Less: Current Liabilities and Provisions			
Current Liabilities	35755.56	38889.21	52435
Provisions	3115.03	3695.02	4742
Total Current Liabilities	38870.59	42584.23	57177
Net Current Assets	19875.48	26521.45	35632
Deferred Tax Assets	1096.57	1025.3	1408
Deferred Tax Liability	10647.9	11702.87	12479
Net Deferred Tax	-9551.33	-10677.57	-11071
Other Assets	3.6	2.33	6840
Total Assets	**197653.46**	**206183.39**	**239271**

Source: Prepared by authors based on Capitaline database.

[1] Three-star assumed operating cash required to be 3% of sales.

EXHIBIT 36.3 RIL Income Statement

(In Rs Crore)	*FY 2008–09*	*FY 2009–10*	*FY 2010–11*
Income			
Net Sales	151335.54	203739.72	265811
Other Income	2129.9	10783.03	2543
Stock Adjustments	2131.48	6035.22	4458
Total Income	155596.92	220557.97	272812
Total Operating Expenses	130260.53	178872.73	232225
Operating Profit (EBITDA)	25336.39	41685.24	40587
Interest	1816.27	2059.58	2411
Depreciation	5650.98	10945.8	14121
Profit Before Tax	17869.14	28679.86	24055
Tax	1273.38	3124.91	4412
Deferred Tax	1645.42	1131.37	371
Net Profit	14950.31	24423.58	19272
Dividend	1897.05	2084.67	2385
Dividend Per Share(Rs)	13	7	8
Earnings Per Share (EPS)	53	81	63

Source: Prepared by authors based on Capitaline database.

EXHIBIT 36.4 RIL Cash Flow Statement

(In Rs Crore)	*FY 2008–09*	*FY 2009–10*	*FY 2010–11*
Cash Flow Summary			
Cash and Cash Equivalents at the Beginning of the Year	4474.16	22742.1	13891
Net Cash from Operating Activities	16287.45	20494.27	33338
Net Cash Used in Investing Activities	-23056.08	-18211.82	-32040
Net Cash Used in Financing Activities	25036.57	-11133.72	14950
Net Inc/(Dec) in Cash and Cash Equivalent	18267.94	-8851.27	16248
Cash and Cash Equivalents at the End of the Year	22742.1	13890.83	30139

Source: Prepared by authors based on Capitaline database.

Assessing RIL's Options

By 2011, market participants were feeling increasingly concerned about idle cash sitting on RIL's balance sheet. The company was in constant pursuit to deploy it in more productive ways. It had made substantial new investments

EXHIBIT 36.5 RIL's Cash Balance and Loans and Advances

	Mar 2008	*Mar 2009*	*Mar 2010*	*Mar 2011*
Cash and Bank (in Rs Crore)	4474.16	22742.1	13890.83	30139
Loans and Advances (in Rs Crore)	21820.27	11049.39	10738.61	8454

Source: Prepared by authors based on Capitaline data.

EXHIBIT 36.6 RIL's Dividend History

Announcement Date	*Effective Date*	*Dividend Type*	*The Dividend*
21-04-2011	06-05-2011	Final	80%
26-04-2010	10-05-2010	Final	70%
07-10-2009	16-10-2009	Final	130%
21-04-2008	08-05-2008	Final	130%

Source: Prepared by authors based on Capitaline data.

in expanding petrochemical operations and new areas such as retail and telecom, the cash pile on the balance sheet was mounting.

According to Three-star, in such a scenario, RIL was faced with the choice of holding back the cash reserves in anticipation of future investment opportunities or distributing the excess cash to its shareholders in the form of dividend payments or share buybacks. RIL could also consider the option of repaying all or a part of its debt.

Holding Cash

The option of holding on to cash reserves would deprive investors of employing their part of cash into more productive asset classes. Also, without clarity on the opportunities for deploying this idle cash, RIL would be unfair to its investors. The investors would react by resulting in a correction in the stock price.

Debt Re-payment

RIL also had the option of repaying all or a part of its debt. Petroleum Refining was a highly levered business. In repaying its debt, an organisation would drift from its target debt-to-equity ratio and increase its Weighted Average Cost of Capital (WACC).

EXHIBIT 36.7 RIL's Capex History

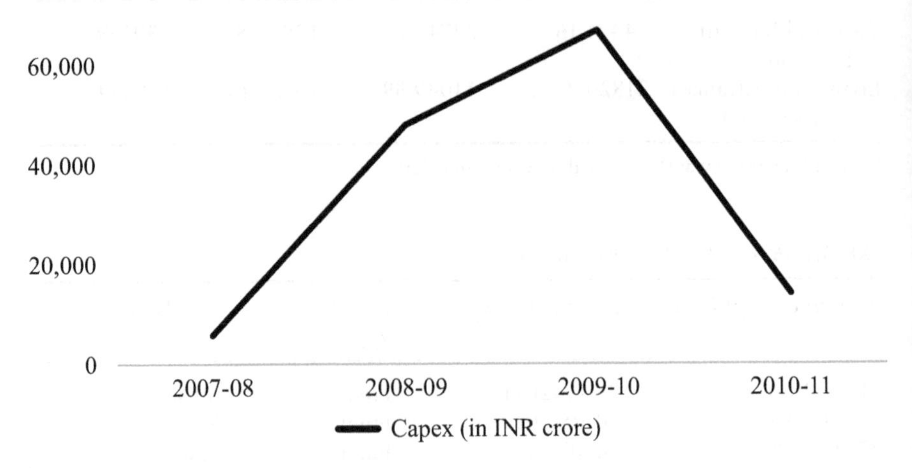

Source: Prepared by authors based on Capitaline data.

Dividends

Distributing income amongst shareholders in the form of dividends is subject to taxation. The income is taxed at the organisation level at the marginal corporate tax rate, though the dividend income in the hands of investors is not taxed. Also, dividend payments are sticky, meaning paying a "special" or "interim" dividend in one year and not paying in the next year may have a possible negative impact on the markets' reaction to the company's stock.

Share Buyback

Another approach to distributing income was in the form of share buyback. A share buyback would have provided a base price for the stock, indicating the worth of the company's share as viewed by the management.

Dilemma

On the one hand, having surplus cash of such magnitude can be a great advantage for future growth opportunities and leaves the shareholders wondering how long they should wait for the right opportunity to exit the investment. Moreover, on the other hand, distributing it at a higher rate of cash dividends or initiating a share buyback leaves the risk of unfavourable terms in raising finance for growth opportunities in future. The shareholders and investors were eagerly looking forward to RIL management's decision to utilise the cash efficiently.

37

YES BANK

The AT-1 Bonds Saga

In August 2020, Rajendra Sharma, Treasury Head of one of the large Information Technology (IT) services firms, was summoned by the board of directors to make a detailed presentation on the status of Rs 300 crore of surplus cash invested in Yes Bank' Additional Tier-1 (AT-1) bonds and similar investments made in AT-1 bonds of other banks. RBI sent shockwaves among AT-1 bondholders in its March 2020 announcement of a reconstruction scheme for Yes Bank. RBI announced writing off of Rs 8,415 crore of AT-1 bonds issued by the bank. However, shareholders were allowed to continue with their shares with three-year lock-in for 75% of shares. Several investors filed petitions in various courts on two grounds: first, going by the hierarchy of claims, the lender's claim was always superior to owners. Therefore, the cost of debt was lower than the cost of equity. However, writing off AT-1 bonds and allowing shareholders to hold on to their ownership rights with potential upside was the case of reversing the hierarchy of capital providers. Second, there was a miss-selling angle; many petitions claimed that the bonds were sold as "Super Fixed Deposits" offering 9/9.5% yield against long-tenured Fixed Deposits offering 7/7.5% at the time of the issue of the bonds.[1] Axis Trustees representing investors added the miss-selling part to their petition filed in Bombay High Court.

Yes Bank: The Rise and Fall

The bank's journey began in 1999 when Rana Kapoor partnered with his brother-in-law Ashok Kapur and Harkirat Singh at Dutch Rabobank to set up Rabo India Finance. In 2002, they received approval to set up a bank,

DOI: 10.4324/9781032724478-42

and in 2004 Yes Bank was formed. However, Harkirat Singh exited before that in 2003.

The bank came up with its Rs 300 crore IPO in 2005, and it grew at a rapid pace over the next decade. It received several awards and delivered stellar returns to its investors over the ten years ending March 2019 post-global financial crisis (see Exhibit 37.1). However, banks' aggressive lending practices came back to haunt them. In 2017, when the RBI identified a divergence in bad loans to the tune of Rs 6355 crore from earlier reported numbers, and since then, the stock turned volatile.

Further, Rana Kapoor's three-year re-appointment on June 18 was cut short to 6 months. The bank struggled to find a new CEO to be the company's face, while their asset quality weakened and their provisions and mark-to-market losses doubled. Moody's downgraded the lender, and a string of high-profile resignations hit the bank. At that point, everything that could go wrong went wrong.

The final leg of its eventual downfall began in November 2019; by then, Ravneet Gill, former India chief of Deutsche Bank, took over as CEO of Yes Bank and vouched for its revival. However, the hope remained short-lived when RBI flagged another significant divergence in its Gross Non-Performing Assets (GNPAs). Bank decided to raise US$ 2 billion to strengthen the balance sheet, but it failed to raise funds. As a result, the stock price of the bank kept falling, and rating agencies invoked multiple downgrades on the bank's credit rating. On March 5, 2020, a 30-day moratorium was imposed on the bank after delayed results for the third quarter. By then, the stock had fallen

EXHIBIT 37.1 Yes Bank vs Sensex and Bankex

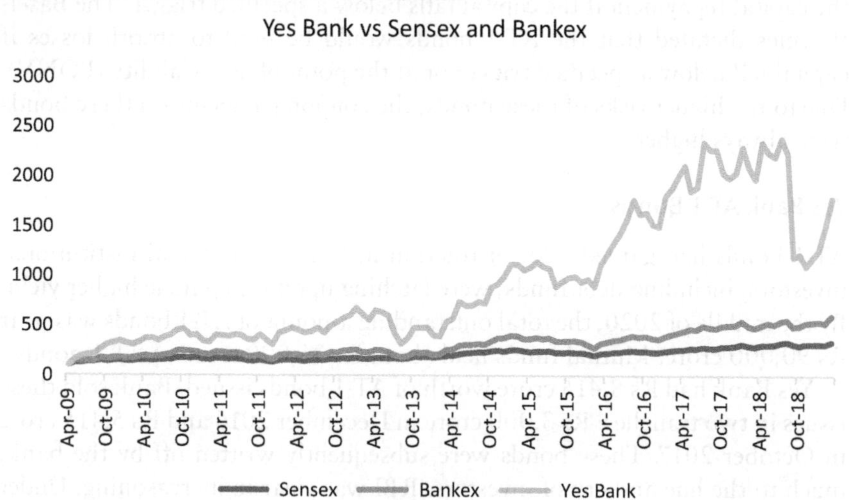

Source: BSE Website and authors compilation

below Rs. 10 per share before stabilising in the range of Rs 10 to Rs 20 per share.

The Government of India (GoI) deemed the bank too big to fail and worked on a package to give it a lifeline. The Reserve Bank of India and the Cabinet approved a package that would involve a consortium of lenders led by the State Bank of India to invest Rs 10,000 crore into the troubled bank, picking up a 49% stake in the process. The consortium of banks would invest with a lock-in period of three years for 75% of their investment. The bank's capital structure was altered to 2,400 crore shares of Rs 2 each (see Exhibits 37.2, 37.3, 37.4, and 37.5 for Financial Statements and Key Financial Ratios).

Basel Norms and AT-1 Bonds

The Basel norms were international banking regulations issued by the Basel Committee on Banking Supervision (BCBS). The norms were introduced to strengthen the global banking system. In addition, these regulations were there to facilitate better coordination among banking regulations across the globe. BCBS consisted of 27 countries (including India) and had its headquarters in Basel, Switzerland. Basel norms have evolved progressively over time, and by 2019 Basel III norms were in force.

Basel III recognised AT-1 bonds as a part of Tier-1 capital. The Basel III norms introduced several changes due to a change in the pillars (see Exhibit 37.6). First, these bonds were issued as quasi-equity security. Banks issued these securities to meet the minimum 10% Tier-1 capital requirements without diluting equity stake, as dictated by the Basel norms. Second, the banks issuing AT-1 bonds had the discretion to skip the coupon payments or even the capital repayment if the capital falls below a specified trigger. The Basel-III rules dictated that the AT-1 bonds would be used to absorb losses if capital fell below a specified trigger or at the point of non-viability (PONV). Due to the higher risks of these bonds, the coupon payments on these bonds were always higher.

Yes Bank AT-1 Bonds

AT-1 bonds had gained a lot of traction in India, and several institutional investors, including debt funds, were latching upon it to pursue higher yield. By the middle of 2020, the total outstanding amount of AT-1 bonds was near Rs 90,000 crore. Mutual funds held about Rs 35,000 crore of AT-1 bonds.

Yes Bank had Rs 8,415 crore worth of AT-1 bonds issued. Bank sold these issues in two tranches: Rs 3,000 crore in December 2016 and Rs 5,415 crore in October 2017. These bonds were subsequently written off by the bank, much to the hue and cry of investors. RBI was clear in its reasoning. Under Section 45 of the Banking Regulation Act, the PONV was triggered, and the

EXHIBIT 37.2 Yes Bank's Income Statement

Particulars		*FY 2016*	*FY 2017*	*FY 2018*	*FY 2019*	*FY 2020*
Interest Income		1,35,334	1,64,246	2,02,674	2,96,248	2,60,666
Interest Expense		89,667	1,06,273	1,25,304	1,98,157	1,92,613
Net Interest Income		**45,667**	**57,973**	**77,370**	**98,091**	**68,053**
	Growth (%)	30.9%	26.9%	33.5%	26.8%	–30.6%
Non-Interest Income		27,121	41,568	52,238	45,902	34,415
Net Total Income		**72,788**	**99,541**	**1,29,608**	**1,43,993**	**1,02,468**
	Growth (%)		**36.8%**	**30.2%**	**11.1%**	**–28.8%**
Operating Expenses		29,764	41,165	52,128	62,643	67,292
Pre Provision Profits		**43,024**	**58,376**	**77,480**	**81,350**	**35,176**
	Growth %		35.7%	32.7%	5.0%	–56.8%
Provisions (excluding tax)		**5363**	**7934**	**15,538**	**57,776**	**3,27,584**
PBT		**37,661**	**50,442**	**61,942**	**23,574**	**–292408**
Tax		**12,268**	**17,140**	**19,697**	**6,371**	**–65259**
	Tax Rate (%)	32.6%	34.0%	31.8%	27.0%	22.3%
PAT		**25,393**	**33,302**	**42,245**	**17,203**	**–227149**
	Growth (%)		31.1%	26.9%	–59.3%	–1420.4%

Source: Prepared by authors based on Capitaline and Bloomberg data.

EXHIBIT 37.3 Yes Bank's Balance Sheet (Rs in Crore)

Particulars		*FY 2016*	*FY 2017*	*FY 2018*	*FY 2019*	*FY 2020*
Equity Share Capital		4205	4565	4606	4630	25,101
Reserves and Surplus		1,33,661	2,15,976	2,52,977	2,64,412	1,92,162
Net Worth		**1,37,866**	**2,20,541**	**2,57,583**	**2,69,042**	**2,17,263**
Deposits		**11,17,195**	**14,28,739**	**20,07,381**	**22,76,102**	**10,53,639**
	Growth (%)		27.9%	40.5%	13.4%	-53.7%
of which CASA Dep		**3,13,428**	**5,18,697**	**7,31,762**	**7,52,533**	**2,80,630**
	Growth (%)		65.5%	41.1%	2.8%	-62.7%
Borrowings		3,16,590	3,86,067	7,48,936	10,84,241	11,37,906
Other Liabilities and Provisions		80,983	1,15,253	1,10,556	1,78,877	1,69,462
Total Liabilities		**16,52,634**	**21,50,599**	**31,24,456**	**38,08,262**	**25,78,270**
Current Assets		82,184	1,95,494	2,47,344	2,68,895	83,831
Investments		**4,88,385**	**5,00,318**	**6,83,989**	**8,95,220**	**4,39,148**
	Growth (%)		2.4%	36.7%	30.9%	–50.9%
Loans		**98,2099**	**13,22,627**	**20,35,339**	**24,14,996**	**17,14,433**
	Growth (%)		34.7%	53.9%	18.7%	–29.0%
Fixed Assets		4,707	6,835	8,324	8,170	10,090
Other Assets		95,259	12,5325	14,9460	22,0980	33,0767
Total Assets		**16,52,634**	**21,50,599**	**31,24,456**	**38,08,262**	**25,78,270**

Source: Prepared by authors based on Capitaline and Bloomberg data.

EXHIBIT 37.4 Yes Bank's Asset Quality (Rs in Crore)

Particulars	*FY16*	*FY17*	*FY18*	*FY19*	*FY20*
GNPA	7,490	20,186	26,268	78,826	32,8776
NNPA	2,845	10,723	13,127	44,849	86,238
GNPA Ratio	0.76	1.52	1.29	3.22	16.8
NNPA Ratio	0.29	0.81	0.64	1.86	5.03
Slippage Ratio	1.21	2.68	4.89	3.58	11.98
Credit Cost	0.57	0.58	0.93	2.6	2.2
PCR (Exc. Tech. Growth (%) write-off)	62	46.9	50	43.1	73.8

Source: Capitaline, Bloomberg and Research Reports.

EXHIBIT 37.5 Yes Bank – Key Ratios

Particulars	*FY 2016*	*FY 2017*	*FY 2018*	*FY 2019*	*FY 2020*
Yield and Cost Ratios (%)					
Avg. Yield on Loans	11.2	10.6	9.2	10.3	9.3
Avg. Cost of Deposits	7.1	6.4	5.5	6.2	6.5
Net Interest Margin	**3.4**	**3.4**	**3.2**	**3.1**	**2.2**
Capitalisation Ratios (%)					
CAR	16.5	17	18.4	16.5	8.5
Tier I	10.7	13.3	13.2	11.3	6.5
Tier II	5.8	3.7	5.2	5.2	2
Business and Efficiency Ratios (%)					
CASA (Current and Savings Accounts) Ratio	28.1	36.3	36.5	33.1	26.6
Cost/Total Income	40.9	41.4	40.2	43.5	65.7
Cost/Core Income	42.4	44.5	41.9	45.3	65.7
Int. Expense/Int. Income	66.3	64.7	61.8	66.9	73.9
Non Int. Inc./Total Income	37.3	41.8	40.3	31.9	33.6
Investment/Deposit Ratio	43.7	35	34.1	39.3	41.7
Profitability Ratios and Valuation					
RoE	19.9	18.9	17.7	6.5	-113.1
RoA	1.7	1.8	1.6	0.5	-7.1
Book Value (INR)	65.6	96.6	111.8	116.2	17.3
Growth (%)	17.3	47.4	15.8	3.9	-85.1
Price -BV (x)	**3.6**	**2.5**	**2.1**	**2**	**1.3**
EPS (INR)	12.1	14.6	18.4	7.5	-77.6
Growth (%)	25.8	20.8	26.3	-59.6	–
Price-Earnings (x)	**19.7**	**16.3**	**12.9**	**31.9**	–
Dividend Per Share (INR)	2	2.4	3.2	2.4	0

Source: Prepared by authors based on Capitaline and Bloomberg data.

EXHIBIT 37.6 Basel II vs Basel III norms

Particulars	*Basel II*	*Basel III*
Pillars	Minimum Capital Requirement	Minimum Capital Requirement Supervisory review and role Market discipline and disclosure
Risks	Credit Risk	Credit Risk Operations Risk Market Risk
Approach	The standard approach of measurement and capital calculation	Multiple approaches for measurement of each of the risk and then the capital calculation
Minimum Common Equity to RWAs	2.00%	5.50%
Capital Conservation Buffer	–	2.50%
Additional Tier 1 Capital	–	1.50%
Minimum Tier 1 Capital to RWAs	4%	7%
Tier 2 Capital	<100% of Tier-1 Capital	2.00%
Minimum Total Capital Ratio	8%	9%
Minimum Total Capital Ratio plus Capital Conservation Buffer	8%	11.50%

Source: Prepared by authors based on information from BIS and RBI websites.

bonds were written off in line with the contact between Yes Bank and AT-1 bondholders and hence there was no merit in any argument against writing off the bonds. Higher returns come with higher risks, and AT-1 bondholders enjoyed higher yields in the past. In the 2017 issue memorandum, there was no provision for conversion of such bonds to equity, thus paving the way for Yes Bank to completely write-off the liability. Thus, AT-1 bondholders lost their entire capital in the process.

Equity shares were not written off first since the company was not under liquidation. Therefore, there was no provision under the AT-1 bonds issue for the write-off of equity shares first. Since seniority of bonds over equity matters only in liquidation, the bonds would be written off while the equity shareholders would continue to hold their shares.

Shareholders in Yes Bank were asked to continue holding 75% of their shares for three years unless they own less than 100 shares. RBIT did that to prevent the excessive speculation that was taking place in the market and ensure that only long-term investors remained invested in the company since it would have to undergo a long process of reconstruction to get back on its feet.

Questions

1. How do you explain the rise and fall of the Yes Bank?
2. What do you understand by AT-1 bonds? How were they different from normal bonds?
3. Do you think writing off AT-1 bonds was legal? Ethical? What were the legal and ethical issues involved in writing off AT-1 bonds?
4. What do you understand by Basel norm, Risk-weighted Assets, Capital Adequacy ratio, Tier-1, and Tier-2 Capital?
5. How would Basel norms contribute to the stability of the banking system?
6. Would you recommend AT-1 bonds to investors? Why? Why not?

Note

1 https://www.moneycontrol.com/news/business/yes-bank-saga-rs-8415-crore-at-stake-will-at1-bond-holders-ever-get-their-money-back-5629921.html accessed on May 28, 2021.

38

INVESTMENTWAVES (C)

Evaluating Cash Dividend vs Homemade Dividend

On a Saturday in February 2020, Anjali Mehra, Head, Business Development and Clients Relations at InvestmentWaves, attended a one-day conference organised by a large private bank in association with a leading stock exchange in India. One of the keynote speakers highlighted the need to force Indian listed companies to distribute at least 30% of their net profit in cash dividends. In other words, the company must maintain at least a 30% dividend pay-out ratio. The speaker cited the famous Graham and Dodd model from the 1950s and claimed that other things being equal, the firm paid higher dividend benefit in terms of the higher valuation of stock in the marketplace. The reasons were simple. First, the higher the cash dividend paid, the faster the payback period; after few years, your stock would become free. Second, cash dividend payment was evidence that the firm earned real cash profit. Third, it also served as a proxy measure for prudent management as high dividend means managers chose to return surplus capital to owners rather than investing in inferior business opportunities.

The session was a superhit. During lunchtime, everyone was busy criticising many successful companies for not paying sufficient dividends from their profits and hoarding cash and keeping investors in need of regular income away from equity investing. Many of her clients were also attending the conference. Anjali found it difficult to answer their questions as InvestmentWaves over the years advised choosing companies based on their merits rather than focusing on dividend pay-out ratio or dividend yield.

Anjali immediately called up Neha Gupta, the Co-Founder and Chief Investment Officer at InvestmentWaves, a fee-only investment advisory firm based in Ahmedabad, India. Anjali updated Neha about the development at

DOI: 10.4324/9781032724478-43

the conference and emphasised that she too started believing that all companies should pay significant dividends. However, not doing so would be an injustice to small investors who wanted to invest in equity and look for regular income. Neha prepared a short note on various propositions on dividend policy and firm value for Anjali and asked her to go through it. A day later, she called Anjali and her team members to explain their position.

Dividend Policy and Firm Value

Two ways to return cash or distribute profit to its shareholders were: cash dividend and share buyback. A firm should consider two significant aspects before deciding what percentage of profit it wanted to distribute in cash dividend. First, how would it impact its valuation and practical constraints regarding funds requirement, availability of other sources of funds, cost of raising new funds, delay and regulatory requirements related to raising new funds and shareholders' preference? Second, shareholders earned their returns as a combination of capital gains and cash dividends and the volatile nature of stock prices; firms, especially in a cyclical business with volatile earnings, would like to maintain a stable rupee dividend policy rather than stable dividend pay-out.

The impact of the dividend pay-out decision had come a full circle in the second half of the twentieth century. It started with Graham and Dodd who proposed their model in the early 1950s, called the traditional model, claiming that given other things equal, higher dividend pay-out would result in higher firm value.

However, two other models refuted the traditional model one-size-fit-all approach. Both Gordon and Walter models concluded that the firm's dividend pay-out decision should be based on its financial performance. The firms with Return on Equity (ROE) higher than Cost of Equity (ke) should not pay dividends and reinvest profits into the business with profitable investment opportunities. The dividend pay-out ratio is irrelevant for the firm earns ROE equal to ke. For the firms with ROE less than ke, they should not hoard shareholders money and ideally pay the entire profit in dividend to invest their money in better investment opportunities. However, these are mere prescriptions. A firm with higher ROE might not find a new investment with high profitability and might choose to distribute significant dividends. On the other hand, the firm with low ROE might find it challenging to mobilise external funds and decide to rely on retained earnings to navigate safely through difficult times.

Modigliani and Miller (MM) argued for the irrelevance of dividend decision under some stringent set of assumptions. However, towards the end of the twentieth century, an extreme proposition emerged that suggested that the firm should not pay dividends at all! It was called the radical approach

EXHIBIT 38.1 Dividend Policy and Firm Value: Models and Propositions

Value of Firm	*Model*	*By whom*	*Proposition*	*notations*
P	m (D +E/3)	Graham and Dodd (1951)	Higher the dividend pay-out higher the firm value given other things equal.	m = constant multiplier D = Dividend Per Share E = Earnings per share where
P	E (1-b)/ (k-br)	Gordon (1962)	The optimum dividend pay-out ratio is a function of return on Investment and ost of capital	E = Earnings per share b = retention ratio k = cost of capital r = return on capital
P	(D + (E-D) r/k)/k	Walter (1963)	Same as Gordon Model	D = Dividend Per Share k = cost of capital r = return on capital
nP	$((n+m) P_1-(I_1 - X_1))/(1+k)$	Modigliani and Miller (MM)	Dividend Policy does not affect firm value	n = number of existing outstanding shares m = number of new shares to be issued P1 = Price at which m shares will be issues I_1 = new investments X_1 = Total dividend paid, nD k = cost of capital

Source: Prepared by authors.

(see Exhibit 38.1 for the value of equity and dividend pay-out ratio under various approaches).

Cash Dividend vs Homemade Dividend

In most countries, capital gains were treated favourably over cash dividends. India had seen different tax treatment for capital gains and dividends over the years. From 2003 to 2018, both dividends and long-term capital gains (LTCG) were tax-exempt in India in the hands of investors. However, the firm had to pay the dividend distribution tax (DDT). Including the basic

DDT, surcharge, and cess, the effective DDT was 20.56%. In 2018, LTCG tax was reintroduced, but Rs 100,000 of LTCG for every financial year was exempted. In the following year, the dividend was taxed in the hands of investors – those who earned more than Rs 10,00,000 dividends from equity or equity mutual funds in a year would pay 10% tax on the dividend income. In the 2020 budget, the government removed the DDT, and the dividend payment from equity would be taxed according to the marginal tax slab of an individual. (see Exhibits 38.2 & 38.3).

InvestmentWaves believed that homemade dividend by selling shares in the market would be tax efficient from an investor's perspective, and it would maximise his post-tax dividend yield. Neha explained it to her team by citing an example of her client.

Mona retired after teaching sociology at an arts college of a private university in Mumbai. While she received a good amount of lumpsum corpus for her superannulation, she did not have a pensionable job. Mona was aware of investing her entire funds into fixed income instruments due to low to negative real returns. She wanted decent exposure in equity to guard against

EXHIBIT 38.2 Personal Income Tax Slabs in India for FY 2020–21 (Old Regime)

Income (in Rs)	*Slab*
0–2,50,000	Nil
2,51,000–5,00,000	5%
5,00,001–10,00,000	20%
>10,00,000	30%

10% surcharge for income above Rs 50,00,000 and 15% surcharge for income above 1,00,00,000 is applicable. In addition, 4% cess is applicable on total tax and surcharge paid.

Source: Prepared by authors based on information from income tax of India website.

EXHIBIT 38.3 Equity Taxation in India

Short-Term Capital Gain	*Long-Term Capital Gain*	*Dividend*
Holding period < 1 year	Holding period > 1 year	NA
Tax rate: 15%	Exempt up to Rs. 1,00,000 per financial year and 10% above that	As per the marginal tax slab of an individual.
Short-term loss can be set off against short-term and long-term losses and can carry it forward for 8-years.	Long-term capital losses can be set off against long-term gains only.	

Source: Prepared by authors based on information from Income tax of India.

inflation, but she wanted a reasonable dividend yield out of her investment to support her annual expenses. She requested Neha to suggest some high dividend-yielding stocks. However, Neha knew that many stocks offered high dividend yield yet failed to create wealth for investors. For instance, Coal India, the largest coal mining public sector undertaking, offered excellent dividend yield but failed miserably in delivering any meaningful returns to its shareholders. On the other hand, many public sector undertakings and promoters dominated firms ended up paying significant dividends, not for economic reasons but making majority shareholders' happy and led to wealth destruction for shareholders in general.

Neha believed that stock picking should not be based on the dividend pay-out ratio or dividend yield of the stock but the quality and fundamentals of the business. She said, "There is no need to chase high dividend stocks; you can always create your dividends."

She explained to Mona that high dividend-yielding stocks were not suitable for her as her annual income would put her in the highest marginal tax bracket. For instance, if she earned a 5% dividend yield on her equity portfolio worth Rs 1 crore, she would end up paying close to one-third of Rs 5,00,000 dividends in tax. However, instead, had she sold Rs 5,00,000 worth stocks with an average LTCG of 20% at the end of the year, she would not pay any tax as LTCG up to Rs 100,000 was tax-exempt. In any given year, if she ended up booking LTCG of more than 1,00,000, she ended up paying LTCG of only 10%, much lower than the 30% marginal tax rate plus 4% cess. Yes, the removal of DDT benefited the real small investors with tax-exempt income as they would get the full dividend income tax-free. In the previous regime, everyone, regardless of their marginal tax bracket, would pay an effective tax of 20.56% on dividend income received as the tax was paid at the firm level rather than the investor's level. So, to that extent, the new tax regime was truly allowing small retail investors to benefit by investing in stocks with high dividends and good fundamentals.

> However, since most of our clients belong to 20% to 30% tax bracket, homemade dividends are always preferred over cash dividends paid by the firm. So yes, if we find a great company paying regular dividends, we would not miss out on that investment opportunity to save tax.
>
> While we might recommend some good dividend-paying stocks to investors in low marginal income tax bracket, on balance, we would prefer homemade dividend rather than cash dividend paid by the firm. The added benefit with the homemade dividend is that we can create it when we want it. Neha concluded.

Questions

1. Compare and contrast different positions/models explaining the relationship between dividend policy and firm value.
2. What is the radical position on the dividend policy of the firm?
3. Do you think replacing DDT by taxing dividends in the hands of investors weakened/strengthen the radical position on dividend policy? How?
4. What practical/economic considerations might force the firm to deviate from the optimum dividend pay-out ratio?

39

DIVIDEND PAYOUT AT MAHINDRA AND MAHINDRA

Minal Dogra, a research analyst at proxy advisory firm Governance-For-Stakeholders (GFS), was examining the data prepared by her associate regarding the dividend distribution of Mahindra and Mahindra Ltd (M&M). The Annual General Body Meeting (AGM) of M&M was scheduled on August 7, 2020, and Minal had to prepare a report on voting recommendations for various resolutions at the AGM for institutional investors, who were the clients of GFS. Minal was presently analysing the proposed dividend of Rs 2.35 per share declared by the Board of Directors of M&M, which was one of the resolutions listed for voting at the AGM.

Established in 1945, M&M was a leading manufacturer of automobiles and tractors in India. It manufactured light commercial vehicles, medium and heavy commercial vehicles, utility vehicles, three-wheelers, two-wheelers, and passenger cars. It was the largest tractor manufacturer in India and one of the leading tractor makers in the world. Along with its many subsidiaries and associate companies, the M&M group was present in diverse sectors, including automobiles, farm equipment, auto components, finance, real estate, and logistics.

Dividend Distribution Policy of M&M

M&M had prepared its dividend distribution policy statement in 2016 and published it on the company's website and annual reports. In July 2016, the Securities and Exchange Board of India (SEBI) had issued regulations making it mandatory for the top 500 listed entities in India by market capitalisation to formulate and disclose their dividend distribution policies.

DOI: 10.4324/9781032724478-44

M&M's dividend distribution policy had included the standard parameters laid out by SEBI and was similar to its peers.[1] It listed the internal and external factors that the company's board would consider while deciding the dividend payouts. The internal factors included profitable growth, cash flow position, accumulated reserves, earnings stability, future cash requirements, capital expenditure, leverage, and current investments. The company would also consider the past dividend history and shareholders' expectations. The external factors included business cycles, economic environment, inflation, industry prospects, government policies, cost of external financing, and taxes on dividend. M&M had also specified that it would endeavour to maintain a dividend payout ratio in the range of 20% to 35% of the standalone profit after tax of the company.

Minal found that M&M had consistently paid dividends every year over the past three decades. The company had also periodically done stock splits and bonus issues, the most recent being a bonus issue in the ratio of 1:1 in December 2017 (see Exhibits 39.1 and 39.2). She noted that two of M&M's peers had also mentioned the target range of dividend payout. Among its peers, only Tata Motors had not been providing dividends during the past three years. Neither M&M nor any peer company had declared a share buyback in the past five years (Exhibit 39.7).

Minal next reviewed the financial statements of M&M to assess its profitability and cash flows (see Exhibits 39.3, 39.4, 39.5, and 39.6). She decided to reorganise the cash flow statement to estimate the free cash flows available for payout to the shareholders.

Having analysed the dividend distribution policy and payout trends, Minal started formulating questions that she wanted to answer before deciding her recommendation. Was the stated policy rational? Was the proposed payout consistent with the stated policy and comparable with the industry peers? Was the company retaining sufficient funds to sustain growth? Was it overinvesting in unprofitable opportunities?

EXHIBIT 39.1 M&M's Dividend Trends

Rs Crore	*2015–16*	*2016–17*	*2017–18*	*2018–19*	*2019–20*
Dividend per Share (Rs)[a]	12.00	13.00	7.50	8.50	2.35
No. of Shares (Crore)	59	59	119	119	119
Dividend Amount	711	772	892	1,013	280
Profit after Tax	3,205	3,643	4,356	4,796	1,331
Market Capitalisation	75,196	79,928	92,021	83,779	30,531
Dividend Payout	22.2%	21.2%	20.5%	21.1%	21.1%
Dividend Yield	0.9%	1.0%	1.0%	1.2%	0.9%

Source: CMIE Prowess IQ, company annual reports, and authors' calculations.

Note: [a] Dividend approved in AGM for the year; dividend for 2019–20 was yet to be approved.

EXHIBIT 39.2 Trend in Share Price

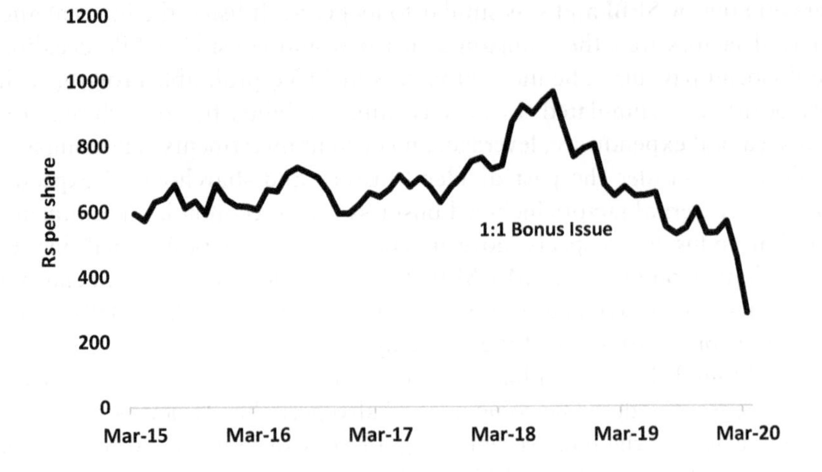

Source: Prepared by authors based on data from CMIE Prowess IQ.

EXHIBIT 39.3 Trends in Profit and Loss and Balance Sheets

Rs Crore	*2015–16*	*2016–17*	*2017–18*	*2018–19*	*2019–20*
Revenues (net of indirect taxes)	40,638	43,684	48,449	53,369	45,311
Other Income	1,156	2,408	1,679	2,532	3,211
Total Income	**41,794**	**46,092**	**50,129**	**55,901**	**48,523**
Cost of Goods Sold	33,380	36,619	39,004	42,837	36,165
Other Operating Expenses	3,087	3,437	4,033	5,000	4,617
Total Operating Expenses	36,467	40,056	43,037	47,837	40,782
EBITDA	5,327	6,035	7,092	8,064	7,741
Depreciation	771	866	889	993	1,105
EBIT	4,556	5,170	6,202	7,071	6,636
Interest and Finance Charges	271	160	127	746	3,494
Profit before Extraordinary Items & Tax	4,284	5,010	6,075	6,325	3,141
Net Prior Period and Extraordinary items	-	288	(27)	(290)	153
Profit before Tax	4,284	4,723	6,102	6,615	2,989
Tax	1,080	1,079	1,746	1,819	1,658

(Continued)

EXHIBIT 39.3 Continued

Rs Crore	*2015–16*	*2016–17*	*2017–18*	*2018–19*	*2019–20*
Profit after Tax	3,205	3,643	4,356	4,796	1,331
Property, Plant and Equipment	7,596	7,771	7,859	10,082	10,395
Capital Work in Progress	1,562	2,040	3,129	2,420	4,009
Non-Current Investments	11,161	14,302	16,645	19,032	17,748
Other Non-Current Assets	4,524	4,849	4,833	4,695	3,649
Non-Current Assets	24,843	28,963	32,467	36,229	35,802
Inventories	2,688	2,758	2,702	3,839	3,401
Trade Receivables	2,570	2,986	3,222	4,016	3,157
Cash & Bank Balance	2,287	1,687	2,894	3,732	4,237
Current Investments	2,386	3,607	3,937	2,984	2,190
Other Current Assets	1,763	1,628	3,786	3,581	2,327
Current Assets	11,694	12,667	16,541	18,152	15,311
Total Assets	**36,538**	**41,629**	**49,008**	**54,380**	**51,113**
Paid-up Equity Capital	296	297	595	596	597
Reserves	22,127	26,489	29,699	33,613	33,871
Total Equity	22,423	26,786	30,294	34,209	34,468
Long-Term Debt	1,495	2,235	2,197	2,033	2,033
Other Non-Current Liabilities	2,716	2,916	3,127	3,857	3,469
Non-Current Liabilities	4,212	5,151	5,324	5,890	5,502
Short-Term Debt	348	539	668	449	900
Current Maturities of Long-Term Debt	1,073	78	94	91	136
Trade Payables	6,675	6,881	8,603	9,678	6,786
Other Current Liabilities	1,807	2,195	4,024	4,063	3,321
Current Liabilities	9,903	9,693	13,390	14,281	11,142
Total Liabilities	14,114	14,844	18,714	20,171	16,645
Total Equity and Liabilities	**36,538**	**41,629**	**49,008**	**54,380**	**51,113**

Source: CMIE Prowess and authors' calculations.

Questions

1. Based on the information provided in the case and the exhibits, state your observations regarding the dividend payout behaviour of M&M based on historical trends and comparison with peers.
2. Analyse whether the dividend payouts made by M&M had been prudent in terms of balancing investor expectations and the need for internal financing.
3. Would you recommend voting for or against the proposed amount of dividend for 2019–20?

EXHIBIT 39.4 Free Cash Flows and Dividends

Rs Crore	*2015–16*	*2016–17*	*2017–18*	*2018–19*	*2019–20*
Cash Flow from Operating Activities	**5,471**	**3,710**	**7,027**	**4,924**	**3,678**
Net Capex	(2,152)	(2,074)	(2,669)	(3,032)	(3,944)
Free Cash Flow Net of Capex	**3,319**	**1,636**	**4,358**	**1,892**	**(266)**
Net Non-Current Investments	**287**	**(2,159)**	**(1,987)**	**(2,020)**	**(620)**
Other Investing Activities	(1,674)	1,452	(455)	2,503	1,988
Cash Flow Net of Investing Activities	1,933	928	1,917	2,375	1,102
Cash Flows from Debt	(950)	(174)	59	(373)	329
Interest Paid	(211)	(148)	(170)	(171)	(157)
Free Cash Flow Available to Equity	771	606	1,806	1,832	1,274
Dividends Paid (including tax)	**(846)**	**(839)**	**(923)**	**(1,012)**	**(1,187)**
Net Increase in Cash and Equivalents	(75)	(233)	883	820	87

Source: Authors' calculations.

EXHIBIT 39.5 Segmental Trends

Rs Crore	*2015–16*	*2016–17*	*2017–18*	*2018–19*	*2019–20*
External Sales					
Automotive	30,807	31,996	32,081	35,328	28,388
Farm Equipment	11,051	13,583	15,762	16,562	15,162
Others	1,781	1,805	1,603	1,725	1,937
PBIT					
Automotive	2,129	1,413	2,148	2,027	1,264
Farm Equipment	1,956	2,562	3,145	3,265	2,926
Others	40	(379)	63	51	73
Capital Employed					
Automotive	5,474	6,346	6,122	7,039	9,349
Farm Equipment	2,806	2,978	2,936	4,548	3,765
Others	414	364	491	514	541

Source: Prepared by authors based on information from CMIE Prowess IQ.

EXHIBIT 39.6 Profile of Significant Non-Current Investments (as of March 31, 2020)

Rs Crore	*Assets*	*Liabilities*	*Total Equity*	*Stake*	*Value of Holding*	
					At Cost	*Market Value*
Mahindra & Mahindra Financial Services	74,071	62,707	11,364	51.39%	1,206	4,673
Tech Mahindra Limited	31,122	8,849	22,273	28.89%	986	14,239
Ssangyong Motor Company	12,467	9,960	2,507	74.65%	2,450	983
Mahindra Vehicle Manufacturers Limited	6,832	2,555	4,277	100.00%	4,065	n.a.
Mahindra Holidays and Resorts	6,419	6,243	176	67.63%	25	1,256
Mahindra USA Inc.	2,422	2,863	(441)	100.00%	755	n.a.
Mahindra Overseas Investment Company	2,380	2,023	357	100.00%	1,826	n.a.
Mahindra Holdings Limited	2,282	2	2,280	100.00%	2,462	n.a.
Mahindra Lifespace Developers Limited	2,000	504	1,496	51.48%	440	509
Mahindra Logistics Limited	1,330	785	545	58.45%	42	948
All Non-Current Investments						
Quoted (equity and debt)					5,235	23,044
Unquoted (equity and debt)					16,635	-
Total					21,870	23,044

Source: Prepared by authors based on Mahindra and Mahindra annual report 2019-20, Bloomberg.

EXHIBIT 39.7 Comparison of Payouts and Financials of Automobile (4-wheeler) Companies

Rs Crore		*M&M*	*Maruti Suzuki*	*Tata Motors*	*Ashok Leyland*
Target Dividend Payout		20% to 35%	18% to 20%.	25% to 40%	Not specified
Average Payout Ratio (3 year)		20.9%	31.8%	0.0%	44.9%
Dividend Payout Ratio	2019–20	21.1%	32.1%	-	61.3%
	2018–19	21.1%	32.2%	-	45.9%
	2017–18	20.5%	31.3%	-	41.4%
Dividend	2019–20	280	1,812	-	147
	2018–19	1,013	2,417	-	910
	2017–18	892	2,417	-	711
Profit after Tax	2019–20	1,331	5,651	(7,290)	240
	2018–19	4,796	7,501	2,021	1,983
	2017–18	4,356	7,722	(1,035)	1,718
Return on Equity	2019–20	3.9%	11.9%	-36.0%	3.1%
	2018–19	14.9%	17.1%	9.5%	25.5%
	2017–18	15.3%	19.8%	--5.0%	25.7%
Debt-Equity Ratio	2019–20	0.09	0.00	1.42	0.46
	2018–19	0.08	0.01	0.84	0.08
	2017–18	0.10	0.00	0.92	0.17
CFO minus Net Capex	2019–20	(266)	248	(4,048)	(427)
	2018–19	1,892	2,019	3,532	(1,023)
	2017–18	4,358	7,920	2,784	5,109
CFO minus CFI	2019–20	1,102	2,941	(6,173)	(1,236)
	2018–19	2,375	3,055	2,472	1,949
	2017–18	1,917	3,503	4,844	2,214

Source: Prepared by authors based on company annual reports and CMIE Prowess IQ.

Note

1 https://www.mahindra.com/resources/investor-reports/FY17/Governance/MM-Dividend-Distribution-Policy-29-9-2016-Final.pdf

40

INVESTOR PAYOUTS AT WIPRO

Raj Purohit, a value investor, was preparing his analysis of Wipro's payout policy before formulating his response to a discussion thread at acepickers .com, an investors forum. The discussion thread had started in response to the observation that Wipro, like a few other Indian IT majors, had increased their total payouts to investors over the past few years. The opinions were evenly divided between those in favour and those against the trend of higher payouts.

A leading provider of information technology (IT) services in India, Wipro divided its business into three segments, IT services, IT products, and India State-Run Enterprise. It provided IT services to customers across diverse industry verticals and geographies worldwide.

Wipro's Dividend Distribution Policy

In its dividend distribution policy objective, Wipro had stated the following:

> *The company believes that returning cash to shareholders is an important component of overall value creation.* [1]

The company also mentioned several considerations the board would consider while recommending the dividend. These included net profit, cash flow generation and cash balance, debt-raising capacity, capital expenditure, investments in mergers and acquisitions, and working capital requirements. Other considerations included macro-economic factors, general business

DOI: 10.4324/9781032724478-45

environment, and corporate actions resulting in significant cash outflows (like share buyback).

Along with the statement dividend distribution policy, Wipro had also appended a statement of capital allocation policy. It stated that the board of Wipro had approved the following capital allocation policy:

> *Effective from the financial year 2021, the company expects to return approximately 45%–50% of the net income cumulatively on a block of 3 years period through a combination of dividends and/or share buy-back and/or special dividends, subject to applicable laws and requisite approvals if any.*[1]

Trends in Cash Flows and Payouts

India's IT sector was estimated to record revenues of US$ 194 billion in fiscal year (FY) 2020–21 according to NASSCOM, the industry association. Export revenues constituted more than 75% of the total revenues. Revenue growth declined from around 19% between FY07 and FY11 to 10% between FY12 and FY16 and further to 6% between FY17 and FY1. The sector had matured, having achieved a significant global customer base and penetration.

Wipro also reported a gradual decline in revenue growth but broadly stable net margins (Exhibit 40.1). The company's return on capital employed in operating assets had gradually reduced. The decline in return on equity had

EXHIBIT 40.1 Revenues, Margins, and Dividends

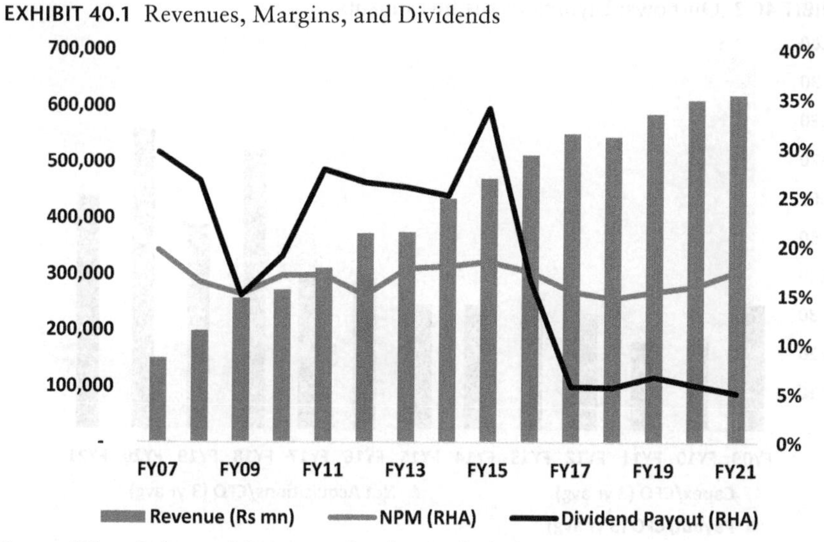

Source: Wipro Ltd annual Reports and authors' calculations.

EXHIBIT 40.2 Asset Composition and Returns

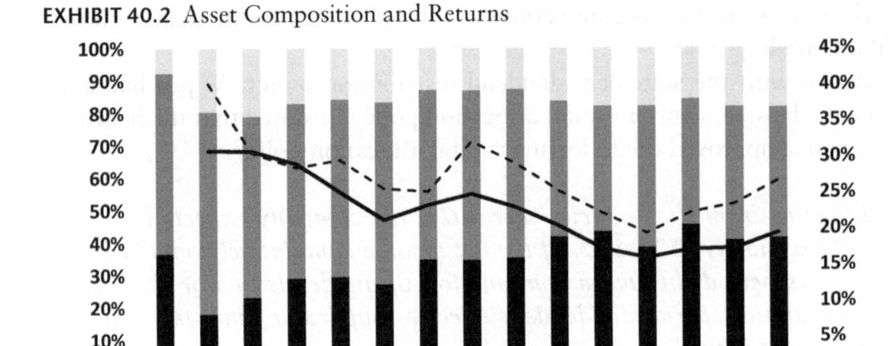

Source: Wipro Ltd annual reports and authors' calculations.

been steeper, partly attributed to the increasing accumulation of cash and current investments (Exhibit 40.2).

Wipro's investments had reduced as a ratio of its cash flows from operations in recent years (Exhibit 40.3). On the other hand, its total payouts had

EXHIBIT 40.3 Outflows: Payouts versus Investments

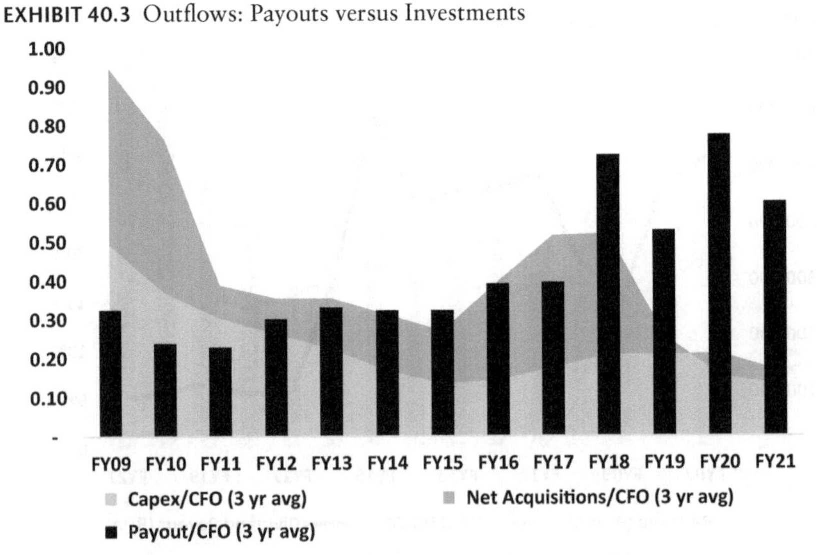

Source: Wipro Ltd Annual Reports and authors' calculations.

EXHIBIT 40.4 Outflows: Dividends and Repurchases

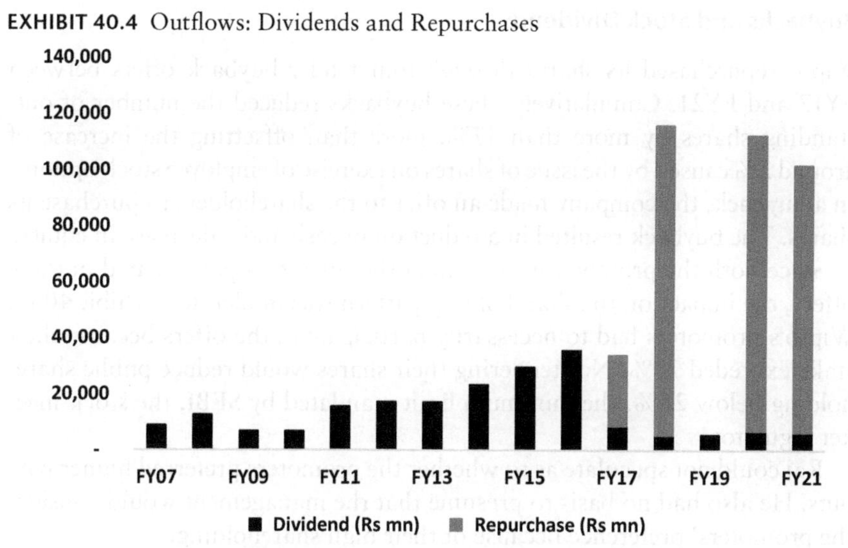

Source: Wipro Ltd Annual Reports and authors' calculations.

increased. Though both dividends per share and dividend payout ratio had fallen sharply from FY16 onwards, the company used large share buybacks to return cash to the shareholders (Exhibit 40.4). Wipro also maintained a moderate level of debt which was less than its cash and current investments and much below its borrowing capacity.

EXHIBIT 40.5 Share Price and Corporate Actions

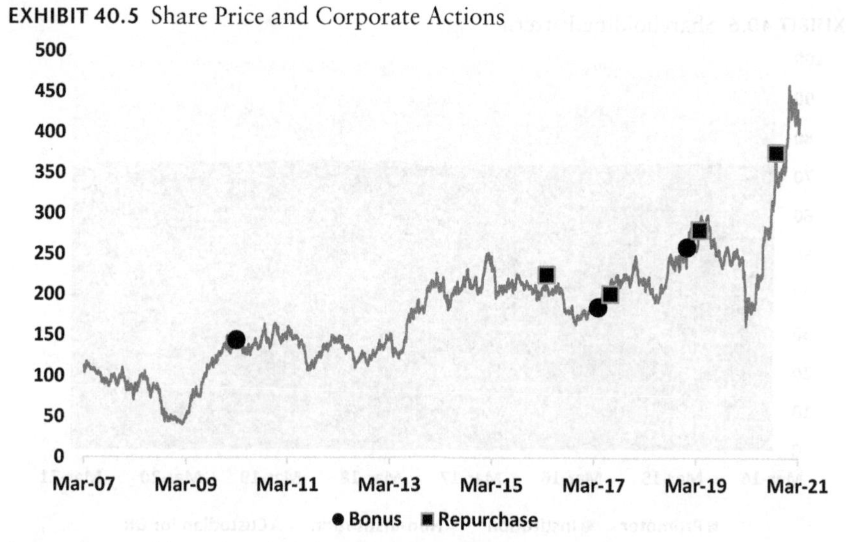

Source: Prepared by authors based on Capitaline AWS data.

Buybacks and Stock Dividends

Wipro repurchased its shares through four tender buyback offers between FY17 and FY21. Cumulatively, these buybacks reduced the number of outstanding shares by more than 17%, more than offsetting the increase of around 2% caused by the issue of shares on exercise of employee stock options. In a buyback, the company made an offer to the shareholders to purchase its shares. The buyback resulted in a reduction in cash and a decrease in equity.

Since both the promoter groups and other investors participated in these offers, the impact on the shareholding pattern was moderate (Exhibit 40.6). Wipro's promoters had to necessarily participate in the offers because their stake exceeded 70%. Not tendering their shares would reduce public shareholding below 25%, the minimum limit mandated by SEBI, the stock market regulator.

Raj could not speculate as to whether the promoters preferred higher payouts. He also had no basis to presume that the management would consider the promoters' preference because of their high shareholding.

Given Wipro's healthy business returns, Raj estimated the use of cash to buy back shares to have been positive for both earnings per share (EPS) and return on equity (ROE). More importantly, the buybacks had provided the company flexibility since, unlike dividends, investors did not typically expect companies to announce buybacks every year.

Tax structure affected the preference for quantum and the form of investor payout. In the absence of taxes, inadequate information and other constraints, dividends and buybacks were irrelevant in theory. However, in

EXHIBIT 40.6 Shareholding Pattern

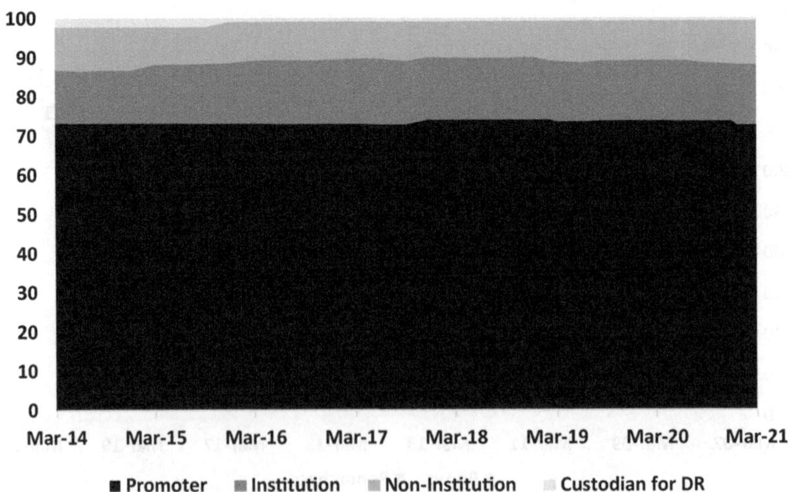

Source: Prepared by authors based on Capitaline AWS data.

practice, taxes were relevant, more so because of the frequent changes in Indian tax rules on capital gains and distributions. Though the government had re-introduced long-term capital gains tax on shares in FY 2018–19, earnings retention (which drove capital gains) still held an advantage through reinvesting and compounding incremental annual tax savings compared with distributions.

The changes in tax rules also affected the relative tax advantages of buybacks versus dividends. For instance, the Union Budget of 2019–20 shifted the tax burden of buybacks from shareholders to companies. On the other hand, the Union Budget of 2020–21 shifted the tax burden of dividends from companies to shareholders. The effect of this change was difficult to assess since tax liability differed according to the tax slab of the shareholder. Raj found that the impact of these changes on Wipro's distribution policy was apparent neither from the stated policy nor from the data.

Information constraints also influenced preference for dividends or share buybacks according to academic research through signalling effects. Managements would increase the level of dividends if they expected prospects to be better. In the case of buybacks, managements were expected to time their buybacks when they believed that the shares had been underpriced. Traders, particularly for companies with constrained information disclosure and dissemination, therefore relied on announcements of share buybacks or increased dividends as favourable signals of managements' optimism regarding future earnings prospects.

Raj was unsure if investors needed to rely on these signals for large, widely followed stock like Wipro, despite its concentrated shareholding. However, he did note that there had been a favourable price reaction in each instance of share repurchase on the next trading day after Wipro intimated to the exchanges that its board would meet to consider the share repurchase. However, the abnormal return had not lasted beyond a week on a cumulative basis (see Exhibit 40.5).

Unlike buybacks which had started only in FY17, Wipro had a long history of bonus issues, two of which it had made in recent years, in June 2017 and March 2019. A bonus issue (also known as a stock dividend) involved an accounting transfer from reserves to paid-up equity but had no impact on cash or capital structure, unlike share buybacks. A bonus issue reduced the EPS but did not affect the ROE. More importantly, it seemed to have no effect on the market value of shares on the ex-bonus date. For example, when the number of bonus shares doubled on an ex-bonus basis on June 13, 2017, the stock price also halved, and thus the issue had no net effect on the value of holdings of any investor.

Raj wondered how bonus shares added value to the investors. After browsing through the internet, Raj learnt about the liquidity and signalling motives of bonus issues. According to the liquidity motive, companies made bonus issues (and stock splits) to bring each share's price down to a more affordable range and increase the trading volumes. Since it involved a significant reduction in reserves (hence capacity to pay dividends out of accumulated reserves), a bonus issue signalled managements' confidence in paying future dividends out of future earnings.

As in the case of buybacks, Raj noticed that the first intimation to exchanges regarding the board meeting to consider a bonus issue had led to a favourable price reaction on three recent occasions, even though the effect was not long-lasting. He was unsure whether the mechanism that worked was signalling or simply a lack of investor awareness. The media often incorrectly mentioned a bonus issue as a "reward" to the investors. However, it seemed like a costless way of managing investor expectations, unlike dividends and buybacks, which involved actual cash outflows.

Finally, Raj compared Wipro's dividend payout policy and trends with other IT majors and found several similarities. Infosys Ltd, a direct peer, had stated a similar set of considerations in its dividend policy statement. It had also offered several share buybacks and a few bonus issues in recent years.

The Decision

Raj believed that companies' capital allocation and payout decisions provided him insights regarding the potential growth in their earnings and cash flows. He had compiled sufficient data and done adequate analysis in the case of Wipro. But he still needed to weigh the multiple considerations, decide, and articulate his position on the discussion thread. Had the change in Wipro's payout policy been positive for the investors?

Questions

1. Assess whether the payout policy of Wipro was optimal for its existing shareholders.
2. What would have been the consequence for Wipro's investors had the company not changed its dividend policy from FY 2016 onwards?
3. Critique the firm's decision to use all the three forms of payout to its investors.

Note

1 https://www.wipro.com/content/dam/nexus/en/investor/corporate-governance/policies-and-guidelines/ethical-guidelines/12769-dividend-distribution-policy-october-2016.pdf

PART V

Business Valuation

41

THE VALUATION OF KRISSKROSS HOTELS

On the morning of April 28, 2019, Eddie Madhvan, the CEO and promoter of KrissKross Hotels, walked excitedly into his CFOs office cabin, waving the day's copy of *The Hindu* newspaper. "Have you seen this article?" he asked Amit Lalani, the CFO. Amit nodded in affirmation as he had already read the article on his mobile app. The Indian hospitality sector seemed to be heading for a boom in the coming year after a decade, the news article had said. It also mentioned that the industry would witness further consolidation.[1]

Eddie and Amit had been in talks with Washburn Property Partners (WPP), a UK-based global alternative asset management company focused on real estate, which was interested in acquiring a significant stake in KrissKross. In another 15 minutes, Amit had to join Eddie in the latter's office to discuss valuation for the potential deal.

Growth Path

Eddie and a team of young executives had set up KrissKross Hotels in 2005 with their first, an upper-midscale business hotel in Mumbai. They had a lucky start as the first few years saw exceptional demand as the overall industry occupancy and average room rates peaked in 2007. They quickly set up new hotels in Jaipur, Ahmedabad, and Indore, targeting the business travellers (Exhibits 41.1 and 41.2). The hotels were efficient and modern with lots of technology, logistic, and workspace facilities but functional in comfort, room space, and amenities.

The global financial crisis and the years that followed saw sharply declining and later stagnant occupancy rates (Exhibit 41.3). It was not until 2014

DOI: 10.4324/9781032724478-47

EXHIBIT 41.1 City-wise Room Revenues of KrissKross Hotels (FY 2018–19)

	Mumbai	*Ahmedabad*	*Jaipur*	*Indore*	*Aggregate*
Rooms	200	150	150	100	600
Average Room Rate	7,000	5,000	5,000	4,000	5,500
Occupancy Rate	75%	65%	65%	65%	68%
Revenue per Available Room	5,250	3,250	3,250	2,600	3,758
Room Revenues (Rs million)	383	178	178	95	834

Source: Prepared by authors.

EXHIBIT 41.2 Segment-wise Break-up of FY 2018–19 Revenues of KrissKross Hotels

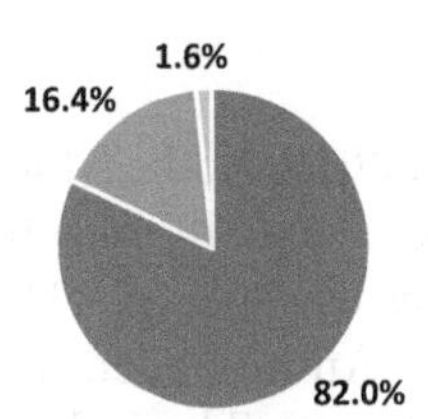

Source: Prepared by authors.

EXHIBIT 41.3 Trend in Hotel Industry Occupancy Rates

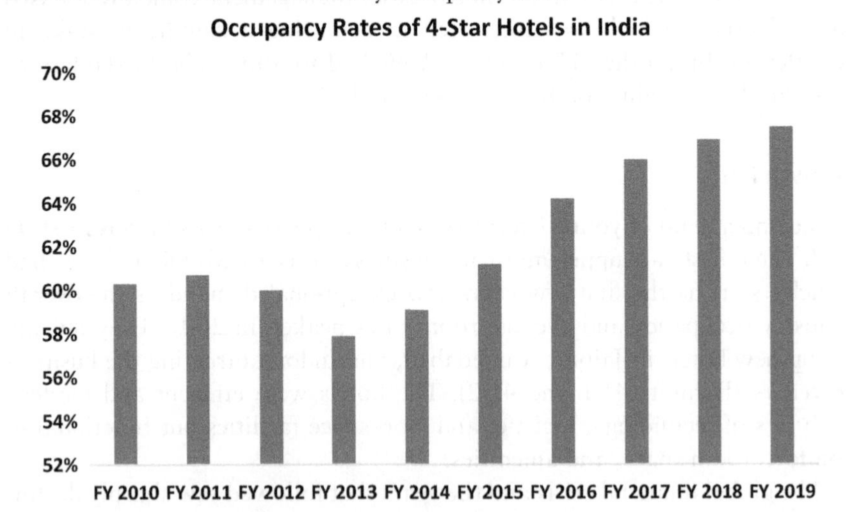

Source: Prepared by authors based on data from Statista.

when the industry occupancy rates started looking up. As demand conditions improved for the industry from 2014 onwards and occupancy rates steadily climbed up, KrissKross did well by historical comparison (Exhibit 41.4). However, Eddie was disappointed whenever he compared growth with some of the more successful players having the same vintage.

Unlike KrissKross, a few other hotel chains had attracted private equity interest much earlier, helping them scale up much faster. Eddie had short-listed Nagpur, Surat, Rajkot, Kota, Raipur, Coimbatore, and Ludhiana as possible destinations for the next set of hotels almost eight years ago. However, the inability to get external equity funding and his conservativeness in using debt had limited the expansion to the existing cities. On the

EXHIBIT 41.4 KrissKross Hotels: Historical Financial Statements (Rs million)

	2016–17	*2017–18*	*2018–19*
Revenue	827	951	1,018
Cost of Food and Beverages	81	94	100
Employee Benefit Expenses	126	139	152
Other Expenses	350	385	424
EBIDTA	270	334	342
Depreciation	96	103	117
EBIT	174	231	225
Interest	30	60	68
Profit Before Tax	144	171	156
Tax	43	51	47
Profit After Tax	101	120	109
	2016–17	2017–18	2018–19
Assets			
Property, Plant and Equipment	1,200	1,380	1,546
Total Non-Current Assets	1,200	1,380	1,546
Inventories	7	8	8
Trade Receivables	138	159	170
Cash and Equivalents	41	48	51
Total Current Assets	186	214	229
Total Assets	1,386	1,594	1,774
Liabilities and Equity			
Total Equity	872	992	1,101
Long-Term Borrowings	500	586	656
Total Non-Current Liabilities	500	586	656
Trade Payables	14	16	17
Total Current Liabilities	14	16	17
Total Liabilities and Equity	1,386	1,594	1,774

Source: Prepared by authors.

EXHIBIT 41.5 Peer Valuations (at the end of FY 2018–19)

	Indian Hotels	*EIH Ltd.*	*Lemon Tree Hotels*	*Chalet Hotels*
P/E	73.2	90.5	226.9	-
P/BV	4.1	4.0	6.4	5.8
EV/EBIDTA	24.4	28.0	49.7	21.4
Revenue (Rs million)	27,804	15,751	2,735	10,027
Market Cap (Rs million)	184,216	117,715	63,895	69,257
Revenue growth (5 yr)	7.6%	4.9%	12.8%	14.9%
EBIDTA Margin	27.3%	25.7%	42.5%	37.5%
PAT Margin	9.1%	6.9%	20.0%	-1.0%
ROE	6.2%	4.0%	6.7%	-1.0%

Source: CMIE Prowess and author's calculations.

other hand, he felt satisfied with the operational efficiency of his hotels and considered their profitability to be reasonably good, though far from excellent.

When WPP approached Eddie for discussing acquiring around 15% stake, he was immediately interested because they could solve the funding issues of KrissKross. It turned out that WPP had very different plans in terms of locations, scale, and selective use of acquisition strategy to complement the long gestation developmental projects. The second plank of WPP's strategy was to "move up" the KrissKross brand's appeal to target more senior business executives as customers, thereby charging better average room rates. Thirdly, WPP believed that KrissKross could reduce business risks by diversifying into leisure-cum-business destinations or even acquiring a small leisure hotel chain.

Though Eddie had his reservations, he believed that WPP knew the industry inside-out, and their selective acquisitions in India had substantially gained in value on an average. Adding to his comfort was that WPP had the image of partners who did not interfere with operational decisions, and their previous acquisitions had not resulted in much executive churn.

For these reasons, Eddie was keen to bring WPP on board. WPP had already conducted due diligence of the financial figures of KrissKross and had all their queries answered. A meeting to kick-start the negotiations on value was scheduled for next week. Eddie and Amit were going to meet their investment banking advisor in two days.

Eddie, who had always believed in his homework, asked Amit to prepare two sets of financial projections and valuations; one based on business-as-usual (BAU) scenario, without WPP on board, and the other based on the scenario with WPP on board.

Value in the Eyes of the Beholder

Eddie looked at Amit's financial projections (Exhibits 41.6 and 41.7) with deep concentration when Amit entered his room. "How has your team been able to make projections for ten years?" Eddie asked Amit. "I can hardly predict the numbers for even one year, and I am always praying that there is no unexpected catastrophe," he added. Amit explained all the assumptions with the rationale that his team had printed in a single sheet. The assumptions were internally consistent; for instance, high revenue growth had to be accompanied by increased capital investment.

Eddie and Amit spent the next fifteen minutes going over the projections based on the scenario with WPP on board. Though WPP's representatives had not explicitly shared plans, their thought process had become evident from their discussions with KrissKross. Amit had provided his team with the assumptions that he believed would be consistent with augmented resources and strategic changes after onboarding of WPP.

Eddie and Amit next discussed the assumptions for cost of capital calculations. "With WPP on board, our risk-taking ability could change. In your view, will our valuation increase or decrease if we take more debt?" Eddie asked. Amit explained that the effect of capital structure on value was complex since both the cost of debt and equity could change, and he would explain that to Eddie later. Eddie agreed to move the discussion ahead.

Eddie wanted to understand the terminal growth assumptions (Exhibit 41.8). He wanted to confirm if the terminal growth rate was real and not nominal since he found the growth rate low. Amit explained to Eddie the conceptual problems with assuming high growth rates in perpetuity.

Finally, Eddie wanted to discuss the results of the valuation. "Do you believe that in the business as usual scenario, our market value should be less than the book value?" he asked Amit. Amit explained that the result was not surprising considering the returns on capital which they got from the projections. However, the explanation did not convince Eddie.

Eddie was happy to see that the value more than doubled in the "With-WPP" scenario but thought that the growth could be even higher if they added new hotel capacity in the metros. Amit explained that though operating cash flows would increase in that case, the rise in investment outflows could offset the same. Finally, it was the free cash flows that mattered. Eddie also asked Amit to figure out what impact would shift to a more asset-light business model by managing hotel properties not owned by KrissKross have on valuation.

As he kept looking into calculations, Eddie remembered his negotiations with a private equity player sometime back. "While you have used a growth in perpetuity approach for estimating the terminal value, that is not how I

EXHIBIT 41.6 KrissKross Hotels: Financial Projections for Business-as-Usual Scenario (Rs million)

	2019–20	*2020–21*	*2021–22*	*2022–23*	*2023-24*	*2024–25*	*2025–26*	*2026–27*	*2027–28*	*2028–29*
Revenue	**1,089**	**1,220**	**1,366**	**1,530**	**1,683**	**1,851**	**2,036**	**2,199**	**2,331**	**2,471**
Cost of Food and Beverages	107	120	134	151	166	182	200	216	229	243
Employee Benefit Expenses	168	181	196	211	228	246	266	287	310	329
Other Expenses	466	503	543	587	634	684	739	798	862	914
EBIDTA	**348**	**415**	**492**	**581**	**655**	**738**	**830**	**897**	**929**	**985**
Depreciation	131	147	164	184	204	225	247	265	279	293
EBIT	**217**	**268**	**328**	**397**	**451**	**513**	**583**	**631**	**650**	**692**
Interest	78	90	102	115	126	137	149	159	166	175
Profit before Tax	**139**	**179**	**226**	**282**	**325**	**377**	**434**	**472**	**484**	**517**
Tax	42	54	68	84	97	113	130	142	145	155
Profit after Tax	**97**	**125**	**158**	**197**	**227**	**264**	**304**	**331**	**339**	**362**
	2019–20	**2020–21**	**2021–22**	**2022–23**	**2023-24**	**2024–25**	**2025–26**	**2026–27**	**2027–28**	**2028–29**
Assets										
Property, Plant and Equipment	1,731	1,939	2,171	2,432	2,675	2,943	3,237	3,399	3,569	3,747
Total Non-Current Assets	**1,731**	**1,939**	**2,171**	**2,432**	**2,675**	**2,943**	**3,237**	**3,399**	**3,569**	**3,747**
Inventories	9	10	11	13	14	15	17	18	19	20
Trade Receivables	181	203	228	255	280	309	339	367	388	412
Cash and Equivalents	54	61	68	76	84	93	102	110	117	124
Total Current Assets	**245**	**274**	**307**	**344**	**378**	**416**	**458**	**494**	**524**	**556**
Total Assets	**1,976**	**2,213**	**2,479**	**2,776**	**3,054**	**3,359**	**3,695**	**3,893**	**4,093**	**4,303**

Liabilities & Equity										
Total Equity	**1,199**	**1,324**	**1,466**	**1,644**	**1,837**	**2,035**	**2,248**	**2,380**	**2,515**	**2,624**
Long-Term Borrowings	759	869	990	1,107	1,189	1,294	1,414	1,478	1,539	1,638
Total Non-Current Liabilities	**759**	**869**	**990**	**1,107**	**1,189**	**1,294**	**1,414**	**1,478**	**1,539**	**1,638**
Trade Payables	18	20	22	25	28	30	33	36	38	41
Total Current Liabilities	**18**	**20**	**22**	**25**	**28**	**30**	**33**	**36**	**38**	**41**
Total Liabilities and Equity	**1,976**	**2,213**	**2,479**	**2,776**	**3,054**	**3,359**	**3,695**	**3,893**	**4,093**	**4,303**

Source: Prepared by authors.

EXHIBIT 41.7 KrissKross Hotels: Financial Projections for With-WPP Scenario (Rs million)

	2019–20	*2020–21*	*2021–22*	*2022–23*	*2023-24*	*2024–25*	*2025–26*	*2026–27*	*2027–28*	*2028–29*
Revenue	**1,089**	**1,252**	**1,503**	**1,803**	**2,074**	**2,322**	**2,555**	**2,759**	**2,925**	**3,100**
Cost of Food and Beverages	107	123	148	177	204	229	251	271	288	305
Employee Benefit Expenses	168	184	212	238	261	288	311	335	362	384
Other Expenses	466	512	589	660	726	799	863	932	1,006	1,066
EBIDTA	**348**	**432**	**553**	**728**	**882**	**1,008**	**1,130**	**1,221**	**1,269**	**1,345**
Depreciation	131	147	167	192	221	250	277	298	313	328
EBIT	**217**	**285**	**387**	**536**	**662**	**758**	**853**	**923**	**956**	**1,016**
Interest	78	89	104	121	135	147	159	167	171	178
Profit before Tax	139	196	282	416	527	611	694	756	785	839
Tax	42	59	85	125	158	183	208	227	235	252
Profit after Tax	**97**	**137**	**198**	**291**	**369**	**428**	**486**	**529**	**549**	**587**
	2019–20	**2020–21**	**2021–22**	**2022–23**	**2023-24**	**2024–25**	**2025–26**	**2026–27**	**2027–28**	**2028–29**
Assets										
Property, Plant and Equipment	1,731	1,939	2,230	2,564	2,949	3,303	3,633	3,814	4,005	4,205
Total Non-Current Assets	**1,731**	**1,939**	**2,230**	**2,564**	**2,949**	**3,303**	**3,633**	**3,814**	**4,005**	**4,205**
Inventories	9	10	12	15	17	19	21	23	24	25
Trade Receivables	181	209	250	301	346	387	426	460	487	517
Cash and Equivalents	54	63	75	90	104	116	128	138	146	155
Total Current Assets	**245**	**282**	**338**	**405**	**466**	**522**	**574**	**620**	**658**	**697**
Total Assets	**1,976**	**2,220**	**2,568**	**2,970**	**3,415**	**3,825**	**4,207**	**4,435**	**4,663**	**4,902**

Liabilities & Equity										
Total Equity	1,199	1,336	1,514	1,776	2,089	2,410	2,653	2,865	3,029	3,205
Long-Term Borrowings	759	864	1,029	1,164	1,292	1,377	1,512	1,525	1,585	1,646
Total Non-Current Liabilities	759	864	1,029	1,164	1,292	1,377	1,512	1,525	1,585	1,646
Trade Payables	18	21	25	30	34	38	42	45	48	51
Total Current Liabilities	18	21	25	30	34	38	42	45	48	51
Total Liabilities and Equity	1,976	2,220	2,568	2,970	3,415	3,825	4,207	4,435	4,663	4,902

Source: Prepared by authors.

EXHIBIT 41.8 Cost of Capital and Terminal Growth

10 Year G-Sec, Govt. of India	7.4%
Equity Market Risk Premium	7.0%
Unlevered Beta, Peer Average	1.40
Marginal Tax Rate	30%
Cost of Debt	11%
D/E, End of FY19 (book value)	0.81
Target D/E (market value)	0.50
Terminal Growth Rate	5.0%

Source: Prepared by authors.

have seen PEs do their valuation," he said. Eddie was referring to the fact that private equity players forecasted an exit value based on estimated exit multiples rather than using perpetuity growth and cost of capital assumptions. Amit argued that it was inappropriate to mix fundamental valuation for the explicit forecast period with relative valuation. The private equity players effectively estimated the probable price at which they could exit to calculate the rate of return on their investments.

"But that is precisely my point," quipped Eddie. "If we are going to negotiate with WPP, why not estimate the value using the way they look at it?" Eddie explained that though he agreed conceptually with Amit on the valuation approach, he would prefer if Amit's team could also estimate the firm value by applying market multiples after just five years of cash flow projections. Amit believed that applying peer-based multiples (Exhibit 41.5) would result in a much higher valuation for KrissKross, but wondered which underlying assumptions would justify using those multiples.

After an hour's discussion, Eddie and Amit decided to end the meeting. Amit promised to come back with responses to Eddie's unanswered queries. As Amit left the room, Eddie had mixed feelings about the meeting. On the one hand, he felt uneasy about the highly subjective nature of corporate valuation. On the other, he found that it provided him with some valuable insights into the value of his business. "In the future, I should think about the value drivers of my business more often," Eddie told himself.

Questions

1. Estimate the value of the firm and the value of equity of KrissKross Hotels in the BAU scenario.
2. Estimate the value of the firm and the value of equity of KrissKross Hotels in the With-WPP scenario. State your observations after comparing the values under both scenarios.

3. Estimate the value of equity in the With-WPP scenario using exit multiples based on five-year projections to estimate the terminal value. State your observations and relative advantages and disadvantages of using this method.

Note

1 https://www.thehindu.com/business/Industry/hospitality-sector-set-for-boom-after-a-decades-lull/article26967976.ece

42

KOTAK MAHINDRA BANK LTD

Challenges in Valuation of Financial Services Firm

In October 2019, Jimit Gupta and Swati Mohapatra were in the middle of their week-long executive education programme at one of the leading business schools in Mumbai – India's financial capital. On the third day of the programme, the instructor gave them the assignment to value Kotak Mahindra Bank Limited (KMBL), India's top private sector bank. While they had learned and had done some exercises to value a simple manufacturing firm, valuing a bank was a new challenge. They tried to fit in the standard discounted cash flow (DCF) valuation template they were provided with to value KMBL but found it challenging to apply.

Jimit and Swati joined Alpha Achievers Capital Partners as sell-side analysts post their MBA in the summer of 2017. They tracked the banking sector, prepared sell-side equity research reports, and primarily used trading multiples to value stocks they followed. However, they knew their research reports became the butt of jokes in the investor's community. James, one of the key clients, recently said: "Your reports are excellent. I have earned much money by just doing opposite to what you recommended in reports."

Divya Shetty, the research head of the institutional desk, keenly followed Prof Damodaran's[1] writings and videos and she increasingly believed that discounted cash flow (DCF) valuation methods were among the best valuation techniques to value a listed firm. According to DCF, value of any firm was discounted value of future cash flows (see Exhibit 42.1 for a comparison of various DCF approaches). While in principle such valuation techniques were relatively simple implementing them required skills and an in-depth understanding of the firm's business model and industry dynamics in question. Given that, Divya worked with the HR team of Alpha Achievers. In turn, they worked with a reputed B-school to design a

DOI: 10.4324/9781032724478-48

EXHIBIT 42.1 Comparison of Various DCF Valuation Approaches

	Relevant Cash Flow	*Relevant Discount Rate*	*Underlying Assumption*	*Output*
FCF (Unlevered free cash flow to firm)-Based Valuation	FCF = EBIT*(1-T) +Depreciation – Capex – Change in Working Capital	Post-tax WACC WACC = kd*wd*(1-T) +ke*we	Debt to equity remains constant WACC is based on market value weights of debt and equity or target debt to equity.	Value of firm or enterprise value of the firm where Value of Firm = Value + Net debt
FCE (Free cash flow to equity)-Based Valuation	FCE = Net Income + Depreciation – Capex – Change in working capital + Net borrowings	Levered cost of equity ke	Debt to equity remains constant WACC is based on market value weights of debt and equity or target debt to equity.	Value of Equity
CCF (Capital Cash Flow)-Based Valuation	CCF = FCF + I*(1-T)	Pre-tax WACC	Varying level of debt and changing debt to equity ratio. Interest tax shield has the same level of risk as a free cash flow to the firm.	Value of Firm = Value of Equity + Net debt
Adjusted Present Value	VL= VU + Present Value of Interest tax shield – Cost of financial distress	Unlevered cost of equity ke	A constant level of debt. Interest tax shield to be discounted at the pre-tax cost of debt.	Value of levered firm based on the value of unlevered firm.

Source: Prepared by Authors.

custom programme on "Corporate Valuation: A Journey from Knowing to Doing." Jimit and Swati were the participants from the first batch of such a programme.

Both Jimit and Swati tried to use a two-stage DCF valuation template based on FCF and WACC to value a manufacturing firm to value KMBL but soon realised it would not work. They looked at the binder provided to them and found a note on "Valuation of Financial Services Firms" by Prof Aswath Damodaran listed for next day pre-class reading. Both met after two hours with their notes on how financial services firms' valuation could be different and ways to do that.

Kotak Mahindra Bank

Established in 1985 by Uday Kotak, Kotak Mahindra Finance Limited (KMFL) became the first Non-Banking Finance Company (NBFC) to get a banking licence in 2003. Since then, Kotak Mahindra Bank had made its mark as the top private sector bank in India. A large financial services conglomerate with business interest spread across Banking, Insurance, Asset Management, Broking, Investment Banking.

KMBL reported Rs 1,408 crore of net income with Rs 205,695 crore in loan book and Rs 312,172 crore in total assets at the end of FY19. It reported 4.48% of Net Interest Margin (NIM). KMBL had a net NPA of 0.78% and impressive CASA deposits of 52.5%. Such a high percentage of CASA deposits kept its cost of funds to as low as 5.5%, resulting in high NIM. In addition, KMBL maintained its Capital Adequacy Ratio (CAR) at 17.9%, with Tier-1 capital at 16.9%, which was much higher than the regulatory capital requirement as per Basel III. It means it could grow without any immediate fundraising requirement, either by issuing debt or equity (See Exhibit 42.2, 42.3, and 42.4 for Income Statements, Balance Sheets, and financial highlights of KMBL).

Valuation of Financial Services Firms

Jimit: How financial services firms are different from a typical manufacturing firm?

Swati: Well, there are three significant differences. First, they are heavily regulated and required to maintain regulatory capital. Second, most of their assets are valued at market value instead of book value for a manufacturing firm. Third, re-investment in a typical firm in the form of capital expenditure and change in working capital is meaningless here. Hence, it would not be possible to calculate FCF or FCE for such firms.

Jimit: How do you calculate WACC for a financial services firm?

EXHIBIT 42.2 KMBL Income Statements

	Q2FY 2020	*Q2FY 2019*	*Q1FY 2020*	*FY 2019*
Net Interest Income	3,350	2,676	3,161	11,206
Other Income	1,224	1,218	1,317	4,657
Fees and Services	1,162	1,032	1,162	4,287
Others	62	186	155	370
Net Total Income	**4,574**	**3,894**	**4,478**	**15,863**
Employee Cost	915	745	902	3,159
Other Operating Expenses	1,150	1,054	1,177	4,356
Operating Expenditure	**2,065**	**1,799**	**2,079**	**7,515**
Operating Profit	**2,509**	**2,095**	**2,399**	**8,348**
Provision on Adv/Receivables (net)	398	221	273	976
Provision on Investments	10	133	44	–14
Provisions and Contingencies	**408**	**354**	**317**	**962**
PBT	**2101**	**1741**	**2082**	**7386**
Provision for Tax	377	599	722	2521
PAT	**1724**	**1142**	**1360**	**4865**

Source: Prepared by authors based on data from Capitaline and Company website.

EXHIBIT 42.3 KMBL Balance Sheets (Rs in Crore)

	30-Sep-19	*30-Sep-18*	*30-Jun-19*
Capital & Reserves and Surplus	45,912	40,103	44,290
Deposits	23,3071	20,5830	23,2931
CA	38,200	30,796	36,543
SA	86,712	72,606	81,580
Term Deposits	**10,8159**	**10,2428**	**11,4808**
Of which: TD Sweep	16,548	13,541	16,375
Borrowings	26,665	32,584	27,242
Other Liabilities and Provisions	11,242	10,319	10,646
Total Liabilities	**31,6890**	**28,8836**	**31,5109**
	30-Sep-19	**30-Sep-18**	**30-Jun-19**
Cash, Bank, and Call	17,780	24,598	18,839
Investments	74,331	67,915	77,259
Government Securities	60,969	55,944	64,532
Others	13,362	11,971	12,727
Advances	2,13,299	1,84,940	2,08,030
Fixed Assets and Other Assets	11,480	11,383	10,981
Total Assets	**3,16,890**	**2,88,836**	**3,15,109**

Source: Prepared by authors based on data from Capitaline and Company website.

EXHIBIT 42.4 Financial Highlights KMBL (Rs in Crore)

	Q2FY 2020	*Q2FY 2019*
PAT	1724	1142
NIM	4.61%	4.19%
Loans	2,13,299	1,84,940
Net NPA	0.85%	0.81%
Total Assets	3,16,890	2,88,836
CAR	18.20%	18%
Tier-1 CAR	17.60%	17.40%
Branches	1512	1425
CASA	53.60%	50.20%

Source: Prepared by authors based on data from Capitaline and Company website.

Swati: Oh! That is a big challenge. First, money for a bank is a raw material rather than a source of fund. Second, if we include deposit as a source of fund, the unlevered post-tax operating income calculation must leave out interest on such deposits. Interest expense might be the single-most-significant expense for a bank, giving distorted cash flow numbers. Besides, for banks with high CASA deposits the cost of fund turn out to be very low. Lower than risk-free rate and which might result in abnormally low cost of capital. Third, Banks operate with very high financial leverage, and a slight increase in bad loans can wipe out a significant amount of equity capital.

Jimit: There is one more issue. Banks have to maintain their debt–equity ratio in book value terms rather than market value terms for a regulatory purpose, and hence we cannot use book value weights to calculate WACC. But why can't we discount back firms' earnings since the bank does not have any Capex or working capital requirement?

Swati: Well, it is not simply possible. Discounting earnings with any positive growth for a bank implicitly assume growth in loan-book; such loan growth is not likely without re-investment in regulatory capital. To that extent, incremental investment in regulatory capital to support growth in loan-book is equivalent to Capex for a manufacturing firm.

Jimit: So, which are the possible discounted cash flow approaches one should use to value financial services firms?

Swati: Well, there are three possible ways. First, using a basic dividend discount model with necessary dividend pay-out consistent with growth. Second, using equity cash flow-based model as I mentioned earlier, using re-investment rate equivalent of Capex.

FCFE = Net income – investment in regulatory capital to support growth in the loan book.

And third, the excess return model, which I believe we should use to value KMBL. Again, the basic model is straightforward.
Value of Equity = Value of Invested equity capital + Present value of expected excess returns to equity shareholders.
The model is solid and straightforward. The firm earns return on equity equals its cost of equity should see the market value of equity converging to current capital invested in the business. The firms with positive excess return on their present and future investments might trade at a market value higher than the value of equity capital invested. Conversely, the firm that earns ROE less than the cost of equity sees its market value dipping below its book value of equity capitals invested.
So the value creation or value destruction is entirely a function of identifying potential investment opportunities that can earn ROE greater than the cost of capital and the firm's ability to find such opportunities over a long period continuously.
*Excess Return on Equity = (Return on Equity minus Cost of Equity) * Equity capital invested.*

Jimit: Good, I have gathered financial information for KMBL and have also come up with some key assumptions to calculate the value of the standalone banking business of KMBL.

Swati: But what about other businesses of KMBL? Most of the subsidiaries are not listed, contributing close to 30% of consolidated profit after tax. So how do we value them?

Jimit: Let us first value the firm on a standalone basis and then look at valuing subsidiaries. Let us see what professor says about our valuation tomorrow.

Questions

1. What is the cost of equity for KMBL? Should we use the different cost of equity in a steady-state? Why? Why not?
2. Project net income, equity cost, and excess return on equity from 2020 to 2029.
3. Calculate the terminal value of KMBL.
4. What is the implied ROE from 2020 to 2029, given the bank would maintain 16% Tier-1 equity capital and its net interest margin remain constant at the Q2FY20 level?

Note

1 Prof. Ashwath Damodaran is a Professor of Finance (as of October 2019) at Stern Business School, NYU. He is popularly known as "Dean of Valuation" given his expertise in corporate valuation.

43

ASHIAN BIOTECH

Acquisition of Myanti Biopharma

On April 3, 2020, Rishi Bhargav, Chief Executive Officer of Ashian Biotech, held a videoconference with his senior management team to discuss the company's future. Lately, he had been under fire from the company's board for not pursuing new opportunities aggressively. Krish Rao, Ashian's founder and chairman, had told Rishi that the board might not renew Rishi's three-year contract, which was coming to an end in December 2020, if the growth plans continued to disappoint them.

Ashian Biotech had grown fast from a small base during 2011–2016. It had made an IPO in December 2015 of Rs 50 crore. However, growth had slowed down considerably during 2017–2020. Earnings had not only stagnated but had even begun to decline in recent years. Despite weakening financial performance, Ashian was still a cash-rich company, as cash and liquid investment balances continued to remain high.

It was in this context that Rishi had called for the videoconference with the senior management team, including Anshuman Mittal (President – New Projects), Bibek Singh (Chief Operating Officer) and George Cherian (Chief Financial Officer). Among other proposals, the management team discussed developing AntiCov, a Covid-19 vaccine. Resuming after a break, the team started discussing a potential acquisition.

Acquisition of Myanti Biopharma

Rishi: Bibek, you were working on the acquisition of Myanti Biopharma. Can you please brief us regarding the progress? Anshuman and George, if you recollect, we started looking at Myanti last year as their products complement ours very well.

DOI: 10.4324/9781032724478-49

Bibek: I managed to reach out to the promoters of Myanti through an investment banking contact. They have shared some financials. The investment banker has given me preliminary forecasts (Exhibit 43.1).

Rishi: How much will it cost us?

Bibek: According to the investment banker, the Myanti promoters expect upward of Rs 30 crore for their stake of 80%. Financial institutions and other private investors hold the remaining stake. We should be able to negotiate their offer downwards.

George: One thing I like about Myanti is that its business risk profile seems similar to ours. But we should not pay anything extra in the name of synergy. What are the key strengths of Myanti?

Bibek: Myanti is well-established in the biopharma business, has skilled people, and a strong product pipeline. I believe that it can sustain growth for a long time. As for synergy benefits, I expect an annual reduction of around 5% of Myanti's employee expenses.

Rishi: Can you explain how we can achieve the reduction in employee costs?

Bibek: Well, I looked at Anshuman's sheet of Ashian's surplus R&D and technical staff currently working on exploratory research initiatives awaiting new projects. I reckon that they can replace equivalent staff at Myanti whom we can offer termination packages. The staff reduction will, of course, take up the upfront costs by Rs 4 crores. The other acquisition-related costs will be Rs 5 crores.

Rishi: It is a pity that we cannot use our shares to acquire because our stock prices are low.

George: Our stock prices are a major concern. They were sliding even before the pandemic, and now they have done worse (Exhibit 43.2). I reckon that we may have to take some debt.

Bibek: I also recollect Krish insisting on bringing debt on Ashian's books. Perhaps we can take debt to pay out a one-time dividend or to repurchase our shares.

George: I did explore the effects of raising some debt. We currently have AAA quality creditworthiness thanks to having no debt. An advisor has provided estimates of how our cost of borrowing will change with debt (Exhibits 43.3 and 43.4). These estimates should give us some idea of how much debt we should take. Remember that our cost of equity will also increase once we take more debt.

Rishi: Look, there is no need for us to take debt just because Krish has raised the point. Instead, we could make a case as to why we should remain a zero-debt company. We can try to fund our requirements completely using our internal sources. This way, we can avoid loan processing or security issuance costs associated

EXHIBIT 43.1 Financial Forecasts of Myanti Biopharma Ltd

Rs Crore	*2019–20*	*2020–21F*	*2021–22F*	*2022–23F*	*2023–24F*	*2024–25F*	*2025–26F*	*2026–27F*	*2027–28F*	*2028–29F*	*2029–30F*
Sales	100.2	105.2	126.3	151.5	174.2	200.4	230.4	253.5	273.7	292.9	310.5
Other Income	0.2	0.2	0.2	0.2	0.3	0.3	0.4	0.4	0.4	0.5	0.5
Total Income	**100.4**	**105.4**	**126.5**	**151.7**	**174.5**	**200.7**	**230.8**	**253.9**	**274.2**	**293.4**	**311.0**
Material Costs	63.8	67.0	79.0	93.3	107.3	123.4	141.9	156.0	168.5	180.3	191.1
Employee Expenses	16.2	17.0	19.6	22.5	25.9	29.8	34.2	37.6	40.6	43.5	46.1
Other Manufacturing Expenses	7.8	8.2	9.4	10.8	12.5	14.3	16.5	18.1	19.6	20.9	22.2
Selling and Admin Expenses	6.5	6.5	7.0	8.1	9.3	10.6	12.2	13.5	14.5	15.6	16.5
PBDIT	6.1	6.7	11.4	17.1	19.7	22.6	26.0	28.6	30.9	33.0	35.0
Depreciation	3.8	4.0	4.3	5.2	6.2	7.1	8.2	9.4	10.4	11.2	12.0
PBIT	2.3	2.6	7.1	11.9	13.4	15.5	17.8	19.1	20.5	21.8	23.0
Interest	3.9	3.8	4.0	4.7	5.4	5.9	6.4	7.0	7.2	7.2	6.9
PBT	(1.6)	(1.2)	3.2	7.2	8.0	9.6	11.4	12.1	13.3	14.6	16.1
Tax	-	-	0.8	1.8	2.0	2.4	2.8	3.0	3.3	3.7	4.0
Profit after Tax	**(1.6)**	**(1.2)**	**2.4**	**5.4**	**6.0**	**7.2**	**8.5**	**9.1**	**9.9**	**11.0**	**12.1**
Equity	11.9	10.7	13.1	17.5	22.5	28.7	35.2	42.3	50.3	59.2	69.3
Debt	27.2	28.3	33.7	38.7	42.1	45.6	50.2	51.6	51.2	49.3	45.8
Capital Expenditure	1.9	6.0	10.8	12.9	13.2	15.1	17.4	16.5	16.6	17.1	17.4
Working Capital											
Inventory	5.8	4.0	4.8	5.8	6.6	7.6	8.8	9.6	10.4	11.1	11.8
Trade Receivables	2.1	2.0	2.4	2.9	3.3	3.8	4.4	4.8	5.2	5.6	5.9
Cash	4.1	2.8	3.4	4.0	4.6	5.3	6.1	6.7	7.3	7.8	8.3
Trade Payables	3.1	2.0	2.4	2.9	3.3	3.8	4.4	4.8	5.2	5.6	5.9

Source: Prepared by authors.

EXHIBIT 43.2 Stock Price Trend of Ashian Biotech vs S&P BSE SmallCap Index

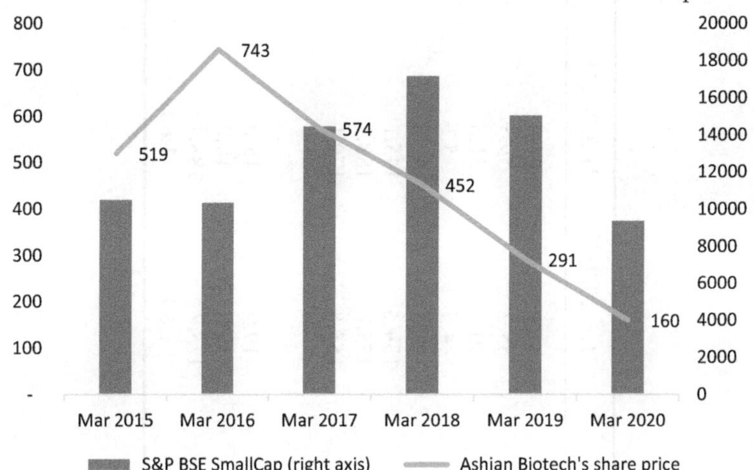

Source: www.bseindia.com and authors' estimates.

EXHIBIT 43.3 Changes in Ashian Biotech's Cost of Debt with Leverage

Debt-Equity (Market Value)	*Pre-tax Cost of Debt*
< 0.40	7.60%
0.40 to 0.90	8.40%
0.90 to 1.20	9.90%
1.20 to 2.00	11.40%

Source: Prepared by authors.

EXHIBIT 43.4 Assumptions for Ashian Biotech's Equity Returns

Risk-Free Rate	6.4%
Equity Market-Risk Premium	7%
Equity Beta (historical, 3-year)	0.80
Marginal Corporate Tax Rate	25%

Note: Debt beta for Ashian Biotech may be assumed to be negligible.
Source: Prepared by authors.

with debt. We could even wait for the equity market conditions to improve and then raise some equity to replenish our war chest of surplus cash and marketable securities.

George: Certainly, though our financial statements and forecasts for 2020–21 suggest that we will continue to retain a war chest for any future projects or acquisitions (Exhibits 43.5 and 43.6). Of

EXHIBIT 43.5 Balance Sheet of Ashian Biotech

Rs Crore	*31.3.2017*	*31.3.2018*	*31.3.2019*	*31.3.2020*	*31.3.2021F*
Property, Plant and Equipment, net	29.8	37.3	39.3	41.1	43.0
Inventories	16.5	30.0	44.0	55.2	59.5
Trade Receivables	9.6	16.5	20.6	30.4	31.0
Cash	3.4	4.2	4.3	4.5	5.1
Marketable Securities	51.1	49.5	51.6	44.4	49.5
Total Current Assets	80.5	100.2	120.4	134.6	145.1
Total Assets	**110.3**	**137.5**	**159.7**	**175.7**	**188.1**
Total Equity	102.1	125.6	143.9	155.8	170.1
Long-Term Debt	-	-	-	-	-
Short-Term Debt	-	-	-	-	-
Trade Payables	8.2	11.9	15.8	19.9	18.0
Total Liabilities	8.2	11.9	15.8	19.9	18.0
Total Equity and Liabilities	**110.3**	**137.5**	**159.7**	**175.7**	**188.1**
Number of shares (crore)	1.60	1.60	1.60	1.60	1.60

Source: Prepared by authors.

EXHIBIT 43.6 Income Statement of Ashian Biotech

Rs Crore	*2016–17*	*2017–18*	*2018–19*	*2019–20*	*2020–21F*
Net Sales	140.5	163.7	177.0	189.4	204.6
Other Income	4.5	4.1	4.2	4.2	3.8
Total Income	**145.0**	**167.7**	**181.2**	**193.6**	**208.4**
Material Costs	76.8	91.0	97.6	105.2	113.6
Employee Expenses	11.9	13.7	22.2	29.9	32.3
Other Manufacturing Expenses	5.8	8.4	9.9	9.5	10.3
Selling and Admin Expenses	12.2	14.0	16.4	20.1	21.7
PBDIT	38.3	40.7	35.1	28.9	30.5
Depreciation	3.1	4.0	5.3	5.9	6.0
PBIT	35.1	36.7	29.8	23.0	24.5
Interest	–	–	–	–	–
PBT	35.1	36.7	29.8	23.0	24.5
Tax	9.0	9.2	7.5	7.1	6.1
Profit after Tax	**26.1**	**27.5**	**22.3**	**15.9**	**18.4**
Dividend	4.0	4.0	4.0	4.0	4.0

Source: Prepared by authors.

course, these numbers are without considering the Covid-19 vaccine project or Myanti purchase.

Rishi: All right then. Let us meet after two weeks with more clarity and details. We will finalise our decisions and then take them to the board by the end of the month.

Unresolved Problems

Despite having covered a lot of ground in the meeting, Rishi was not sure if they would ultimately solve the business growth problem. He had also not shared with his management team how Krish had been reminding him that Ashian Biotech had become cash-rich only because of a well-timed IPO, and it was time to enhance shareholders' value. Of late, Krish had also been grilling Rishi on private jets chartered by the senior management to fly to multiple business locations and other expenses, which he considered wasteful perquisites. Rishi hoped that he continued to enjoy the confidence of other board members.

Questions

1. Evaluate the proposal to acquire Myanti Biopharma Ltd. Explain the estimation of cash flows and the discount rate.

2. Use sensitivity analysis to assess the impact of changes in critical assumptions on the valuation and hence the decisions to acquire the target.
3. Discuss whether and how a change in the capital structure of Ashian Biotech will impact the decision to acquire Myanti Biopharma.
4. Should Ashian Biotech raise debt? Justify your answer with quantitative and qualitative analysis.

44

VALUATION OF 212 DEGREES FAHRENHEIT

Arjan Baweja, a Gurgaon-based restaurateur, checked the email he had received from Vini Lobo, his investment advisor, on a late Saturday afternoon in September 2019.

Email from Vini Lobo to Arjan Baweja dated September 21, 2019

Hello AB,

We can persuade Binita Nair to sell her entire stake in 212 Degrees Fahrenheit. The chain has three quick-service restaurants in Bengaluru and plans to open more QSRs and cafes.

I have asked Hari Kishore, her investment advisor, to send us the business details and the financials. I will keep you updated.

Vini

Email from Hari Kishore to Vini Lobo dated September 25, 2019

Dear Vini,

I am emailing you the business details, current numbers, and financial projections. Binita thinks it will be best to discuss valuation in person after meeting Arjan.

With regards
Hari Kishore

DOI: 10.4324/9781032724478-50

EXHIBIT 44.1 Seller's Forecasts

Rs Crore	*2018–19*	*2019–20F*	*2020–21F*	*2021–22F*	*2022–23F*	*2023–24F*
Revenues	12.0	13.8	15.9	17.5	18.9	19.8
Other Income	–	–	–	–	–	–
Total Income	**12.0**	**13.8**	**15.9**	**17.5**	**18.9**	**19.8**
Material Costs	3.6	4.1	4.8	5.2	5.7	5.9
Employee Expenses	2.0	2.2	2.4	2.5	2.7	2.8
Other Expenses	2.4	2.6	2.9	3.0	3.2	3.4
EBITDA	4.0	4.8	5.8	6.6	7.3	7.7
Depreciation	0.9	1.0	1.1	1.2	1.3	1.4
EBIT	3.1	3.9	4.7	5.4	6.0	6.3
Interest	1.1	1.1	1.3	1.5	1.7	1.7
Profit Before Tax	2.0	2.8	3.3	3.9	4.3	4.5
Tax	0.5	0.7	0.8	1.0	1.1	1.1
Profit After Tax	**1.5**	**2.1**	**2.5**	**2.9**	**3.2**	**3.4**
Equity	5.0	5.4	5.9	6.5	7.1	7.8
Debt	5.5	6.7	7.6	8.4	8.6	8.8
Capital Employed	**10.5**	**12.2**	**13.5**	**14.9**	**15.8**	**16.6**
Net Fixed Assets	9.5	11.0	12.2	13.4	14.2	15.0
Net Working Capital	1.0	1.2	1.3	1.5	1.6	1.6

Source: Prepared by authors.

Note: Revenue growth from FY 2024–25 is expected to be at the rate of 5% per annum.

EXHIBIT 44.2 Valuation Assumptions (Public Company Inputs)

Risk-free Rate	6.8%
Equity Market Risk Premium	7.5%
Unlevered Beta[a]	1.02
Cost of Debt	15%
Target Debt–Equity Ratio (Market Value)	0.30
Marginal Tax Rate	25%

Source: Prepared by authors.

Note: [a] Based on average of listed peers.

EXHIBIT 44.3 Forecasts Revised by Private Buyer (First Cut)

Rs Crore	*2018–19*	*2019–20F*	*2020–21F*	*2021–22F*	*2022–23F*	*2023–24F*
Revenues	12.0	13.2	14.5	16.0	16.8	17.6
Other Income	–	–	–	–	–	–
Total Income	**12.0**	**13.2**	**14.5**	**16.0**	**16.8**	**17.6**
Material Costs	3.6	4.0	4.4	4.8	5.0	5.3
Employee Expenses	2.0	2.7	3.0	3.1	3.3	3.4
Other Expenses	2.4	2.6	2.9	3.0	3.2	3.4
EBITDA	4.0	3.9	4.3	5.0	5.3	5.5
Depreciation	0.9	1.0	1.1	1.2	1.3	1.3
EBIT	3.1	3.0	3.2	3.9	4.0	4.2
Interest	1.2	0.8	1.0	1.1	1.2	1.3
Profit Before Tax	1.9	2.1	2.3	2.8	2.7	2.9
Tax	0.5	0.5	0.6	0.7	0.7	0.7
Profit After Tax	**1.4**	**1.6**	**1.7**	**2.1**	**2.1**	**2.2**
Equity	5.0	5.2	5.5	5.8	6.1	6.4
Debt	5.5	6.5	7.3	8.3	8.5	8.6
Capital Employed	**10.5**	**11.7**	**12.8**	**14.1**	**14.6**	**15.1**
Net Fixed Assets	9.5	10.6	11.6	12.8	13.2	13.6
Net Working Capital	1.0	1.1	1.2	1.3	1.4	1.5

Source: Prepared by authors.

Notes:

1. Revenue growth estimates provided by seller have been revised downwards. There seem to be issues in method of accounting revenues in 2018–19. The estimate for 2019–20 is lowered to reflect adjustment to the base. Growth estimates in subsequent years have been reduced to make them more realistic.
2. Revenue growth from FY 2024–25 is expected to be at the rate of 3% per annum.
3. Increase in expenses, net fixed assets, and net working capital have been adjusted in line with revised revenue growth assumptions.
4. The owner is showing low salary (Rs 10 lakh) and is taking out the money as dividend and excessive interest (at 20%) on unsecured loans. The revised forecasts incorporate an addition of Rs 50 lakh to the owner-manager's salary in 2019–20 and growing thereafter and reduction in interest rate to 15%.

EXHIBIT 44.4 Valuation Assumptions of Private Buyer

Risk-Free Rate	6.8%
Equity Market Risk Premium	7.5%
Unlevered Total Beta[a]	2.22
Cost of Debt	15%
Target Debt-Equity Ratio (market value)	0.30
Marginal Tax Rate	25%
Illiquidity Discount for Small Unlisted Restaurant Chain	30%

Source: Prepared by authors.

Note: [a] Unlevered total beta is estimated by dividing the peer average unlevered beta by the average correlation between the stock returns of listed peers and the market index (see http://pages.stern.nyu.edu/~adamodar/pdfiles/valn2ed/ch24.pdf).

Email from Vini Lobo to Hari Kishore dated 30 September 2019

Hello Hari,

Your business plans and numbers look surprisingly good. My team is more conservative about future revenues and margins. We have high regards for Binita's abilities in personally supervising the restaurants. We believe that the growth will be much lower than you have projected once she leaves. The forecasts as revised by us (first cut) are attached.

Arjan is very keen that this deal should go through. We are looking forward to hearing from you.

Vini

Email from Vini Lobo to Arjan Baweja dated 03 October 2019

Hello AB,

I spoke with Hari yesterday. They insist on their revenue and EBIDTA forecasts. I think we can use the following inputs to set the upper limit for bargaining when we meet Binita:

1. If Binita can agree to stay on an employment contract for three years, we can go with their numbers, except for the adjustment due to Binita's salary, which is, of course, negotiable.
2. We can agree to exit EV multiple of up to 1.5x 2023–24 revenues.
3. We can reduce the illiquidity discount from 30% to 20%.

Vini

Questions

1. Value the company based on Exhibits 44.1 and 44.2, as if it were a public company being purchased by a well-diversified investor.
2. Estimate the plausible value of the company to the buyer, considering Exhibits 44.3 and 44.4 and the lack of diversification of both the seller and the buyer.
3. Estimate the plausible value of the company the buyer can set as upper limit while bargaining, considering Vini's email to Arjan dated 03 October 2019.

45

PVR'S ACQUISITION FOR SPI CINEMA

An Expensive Southern Excursion?

At 6.00 p.m., August 12, 2018, Kathy Rose received a call from her boss Krish Subramanian. It was Sunday evening, and Kathy was out with her friends heading towards the famous Marina Beach in Chennai, a southern Indian city. Both Kathy and Krish worked for Sevenstar Capital Partners as buy-side analyst and fund manager, respectively. Kathy looked after India's entertainment sector, and Krish managed a US$ 1 billion worth of India-focused portfolio. It was rather unusual for Krish to call her over the weekend, and she knew something needed urgent attention. As it turned out, it was urgent. Krish told her that he wanted a base case valuation and sensitivity analysis for SPI Cinema Pvt. Ltd, (SPI), the company was running the iconic chain of Sathyam cinemas in Chennai and holding a dominant Tamilnadu movie exhibition business presence. PVR announced Sathyam Cinema's acquisition at close to Rs 1,000 crore in cash plus equity transaction. According to PVR, the deal would be EPS accretive from year one. It would further strengthen PVR's position as the market leader in the Indian Multiplex industry; Krish was concerned about the price paid for SPI's acquisition. Based on PVR's closing price on August 10, 2018, PVR was valued at Enterprise Value (EV) of Rs 10.5 crore per screen, whereas it paid Rs 13.2 crore[1] EV[2] (per screen) for the acquisition of SPI.

PVR was one of the significant holdings in Kirsh's portfolio, and the stock had run up to Rs 1,300 from Rs 1,100 just a fortnight back. He wondered whether he should trim PVR's weight in his portfolio given the aggressive heavy Capex growth strategy of PVR due to growing concerns of stiff competition from over the top (OTT) content providers such as Amazon Prime, Hotstar, and Netflix. However, one possibility was that OTT might turn out to be another irritant like TVs and DVDs, a couple of decades back and the

DOI: 10.4324/9781032724478-51

Indian Premier League (IPL) before a decade. Each of them had threatened to change the movie-going habits of Indian consumers, but they did not. Yes, single-screen cinemas lost out to multiplexes, but consumers' preference towards going out for movies had not changed. SPI's acquisition was one major event to assess whether PVR was prudent or reckless in chasing growth, and SPI valuation would answer whether PVR ended up overpaying for SPI.

Indian Multiplex Industry

With 2,089 movies released in the calendar year 2017(CY17), India led the global chart with South Korea, a distant second with 1,765 movie releases. While India topped the list of movies released, India was at the fifth position in the box office collection worth $ 1.6 billion. Despite the large market size, India remained an under-screened market with seven screens per million compared to 111 for the USA and 36 for China. Till CY15, multiplex screens were just about 15% of the total screens. However, the CY17 share of multiplex screens jumped to 26% and would further expect to go up to 40% by CY23. Multiplex screens gaining traction, India continued to remain a diverse nation and regional cinema, especially in southern India, contributed significantly to box office collection. Bollywood (Hindi Cinema) led the charts, contributing 40% of the total box office collection in CY17. The number of movies crossing the Rs 1 billion box office collection mark increased from seven in 2015 to thirteen in 2018. It was a sign of increased average ticket price and a healthy pipeline of blockbuster movies of Indian cinema (see Exhibit 45.1).

Introduction of Goods and Services Tax (GST) in 2017 helped the Indian multiplex industry as many taxes in entertainment tax, service tax, and the value-added tax had gone and replaced by GST. GST rates of 28% for ticket price above Rs 100; 18% for ticket size below Rs 100; and 18% for the food and beverage sales were applicable. However, in the subsequent revision, the rates were slashed to 18%, 12%, and 5% for ticket above Rs 100, less

EXHIBIT 45.1 Trends in Indian and Global Multiplex Industry CY 2017

	Gross Box Office Collection ($ billion)	*No of Movies Released*	*No of Screens per Million Residents*
US + Canada	11	777	111
China	7.9	NA	36
Japan	2	1,187	28
UK + Ireland	1.6	760	60
India	1.6	2,089	7
South Korea	1.6	1,765	54

Source: PVR Investor Presentation.

than Rs 100 and F&B, respectively, provided a much-needed tailwind for the industry.

PVR Cinema

From the launch of its first screen in 1997, PVR had come a long way. With the SPI acquisition in August 2018, it crossed 700 screens and was well set to reach the 1,000-screen target set for itself by 2020.[3] With 748 screens and 161 properties, PVR had its presence in 64 cities and 21 Indian states. PVR registered an impressive CAGR of 25% from 2012 to 2018 in terms of the number of screens. It was a market leader with more than 25% market share, followed by its closest rival, Inox leisure (close to 20% market share). PVR had growth using a mix of organic and inorganic growth opportunities. Before SPI's acquisition, PVR acquired Cinemax in 2012 and DT Cinema in 2015.

PVR reported an operating profit (EBITDA) of Rs 433.18 crore on Rs 1932.28 crore of revenue from operations for FY18. The assets on the balance sheet at the end of FY18 were worth Rs 1,917.28 crore. It earned close to 55% of revenues from the sale of tickets, 28% from the sale of F&B, and 10% from advertising. Convenience fees and movie production and distribution were other sources of revenue. While the operating margin was hovering around 18–19% for the past three years, PVR expected it to stabilise at around 20% due to favourable GST rates. Thus, while FY18 turned out to be a sluggish year, FY19 looked like it would be one of the best years (see Exhibit 45.2 for financial PVR's income statement and balance sheets).[4]

SPI Cinema

Promoted by Kiran Reddy and Swaroop Reddy in 1975, SPI was a leading player in South India. By August 2018, it had 76 screens across 17 properties in 10 cities. Twelve more screens were in the pipeline and were likely to open in twelve months. Thirty-one of these screens were in Chennai and under the brand name Sathyam, and it was an undisputed leader in the Chennai market. Other than Sathyam, SPI operated screens under Escape, Palazzo, The Cinema, and S2 Cinema. The brands enjoyed goodwill and strong brand loyalty. SPI reported Rs 63 crore or operating profit on revenue of Rs 309.6 crore. It was on its way to deliver revenue of Rs 410–425 crore and Rs 90–100 crore in operating profit for the year FY19 (see Exhibit 45.3 for SPIs FY18 financial performance and projected Q3FY19 financial information).

PVR–SPI Transaction

In early August 2018, PVR announced that it would acquire SPI for an enterprise value close to Rs 1,000 crore. In a multi-layered transaction, it would

EXHIBIT 45.2 PVR's Income Statement, Balance Sheet, and Key Metrics

Key metrics	*FY 2016*	*FY 2017*	*FY 2018*
Properties	112	126	134
Screens	516	579	625
Seats	1,18,124	1,32,026	1,39,509
Cities	46	50	51
Admits (In lakhs)	696	752	761
Occupancy %	34.30%	32.90%	31.30%
Average Ticket Price (ATP) in Rs.	188	196	210
Spend per Head (SPH) in Rs	72	81	89
P&L Account (Rs in lakhs)	**FY 16**	**FY 17**	**FY 18**
Income from sale of movie tickets	99,480	1,12,488	1,24,707
Sales of Food and Beverages	49,774	57,942	62,495
Advertisement Income	21,454	25,176	29,693
Convenience Fees	3,329	5,816	5,971
Other Operating Income	10,919	10,521	10,545
Other Income	6,348	6,225	3,134
Total Revenues	1,91,304	2,18,168	2,36,545
Film Exhibition Cost	41,975	46,516	53,766
Consumption of Food and Beverages	12,483	14,010	15,907
Employee Benefit Expense	18,594	22,051	25,407
Rent and CAM	41,989	50,220	52,373
Other Operating Expenses	40,671	47,784	45,775
Total Expenses	1,55,712	1,80,581	1,93,228
EBITDA	35,592	37,587	43,317
EBITDA Margin	18.60%	17.23%	18.31%
Depreciation	11,511	13,838	15,369
EBIT	24,081	23,749	27,948
Finance Cost	8,395	8,058	8,371
PBT Before Exceptional Item	15,686	15,691	19,577
Exceptional Item	-1,156	-407	-59
Share of Net Profit/(loss) of Joint Venture	-	-	-72
PBT After Exceptional Item	14,530	15,284	19,446
Tax	4,668	5,700	7,044
PAT	9,862	9,584	12,402
PAT Margin	5.15%	4.39%	5.24%
EPS – Basic	21.05	20.5	26.68
EPS – Diluted	21.03	20.5	26.57
Balance Sheet (Rs in Lakh)	**FY 2016**	**FY 2017**	**FY 2018**
Shareholder Funds	92,132	1,00,551	1,07,617
Total Debt	66,002	81,958	83,052
Other Non-Current Liabilities	672	801	1,060
Total Sources of Funds	1,58,806	1,83,310	1,91,729
Non-Current Assets	1,44,127	1,94,530	2,05,109
Net Fixed Assets (Including CWIP)	1,07,557	1,15,030	1,22,864
Goodwill	8,579	43,365	43,447
Right of Use	0	0	0

(*Continued*)

EXHIBIT 45.2 Continued

Key metrics	*FY 2016*	*FY 2017*	*FY 2018*
Others	36,135	38,798	69,322
Current Assets	45,595	28,039	29,775
Less: Current Liabilities	30,916	39,259	43,155
Net Current Assets	14,679	-11,220	-13,380
Total Assets	1,58,806	1,83,310	1,91,729

Source: PVR Investor Presentation.

EXHIBIT 45.3 SPI Key Metrics FY18 and Q3FY19 Projections

SPI FY18 Key Metrics		*SPI Cinema : Q3FY19 Projections (Rs in million)*	
		Income from sale of movie tickets	563.3
Admits (mn)	12.3	Sale of food and beverages	384.4
ATP (gross INR)	141	Advertisement income	113.3
SPH (gross INR)	83	Convenience fees	100
Occupancy	58%	Other operating revenue (gaming, movie production, management fee etc.)	202.9
P&L (INR mn)		Revenue from operations	1,363.9
Total revenues	3,096	Other income	6.1
EBITDA	633	Total income	1,370
EBITDA Margin	20.40%	EBITDA	307.4
		EBITDA margin	22.40%
		Location	16
		Screens (72 operational and 4 under construction)	76
		Seats	18825
		Admits (mn)	4.4
		Occupancy	57%
		ATP (gross INR)	172
		SPH (gross INR)	89

Source: PVR Investor Presentation.

acquire 71.7% of equity from SPI promoters at Rs 633 crore for the remaining 28.3% of SPI's stake PVR would issue its equity shares, amounts to 3.3% of diluted equity of PVR. It would also assume Rs 160 crore of SPI's debt. (see Exhibit 45.4 for details of the transaction).

The transaction would put PVR in a pole position in Tamilnadu state. It presented an excellent opportunity to expand in the under-penetrated southern multiplex market. Forty-nine per cent of the total 9,530 screens

EXHIBIT 45.4 Transaction Details and Funding Plan (amount in INR mn)

(A) Cash Consideration for Acquiring 71.7% Equity in SPI Cinemas		6,330
	Funded through:	
	Internal accruals	3,850
	Net debt issuance	1,550
	Deferred consideration	1,000
(B)		1.6 million shares of PVR Ltd
(C) Existing debt of SPI Cinemas		1,600

Source: PVR Investor Presentation.

in India were located in south India (including both single screens and multiplex screens). West, north, and east accounted for 24%, 15%, and 12% of the screens. Of all the screens, 2,750 were multiplex screens. The multiplex screens as a percentage of total screens were as high as 60% and 47% for north India and Western India, whereas it was 14% each for southern and eastern India. Southern India, home to half of India's movie screens, had massive scope for multiplex penetration, and PVR was known for creating best-in-class movie watching experience. The transaction would add 88 screens (76 operational plus 12 in the pipeline) to PVR's southern screen portfolio and would make South India the most represented region with 35% of screens from 26% before the transaction. Besides, PVR was planning to add another 100 screens in south India over the next five years. The additional advantage of diversification of content risk. The acquisition would increase regional cinema's contribution from 19% to 22% in PVR's total revenue. Tamil, Kannada, and Telugu formed 37% of the total India box office.[5]

Did PVR Pay Too Much?

Kathy realised that while she would get all the details about PVR, it would be challenging to get all SPI details. However, she went about using available information from information in Exhibit 45.4 and build from thereon by using information about PVR as a proxy and make necessary adjustments to value SPI. Besides, Kathy gathered data on risk-free rate, PVR's beta, the risk premium for the Indian market, credit rating for SPI cinema bank facility, and corresponding yield spread (see Exhibit 45.5). Finally, she had to forecast cash flows and cost of capital to come up with an enterprise value of SPI and ascertain whether PVR ended up overpaid or not. Thoughts were running at the speed of the fighter jet in her mind.

EXHIBIT 45.5 Kathy's Inputs for SPI's Valuation

Risk-Free Rate (10-Year G-sec Yield)	7.85%
Expected Market Risk Premium	8%
PVR Beta (Average of 1,2,3-Year Beta)	1.15
Terminal Growth Rate	Expected risk-free rate after 10 years
High Growth Period in Base Case Scenario	10 years
SPI Credit Rating (for long-term bank facility)	AA- (Stable)
Yield Spread for AA- (Stable) long-term debt	150 bps
Effective Rate	30% on an average
Capex (Base case estimates)	10% of revenue from operations during the high growth period

Source: Prepared by authors.

- How to project cash flows for SPI?
- What should be the high growth period? What should be the growth in cash flow over that period?
- What should the terminal growth rate?
- What should be a reasonable estimate of the cost of capital for SPI?
- What should be the base case value of SPI? How could she factor in the possible impact of increased competition from OTT content providers?
- What would be her recommendation for Krish? Hold, trim position or buy more PVR shares?

Notes

1 Rs 1 crore = Rs 10 million = Rs 100 lakh, US$ 1 billion = US$ 100 crore = Rs 700 crore (approx.)
2 https://www.livemint.com/Money/EfrlUQNJGfRw1c7OpnIfbO/PVR-pays-a-premium-for-south.html accessed on March 25, 2021.
3 https://qrius.com/how-pvr-stands-to-gain-from-spi-cinemas-acquisition/ accessed on March 25, 2021.
4 https://static1.pvrcinemas.com/pvrcms/pvrinvestor/PVR_Investor_Presentation_March19.pdf accessed on March 25, 2021.
5 https://static1.pvrcinemas.com/pvrcms/pvrinvestor/PVR_Investor_Presentation_March19.pdf accessed on March 25, 2021.

46

RELIANCE INDUSTRIES LIMITED (A)

Valuation of RIL's O2C Business

On March 23, 2021, Madhumita Gogoi, Head of Institutional Equities Research at PerfectPoint Investment Partners – called for a meeting of her Oil and Gas analysts – Trisha Iyer and Mahima Choudhry, to discuss the valuation impact of the recently announced corporate reorganisation by Reliance Industries Limited (RIL). PerfectPoint was a Mumbai-based Investment Advisory and Research firm with institutional clients from Asia, Middle East, Europe, and the USA. Its clients include Sovereign Wealth Funds, Pension Funds, and select Endowment Funds. Most institutional clients had a long-term investment horizon and wanted to invest in stocks of a growing business with solid fundamentals run by strong management.

The discussion agenda was to advise one of the large pension funds on-sell, hold, or add more to RIL stock after the announcement of RIL to reorganise its oil to chemicals (O2C) business into a separate entity. Of course, the new entity would remain a wholly owned subsidiary of RIL and hence would not change the consolidated financials of RIL. However, a few experts raised concern about RIL becoming a mere holding company. Therefore, they might erode its premium valuation in the market as creating a separate O2C subsidiary might signal the first step in breaking up Telecom, Retail, and O2C businesses.

Reliance Industries Limited (RIL)

Founded by Dhirubhai Ambani, Reliance Industries went through multiple reorganisations. It emerged as one of the world's largest refining and

DOI: 10.4324/9781032724478-52

petrochemical companies after expanding its Jamnagar refining complex capacity in 2008. Since then, Reliance had turned its focus on new growth areas such as digital/telecom and retail. By 2020, heavy Capex that it had incurred over the last decade increased the debt burden, and from zero net debt company in 2012, RIL had debt worth Rs 3,060 billion by the end of December 2019. The net debt was Rs 1,530 billion. The net debt to equity ratio jumped above 0.5.

As part of a debt reduction plan and to become a debt-free company on a net basis by the end of FY21, RIL looked for opportunities to monetise its assets. The first step in this direction was to sell 20% of its refinery and petrochemicals business to Saudi Aramco at US$ 15 billion, which valued its refining and petroleum and upstream oil and gas business at US$ 75 billion. However, the deal got delayed, and then global energy markets were rocked by Covid-19 with a sharp fall in oil prices and energy demand that pushed global crude oil prices and refining margins to historic lows. All these rocked the valuation of Aramco and RIL.

Cut March 2021; a lot had changed over one year. After falling to a low of Rs 841 per share on March 23, 2020, RIL stock outperformed broader Indian markets by a considerable margin, trading at close to Rs 2,000 on March 23, 2021, after making a high of Rs 2,400 during the year. The turn of fortune on Dalal street was not a surprise. After Aramco's flip-flop, RIL aggressively monetised its telecom and retail business by selling the stake to strategic investors and private equity investors and came out with the largest rights issue in the history of Indian equity markets (see Exhibit 46.1 for RIL's fundraising during 2020–21).

RIL's O2C Business and Proposed Reorganisation

Reliance's O2C business spinoff into a wholly owned subsidiary was the first step towards monetising the business. The spinoff assets would include the entire refining and petrochemicals business, midstream assets, and fuel retail marketing (51:49, RIL–BP joint venture). The standalone O2C business would own assets worth US$ 42 billion with initial funding support

EXHIBIT 46.1 Reliance Industries Fund Raising in FY21

Fundraising	*US$ billion*
Investments in Jio Platforms for 33% stake	20
Investments in Reliance Retail for 10% stake	6
Rights Issue	7.27
Total	**33.27**

Source: Prepared by authors based on company reports and regulatory filings.

EXHIBIT 46.2 Proforma Standalone O2C Business as of January 1, 2021

Assets (US$ Billion)		*Liabilities (US$ Billion)*	
Long-Term Assets	40	Total Equity	12
Net Working Capital	2	Long-term loan from RIL	25
		Non-current liabilities	5
Total Assets	42	**Total Liabilities**	42

Source: Prepared by authors based on company reports and regulatory filings.

provided by RIL in the form of a US$ 25 billion long-term loan with interest linked to SBI MCLR rate (7% in March 2021) (see Exhibit 46.2 for the proforma Balance sheet of proposed O2C subsidiary).

RIL's Jamnagar refinery and the petrochemical complex had a refining capacity of 1.4 MMbls/d vs average peers at 2.62 MMbls/d. Reliance had one of the most complex refineries in the world. Hence, it could process heavy crude and enjoyed superior Gross Refining Margin (GRM) than most global peers and benchmark Singapore Complex GRM for 20 years in a row. The average GRM over the five years ending FY19 was US$ 10/b. The GRM for FY21 would be around US$ 5.25/b and would improve to US$ 7.5/b and would further improve to US$ 9.25/b and remain steady after that. The general shift towards Electrical Vehicles and green fuel would keep a lead on oil prices and GRMs.

RIL's petrochemical facility was one of the largest globally, only behind Aramco and Sinopec (produced 38.8 MT of petrochemicals in FY20). It enjoyed a superior margin of US$ 92/T compared to US$ 88/T for global peers.

O2C business was the most significant contributor with close to 60% of EBITDA during FY20; the collapse in energy prices in the early part of FY21 led O2C to contribute to 39% of total EBITDA recovery FY22 onwards. However, rapid growth in digital (telecom +) and retail businesses would result in O2C EBITDA being around one-third of total EBITDA by the end of FY26.

What Should We Expect Post O2C Reorganisation?

Post O2C business spinoff, RIL would bring strategic and financial investors before listing its O2C business via IPO. The process should start with Aramco's long-pending investment in the O2C business. Powered by new fundraising and cash flows from the refining and petrochemicals business, O2C business would generate sufficient funds and operating cash flows to meet potential expansion in high-value downstream chemicals and investments

EXHIBIT 46.3A Petrochemical EV/EBITDA for Comparable Global Peers

EV/EBITDA	*2021E*	*2022E*	*2023E*
Akzo Nobel	12.2	11.4	12
Sabic	11.7	10.3	11.4
BASF Se	9.5	8.8	9.3
Dow Chemicals	8.1	7.9	8
Lyondellbasell	8.8	8.3	8.7

Source: Compiled by authors based on Bloomberg data and research reports.

EXHIBIT 46.3B Refining EV/EBDITA for Comparable Global Peers

EV/EBITDA	*2021E*	*2022E*	*2023E*
SK Innovation	19.2	14.7	18.2
Thai Oil	14.7	13.2	14.3
S Oil	11.9	10.5	11.5
Philips 66	12.2	8.5	11.3
Valero Energy	12.4	6.9	11

Source: Compiled by authors based on Bloomberg data and research reports.

into CCUS and H2 production.[1]And at the same time had enough flexibility to upstream cash flows to its parent, RIL.

Valuation of O2C Business

Madhumita was happy that both Trisha and Mahima did their homework before joining her for the meeting. Trisha collated EV/EBITDA multiples of global refining and petrochemicals peers of RIL, whereas Mahima came up with the financial projections for the O2C business till FY26. This information would allow them to value RIL's O2C business using relative valuation and DCF valuation techniques (see Exhibit 46.3a and 46.3b for trading multiples and Exhibit 46.4 for financial projections of O2C business). Before starting the formal exercise, the valuation of the O2C business, Madhumita listed down a few questions on her excel sheet and turned her laptop screen towards her colleagues.

Questions

1. Which method should we use to value O2C business? Trading multiples or DCF?
2. How do we value O2C business using EV/EBITDA multiples?
3. How do we value O2C business using the DCF approach?

EXHIBIT 46.4 Financial Projections and Assumptions for RIL's O2C Business

Petrochemicals	*2018A*	*2019A*	*2020A*	*2021E*	*2022E*	*2023E*	*2024E*	*2025E*	*2026E*
Revenue	1202.2	1,687	1,409	1172.4	1,600	1,600	1,750	1,900	2,000
EBITDA	250.8	378.36	303.12	231	312	367.8	408	456	480
EBIT	209	315.3	252.6	192.5	260	306.5	340	380	400
Refining and Marketing	2018A	2019A	2020A	2021E	2022E	2023E	2024E	2025E	2026E
Revenue	2563.6	3205.5	2,991	2,000	2,700	3,100	3,500	3,800	4,100
EBITDA	294.84	232.2	247.8	42	210	270	300	330	369.6
EBIT	245.7	193.5	206.5	35	175	225	250	275	308

Key Assumptions

1. Topline growth beyond 2026 would stabilise at 4.5%.
2. Operating margin (EBIT/Sales) for Petrochemicals and Refining and Marketing would stabilise at 20% and 7.5% beyond 2026.
3. The effective tax rate applicable for O2C business would be 25%.
4. The target debt/equity ratio for O2C business would be 1:1 with pre-tax cost of debt of 7.25%, EMRP = 7.5%, beta: 1.1 and rf = 6.25%.
5. Capex Assumptions: 5% of Revenues for Petrochemicals and 2.5% of Revenues for Refining and Marketing Segment (Actual Capex would be lumpy).
6. Change in working capital requirement would remain negligible and could be ignored.

Source: Company reports, Infrontanalytics.com and Trisha's estimates.

4. How do we calculate the weighted average cost of capital, free cash flow to firm, and terminal value for the O2C business?
5. How sensitive is the valuation to the critical assumptions like weighted average cost of capital and terminal growth?
6. Are these likely to throw very different valuation? If yes, how would you reconcile them?

Note

1 RIL announced its plan to become a net-zero carbon entity by 2035. CCUS means carbon capture utilisation and storage, and H2 means hydrogen gas.

47

RELIANCE INDUSTRIES LIMITED (B)

Valuation of Jio Platforms

On March 24, 2021, 9.00 a.m., Madhumita Gogoi, Head of Institutional Equity Research at PerfectPoint Investment Partners, was waiting for Chitra Iyer, telecom and digital sector analyst at PerfectPoint. PerfectPoint was a Mumbai-based Investment Advisory and Research firm with a global client base. The clients include Sovereign Wealth Funds, Pension Funds, and select Endowment Funds. Most institutional clients had a long-term investment horizon and wanted to invest in stocks of a growing business with solid fundamentals run by capable management.

A few days back, a large Pension Fund had a Zoom call with Madhumita to seek advice on whether to sell/hold/add Reliance Industries Ltd (RIL) stock. Madhumita decided to review RIL investment potential using the bottom-up Sum of the Parts (SOTP) valuation. After putting the O2C piece of business valuation in place with the help of her Oil and Gas analysts team, she took up the valuation of Jio Platforms.

RIL

Founded by Late Dhirubhai Ambani in 1973, RIL had come a long way in 47 years. With a market capitalisation of close to Rs 13.5 trillion[1] in March 2021, RIL emerged as one of the most prominent Indian companies with business interests spread across Oil-to-Chemicals (O2C), Digital &Telecom, Retail, a relatively smaller upstream oil Gas Exploration as well as proposed new renewable energy business, RIL's stock hit the lows of Rs 841 on March 23, 2020, during a panic sell-off in global markets, the same day Nifty touched an intraday low of 7511, about a 40% fall from its Feb 2020 peak.

DOI: 10.4324/9781032724478-53

Plummeting global energy demand and free fall in global crude oil prices threatened RIL's deleveraging plans. A sizeable proposed investment of US$ 15 billion for a 20% stake in RIL's downstream business by Saudi's Aramco got delayed, and RIL's target to achieve net-zero debt status by March 2021 appeared to be an impossible goal to achieve.

Jio Platforms

A mounting debt of RIL due to heavy investments in its digital and retail business led many blue-blooded brokerage houses to have underweight on RIL. Credit Suisse was one of them. However, RIL chairman Mukesh Ambani, in 2019, AGM announced to make RIL debt-free over the next 18 months pushed most of them to reverse their stance. Jio Platforms, born as RIL, announced a new organisation structure on October 25, 2019. It created a super subsidiary that would house the company's telecom and digital assets. Close to Rs 1.08 crore of debt of digital business was transferred to RIL's standalone balance sheet in exchange for optionally convertible preference shares in Jio Platforms. With such debt transfer, Jio would become debt-free (except for spectrum charges). (see Exhibit 47.1 for Jio Platforms Debt levels).

After Aramco's flip-flop, RIL turned to plan B and aggressively pursued monetising its telecom and retail assets by selling the stake to strategic investors and private equity investors, followed by the launch of India's biggest rights issue ever. It all started with a Facebook investment of US$ 5.7 billion for a 9.99% stake in Jio Platforms in April 2020. It led to a flurry of investments flowing into Jio platforms by marquee strategic and financial investors. (see Exhibit 47.2 for Investments in Jio Platforms). Investors pumped in a total of US$ 20 billion for a 33% stake in Jio platforms in a matter of a quarter after Facebook investment. Such a significant capital infusion helped RIL closing in towards achieving debt-free status by the end of FY21. No surprise, RIL stock outperformed the benchmark Nifty Index by a considerable margin over one year ending March 22, 2021 (see FExhibit 47.3 for RIL vs Nifty performance).

EXHIBIT 47.1 Reliance Jio's Total Debt FY 2017–2020

Total debt of Reliance Jio Infocomm Limited from the financial year 2017 to 2020 (in billion Indian rupees)	
FY 2017	474.63
FY 2018	583.92
FY 2019	762.12
FY 2020	232.42

Source: Statista.

EXHIBIT 47.2 Investments in Jio Platforms

Investor	*Type*	*Investment (US$ Billion)*	*% stake*
Facebook	Strategic	5.7	9.99
Google	Strategic	4.5	7.73
Vista Equity Partners	Financial	1.5	2.32
KKR	Financial	1.5	2.32
PIF	Financial	1.5	2.32
Silver Lake	Financial	1.35	2.08
Mubadala	Financial	1.2	1.85
General Atlantic	Financial	0.87	1.34
ADIA	Financial	0.75	1.16
TPG	Financial	0.6	0.93
L Catterton	Financial	0.25	0.39
Intel	Financial	0.25	0.39
Qualcomm	Financial	0.1	0.15
Total		20.07	32.97

Source: Prepared by authors based on company reports.

EXHIBIT 47.3 RIL vs Nifty from March 2020 to March 2021

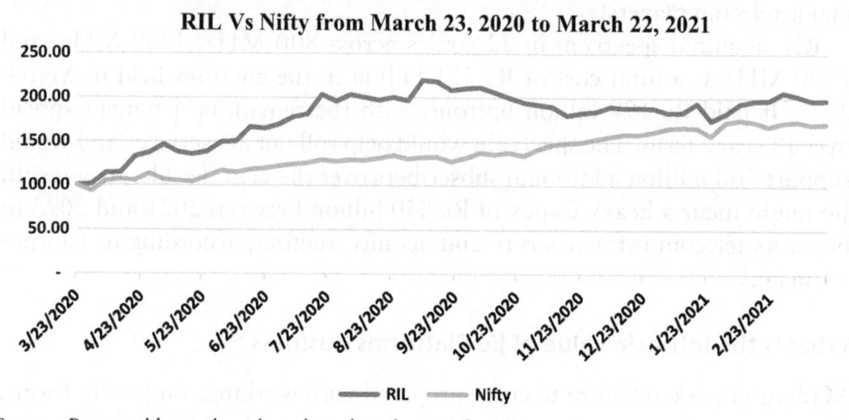

Source: Prepared by authors based on data from Yahoo Finance.

Jio Platforms in March 2021

By the end of Dec 2021, Reliance Jio had 410.8 million subscribers, showing net addition of 5.2 million subscribers in Q3FY21. Monthly Average Revenue per User (ARPU) increased to Rs 151/month, up 4% q-o-q and 18% on y-o-y basis. Per capita data consumption increased to 12.9 GB per month, up 8% from 12GB in Q2FY21. Average voice consumption for Q3FY21 was 796 minutes per user/month, up 8% from a corresponding number

EXHIBIT 47.4 Market Share of Indian Telecom Players

Market Share	*Number of Subscribers*		*Mobile Revenue*	
	2020A (%)	2025E (%)	2020A (%)	2025E (%)
Reliance Jio	36	45	37	45
Bharti Airtel	26	26	31	33
Vodaphone-Idea	27	17	27	19
BSNL + MTNL	11	11	4	2

Source: Company reports and authors' estimates.

of 776 minutes in Q2FY20. Reliance Jio had more than one-third market share, both in terms of the number of subscribers and subscribers' revenue in a rapidly consolidating and growing Indian telecom market reduced to four players by the end of 2021. Vodaphone Idea had to pay US$ 7 billion towards AGR dues over ten years, putting a serious cap on its ability to acquire spectrum, build telecom infrastructure, and roll out 5G services. In fact, over the past few quarters, both Jio and Bharti gained significantly in 4G upgrades. The trend might continue post 5G services launch and more subscribers going for 4G upgrades (see Exhibit 47.4 for the market share of major telecom players).

RIL acquired spectrum in 22 circles across 800 MHz, 1800 MHz, and 2300 MHz at a total cost of Rs 571 billion in the auctions held in March 2021. It paid Rs 199 billion upfront, with the remaining payment spread over 18 years' term. The spectrum would help roll out 5G services and would support 300 million additional subscribers over the next decade. As a result, Jio might incur a heavy Capex of Rs 850 billion between 2021 and 2023 to boost its telecom infrastructure and acquire auction, according to Chitra's estimate.[2]

What Is the Intrinsic Value of Jio Platforms Business?

Madhumita asked Chitra to come prepared with workings on Jio Platforms. Chitra entered the conference room, equipped with a few handouts on Reliance Jio subscribers and ARPU estimates from 2021 to 2030. According to her, further 4G upgrades and growth in data consumption would lead to a sharp increase in both subscribers and ARPU in 2023. Beyond 2030, subscriber growth would stabilise at around 2%, and ARPU growth at 3%. The increase in ARPU combined with favourable operating leverage would increase the EBITDA margin from 44% in 2021 to 55% in 2030. It would stabilise at the same level after that. She also compiled average EV/EBITDA multiples of the global technology and telecommunications sector. However,

EXHIBIT 47.5 Jio Subscribers and ARPU Estimates and Key Assumptions

Year	*Subscribers (million)*	*ARPU/month*
2020A	388	127
2021E	419	148
2022E	452	165
2023E	500	189
2024E	530	210
2025E	545	227
2026E	557	243
2027E	568	260
2028E	580	275
2029E	592	290
2030E	604	300

Other Assumptions:

1. Jio Platforms beta would be in line with global telecom majors average beta of 0.87 or 1 as a conservative estimate.
2. The target debt/equity ratio for Jio Platforms would be 0.75:1 to 1:1 with pre-tax cost of debt of 7.25%, EMRP = 7.5%, and rf = 6.25%.
3. The depreciation would be 10% of the revenue, and Capex beyond 2023 would be 110% of depreciation.
4. Change in working capital requirement would remain negligible and could be ignored.

Source: Company Reports, Infrontanalytics.com and authors' estimates.

given the growth phase of telecom and digital services in India, Indian firms might deserve higher multiples. For example, Bharti Airtel traded at EV/EBITDA of 14 during FY19 and FY20. She felt that Jio Platforms deserved even higher trading multiples than Bharti Airtel. Madhumita was quite happy with the homework done by Chitra. She had taken the printouts of the questions prepared for the discussion with Chitra (see Exhibit 47.5 for estimates of subscribers, ARPU and EV/EBITDA multiples).

Questions

1. Which method should we use to value Jio Platforms? Transaction value, trading multiples or DCF?
2. How do we value Jio Platforms business using EV/EBITDA multiples, given the expected expansion in EBITDA margins?
3. How do we value Jio Platforms business using the DCF approach?
4. How do we calculate the weighted average cost of capital, free cash flow to firm, and terminal value for Jio Platforms business?

5. How sensitive is the valuation to the critical assumptions like weighted average cost of capital and terminal growth?
6. How do you read the difference in valuation of Jio Platforms using different methods?

Notes

1 1,000 million = 1 billion = 100 crore, 1,000 billion = 1 trillion and US$ 1 = Rs. 73.
2 The Capex includes Rs 199 billion spent in 2021 and annual instalments of March 2021 auction spent.

48

RELIANCE INDUSTRIES LIMITED (C)

Valuation of Reliance Retail

On March 25, 2021, 9.00 a.m., Madhumita Gogoi, Head of Institutional Equity Research at PerfectPoint Investment Partners, was waiting for Sanjana Singh to join her for a scheduled Zoom meeting. While waiting, she glanced through her notes and spreadsheet workings from her meetings with her Oil and Gas and Telecom analysts over the last two days. PerfectPoint was a Mumbai-based Investment Advisory and Research firm with a global client base. Its clients include Sovereign Wealth Funds, Pension Funds, and select Endowment Funds. Most institutional clients had a long-term investment horizon and wanted to invest in stocks of a growing business with solid fundamentals run by capable management.

A few days back, a large Pension Fund had two hours long telephonic discussion with Madhumita to seek advice on whether to sell/hold/add more Reliance Industries Ltd (RIL) stock. The client was also asking about buying stocks of Reliance Retail, one of the fastest-growing arms of RIL. Shares of unlisted business segments with potential for eventual IPO were traded in private markets. Reliance Retail was one of them. Madhumita decided to review RIL's valuation by applying sum-of-the-parts (SoTP) valuation approach. After finishing the valuation of O2C and Jio Platforms, she had taken up Reliance Retail's valuation on hand. She had applied net asset value (NAV) valuation for relatively small upstream business and estimated it at nearly USD 1 billion at an average estimated oil price of US$ 50 per barrel. So once she finished retail business valuation, the SOTP valuation of RIL would be complete.

DOI: 10.4324/9781032724478-54

RIL in March 2021

Founded by Late Dhirubhai Ambani in 1973, RIL grew by leaps and bounds and underwent several reorganisations. With a market capitalisation of close to Rs 13.5 trillion in March 2021, RIL emerged as one of the most prominent Indian companies with business interests spread across Oil-to-Chemicals (O2C), Digital & Telecom, Retail, a relatively small upstream oil Gas Exploration as well as proposed new renewable energy business, RIL's stock hit the lows of Rs 841 on March 23, 2020, during a panic sell-off in global markets, the same day Nifty touched an intraday low of 7511, about 40% fall from its Feb 2020 peak. Plummeting global energy demand and free fall in global crude oil prices threatened RIL's deleveraging plans. A sizeable proposed investment of US$ 15 billion for a 20% stake in RIL's downstream business by Saudi's Aramco got delayed, and RIL's target to achieve net-zero debt status by the end of FY21, which its chairman announced in August 2019, appeared to be an impossible goal to achieve.

However, amidst the uncertainty surrounding Aramco's investment and economic standstill caused by the nationwide lockdown in India, RIL turned to its alternative fundraising plan. It aggressively started monetising its telecom and retail business by selling stakes to strategic and private equity investors, followed by the launch of India's biggest rights issue ever. It all started with a Facebook investment of US$ 5.7 billion for a 9.99% stake in Jio Platforms in April 2020. It led to a flurry of investments flowing into Jio Platforms and Reliance Retail by marquee strategic and financial investors (see Exhibit 48.1 for Investments in Reliance Retail). It led to RIL being able to achieve its zero net debt status by 2021. No surprise, RIL stock outperformed the benchmark Nifty Index by a considerable margin over one year ending March 22, 2021 (see Exhibit 48.2 for RIL vs Nifty performance).

EXHIBIT 48.1 Investments in Reliance Retail in 2020

Investor	*Type*	*Investment (US$ billion)*	*% Stake*
KKR	Financial	0.75	1.2%
PIF	Financial	1.3	2.0%
Silver Lake	Financial	1.25	2.0%
Mubadala	Financial	0.83	1.3%
General Atlantic	Financial	0.5	0.8%
ADIA	Financial	0.75	1.2%
TPG	Financial	0.25	0.4%
GIC	Financial	0.75	1.2%
Total		**6.38**	**10.1%**

Source: Prepared by authors based on company reports.

EXHIBIT 48.2 RIL vs Nifty from March 2020 to March 2021

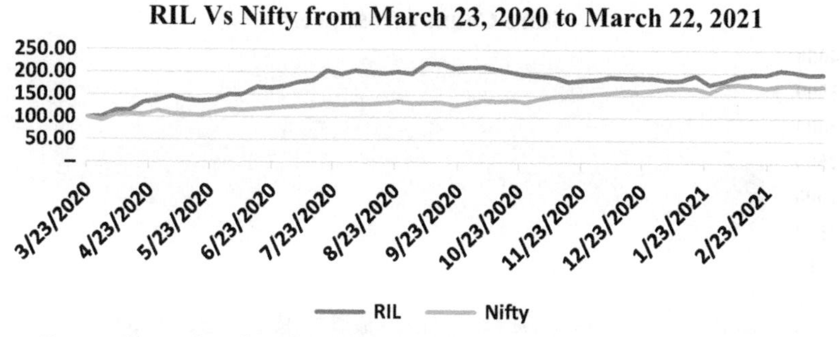

Source: Prepared by authors based on Yahoo Finance data.

Indian Retail Sector

The Retail Industry in India had become one of the most dynamic and fast-paced industries due to the entry of new players. It accounted for more than 10% of the GDP and contributed to 8% employment in 2021. The industry was expected to be worth US$ 1.75 trillion by 2026. The retail e-commerce market was expected to grow at 30% CAGR for the next five years – recent policy changes allowed for a 100% FDI under the automatic route for single-brand retail trading. As a result, India would become the world's fastest-growing e-commerce market, driven by investment and a high number of internet users.[1]

E-commerce was expanding in India. Consumers had the ever-increasing choice of products at the lowest rates. Retailers could choose a digital/online channel to sell their products, enabling them to spend less money on real estate. The long-term outlook looked optimistic, supported by rising income, favourable demographics, entry of foreign players like Wal-Mart, and increasing urbanisation.

Reliance Retail in March 2021

Reliance Retail was the largest retailer in India with a core revenue base of US$ 12 billion, a network of 12,201 stores (over 3,500 core) spread across 7,000 cities. It was the only large retailer with a diversified presence across consumer electronics, fashion and grocery. Reliance Retail had three distinct segments: core, non-core, and e-commerce. The core business consisted of brick-and-mortar stores (grocery, fashion, and electronics), the non-core made up the distribution services provided by Reliance Retail for Jio's telecom services (connectivity). The e-commerce segment included B2C (JioMart, Ajio.com, reliancedigital.in, etc.) and its new B2B e-commerce venture that would serve as a distributor to Kirana (local grocery) stores.

EXHIBIT 48.3 Reliance Retail Stores in Comparison to Peers

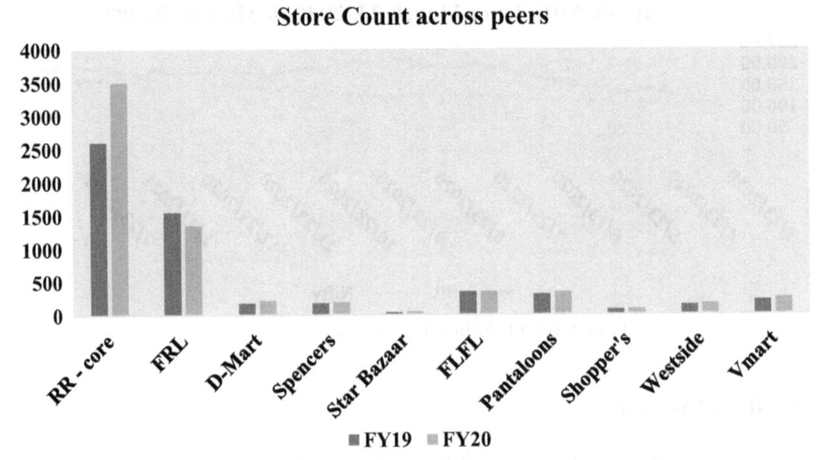

Source: Prepared by authors based on company filings and research reports.

Reliance Retail had nearly 20% share in the grocery segment, a 5% share in the fashion segment, and a 12% share in the consumer electronics segment. Its retail footprint was bigger than any competitor (see Exhibit 48.3 for stores comparison).

Reliance Retail reported a total of Rs 1,629 billion in revenue for FY20.[2] The revenues and EBITDA grew 25% and 56% y-o-y in FY20.[3] Lower footfalls caused by Covid-19-related lockdown in the first half of FY21 adversely impacted retail business. Petro retail business that contributed to 9% of total retail revenues was transferred to O2C after investment from British Petroleum for 49% stake and hence would not be part of Reliance Retail business from FY21 onwards (see Exhibit 48.4 for the FY19 and FY20 revenues and EBITDA breakup excluding Petro retail business).

It pushed private label brands to seek higher margins and win customer loyalty. In-house brands contributed to nearly 40% of the footwear sales, 15% of the grocery sales, and 75% of apparel sales. It also believed that private labels would be instrumental in their profitability and growth as it embarked on its Kirana linking programme.

Reliance Retail's Acquisition of Future Retail

In August 2020, Reliance Retail announced the acquisition of the Future Group business for roughly Rs 24,700 crore. The acquisition was made at a valuation of <1x EV/Sales and <10x EV/EBITDA on 9mFY20 numbers, which was an attractive buy for RIL.

The deal was put on hold when Amazon filed a case in the Singapore Arbitration Court (SIAC) claiming they had the right to buy Future Group.

EXHIBIT 48.4 Reliance Retail FY19 and FY20 Core and Non-Core Retail Revenues and Margin Breakup

	Revenue (Rs in billion)			
	FY 2019	*FY 2020*	*Q4FY20 EBITDA Margins*	*Reliance Retail Core + Non-Core Revenue Mix FY 2020*
Grocery	234	346	8.0%	23.27%
Fashion and Lifestyle	110	136	7.0%	9.15%
Consumer Electronics	392	446	29.0%	29.99%
Connectivity	437	559	2.2%	37.59%
Total	**1,173**	**1,487**		

Source: Company Reports.

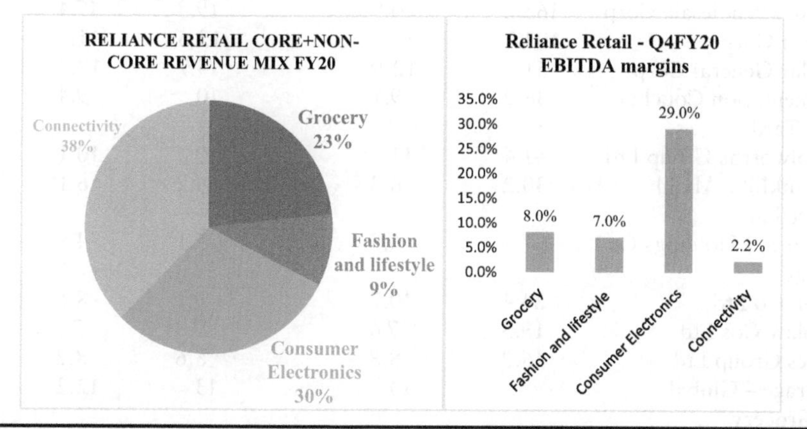

Source: Prepared by authors based on company filings and research reports.

The case was still under arbitration. Reliance Retail's core revenues could increase by 30% if the deal went through, which will be led by 40% growth in grocery and almost a 100% growth in fashion. EBITDA could increase by 25% without accounting for any synergy gains.[4] Future Group stores could also be used as fulfilment centres thus, helping Reliance Retail's e-commerce growth. The acquisition would also improve Reliance Retail's bargaining power with suppliers, vendors, and logistics partners.

Valuation of Reliance Retail Business

Madhumita had asked Sanjana to come prepared with workings on Reliance Retail. Sanjana compiled trading multiples of Indian listed retail firms and global grocery retailers (Exhibit 48.5). She proposed that the core retail

EXHIBIT 48.5 Trading Multiples of Indian Retailers and Global Grocery Retailers

Indian retailers	*Mcap (US$ bn)*	*EV/EBITDA FY21E*	*FY22E*	*FY23E*
Trent	3.7	151.1	33.4	26.2
Titan	17.3	82.5	46.7	37.6
DMart	23.4	101.8	54.6	39.4
Jubilant Foodworks	5	47.6	31.3	25
ABFRL	2.1	72.2	16	13.3
V-Mart Retail	0.7	45.2	20.7	16.2
Shoppers Stop	0.3	85.7	8.5	7.3
Bata India	2.2	80.2	22.7	17.9
Relaxo Footwears	2.9	46.8	41.4	34.1
Average – India		**89**	**44.9**	**34.3**
Global Grocery Retailers				
Walmart Inc	393.6	12.3	12.8	12.1
Costco Wholesale Corp	165.2	20.9	19.3	17.4
Target Corp	102.7	12	12.5	11.8
Dollar General Corp	51	12.9	14.7	13.3
Alimentation Couche – Tard	36.2	9.1	10	9.4
Woolworths Group Ltd	41.4	11	10.5	10.1
Koninklijke Ahold Delhaiz	30.2	6.3	6.2	6.1
Seven & I Holdings Co Ltd	37	6.3	5.1	4.9
Aeon Co Ltd	24.4	10.7	9.1	8.6
Loblaw Cos Ltd	19.3	7.6	7.3	7.3
Coles Group Ltd	16.2	8.8	8.6	8.2
Average – Global Grocery		**13**	**13**	**12.2**

Source: Prepared by authors based on Bloomberg, company filings and research reports.

business be valued at FY23 trading multiples of relevant Indian peers. In contrast, a non-core retail business could be valued at a lower trading multiple, more in line with global grocery retailers given the low-margin nature of connectivity business, whereas e-commerce business should be valued using GMV[5] multiple based on FY25E GMV. According to the Technopac Indian retail market, an unorganised sector would continue to be dominated by food and grocery chains that would command a dominant 80% share of the total retail pie. The total retail market was worth US$ 676 billion in 2018 (88% unorganised, 8.4% organised-offline, and 3.6% e-commerce). It was expected to grow to US$ 1,277 billion by 2025 (75% unorganised, 14.6% organised-office, and 10.4% e-commerce) by 2025. Reliance e-commerce would penetrate through unorganised retail and capture approximately

10% of total e-commerce GMV by 2025, 80% of which would be contributed by B2C and 20% by B2B. Sanjana noted that the Walmart–Flipkart deal was valued at around two times one-year forward GMV. However, given the premium valuation involved in Flipkart's acquisition and the low-margin nature of reliance on retail B2B business, the e-commerce piece of Reliance Retail should be valued at a slightly lower valuation. Therefore, the appropriate discount rate for such a business should be 15%. She believed that the core and non-core retail business would grow at a rate similar to that reported between FY19 and FY20. Madhumita was very happy with the work done by Sanjana.

Questions

1. How would you value Reliance Retail? In aggregate or using the SoTP valuation approach? Why?
2. What is the intrinsic value of Reliance Retail?
3. Do you agree with the 15% discount rate estimate for the e-commerce leg of Reliance Retail? Why? Why not?
4. How would your valuation change if Reliance Retail–Future Retail deal goes through?
5. How do you read the difference in valuation of Reliance Retail using trading and transaction multiples?

Notes

1 Source: IBEF and Invest India.
2 It includes 9% contribution by Petro retail that moved out of Reliance retail post-acquisition of 49% stake in Petro retail business.
3 Company Annual Report.
4 Source: Jefferies Research Report.
5 GMV is an acronym for Gross Merchandise Value.

49

SWIFT COMMUNICATIONS

Valuing Synergy Gains in an Acquisition

In mid-2021, Ridham Khanna, Senior Associate at Moonlight Bank's Transaction Advisory Group, was busy preparing his summary valuation report for Swift Communications Technology Services Ltd (SCTSL). After rapid consolidation in Indian Telecom Service Providers over the last decade, especially after Reliance Jio's entry, it seemed there would be a wave of consolidation in Telecom services technology providers. Moonlight developed expertise in facilitating transactions in several sectors, including telecom. It advised SCTSL to acquire Quick Singling Services Ltd (QSCL), which was slightly bigger via the equity-swap transaction; Moonlight promised to structure the transaction such that management control and board majority would remain with SCTSL. While the deal was about to close, a prominent institutional investor raised concern that SCTSL might be overpaying for QSCL. While they were supportive of the overall transaction, the Special Committee of Independent directors called for a supplementary report from Moonlight to relook at the valuation before signing the Definitive Merger Agreement (DMA) with QSCL.

Indian Telecom Industry in 2021

With a subscriber base of 118 crore and 75.8 crore internet subscribers at the beginning of 2021, India was the world's second-largest telecom market. Indian mobile/digital economy and data usage was growing, and India became the second-largest market surpassing the USA in terms of data downloads. Gross revenue of telecom sector was nearly Rs 700 crore by the end of FY21. India would add 500 million new internet users over the next five years, further boosting the digital economy and connectivity.[1]

DOI: 10.4324/9781032724478-55

The entry of Reliance Jio in the Indian Telecom Services market in 2016 had two significant impacts: first, it led to an explosion in mobile subscribers and data usage, and, second, the price war resulted in shunting out of the smaller players, and that resulted in a wave of consolidation in the industry. By 2021, India remained a three-player market with Reliance Jio, Bharti Airtel, and Vodafone Idea (and BSNL, a state-owned player). However, Vodafone Idea struggled to keep its market share due to financial challenges, and BSNL continued to lose ground.

Such a large and growing market required an extensive backbone of technology solutions, equipment and signalling solutions. In addition, while that market was large, it was a matured and highly competitive market with a wave of consolidation just begun.

The Transaction

In early June 2021, SCTCL was on the verge of inking a deal to acquire QSCL. The proposed acquisition would use an equity swap to ensure a better alignment of shareholders' interests post-acquisition. SCTCL shares traded at Rs 30, whereas QSCL shares traded at Rs 25. According to proposed deal terms, QSCl shareholders would get 1.25 shares of SCTCL for one share of QSCL by them. The merged entity would rename itself as Modern Communication Technology Solutions Ltd (MCTSL).

Table 49.1 provides relevant financial information for the two merger candidates based on FY21 data.

Both firms had reached a constant growth phase. QSCL and SCTSL would continue to grow at an average rate of 5% and 5.5%, respectively, had they opt to operate independently. Capital spending would be 110% of depreciation in both firms given the fast-changing technology pace in

TABLE 49.1 QSCL and SCTCL Financial Information

	QSCL(Rs crore)	*SCTCL(Rs crore)*
Revenues	900	700
Cost of Goods Sold (w/o depreciation) as % of Revenue	85%	87%
Depreciation	30	15
Tax Rate	25.00%	25.00%
Working Capital	10% of Revenue	9% of Revenue
Cash	20	10
Market Value of Equity	380	420
Outstanding Debt	75	50

Source: Prepared by authors.

their business. The estimated beta for QSCL was 1.4, and SCTSL was 1.3. Both firms were rated BBB by leading credit rating agencies in India. Both firms recently rolled over their debt, and the interest rate on recently raised long-term debt was 10.0%. The prevailing annual risk-free rate in India is 6.5%. Moonlight estimated the market risk premium at 7.5%

Post-merger, the combined entity would rationalise its overhead expenses, and the cost of goods sold (COGS) for the combined entity would be 84% of the total revenues. SCTSL was confident that the combined entity would grow at 5.5% as size advantage kicks in; a larger size would make them eligible to bid for large contracts and result in a higher deal win rate.

The combined entity had a target debt to value ratio of 20%. (At that level of debt, the combined entity's credit rating would upgrade to A, and the applicable cost of debt would drop to 8.75 %.). The beta of the combined entity would be 1.25 at the given level of debt. However, in the absence of any further borrowings, the cost of debt would be 8.5%.

Questions

1. What would be the intrinsic value of SCTSL and QSCL as standalone entities?
2. What would be the equity value of the combined entity with synergy benefits but without additional borrowing?
3. What would be the equity value of the combined entity with synergy benefits and an increase in debt to target debt/value level?
4. Do you agree with Institutional Investors concern? Why? Why not?

Note

1 IBEF Website.

50

ITC LTD

EVA Analysis of FMCG and Hotel Divisions

On October 1, 2019, Debashis Banerjee, an analyst at one of the leading Investment Management firms in India, was busy working on his analysis of ITC. He had been assigned a task to perform a detailed financial analysis of ITC to help his firm decide whether ITC was a "value buy" opportunity or a "value trap." Despite having stellar performance on both the financial and market front (Exhibit 50.1), ITC had been struggling to hold its ground and underperformed the market for nearly two years. While implementation of GST and Environment, Social and Governance (ESG) concerns were presented as explanations for such underperformance, Debashis thought there was something beyond the popular narrative. He agreed that there had been growing concern surrounding ESG among global institutional investors; however, ITC, except its flagship Cigarettes business, which falls under the sin goods category, was doing an excellent job on the ESG front. As far as taxes were concerned, being there in the business of sin goods, it was always there on the receiving end of the government's stick in the form of higher taxes in every year's budget, and yet it delivered excellent performance over the years.

Debasish suspected that more than ESG and tax concerns, capital allocation might be haunting investors. So he decided to go beyond traditional financial ratios and apply value-based performance metrics, especially Economic Value Added (EVA). He was seeking answers to critical questions. Was ITC creating value for its shareholders? Were capital hungry FMCG and hotel businesses creating value?

DOI: 10.4324/9781032724478-56

EXHIBIT 50.1 ITC's Long-Term Financial and Market Performance (Rs Crore)

	2008–09	*2018–19*	*10-Year CAGR 08–09 to 18–19*
Net Revenue	15,612	44,415	11.00%
PBT	4,826	18,444	14.30%
PAT	3,264	12,464	14.30%
Capital Employed	14,780	60,005	15.00%
Segment RoCE	39.70%	70.30%	
Market Capitalisation	69,751	3,63,714	18.00%
Total Shareholder Returns			20.30%
Sensex (CAGR 08–09 to 18–19)	14.80%		

Source: Company Corporate Presentation.

ITC Ltd: Company Background

Established in 1910, ITC was a large Indian conglomerate with business interests spread across FMCG (including cigarettes), Hotels, Paperboard and Packaging and Agribusiness. ITC had delivered double-digit CAGR in the last ten years on all metrics – top-line growth, bottom-line growth, and growth in market capitalisation. At the end of FY19, ITC's revenue, profit after tax and market capitalisation were Rs 44,415 crore, Rs 12,464 crore, and Rs 3,63,714 crore, respectively. ITC enjoyed pole position in the hotel business and had established a strong presence in the FMCG business with several category winners and strong brands in sub-segments of FMCG business. Despite the stellar long-term performance, ITC was facing challenges on three fronts. First, sluggish volume growth in flagship cigarette's businesses; second, the growing preference among global investors for ESG compliant companies and avoiding companies such as ITC involved in the business of sin goods; and third, frustratingly long wait for returns in capital guzzler hotel and FMCG businesses. While there was a visible ray of light at the end of the tunnel by the end of FY19, both FMCG and hotel businesses reported their highest ROCE in the last five years; the ROCE for FMCG hotel businesses were 5.3% and 3.0%, respectively. The total capital employed by ITC at the end of FY19 was about Rs 26,500 crore spread across five major business segments; FMCG and hotels accounted for near half of the total capital employed. ITC could slowly diversify its revenue stream. FMCG-other, paper and agri-business contributed meaningfully to the revenue mix; it largely remained a cigarette company with cigarettes business contributed 85% of FY19 net profit (Exhibit 50.2). FMCG-others and hotels combined contributed to just 2.8% of the company's profits.

EXHIBIT 50.2 ITC Ltd: Major Business Segments Data

Operating Margin

	Cigarettes	FMCG-Others	Hotels	Agri-business	Paper & Packaging
FY15	63.7%	0.1%	12.6%	10.7%	18.3%
FY19	67.3%	2.6%	10.9%	8.3%	21.2%

Capital Employed in a Year (Rs in Crore)

	Cigarettes	FMCG-Others	Hotels	Agri-business	Paper & Packaging
FY15	6,230	3,420	4,230	2,180	5,310
FY19	3,970	6,200	6,670	3,400	6,200

Return on Capital Employed (ROCE)

	Cigarettes	FMCG-Others	Hotels	Agri-business	Paper & Packaging
FY15	33.30%	0.8%	1.1%	42.2%	17.1%
FY19	26.70%	5.3%	3.0%	25.2%	20.4%

Source: Company corporate presentation.

Value-Based Financial Performance Metrics

While accounting measures and return ratios were helpful, they were criticised for not capturing whether the firm or its division created value for shareholders. Which, means that if a firm earns Return on Invested Capital (ROIC) less than its Weighted Average Cost of Capital (WACC), it destroys value for its shredders. The firm makes ROIC greater than WACC would create value for the firm. Stern-Stewart Corporation gave a measure called EVA that measured whether the firm created value from its investments or otherwise. EVA provides a dollar value of value created by the firm.

EVA = Net Operating Profit After Tax (NOPAT)– Capital Employed * Weighted Average Cost of Capital (WACC)

A positive EVA number indicated the firm's crated value after meeting the long-term opportunity cost of funds. While implementing, many firms came up with their variations. For instances, some of them measured EVA rate[1] rather than EVA for measuring the performance of a unit or division. Another measure that ensured that the firm generated EVA and how it changes over time. Change in EVA scaled to Sales. For instance, if the EVA created by a firm in a given year was Rs 1 billion and EVA for the previous year was Rs 500 million, the sales in the prior year were Rs 25 billion EVA momentum ratio was 2%. Positive ratio meant firm created value, and negative ratio meant it destroyed value on an incremental basis.

MVA

Another measure was Market Value Added (MVA); MVA was simple to measure; one could measure MVA as follows.

MVA = Total Value of Firm – Total Capital Invested

It showed how much value the firm had created. Conceptually, MVA was noting, but the present value of all the future expected EVAs.

CVA

Boston Consulting Group (BCG) came up with Cash Value Added (CVA) to measure cash flow based value-added metrics rather than profit-based. There were two ways to calculate CVA.

CVA= Gross cash flow – Economic depreciation – capital charge

Ord

CVA = (CFROI – Cost of Capital) × Gross Investment

Where

- CFROI is cash flow return on investment, or [(gross cash flow - economic depreciation) / gross investment]
- Economic depreciation is [WACC / (1+WACC)^n -1]
- Gross cash flow is adjusted profit + interest expense + depreciation
- The capital charge is the cost of capital x gross investment
- Gross investment is net current assets + historical initial cost

While EVA focused on the entire intrinsic value of the business, CVA concentrated only on the company's cash value.

After careful comparison, Debashis zeroed down on using EVA for his measure of value creation.

Ready to Go

Debashis gathered the necessary financial information from financial statements of ITC and other market sources to calculate ITC's EVA. However, he realised that calculating EVA for FMCG and hotel divisions would not be easy given the challenges involved in calculating the cost of capital for unlisted divisions. Therefore, he complied financial information of FMCG and hotel peers to facilitate his task. (see Exhibit 50.3 & 50.4 for financial information on listed Hotel and FMCG firms). In addition, he compiled

EXHIBIT 50.3 Financial Data for ITC Ltd and Selected Listed Hotel Companies in India at the End of March-2019 (Rs Crore)

Company Name	*EBITDA*	*EBIT*	*PAT*	*Total Debt*	*Net worth*	*Net sales*	*ROCE (%)*	*RONW (%)*	*levered beta*	*M-Cap*	*P/E*	*P/B*	*EV*	*Credit rating*
Chalet Hotels Ltd	388.83	247	-9	1411.03	1473	987	8.86%	–0.53%	1.1	6925.71	–	4.87	8892.5421	BBB
Country Club Hospitality & Holidays Ltd	48.46	3.85	-53.67	350	946.96	264.57	0.27%	–5.58%	1.4	106.74	–	0.11	546.6288	NA
E I H Ltd	474.71	342.15	136.66	499.78	2993.39	1,810.82	7.77%	4.65%	1.42	11577.15	88.01	3.87	11886.7384	AA
Indian Hotels Co. Ltd	916.71	588.86	244.59	1723.2	4348	4,512.00	8.97%	5.74%	1.1	18356.85	64	4.22	20442.633	AA
Kamat Hotels (India) Ltd	74.1	55.76	16.6	260.17	-147.84	236.09	13.09%		1.7	116.39	6.89	-0.78	614.289	NA
Lemon Tree Hotels Ltd	183.28	129.17	55.58	1135.95	875.02	549.51	7.33%	8.45%	1.1	6349.88	112.63	9.13	7514.48	A-
Mahindra Holidays & Resorts India Ltd	239.43	138.09	59.49	584.86	281.57	2,238.99	14.96%	65.31%	1.15	3190.26	52.8	–6.16	3941.0178	AA
Royal Orchid Hotels Ltd	49.48	35.16	13.11	91.35	177.48	203.83	12.99%	7.92%	1.6	323.67	27.1	1.91	383.9648	BBB
Taj G V K Hotels & Resorts Ltd	76.41	59.71	24.31	160.11	391.86	316.87	10.08%	6.39%	1.3	1488.85	54.75	3.8	1684.0764	A+
ITC	20606.13	19209.52	12824.2	NA	59140.87	48352.68	34%	23.80%	0.5	363712.7	28.88	6.36	359576.969	AAA
ITC-Hotels	374	178	122.82	?	?	1,665.00	?	?	?	NA	NA	NA	NA	?

Source: Prowess IQ

EXHIBIT 50.4 Financial Data for ITC Ltd and Select FMCG Companies in India at the end of March 2019 (Rs Crore)

Company Name	*EBITDA*	*EBIT*	*PAT*	*Total Debt*	*Net worth*	*Net sales*	*ROCE*	*RONW*	*Levered beta*	*M-Cap*	*P/E*	*P/B*	*EV*	*Credit rating*
HUL	9430	8865	6060	99	7867	39311	114.67%	84.15%	0.5	496400	73.56	60.43	441795.5	AAA
Marico	1429	1298	1132	349	2976	7334	41.99%	41.25%	0.5	44537.25	39.98	15.06	44341.87	AAA
Dabur	2035.73	1858.83	1445.29	524.28	5631.68	8,514.99	27.49%	25.88%	0.55	72250.5	50.09	13	72614.4891	AAA
Britannia	1939.87	1777.99	1156.43	138.02	4253.25	11,054.67	44.36%	30.32%	0.7	74059.26	63.89	17.49	74103.034	AAA
Nestle	2876.57	2540.9	1606.93	35.14	3673.74	11292.27	70.93%	0.453	0.6	107096.1	66.65	29.15	105512.5876	AAA
Godrej Consumer	2478	2308	1828	2875.72	7266.92	10314.34	22.76%	34.65%	0.8	70240.47	30	9.68	80435.88	AA
Colgate Palmolive	1273.71	1114.54	775.57	77.71	1446.75	4,462.43	74.97%	52.37%	0.6	34288.08	44.13	23.72	33906.1602	AAA
Emami	762.12	436.81	304.73	109.87	2076.06	2,964.63	18.87%	14.90%	0.85	18157.4	59.88	8.75	18062.244	A
ITC	20606.13	19209.52	12824.2	NA	59140.87	48,352.68	34.39%	23.80%	0.5	363712.68	28.88	6.36	359576.9685	AAA
ITC FMCG-others	758	386	266	NA	?	12505	?		?	NA	NA	NA	NA	?

Source: Prowess IQ.

EXHIBIT 50.5 Yield Spread, Risk-free Rate, and Market Risk Premium Estimates

Credit Rating	*The Yield Spread at in September 2019 (basis points))*
AAA	125
AA	175
A	250
BBB	330
BB	420
B	520
Prevailing 10-year GSEC Yield	7%
Additional Information	
91 days T-bill Yield	5.50%
Expected Market Risk Premium	8%
Applicable Marginal Tax rate for divisions (if operated independently)	25%

Source: Authors' estimates based on market information.

information about prevailing yield spread, risk-free rates and expected market risk premium (see Exhibit 50.5).

He was ready to calculate EVA for ITC and its FMCG and Hotel divisions. However, he knew that his calculations would not be precise for FMCG business as many expense items in FMCG business would eventually contribute to the brand equity and hence should be capitalised rather than expensed.

Questions

1. Estimate the cost of capital for ITC and its FMCG and hotel divisions.
2. Calculate the capital charge for ITC and its FMCG and hotel divisions.
3. Calculate the EVA for ITC and its FMCG and hotel divisions.
4. Was ITC creating value for its investors? Could you say the same about its Hotel and FMCG divisions?
5. What do you understand by the concept of EVA rate, EVA momentum MVA, and CVA? Compare these measures.

Note

1 EVA rate = NOPAT / (Capital Employed times WACC).

51

VENU'S ESOP CHOICES (A)

ESOPs of a Listed Company

Venu Rao, an Executive MBA graduate from NITSOM, Hyderabad, was considering two compensation alternatives he had to choose between in the job offer letter he had received from Esquire Finn AMC Ltd., a publicly listed investment management company. The company had offered him an annual compensation of Rs 35 lakh. In addition, he could choose to receive a joining bonus either in cash of Rs 2 lakh under Alternative A or 400 employee stocks options (ESOPs) under Alternative B.

Terms of the ESOP Plan at Esquire Finn AMC

The terms of the grant of 400 ESOPs under Alternative B were as follows:

1. The options would start vesting after 12 months from the grant date (April 1, 2021); 25% of the options would vest at the end of every year for four years.
2. The options must be exercised within ten years from the date of the grant. The shares arising from the exercise would not be subject to any lock-in period.
3. The options would lapse if the employment were terminated before the date of exercise.
4. The exercise price of the options would be the market price as of the date of the grant.

Evaluating the ESOP at Esquire Finn AMC

Venu found the terms of Esquire Finn standard and like those of several other large publicly listed companies. He realised that the ESOPs would

DOI: 10.4324/9781032724478-57

have little intrinsic value initially since the exercise price was the same as the price on the date of the grant, which was a few days away. The fair value of the ESOPs, therefore, consisted almost entirely of the options' time value.

Venu wondered whether he could use either Black Scholes or binomial model for ESOP valuation. He realised that there were significant differences to consider from the usual application of the pricing models. First, there was an extended vesting period and not a single date. The number of options Venue could exercise depended upon how long he remained employed with the company. Second, unlike standard options, ESOPs resulted in dilution of shares upon exercise. Third, ESOPs could not be traded, unlike ordinary stock options. He found that despite these complexities, the Black Scholes model could be used with adjustments to provide an approximate value of the ESOPs.[1]

Further, there were practical complexities that he had to consider while comparing the two compensation alternatives. The ESOPs were taxable on the exercise date depending upon the difference between the market price and exercise price and on the date of sale based on capital gains from the exercise date to the time of sale of shares. In comparison, cash compensation would directly add to the annual taxable income. Also, if the value of ESOPs became large relative to Venu's total savings, that would make his wealth highly concentrated in a single asset.

Venu searched and noted down the information that would be relevant for valuing Esquire Finn's ESOPs. The historical realised volatility of Esquire Finn's stock was 33% per annum, but the implied volatility based on the traded options of the company was currently 35%. The expected dividend yield of the company was 1.5%. The current risk-free rate corresponding to the estimated life of the options was around 5.5%. Since the grant was only a few days away, he assumed the current stock price of Rs 2,300 to be a good proxy for the exercise price based on the terms of the grant.

Venu estimated the chances that he would remain employed with Esquire Finn for different tenures to determine the potential benefits he could derive from each instalment of the options grant. Further, to simplify the estimate of time to maturity, Venu assumed that he was most likely to exercise the options earlier than the maximum limit of 10 years from the grant date. Though a longer holding period was optimal from a valuation standpoint, he considered early exercise a reasonable assumption since he could leave the company before ten years or decide to encash his options early for liquidity reasons.

Decision-Making

Venu wondered if it was a great idea to choose ESOPs instead of a cash joining bonus which was a bird in the hand. He had made great efforts to get the necessary information. Now he had to prepare his estimates to decide.

Questions

1. If Venu decides to join the listed AMC, which compensation package will you recommend and why? You can use the Black Scholes model with the following additional assumptions:
   a. Assume the probability that Venu will remain employed and eligible at the time of vesting are as follows: one-year vesting (90%), two-year vesting (70%), three-year vesting (60%), four-year vesting (50%).
   b. Assume the average time of exercise of the stock options to be the mid-point between the date of vesting and ten years from the grant date.
   c. Given the small ratio of ESOPs to the total number of shares, ignore the dilutive effect of these options on the stock price.

2. How will your answer change if Venu is confident that he will remain with the company for ten years? You can assume the average time of exercise to be 7.5 years from the date of the grant.
3. Do the options cost anything to the company? Who bears the cost of the ESOPs received by Venu?
4. What is the benefit of providing the ESOPs to the company?

Note

1 Damodaran, A. (2005). Employee stock options (ESOPs) and restricted stock: valuation effects and consequences. *Available at SSRN 841504*.

52

VENU'S ESOP CHOICES (B)

ESOPs of a Start-Up

Venu Rao, an Executive MBA graduate from NITSOM, Hyderabad, had received two job offers. The first had been from Esquire Finn AMC Ltd., a publicly listed company. Venu had already evaluated this offer, including the choice of receiving the joining bonus as either cash or as employee stock options (ESOPs).

The second job offer was from MetaQ, a robo-advisor established in 2018. The firm had offered him an annual salary of Rs 20 lakh and 2,000 employee stock options. The firm had shared the terms of the ESOPs with the offer letter. One of the co-founders was also going to explain the ESOP plan to him, as was customarily done by the firm for new employees.

Terms of the ESOPs at MetaQ

Venu was offered 2,000 employee stock options by MetaQ, under the following terms:

1. The options would vest 12 months from the date of the grant (April 1, 2021); 25% of the options would vest at the end of every year for four years.
2. The options must be exercised within ten years from the date of the grant. The shares arising from the exercise would not be subject to any lock-in period.
3. The options would not lapse even if the employment were terminated before the date of exercise.
4. The exercise price of each option would be the face value of each share (Rs 10).

DOI: 10.4324/9781032724478-58

5. Accelerated vesting: All existing unvested options held for more than a year from the grant date would be vested immediately before listing or in the event of a strategic sale.

Appended with the terms was a detailed description of the ESOP programme at MetaQ. Details about the company, including business description, goals, and funding received, had also been annexed.

Challenges in Valuing MetaQ ESOPs

Venu had previously evaluated the ESOPs offered by Esquire Finn AMC Ltd, a publicly listed company. He had found that despite the many practical complexities, he could adapt the Black Scholes model to provide an approximate value of the ESOPs. Further, he could quickly gather information to estimate the critical option pricing variables such as current stock price and volatility. By making some reasonable assumptions, Venu had been able to assess the value of the options.

However, Venu encountered several problems in estimating the value of the ESOPs in the case of MetaQ. Since the company was unlisted, he had to rely on peer companies for an estimate of volatility. But MetaQ's robo-advisory business was different from any listed peer. Further, Venu believed that a start-up's high business uncertainty could result in much higher volatility than in an established company. As for the current stock price, all he had was an estimated implied value of Rs 900 per share from a recent round of funding last year.

The most challenging part of valuation was determining the time to expiry of the options. Though the ESOPs would start vesting after one year, it made little sense to exercise them early without any visibility regarding monetisation. Exit events such as an IPO or acquisition could be uncertain and distant. In the absence of clarity regarding how the shares received on ESOP conversion could be liquidated, the ESOPs did not appear worthwhile to Venu.

Venu was also concerned about some recent news articles regarding employee experience with ESOPs at start-ups. In the face of the Covid-19 pandemic and the consequent cash flow challenges, several start-ups had cut salaries and substituted them with ESOPs. In several cases, the ESOP documents were not shared or with the employees or had clauses in fine print that allowed the employers to withhold vesting.[1]

Discussion with Vijay Sachdeva of MetaQ

Venu had an online meeting with Vijay Sachdeva, Co-founder and Director of MetaQ, on March 28, two days before the deadline, to submit his acceptance of the job offer. At Vijay's behest, Venu stated his queries regarding the offer letter.

Vijay decided to address the questions related to the ESOP valuations first. He explained that unlike in a publicly listed company, the best practice among start-ups was to keep the exercise price much below the current value. This difference ensured that the option was deep in the money and not at the money, unlike ESOPs of listed companies. In the case of ESOPs offered by MetaQ, the intrinsic value was the relevant component, whereas the time value was minuscule.,

Vijay provided an estimate of the company's current value as Rs 1080 per share, assuming a 20% increase from last year's fund-raising. According to him, this value was conservative given that MetaQ had consistently met all the monthly targets. He also suggested that Venu assume as typical values nil dividends, high volatility of 50%, and a risk-free rate of 5%. Even if he were to change these assumptions significantly, that would make little difference to the value of the options. Venu could set the exercise period close to the liquidity event to avoid tax without receiving any cash flow. (As per Indian tax rules, ESOP employees incurred taxes at the time of exercise on the difference between fair value and exercise price. Later, they incurred tax again on capital gains when they sold the shares).

MetaQ had followed the best practices among start-ups to make the ESOPs attractive. The ESOP plan was generous, with even somebody like Venu, who was not part of the core management team, receiving options representing 0.2% of the shares. The ESOPs were very affordable, with the exercise price at a fraction of the fair value of shares. The ESOPs would not lapse even after the employment ended and could be exercised anytime till ten years of the grant date.

Vijay further mentioned that, unlike several start-ups offering ESOPs only to preserve cash, MetaQ's objective was to engender a sense of ownership and an entrepreneurial culture in employees. The ESOP programme had been carefully drafted, planning for a horizon of ten years, and had the complete buy-in of the investors. The venture capitalists had committed to support secondary liquidity event every three years where employees could sell back their options.

There would be further "top-up" plans, with new option grants being given again at a frequency of around three years. Being a robo-advisor, MetaQ envisaged only a few employees and had only two co-founders. Fewer employees meant that Venu could look forward to a larger share of the pie going forward. Unfortunately, MetaQ had not registered with the Inter-Ministerial Board constituted by the Indian government. Hence, its employees could not avail deferment of taxes provided in the Union Budget of 2020–21.

According to Vijay, a start-up had massive potential for wealth creation. Successful start-ups in India had resulted in employees becoming much more prosperous than their peers who had started with high salaries in well-established companies. He was confident that MetaQ's valuation would grow three times within the next three years, and if Venu stayed on, he could undoubtedly reap a rich harvest.

To make the employees feel confident about the valuation prospects of the company, MetaQ shared monthly reports on the achievement of milestones and financial targets with all the employees. The high level of transparency regarding business plans and achievement was highly appreciated, even by the VCs. They realised that the scalability of the business depended upon employee retention and motivation.

Before ending the meeting, Vijay clarified that though the company offered ESOPs to all the employees at an early stage, ESOPs in future would have to be earned based on performance since MetaQ was very intent on fostering a performance-driven culture.

The discussion with Vijay rejuvenated Venu. He found the approach followed by MetaQ was as per the best practices recommended by successful start-ups such as Urban Company,[2] the India-based home services company and Wealthfront, the US-based robo-advisor.[3]

However, he still had some niggling doubts. Many more start-ups failed than succeeded, which meant lottery-like payoffs of their ESOPs. Further, despite Vijay's pitch, MetaQ's compensation plan might be motivated by cash preservation rather than aligning employees' interests with shareholders. It was also easier to be transparent about its business performance only while the going was good. Finally, the management could provide no guarantee about providing regular liquidity for the ESOPs despite best intentions. Venu had to take a leap of faith and see the track record of MetaQ over time.

Decision-Making

For Venu, joining the start-up held great appeal from both an emotional and a learning perspective. Moreover, he did not mind the lottery-like payoff for his efforts at a relatively early stage of his career. Nevertheless, he wanted to estimate the value of his ESOPs objectively. He had learnt how evaluating an ESOP plan of a start-up was different from evaluating an ESOP plan of a publicly listed company.

Questions

1. Compare the relative importance of an ESOP programme to a start-up like MetaQ with an ESOP programme of a publicly listed company. What are the differences which employees must consider while evaluating the ESOPs of a start-up compared with the ESOPs of a publicly listed company?

2. Estimate the value of the ESOPs offered by the start-up to Venu under the following assumptions:
   a. The probability that Venu will remain employed with the start-up after one, to, three, and four years to be eligible for the ESOP vesting would be 80%, 60%, 40%, and 20%, respectively.
   b. There would be opportunities to liquidate the ESOPs after two years and after four years. Venu would utilise them by exercising the ESOPs shortly ahead of the liquidity event.
   c. The current value of the start-up was Rs 1,080 per share on a fully diluted basis.

Notes

1 https://www.livemint.com/industry/retail/the-pitfalls-of-esop-lifelines-at-start-ups-11592322029892.html
2 https://mystartupequity.com/blog/can-esops-help-startups-survive-the-downturn/
3 https://blog.wealthfront.com/the-right-way-to-grant-equity-to-your-employees/

PART VI
Long-Term Financing

53

ROSSARI BIOTECH

An IPO in the Indian Stock Market

On July 11, 2021, Lizzy George was preparing an initial public offer (IPO) note on Rossari Biotech IPO. Lizzy worked with Hexagon, a rapidly growing discount brokerage house, boasting of its ability to nudge investors to make fewer behavioural mistakes while trading and investing. Hexagon had developed several tools to alert traders and investors to prevent them from committing potential behavioural mistakes. Hexagon added more than one million clients in the single quarter ending June 2020. Most of them were early-career technology and consulting professionals and were new to the world of equity markets. Hexagon was trying to offer them insights into the basics of trading and investing through its research reports, weekly newsletters, and webinars. Many clients invested in recent IPOs and enjoyed good listing gains; however, they wanted to know more about IPOs. Lizzy thought a research note on Rossari Biotech IPO would be an excellent medium to educate investors about IPOs in the Indian markets.

IPO

The firm could raise external equity funds in several ways: Angel Investors, Venture Capital, Private Equity, Rights Issue, Follow on Public Offer (FPO), and Private Placement. While Angel Investors and Venture Capital financing were for early-stage start-ups, the private equity funding was available to both grown-up start-ups, unicorns, and listed firms. The firm wanted to go public and become a listed entity on stock exchanges that would raise funds through the first-time offering of new securities to the public in primary markets, called IPO. The firms already listed could further tap FPOs, Rights

DOI: 10.4324/9781032724478-60

EXHIBIT 53.1 Pros and Cons of IPO for Issuing Firm

Pros	*Cons*
1. Company gets additional capital without any fixed obligation.	1. High IPO Costs.
2. Stringent financial reporting rules and periodic audits.	2 More publicity and media coverage
3. Company can issue ESOPs to employees.	3. Dilution of equity.
4. There may not be enough interest in the IPO.	4. Additional capital can be used to repay debt or for growth purposes.
5. Distractions due to the IPO process may lead to missed opportunities in business.	5. Company finds it easier to raise loans or negotiate with vendors

Source: Prepared by authors.

Issue, or Private Placement to raise additional equity capital (see Exhibit 53.1 for Pros and Cons of IPO for an issuer).

IPO Process

The IPO process in India had changed a great deal over the years. The duration between the IPO launch date and the listing date had reduced significantly, and the movement of funds had become seamless. The firm intended to launch an IPO had to prepare itself for a few years to meet the Securities and Exchange Board of India (SEBI)'s norms. The firm typically worked with Pre-IPO consultants for the same. They then hired Book Running Lead Managers (BRLM), typically a merchant banker or an investment bank (more than one for large issues) and filed a draft offer document with SEBI, which subsequently became an offer document once SEBI approved it. After that, the firm added the issue size and price band (or fixed issue price) to the offer document and became a red herring prospectus. Soon after, the firm, in consultation with its BRLM and stock exchanges, decided the launch date of the IPO. Several other intermediaries were roped in. Registrar of the issue (to collect and process applications, allotments, and refunds), Underwrites (subscribe to IPO in case of a shortfall), bankers (for fund management), and many more. The IPO would remain open for subscription for a minimum of three days and a maximum of seven days; it could go up to ten days if the firm decided to revise its price band in between. For an IPO to succeed, it must get 90% subscriptions; the IPO would fail otherwise or subscribed by underwriters to meet the shortfall (see Exhibits 53.2 and 53.3 for IPO and IPO application process).

EXHIBIT 53.2 Key Steps in IPO Process in India

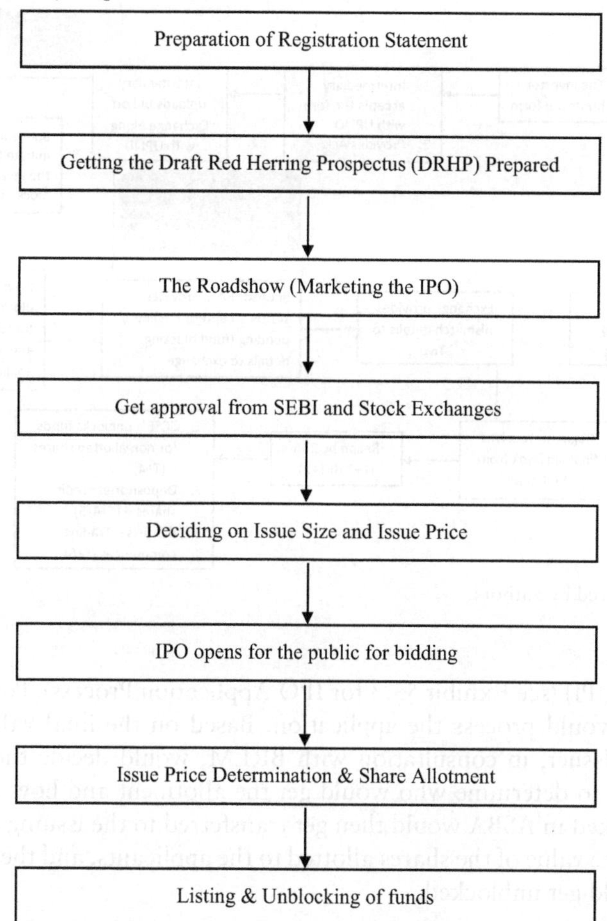

Source: Prepared by authors.

A day before the IPO opened for public subscription, the company would accept bids from a group of anchor investors. The purpose of these anchor investors was to instill confidence about the IPO in public. The investors were allowed to bid in three different categories: Retail Individual Investor (RII), Non-Institutional Investor (NII), and the Qualified Institutional Bidder (QIB). Thirty-five per cent of the issue would be reserved for RII, and they would be allowed to bid at the cut-off price (the price at which the company allots the securities). Fifteen per cent of the issue would be reserved for the NIIs and 50% for the QIBs. The investors would apply via Application Supported by Blocked Amount (ASBA) or Unified Payment

EXHIBIT 53.3 IPO Application Process in India

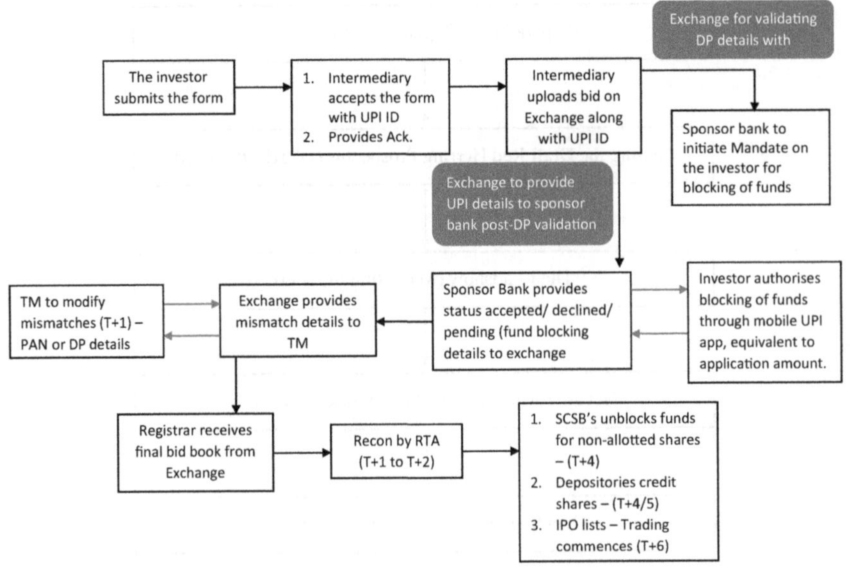

Source: Prepared by authors.

Interface (UPI) (see Exhibit 53.3 for IPO Application Process). Post that, the Registrar would process the application. Based on the final valid applications, the Issuer, in consultation with BRLM, would decide the "basis of allotment" to determine who would get the allotment and how much. The funds blocked in ASBA would then get transferred to the issuing firm to the extent of the value of the shares allotted to the applicants, and the remaining funds would get unblocked.

Rossari BioTech: The IPO

Founded in 2003 as a partnership firm, Rossari Biotech become a company in 2009. In less than two decades, Rossari Biotech became the leading speciality chemical manufacturing company in India, with customers ranging from the Textile, FMCG, Poultry and Animal feed industry. The company had 1948 different products that it sold and two R&D facilities to research for more. Their products could be categorised into four segments: Home, Personal Care & Performance Chemicals, Textile Specialty Chemicals, and Animal Health and Nutrition Products. In FY20, Rossari Biotech earned Rs 65.5 crores in earnings on sales of Rs 605 crores and on total assets worth Rs 471 crores. Their flagship, core textile chemicals business had

EXHIBIT 53.4 Rossari Biotech IPO Terms

IPO Open	13-Jul-20
IPO Close	15-Jul-20
IPO Size	Approx. Rs 500 crore
Face Value	Rs 2 per equity share
Price Band	Rs 423 to Rs 425 per share
Listing on	BSE & NSE
Retail Portion	50%
Issue Size	1,16,82,033 equity shares of Rs 2 each
Fresh Size	11,82,033 equity shares of Rs 2 each
Offer for Sale	1,05,00,000 equity shares of Rs 2 each
Lot Size	Minimum 35 Shares and Maximum 455 Shares
Minimum Amount	Rs 14,875.00
Maximum Amount	Rs 1,93,375.00
Basis of Allotment	20-Jul-20
Refunds	21-Jul-20
Credit to Demat Account	22-Jul-20
Listing Date	23-Jul-20

Source: Stock Exchange filings.

done well and had grown at 10–25% in the past six to seven years. Rossari Biotech launched IPO to offer with a large chunk of offer for sale (OFS) component and a relatively smaller portion of the fresh issue of capital that would be used to repay debt and general purpose (see Exhibit 53.4 for IPO details).

IPO Recommendation

Before finalising her IPO recommendation on the Rossari Biotech issue, Lizzy performed SWOT analysis for Rossari Biotech and compiled financial information of Rossari Biotech and its select listed peers (Exhibit 53.5 and 53.6). While Hexagon would give it recommendation based on their analysis, they would also keep track of Grey Market Premium (GMP)[1] and subscription data on the second half of the last day of IPO and provided final subscription recommendation based on that.

Questions

- What are the various ways a firm can raise external equity?
- What are the pros and cons of IPO for an issuer?
- Explain the IPO and IPO application process in India.

EXHIBIT 53.5 SWOT Analysis of Rossari Biotech

Strengths		*Weaknesses*	
1	Pan-India distribution network.	1	No long-term agreement with the raw material suppliers
2	Robust technical and R&D team.		
3	India's No. 1 largest textile speciality chemical company.		
4	Flexible manufacturing capabilities for powders, granules, and liquid.		
5	Rossari promoters with 80+ years of cumulative experience in Textile Chemical Engineering.		
Opportunities		Threats	
1	Capacity expansion to meet the increasing demands.	1	Heavy reliance on a limited number of customers.
2	Fast launches of new customisable and sustainable products.	2	Exposure of workforce to potentially dangerous circumstances with highly toxic, flammable, and explosive chemicals.
3	Pent-up demand due to the lockdown.		

Source: IPO prospectus, brokerage reports and authors' analysis.

- What is the difference between the OFS and Fresh issue component of an IPO? Does the split between OFS and Fresh issue component of IPO contain any information?
- If you were in Lizzy's place, would you have recommended Rossari Biotech IPO to the client? Why? Why not?
- Do you think GMP and waiting until the last day subscription data would offer a margin of safety against the potential downside of IPO listing?

EXHIBIT 53.6 Rossari Biotech with Select Listed Peers: Financial Comparison (as of July 2020)

Particulars	*Revenue*	*EBITDA*	*Net Profit*	*EBITDA margin (%)*	*Net Margin (%)*	*EPS (Rs.)*	*BVPS(Rs.)*	*RoE (%)*	*RoIC*	*P/E*	*P/B*	*EV/ EBITDA*
Rossari Biotech Ltd												
FY18	292	45	29	15.3	9.9	5.6	18.2	30.7	26.4	76.1	23.4	49.8
FY19	516	77	45	14.9	8.8	8.7	24.9	35.1	37.1	48.7	17.1	28.6
FY20	600	105	65	17.5	10.9	12.6	55.2	22.8	31.6	33.7	7.7	20.3
FY21 (E)	680	112	75	16.5	11.1	14.5	75	19.3	35.1	29.3	5.7	18
FY22 (E)	840	138	94	16.4	11.2	18.2	85.9	21.1	41.8	23.4	4.9	14.4
Sudarshan Chemical Industries Ltd (CMP: Rs 392 Mkt Cap: Rs 2714 cr)												
FY18	1306	187	85	14.3	6.5	12.2	63.6	19.3	15	32	6.2	16.8
FY19	1453	211	135	14.5	9.3	19.5	82	23.8	15.7	20.1	4.8	14.6
FY20	1681	246	145	14.7	8.6	20.9	86.8	24.1	16.6	18.8	4.5	12.8
FY21 (E)	1737	256	93	14.7	5.3	13.4	99.5	13.5	16	29.2	3.9	12.5
FY22 (E)	2069	337	139	16.3	6.7	20.1	116.4	17.2	19.4	19.5	3.4	9.5
Aarti Industries (CMP: Rs 927.9 Mkt Cap: Rs 16167 cr)												
FY18	3759	691	333	18.4	8.9	19.1	97.1	19.7	14.5	48.6	9.6	26.4
FY19	4659	963	492	20.7	10.6	28.2	151.8	18.6	16.9	32.9	6.1	19
FY20	4186	977	536	23.3	12.8	30.8	171	18	17.4	30.2	5.4	18.1
FY21 (E)	4534	1057	549	23.3	12.1	31.5	198.6	15.9	15.4	29.4	4.7	17.1
FY22 (E)	5459	1334	725	24.4	13.3	41.6	234.8	17.7	18.2	22.3	4	13.5
Atul Ltd (CMP: Rs 4587 Mkt Cap: Rs 13606 cr)												
FY18	3240	505	276	15.6	8.5	93.2	756.5	12.3	17.9	49.2	6.1	26.9
FY19	4038	767	436	19	10.8	147	912.2	16.1	26	31.2	5	17.5
FY20	4093	902	666	22	16.3	224.7	1063.7	21.1	30.1	20.4	4.3	14.4
FY21 (E)	4033	876	584	21.7	14.5	196.9	1265.7	15.6	23.7	23.3	3.6	15
FY22 (E)	4825	1102	745	22.8	15.4	251.3	1503.4	16.7	24.4	18.3	3.1	11.9
Galaxy Surfactants Ltd (CMP: Rs. 1609 Mkt Cap: Rs 5705 cr)												
FY18	2413	288	158	11.9	6.5	44.6	202.7	22	23	36.1	7.9	20.9
FY19	2732	353	191	12.9	7	53.9	247.3	21.8	27.3	29.9	6.5	16.8

(Continued)

EXHIBIT 53.6 Continued

Particulars	*Revenue*	*EBITDA*	*Net Profit*	*EBITDA margin (%)*	*Net Margin (%)*	*EPS (Rs.)*	*BVPS(Rs.)*	*RoE (%)*	*RoIC*	*P/E*	*P/B*	*EV/ EBITDA*
FY20	2596	369	230	14.2	8.9	65	301.2	21.6	22.7	24.8	5.3	16.2
FY21 (E)	2744	358	212	13	7.7	59.7	351.6	17	23.8	26.9	4.6	16.7
FY22 (E)	3155	442	272	14	8.6	76.7	417	18.4	24.9	21	3.9	13.5
Deepak Nitrite (CMP: Rs 516.1 Mkt Cap: Rs 7039 cr)												
FY18	1611	196	79	12.2	4.9	5.8	67.6	8.6	7.8	89.1	7.6	40.5
FY19	2675	414	174	15.5	6.5	12.7	78.6	16.2	15	40.5	6.6	19.8
FY20	4230	1026	611	24.3	14.4	44.8	115.2	38.9	34.3	11.5	4.5	7.8
FY21 (E)	3940	938	535	23.8	13.6	39.2	146.2	26.8	28.1	13.2	3.5	8.2
FY22 (E)	4507	1057	623	23.4	13.8	45.6	181.4	25.2	29.4	11.3	2.8	7
Vinati Organics (CMP: Rs 1009 Mkt Cap: Rs 10379 cr)												
FY18	729	199	144	27.4	19.7	14	77.5	18.1	25.8	72.1	13	51.5
FY19	1108	404	282	36.4	25.5	27.5	102.3	26.9	39.4	36.7	9.9	25.5
FY20	1029	414	334	40.2	32.4	32.5	124.5	26.1	38.1	31.1	8.1	24.4
FY21 (E)	1153	415	294	36	25.5	28.6	147.5	19.4	39.3	35.3	6.8	24.9
FY22 (E)	1547	570	411	36.9	26.6	40	170.5	23.5	40.5	25.2	5.9	18.1
Himadri Specialty Chemical Ltd (CMP: Rs 48.9 Mkt Cap: Rs 2048 cr)												
FY18	2021	452	247	22.4	12.2	5.9	33.8	17.5	21.2	8.3	1.4	5.8
FY19	2422	560	324	23.1	13.4	7.7	39	19.9	26.1	6.3	1.3	4.3
FY20	1930	354	183	18.4	9.5	4.4	43.1	10.1	27.4	11.2	1.1	6.9
FY21 (E)	2100	414	206	19.7	9.8	4.9	49.1	10	28.7	9.9	1	5.9
FY22 (E)	2590	532	309	20.5	11.9	7.4	56.4	13.1	30	6.6	0.9	4.6
Nocil Ltd. (CMP: Rs 92.3 Mkt Cap: Rs 1529 cr)												
FY18	977	265	170	27.2	17.4	10.3	63.6	16.1	30.1	9	1.5	4.8
FY19	1030	293	185	28.4	17.9	11.2	70.3	15.9	26.2	8.3	1.3	4.7
FY20	846	178	131	21.1	15.4	7.9	71.6	11	12.7	11.7	1.3	8.3
FY21 (E)	897	186	117	20.7	13.1	7.1	77.3	9.2	13.6	13	1.2	8
FY22 (E)	1124	244	161	21.7	14.3	9.7	83.4	11.7	14.6	9.5	1.1	6.1

Source: Prepared by authors based on IPO prospectus, prowess, brokerage IPO notes.

Note

1 GMP was the premium in an unorganised informal market where IPO traded from its announcement to its allotment and listing. Moreover, it was not a legal market. Hence, Hexagon never recommended its clients to participate in it, yet offered an essential source of information to estimate listing gains of an IPO.

54

RELIANCE INDUSTRIES LTD

The Tale of India's Largest Rights Issue

On May 15, 2020, Rehana Ahmed, a buy-side analyst at Prestige Asset Managers, was busy preparing her note on the recently announced rights issue by Reliance Industries Ltd (RIL).

"The board approved the issuance of equity shares of Rs 10 each of the company on rights basis to eligible equity shareholders as on the record date of an issue size of Rs 53,125 crore," said RIL in its update to the stock exchanges and media.[1] It would be the largest rights issue by any Indian company in Indian markets.

The issue was priced at Rs 1,257, at 14% or Rs 210 discounts to its closing price on April 30, 2020. May 14, 2020, was set as the record date. On May 13, 2020, the RIL stock traded Ex-right and closed at Rs 1,437 per share, nearly 4% lower compared to the previous day close of Rs 1,496, RIL's last issued rights issue in 1991.

Prestige Asset Managers had substantial holdings in RIL. So Anthony George, the fund manager at Prestige, had to decide (a) whether to participate in RIL's rights issue or let it give a pass and sell rights entitlements in open markets and (b) if they participate, how many shares should they apply.

Reliance Industries Ltd

Founded by Dhirubhai Ambani, RIL came up with its IPO in 1977. Over four and a half decades, RIL had gone through multiple reorganisations to become an oil-to-telecom conglomerate with business interests spread across Oil to Chemicals (O2C), Digital and Telecom; Retail and E-commerce, Upstream Oil and Gas and proposed renewable energy business. From a zero net debt company in 2012, RIL piled up a total debt of Rs 3,060 billion,

DOI: 10.4324/9781032724478-61

and the net debt of the net debt was Rs 1,530 billion by the end of December 2019. The net debt-to-equity ratio jumped above 0.5 in book value terms. While the debt levels were not excessive, given the Capex heavy nature of both telecom and retail businesses was bothering markets, and many brokerages turned cautious on RIL stock in the middle of 2019.

However, in his RIL's 42nd speech in August 2019, RIL's Chairman, Mukesh Ambani, pledged to make RIL a zero net-debt company over the next 18 months, the end of FY21. It changed analysts view about RIL and most of them upgraded RIL's stock.

Soon after, RIL announced USD 15 billion investment by Suadi's Aramco into its Oil-to-Chemicals business for a 20% stake. This transaction itself would knock off two-third of RIL's net debt. However, the transaction hit roadblocks and then Covid-19 led stock and commodity market crash pushed RIL and Aramco's stock prices and market valuations in a tailspin. Such adverse developments made markets participants believe that RIL's goal of becoming debt-free would remain a distant dream. As a result, IL's stock nosedived to Rs 841 per share, close to a 40% decline in less than two months.

FPO vs Rights Issue

There are multiple ways in which a publicly listed firm could raise equity.

Follow-on public offer (FPO) in which the firm offers shares to the public, usually at a discount to the prevailing market price, via a competitive bidding process by setting a floor price. Such an offering would not differentiate between existing shareholders and other investors and might dilute holdings for existing investors if they cannotnot win the bidding process. Besides, those who cannot not take part in the new issue might face erosion of wealth. Stock price post FOP should settle at a weighted average of pre-FPO stock price and FPO issue price.

On the other hand, the rights issue entitles existing shareholders in the form of rights entitlements (RE). They get a choice to apply for new shares or sell them RE in the open market to avoid potential wealth erosion. Anyone who is not the shareholder of the issuing firm as on record date and still wants to apply in rights issue has to acquire RE from the market to become eligible to participate in rights issues.

Other than the first right to subscribe to share given to existing shareholders, the rights issue differed from FPO in two ways. First, contrary to FPO, the issue price is fixed in the rights issue, and second, since there is no competitive bidding involved, RE owners are guaranteed the allotment of shares in proportion to RE owned and used by them to subscribe to the issue.

Both FPO and right point are typically issued at a discount for two apparent reasons. First, the issue of new shares either by FPO or rights issue results in the number of outstanding shares in the market and hence given everything else remain the same, an increase in the supply of shares should push equilibrium price lower. Second, for most liquid stocks with sufficient free float, one could buy stock from the market instead of facing the uncertainty of allotment in FPO or waiting for process completion in case of the rights issue and running price risk.

RIL's Rights Issue

On April 21, 2020, RIL announced a USD 5.7 billion investment by Facebook into its Jio Platforms business for a 9.99% stake in a sudden turn of event. Several other strategic and financial investors followed suit. As a result, RIL stock rallied to Rs 1,467, from lows of Rs. 841, it hit just about a month back, fueled by these investments into its telecom and retail businesses. While the stake sale in Jio platforms and retail business was underway, RIL announced Rs 53,000 crore (approx. US$ 7.5 billion) rights issue on April 30, 2020. It surprised many, given the backdrop of volatile equity and commodity markets and nationwide lockdown.

SEBI's circular in January 2020 announced dematerialised trading of the rights entitlements. The Registrar and Transfer Agent (RTA) of the rights issue would credit the rights entitlement receivable by the shareholders to their respective Demat accounts.

Eligible shareholders would get a credit of the RE in their Demat accounts before the rights issue opens. The RE would be as temporary Demat securities, which would lapse if not renounced/exercised. While you could buy or sell RE through recognised stock exchanges, it would not be possible to transact RE intraday, and it would be settled on a trade-to-trade (T2T) basis (see Exhibit 54.1 for Terms of RIL's rights issue).

The existing shareholders could subscribe to one equity share for every fifteen shares held. The promoters committed to subscribe to their full quota and fill the gap if the issue remained undersubscribed. That showed promoters' confidence in the company's future. Anyway, they owned over 50% at the time of the launch of the rights issue.

Suppose existing shareholders did not want to subscribe to the issue by putting in additional money. In that case, they could use the exchange trading window to sell them RE to non-shareholders who wanted to participate in the rights issue or some of the existing shareholders who wished to participate beyond their entitlement. They could do it anyway, but they would get allotment for the shares subscribed beyond their entitlement only if the issue remained undersubscribed.

Most firms opted for rights issue when they needed liquidity, and other sources of funds might have dried up. The rights issue was the tool of fundraising by going back to existing owners of the firm. However, in RIL's case,

EXHIBIT 54.1 Terms of RIL's Rights Issue

Number of Shares Outstanding as of April 30, 2021	633.87 crore
Right Issue Ratio	1:15
Number of Rights Shares to be Issued	42.26 crore
Ex-right Date	May 13, 2020
Record Date	May 14, 2020
Issue Opening Date	May 20, 2020
Issue Closing Date	June 3, 2020
Date of Allotment of Shares	June 10, 2020
Date of Credit to Demat Accounts	June 11, 2020
Date of Listing of Newly Issued Partly Paid Shares	June 12, 2020
Investment Schedule	Issue Price: Rs 1,257 (Rs. 10 shares @ Rs. 1,247 premium) Instalment 1: Subscription money: Rs. 314.25 Instalment 2: First Call: Rs. 314. 25 (May 21, 2021) Instalment 3: Second and Final call: Rs. 628.5 (November 21, 2021)
Total Money to be Raised	Rs. 53, 121 crore
Post Rights Shares Outstanding	676.13 crore
Capital Dilution Due to Rights Issue	6.67%

Source: Company filings.

liquidity was never an issue. Announcement of Investments in Reliance Jio Platforms by marquee names like Facebook, RIL was sitting on comfortable liquidity position. The rights issue was more part of attaining a net-zero debt target before the end of FY21.

RIL did not need immediate liquidity, and investors might be constrained with liquidity due to economic challenges posed by Covid-19-related lockdowns imposed in various parts of the world; RIL offered rights issue with the staggered payment schedule. Investors would pay only 25% of the issue price for the rights shares in May 2020, whereas they would by another 25% in May 2021 and the remaining 50% in 2021. RIL would issue partly paid shares, and that would trade separately than RIL's shares. In May 2021, RIL would again fix the record date, and those who owned partly paid shared on record date would pay the money required for the first call within a window (typically fortnight). It would repeat the same process in November 2021 for the second and final call. Then the fully paid rights shares would start trading with RIL's shares, and partly paid shares would cease to exist.

SEBI's Janury 2020 change in the process of a rights issue facilitated RIL's rights issue in an entirely online mode. In the old system, each shareholder had to be sent a physical letter with forms to subscribe, transfer/renounce rights in favour of someone else, and all these would not have been possible given COVID-19 lockdown in the country.

Rights Issue in India – A Mixed Bag

Rights issues in India had been a mixed bag. Many of them received an inadequate response. Incidentally, two of the most significant rights issues were from Telecom firms only. Bharti Airtel came up with a rights issue of Rs 25,000 crore in February 2019 at a 30% discount to the prevailing market price. The rights issue had an entitlement ratio of 19 rights shares for every 67 shares held, which means an implied dilution of 23.85%. Despite such significant dilution, Bharti Airtel's stock performed well in the market during and after rights issues. It could successfully raise ample funds to stay relevant in the three-player Indian telecom market.

On the other hand, around the same time, Vodafone Idea announced a rights issue of Rs. 25,000 crores at Rs. 12.5 per share at a steep discount of 61% to the prevailing price. Shareholders were entitled to 87 new shares for every 38 shares held by them, resulting in 229% dilution. There was always a debate about whether the steep discount was a part of the strategy to get the issue fully subscribed or a negative signal. The issue got fully subscribed as promoters absorbed the issue beyond their entitlement to cushion the issue. The stock price fell below its issue price after the issue.

Evaluating Alternatives

Rehana knew that Prestige already had an overweight position in RIL, and her fund manager continued to hold such a position even after the record data. Now she had to give her recommendation on RIL's rights issue opening in less than a week. She noted down the following alternatives.

a) Subscribe to the issue in full.
b) Subscribe to the issue in full and also apply for additional shares.
c) Subscribe to the issue in full and acquire additional RE from the market during the trading window and subscribe for additional shares.
d) Sell RE in the market during the issue.

Questions

1. What are the different ways a listed firm can use to raise funds from the public/shareholders?

2. What are the key differences between FPO and the Rights Issue?
3. What do you understand by rights entitlement and partly paid shares in the context of RIL's rights issue? What are the consequences of not using/selling RE for existing shareholders?
4. What should be the ideal stock price adjustment to the stock price on the ex-rights day? Explain the same using RIL's issue.
5. Which of the four alternatives (a, b, c, d listed above) should Rehana recommend to her fund manager? Why?

Note

1 Corporate Announcement by Reliance Industries on April 30, 2020 to BSE. https://www.bseindia.com/xml-data/corpfiling/AttachHis/DC94A36A-DC93-43CC-989A-14A21648B3FC-185520.pdf

55

BHARTI AIRTEL'S FCCB

Alex Shen had two hours left to bring out his credit analysis on Bharti Airtel's foreign currency convertible bond (FCCB) issue, which opened on January 8, 2020. Alex was a Singapore-based fixed income credit analyst at Washburn Asset Management. His role was to analyse the bond issues of Asia-based issuers of fixed income securities. Alex had to prepare a report that covered the credit profile of the issuer, the features of the instrument, key valuation metrics, and an opinion regarding the issue price.

Company Background

Bharti Airtel Ltd (BAL) was one of India's leading telecom service providers and the third-largest telecom operator globally by the number of subscribers. It provided mobile, fixed-line, broadband, enterprise, and direct-to-home services. It had 327 million wireless subscribers in India at the end of December 2019 and additional subscribers in Africa and South Asia. The key shareholders included the Mittal family through Bharti Telecom Ltd (36%) and Singtel, Singapore through its subsidiaries (20.2%).

BAL enjoyed a well-established market position and a large, diversified revenue base. However, increasing intensity of competition with Reliance Jio entering mobile services, accompanied by sharp declines in tariff, started affecting both customer base and revenues. Both revenues and EBITDA margins declined from 2016–17 to 2018–19 (Exhibit 55.1). Despite the decline, BAL had a significant EBITDA at US$ 1.8 billion in 2018–19. However, BAL reported a net loss of US$ 529 million over revenue of US$ 19.2 billion in the financial year ending March 2019, mainly due to the provision

DOI: 10.4324/9781032724478-62

EXHIBIT 55.1 Bharti Airtel (Consolidated): Key Financial Information

US$ Million	*Mar-17 (12m)*	*Mar-18 (12 m)*	*Mar-19 (12m)*	*LTM Sep 2019*
Market Cap	21,573	24,467	19,208	20,762
Cash and Equivalents	27	72	270	410
Total Debt	9,265	10,042	12,087	12,527
Enterprise Value	30,811	34,437	31,025	32,879
Revenue	9,289	8,324	7,097	7,181
EBITDA	3,596	2,808	1,823	2,168
Net Income	980	73	-529	-692
EPS	0.23	0.02	-0.12	-0.14
Cash from Operations	3,329	2,204	1,048	n.a.
Capex	-2,329	-2,997	-2,663	n.a.
Free Cash Flow	1,000	-793	-1,615	n.a.

Source: Prepared by authors based on data from Bloomberg.

of adjusted-gross-revenue (AGR)-related liability. It continued to report net losses in the first two quarters of the financial year 2019–20.

Over the past several years, BAL's cash flow from operations had been inadequate to finance its large capital expenditure requirements in fibre and spectrum acquisition. As a result, the company reported negative free cash flows, which consistently required external financing. In the past, BAL had raised significant amounts of funds at competitive rates in India and international markets to meet its cash flow deficits. In addition, the cash flow situation was expected to improve due to an increase in industry tariffs by telcos in December 2019, an anticipated decline in spectrum requirements in the future, and divestment of stakes in subsidiaries and affiliates.

AGR Dues

The telcos in India were required to pay a license fee to the Department of Telecommunications (DoT), Government of India. The license fee was initially fixed but was substituted by a revenue-sharing-based regime in 1999, under which telcos had to pay a percentage of their adjusted gross revenues (AGRs). Typically, telcos paid 3–5% of AGR as spectrum charges and 8% as license fees. The AGR was determined by excluding certain specified revenue items from gross revenues. Subsequently, the telcos entered litigation with DoT regarding the definition of AGRs and did not pay the disputed amounts.

On October 24, 2019, the Supreme Court of India (SC) ruled against telecom operators (telcos), including BAL, over the AGR issue.[1] The SC held that there was no scope for ambiguity in the definition of AGR, which was

EXHIBIT 55.2 Bharti Airtel's Stock Price History

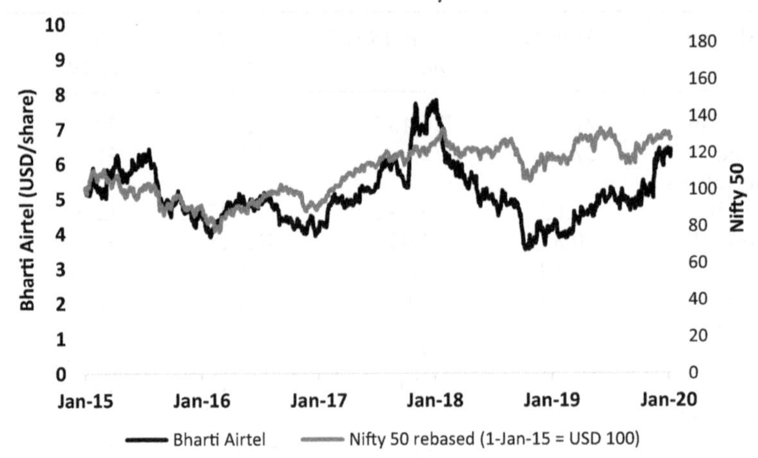

Source: Prepared by authors based on data from Bloomberg.

intended to be broad, comprehensive, and inclusive from inception. Apart from the payment of the disputed revenue share from the beginning, telcos had to pay interest and penalty on account of payment delays. The SC's adverse ruling led to DoT raising a claim of US$ 4.9 billion in unpaid dues from BAL. However, the exact amount and timing of payments were unclear, and the SC was expected to rule on a review petition filed by BAL in January 2020.

In response to the SC's adverse ruling, credit-rating agency Fitch placed the BBB ratings of BAL on Rating Watch Negative (RWN). The RWN reflected uncertainty about the amount and timing of the AGR dues.[2]

The FCCB Issue

On January 8, 2020, Bharti Airtel informed the stock exchanges in India about a proposed placement of equity shares through a qualified institutional placement (QIP) and FCCBs.[3] The funds raised from FCCBs were expected to be up to an amount of US$ 1 billion.

The company also issued the preliminary offering circular specifying the terms of the FCCB issue (Exhibit 55.3). The FCCB had a low coupon of 1.5% per annum and a maturity of slightly more than five years. It had no call or put options.

Alex Shen's Analysis

Alex analysed the likely impact of the QIP and FCCB issues, if subscribed, on BAL's credit profile. He noted that the effect would be largely positive as it will help meet the AGR payments while maintaining the debt ratios within the range required to maintain the current ratings. But he wanted to understand why BAL wished to raise an FCCB instead of raising the entire amount as equity through QIP.

Alex also estimated the key FCCB valuation metrics, including investment premium and conversion premium. Finally, he valued the FCCB by adding the value of the bond component and the value of the embedded options. Since the conversion was allowed during almost the entire tenure of the bond, Alex decided to use the binomial pricing model for valuing the options component.

Questions

1. Analyse the merits of Bharti Airtel raising part of its funds through an FCCB.
2. Estimate the following valuation metrics based on information available in Exhibits 55.3 and 55.4:

EXHIBIT 55.3 Terms of Bharti Airtel's FCCB.

Issue date & size: 1 million FCCBs with a face value of USD 1000, worth USD 1000 million. The issue opened on January 8, 2020, with the first settlement date on January 17, 2020. The FCCB would be listed on Singapore Exchange.
Coupon: Fixed coupon of 1.50 per cent, paid semiannually in equal instalments of USD 7.50 on February 17 and August 17 every year. However, the first coupon of USD 8.75 to be paid on August 17, 2020.
Redemption: 102.66 per cent of par value to be repaid on February 17 2025.
Conversion: Each FCCB to be convertible into 134.8807 equity shares of Bharti Airtel having a face value of Rs 5 each. The initial conversion price of Rs 534 per conversion equity share (which was at a premium of 20% to the QIP issue price). The conversion would be allowed during the period between February 27, 2020, to February 7, 2025.
Seniority: Senior, unsecured
Credit Rating: BBB-/CreditWatch Negative (Fitch)

Source: Prepared by authors based on data from Bloomberg.

EXHIBIT 55.4 Key Valuation Information & Assumptions (Jan 8, 2020)

US Government Treasury Rate (5-year): 1.66%
Credit Spread (5-year): 275 basis points (assumption)
Stock Price (closing, January 10): INR 458.85 per share (USD 6.40 per share)
Implied volatility (1 year): 35% (assumption)
Expected dividend yield: 45 basis points (assumption)

Source: Prepared by authors.

a. Bond Floor b. Investment Premium c. Parity/conversion value, d. Conversion premium on parity.

3. Estimate the value of the FCCB on January 8, 2020.

NOTE ON CONVERTIBLE BONDS

A convertible bond allows the bondholder to convert the bonds into shares based on pre-specified terms. The bond's conversion ratio (CR) specifies the number of shares it can get converted into. A convertible bond is equivalent to a combination of debt and call option on the firm's shares. It is also equal to CR shares with a put option on the shares. Most convertible bonds allow conversion before maturity, in which case the embedded options are American style.

The following diagrams illustrate convertible bonds' terminal payoff and the payoff before maturity.

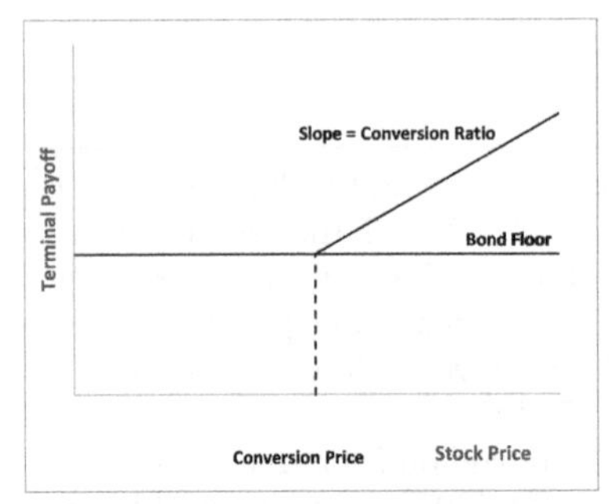

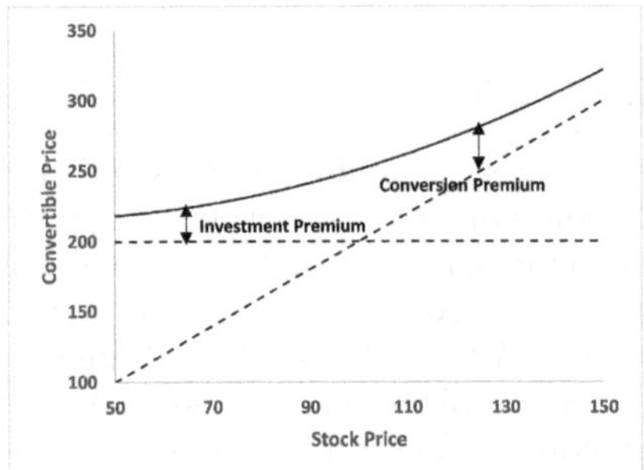

FIGURE 55.1 Convertible Bonds' Terminal Payoff and the Payoff before Maturity

Key valuation concepts and metrics associated with convertible bonds:

- Bond floor = present value of bond cash flows
- Investment premium = (convertible price – bond floor)/bond floor
- Conversion ratio = number of shares converted per bond
- Parity (or conversion value) = conversion ratio x current market price of shares
- Conversion premium on parity = (convertible price – parity)/conversion value

One may note that the convertible price is usually higher than both the bond floor and the conversion value. The convertible value exceeds the bond floor by the value of the implicit call options and the conversion value by the value of the implicit put options.

Notes

1 https://dot.gov.in/sites/default/files/SC%20Main%20judgment%2024-10-2019.pdf?download=1
2 https://www.fitchratings.com/research/corporate-finance/correction-fitch-places-bharti-on-rating-watch-negative-on-supreme-court-ruling-07-11-2019
3 https://assets.airtel.in/static-assets/cms/Opening_of_Qualified_Institutional_Placement_and_FCCB_Issuance_15012020.pdf

56

BPL LIMITED

In Search of Innovative Financing Options

In September 2020, Bhanu Pratap Sharma, CFO of Baramati Power Ltd (BPL) and his team members were busy evaluating financing options to refinance debt and financing organic and inorganic growth opportunities. The year gone by was quite turbulent, and it stretched the finances of the best of the businesses. Prolonged lockdowns led to a crash in demand, and that in turn adversely affected the revenues and cash flows of BPL. The finance team led by Bhanu had the task to explore innovative financing options to ensure minimum equity dilution and avoid excessive borrowing to prevent adverse impact on credit rating that might increase the cost of capital. The presence of such constraints reduced the flexibility for fundraising. Prevailing global market scenario, liquidity conditions, regulatory environment and investors appetite were the critical factors in structuring funding instruments.

BPL: Company Overview

Baramati group had been part of a reputed Indian business house with business interests spread across automobile, consumer staples, information technology, power, and steel.

BPL had been among the largest integrated power companies in India, with a presence in the power generation and transmission and distribution business. BPL had been investing aggressively towards adding power generation capacity in coal-fired and natural gas-fired power plants. In addition, it was aggressively building its unconventional energy business. In order to ensure the availability of supply of high-quality coal, it acquired a majority stake in Indonesian Coal Mines through its wholly owned subsidiary BPL Investments in Indonesia. The acquisition was funded by borrowing nearly

DOI: 10.4324/9781032724478-63

EXHIBIT 56.1 Criteria for Credit Rating Agencies for Assigning Equity Credit to a Hybrid Issue

	Low Equity Credit	*Medium Equity Credit*	*High Equity Credit*
Coupon Deferral	**Nearly fixed** Deferral triggered only under exceptional circumstances.	**Optional deferral** Coupon deferral triggers relate to capital ratios. Deferral would be triggered if ratios breach certain preset levels.	**Mandatory suspension** Greater flexibility to defer coupon payments.
Settlement	**Cumulative** Payments deferred are accumulated and must be paid before distributing dividends on common equity – Dividend stopper covenant.		**Non-cumulative** – Payments deferred need not be serviced.
Ranking	**Subordinated to senior debt** Senior to common equity	**Preferred** – Ranked at par with preference share, just before the equity.	**Equity** – At par with equity shares. It might lead to a question mark on tax-deductibility of coupon paid.
Maturity	**Low maturity** (< 30 years)	**> 30 years but not irredeemable** – higher it is better it is.	**Irredeemable**
Refinance–Replacement Capital Covenant	**Weak replacement language –** Issue can be refinanced using debt issuance as well.	If the issuers call back the hybrid, the hybrid must be replaced by issuing security with the same or higher equity credit (hybrid or equity issue). However, in case of credit rating upgrade by one notch, replacement capital covenant does not remain binding on the issuer.	**Strong replacement language** – If the issuer calls the security, the hybrid must be replaced by issuing another similar hybrid or equity of the same size.

Source: Prepared by authors based on information on credit rating agencies websites.

US$ 250 million towards the end of 2016 via five-year US$ bonds issued in the Singapore market. The same was due for repayment in May 2021.

The world was struggling to tackle the Covid-19 pandemic, and the wait for the vaccine was not yet over. India was going through terrible times with Covid-19 and the rapidly raising cases. However, global equity markets recovered from their March 2020 lows and cut most of their losses. Many firms raised funds to meet liquidity shortages created by a sudden drop in operating cash flows due to nationwide lockdown and collapse in economic activities.

BPL had to raise funds soon to refinance existing debt and exploiting growth opportunities in the future. However, it was not an easy task. The power sector in India had been in chaos for the last decade, and the stock prices of power company reflected the same. Raising a large sum of money would lead to significant dilution, whereas raising debt would result in a credit-rating downgrade and the resultant increase in the cost of capital. BPL needed alternative capital in debt but with equity-like features.

Hybrid Capital Instruments

Hybrid or perpetual securities were debt instruments with equity-like features. The structure of the instrument would determine equity credit available. Such instruments would help debt-ridden issuing firms strengthen their capital structure due to the soothing effect of equity credit associated with such instruments. For yield-seeking investors, such instruments would allow earning a much higher yield compared to senior debt.

The hybrid capital instruments would benefit the issuer in various ways: first, equity credit associated with this instrument would have a benign impact on credit rating; second, the shareholders of the firm would benefit due to the reduced leverage without equity dilution; and third, it would serve as tax-deductible equity and allow management to optimise its cost of capital.

The availability of equity credit would depend on key structure elements: first, coupon deferral clause-option to defer coupons; second, call option – typically NC5[1] and option with the issuer to call back hybrid after five to ten years; third, the Replacement Language – the nature of the funding instrument could be used if the call option was exercised; fourth, coupon step-up to disincentivise issuer not to exercise the call option, there would be 100 bps–500 bps coupon pick up after five to ten years (see Exhibit 56.1 to see how credit rating agencies assign equity credit).

History of Indian Hybrids and Perpetual Bonds

Many Indian firms used hybrid and perpetual bonds to raise funds both in Indian and foreign currency. Reliance Industries issued 100-year

EXHIBIT 56.2 Issue of Foreign Currency Denominated Hybrid and Perpetual Securities by Select Non-Banking Indian Issuers between 2011 and 2020

Issuer	*Instrument Rating (S&P and Moody's)*	*Issue Size (US $ million)*	*Coupon*	*Structure*
Bhira Investments	NR-NR	450	8.50%	60 NC5
Ballapur	NR/NR	200	9.75%	Perp NC5
Tata International	NR/NR	110	6.65%	60 NC5
Reliance Industries	BB+/Baa 3	250	US Treasury yield + 380 bps	100-year

Source: Compiled by Authors based on exchange filings.

US$-denominated Yankee bonds way back in 1997 before the South-East Asian Crisis rocked the market for emerging market debt. The demand for emerging market securities dried up entirely.

The market revived nearly 15 years later when global investors warmed up again to invest in emerging market papers. Since then, many Indian firms raised funds using long-term hybrids and perpetual bonds denominated in foreign currency under the External Commercial Borrowings (ECB) route. Some other firms used their foreign subsidiaries to issue foreign currency-denominated hybrids (see Exhibit 56.2). Tata Steel raised Rs 1,500 crores via perpetual bonds in Indian markets in 2011 to become the first non-banking firm in India to issue perpetual bonds. Later, Tata Power issued a 60-year hybrid NCD in 2018 to raise Rs 1500 crore.

BPL: Evaluating Options

BPL had to decide several aspects before finalising the structuring of the instrument. Should they issue perpetual bonds or hybrid with long maturity? Should they go for a bond issue in Indian markets or raise funds via US$-denominated bonds overseas? Should it use the ECB route or issue bonds through an overseas subsidiary?

BPL wanted to tap the Indian hybrid perpetual securities market in line with Tata Steel and Tata Power. However, RBI had recently written off Rs 8,315 crore worth Additional Tier-1 (AT1) perpetual bonds of YesBank, a domestic Indian bank, to keep the bank afloat. This move had significantly dampened the appetite for hybrid and perpetual securities in Indian markets. The other reason why BPL might consider the issue in foreign currency was the US$250 million repayment/refinancing due for the borrowing by its overseas subsidiary.

BPL had two options: raise funds under the ECB route or raise funds via its overseas subsidiary, BPL Investments Limited.

BPL was eligible to raise US$ 750 million with an all-in-cost ceiling of benchmark plus 450 basis points. BPL was looking at raising US$ 500 million, and that would be well within the limits of the ECB ceiling. However, the concern was the all-in-cost ceiling. Given that the global central banks expanded balance sheets rapidly in the past few months to blunt the economic impact caused by the Covid-19 pandemic, such action had flooded the markets with liquidity and resultant crash in yields across the globe. The most popular Benchmark, London Interbank Offer Rate (LIBOR), dropped 30 bps by the end of August 2020 (see Exhibit 56.3). Given the low yield environment, while the total cost of funds would be lower, the yield spreads had increased, especially for the papers with low credit rating. It would be challenging to meet the all-in-cost ceiling criteria for a long-dated hybrid under the ECB route by an Indian company with a rating just about or a notch below investment grade rating.[2]

BPL Investments was an unrated entity. It needed a credit booster in the form of a guarantee by the Indian parent BPL for better pricing and marketability of the hybrid. However, RBI Overseas Direct Investments (ODI) norms did not allow open-ended guarantee. It had two conditions. The guarantee must be dated (for a specific period), and the cumulative guarantee must not exceed 400% of the total net worth of the Indian parent. Second,

EXHIBIT 56.3 3-Month LIBOR, based on US$

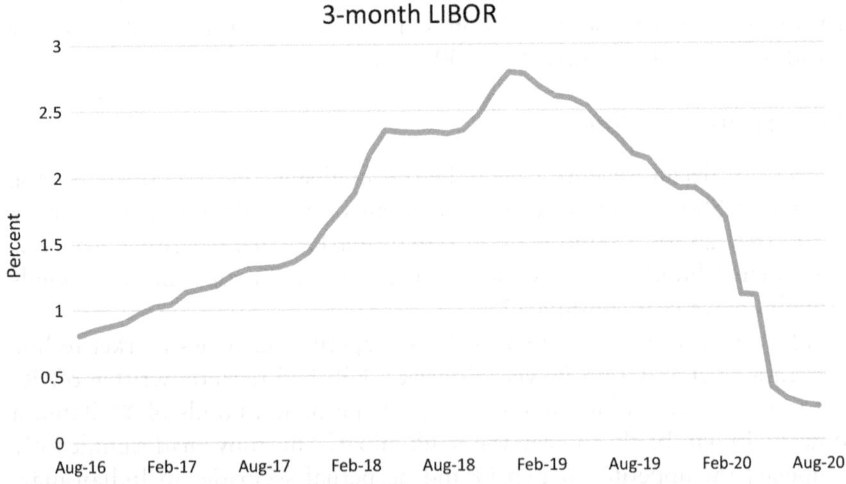

Source: Prepared by Authors based on European Central Bank Data, https://data.ecb.europa.eu/data/datasets/RTD/RTD.M.S0.N.C_USL3M.U.

EXHIBIT 56.4 BPL Investments Hybrid Issue Terms

Issuer	BPL Investment Limited
Guarantor	BPL Limited
Guarantor Ratings	BB-(S&P)/Ba3 (Moody's)
Guarantee	US$ 1 billion
Ranking	Subordinated
Issuer Ratings	Not Rated
Accounting Treatment	Debt
Rating Agency Treatment	50% Equity Credit
Issue Amount	US$ 500 million
Coupon	5-year S Treasury yield + 575 bps
Tenor	60-year
Call Option	End of year five and every interest payment after that
Step-up	100 bps at the end of year 10 if not called
Additional Step-up	200 bps step up if BPL could not renew after 10 years
Replacement Capital Covenant ("RCC")	Yes, RCC would go off in case of a rating's upgrade by 1 notch
Coupon Deferral	Optional deferral, cash cumulative, compounding

Source: Prepared by authors based on information from exchange filings, RBI website and issuance of foreign currency hybrid and perpetual bonds by Indian firms.

the Indian parent must apply to top-up the guarantee if the guarantee got utilised in the intervening period. The BPL had a total net worth of US$ 250 million at the end of FY20.

The Final Structure

To meet the regulatory constraints and get the best possible pricing, BPL Investments went ahead with the issue of a 60-year hybrid worth US$ 500 million bonds with a coupon rate of 5-year US Treasury plus 575 basis points. BPL Investments could achieve such tight pricing by fixing the first call date five-year after the issue date. There was a coupon step-up of 100 bps if the issuer failed to call back the option after 10 years. The bond had a coupon deferral clause if the issuer did not earn profit in a given year. However, deferral would be cumulative, and BPL Investments would not pay a dividend to its shareholders until all cumulative deferred coupons were paid to hybrid bond investors. The hybrid qualified for 50% equity credit by the credit-rating agencies. The bonds would be positioned just above equity shares at par with preference in capital structure.

Given that BPL Investments was an un-rated entity, it would have been difficult to market the issue. To enhance the credibility of the issue, BPL guaranteed the hybrid with a 200% of guarantee. RBI not only insisted on a limited period guarantee (which meant it was difficult to issue perpetual bonds), it would not allow a 60-year guarantee in one go. BPL had to renew the guarantee every ten years. BPL committed to renewing the guarantee every ten years if BPL Investments had not called back the bond. If BPL could not renew or top-up the guarantee as required, the hybrid would have another 200-bps step-up coupon to reflect the risk of an un-rated issuer. The hybrid securities would be placed below all other bonds but just above in (see Exhibit 56.4 for the terms of the issue).

Given the rock bottom bond yields prevailing in the global markets with nearly US$20 trillion worth of bonds trading in negative yield territory, institutional investors and high net worth global investors in search of higher yields found the BPL investments issue quite attractive. As a result, the issue got oversubscribed by 1.5 times, with investors from the USA, Singapore, Hongkong, and Middle East participating aggressively. Bhanu was pleased with the outcome as it felt it raised tax deductible equity capital at the cost of debt. As a result, the consolidated debt-to-equity for BPL was nearly 2.25, and the hybrid issue with 50% equity credit would bring it below the targeted level of 2.

Questions

1. Why was BPL looking beyond plain vanilla debt or equity to raise funds?
2. What do you understand by perp or hybrid securities? Are they debt or equity?
3. Why do perpetual/hybrid securities have the potential of being a win–win for both issuer and investors?
4. Should BPL go for INR perpetual/hybrid or consider foreign currency perpetual/hybrid securities? Explain your choice.
5. Why did BPL opt for issuing foreign currency hybrid through its overseas subsidiary rather than issuing itself?
6. Which factors were instrumental in determining the final structure of the hybrid bonds issued by BPL Investments Ltd?

Notes

1 NC5 means Not Callable for 5 years.
2 BPL's Investment Banker's informal inquiry with rating agencies indicated how they might rate BPL's hybrid issue under the ECB route.

57

FINANCING JOYZZ NUTRIXX

Sejal Dalal and Jenny Kaur were discussing the business plan of their proposed nutrition supplements venture "Joyzz Nutrixx" (JN) with Sumana Rane at a coffee shop in Ahmedabad. Sumana, who had founded and managed a successful IT venture, had agreed to mentor the young entrepreneurs.

Funding Avenues

As the discussion moved to finance, Sejal told Sumana that they were taking the help of Raghav Jariwala, an ex-investment banker, in preparing their financial projections and a presentation that they could use in a pitch to prospective investors. They had prepared a list of funding sources based on search and interactions. They wanted Sumana's comments regarding that list.

Jenny showed Sumana the following list of prospective funding sources:

1. The co-founders' limited savings.
2. Nalin, a friend of Jenny, was ready to invest Rs 1 crore in the venture. However, they were not sure of his interest in the business.
3. Nalin also promised to get bank funding through his uncle, who was in a senior position in a bank.
4. The promoter of a mid-sized healthcare firm, who Sejal and Jenny met through a friend, had shown interest in taking a stake.
5. A venture capital (VC) firm with whom Raghav had business dealings and who he thought would be a good fit, given the sector and size of funding required.

DOI: 10.4324/9781032724478-64

6. An angel investor had responded to Sejal's email and had shown interest in discussing the idea further. Raghav thought that they should make a strong pitch to him too.
7. A shortlist of private equity funds focused on the healthcare sector and had been active recently.
8. A shortlist of crowdfunding platforms.

Sumana explained to the co-founders that they would need to narrow down this shortlist since not all the sources were suitable at an early stage. Further, there would be trade-offs they must consider regarding what an investor brought to the table in terms of funding, knowledge, and network versus what the investor would expect in terms of valuations, exit, control, and involvement. She forwarded them from her tablet a file that summarised the differences between each investor category (Exhibits 57.1 and 57.2).

Raising Venture Capital

After a few months, the co-founders had registered their venture with an initial capital of Rs 1 crore. They funded their equity contributions using an unsecured personal loan jointly taken from Nalin. The discussions with the strategic investor had failed. They were still pursuing angel investors and VCs.

They invited Raghav to their makeshift office. He had prepared the baseline financial projections for JN based on the opportunity sizing and other

EXHIBIT 57.1 Start-up Financing Alternatives: Forms of Capital

Equity: The equity investor is interested in capturing the upside in the venture's value but agrees to accept the losses. Equity is the most common form of capital for start-ups since they have high risks and a high potential to create value. The equity investor may be involved in the management and oversight of the venture and may monitor its performance closely. The investor could bring equity as convertible preference shares and convert them into shares on exit.

Debt: Suitable for ventures with stable cash flows, are less risky and have collateral assets to offer. Banks are unlikely sources at an early stage. Venture capitalists may provide debt incrementally with equity funds, though rarely. Incubators and crowdfunding are suitable for raising moderate amounts but are applicable only in select areas. Debt investors are not interested in high returns or control. Raising debt requires more predictability of cash flows.

Convertible debt: Convertible debt, which has a mix of debt and equity characteristics, may be commonly used. The investor is interested in converting the debt into equity later or participating in the upside while protecting itself on the downside.

Source: Prepared by authors.

EXHIBIT 57.2 Start-up Financing Alternatives: Investor Categories

Sources	*Potential benefits*	*Potential limitations*
Family and Friends	Can provide moderate amounts as equity/ convertible debt with high flexibility in terms of returns and control.	Need to separate personal and business relationship
Angel investor(s): Can be one or several	Usually, entrepreneurs themselves; can provide funds, connections, and expertise; usually provide smaller amounts than VCs.	Require several rounds of discussions and screening
Venture Capitalists (VCs): Invest using professionally managed funds	Can provide significant funds as equity (sometimes with debt) and expertise; benefits of professional oversight – more rigorous due diligence, analysis, and monitoring	May place substantial emphasis on valuations (tough bargaining, high pressure on driving valuations), exit and control through a seat on the board (reduce flexibility in decision-making)
Private Equity Investors (PEs)	Can provide large funds (equity/debt) and expertise, more rigorous due diligence, analysis, and control	Not for seed funds, interested in later rounds; emphasis on valuations, exit, and monitoring
Strategic Investor	Can provide significant funds, network and expertise	Potential conflicts of interest due to a presence in related business, differences with founder's vision
Banks	Can provide debt funds against tangible assets or cash flows	Not feasible for seed funds in the absence of cash flows or assets
Incubators: set up by governments, educational institutes, social enterprises	Can provide mentoring, networking opportunities, and seed funding	Applicable for specific sectors such as agriculture, skilling, financial inclusion
Crowd-funding	Smaller amounts of debt funds from many contributors (crowd-funding equity is not legal in India)	Applicable for social causes or ideas that resonate with many

Source: Prepared by authors.

details in the business plan shared with him by the co-founders. He further explained the plausible funding scenario that they could assume as they entered discussions with the seed investor.

1. The estimated net income of JN in year five would be around Rs 7 crore. The exit P/E multiple based on comparable transactions would be around 12.
2. The VC could be looking to earn an annual return of around 35% and an exit in about five years. JN could expect to fund Rs 6 crore upfront from the VC.
3. The co-founders should ensure that they retain a significant stake themselves. They may also want to keep some stake, say around 10% of the terminal value in the form of employee stock options, for their senior employees in the future.
4. There could be multiple rounds of funding depending upon success in terms of revenue build-up and scaling up of the venture.
5. The equity funding was more likely to be through convertible preference shares with no dividends but 1:1 conversion into shares after five years.

Raghav asked the co-founders if they had any questions before he shared his estimates of pre-money and post-money valuation of JN. He also forwarded them a note on the venture capital valuation method (Exhibit 57.3). Sejal wanted to know how much stake each party would get in the business and how they should price the shares. Jenny wondered why they should not raise more funds from the VC upfront as that would give them a lot of flexibility in their investment plans for the business.

Questions

1. Select from the list of investors prepared by the co-founders who could be prospective investors in the seed round. Discuss the merits and demerits of raising funds from each of the selected investors.
2. Use the worked example of venture capital valuation provided in Exhibit 57.3 to answer the following.
   a. Estimate the share of the co-founders, and the VC, based on Raghav's assumptions, if there were only a single round of equity fundraising. If 100,000 shares were to be issued before approaching the VC, what share price would the VC be willing to pay? Hence, what would be the pre-money and post-money valuation of the company?

EXHIBIT 57.3 Illustration of Venture Capital Valuation Method

Exit Value Assumptions	
Projected Net Income after Five Years (Rs crore)	10
Comparable Companies P/E	15
Value of Company after Five Years	**150**
Funding Assumptions	
Shares Issued before Round 1	1,000,000
Equity from Round 1 Investors (Rs crore)	5
Returns Expected by Round 1 Investors	40%
Additional Funds Required by Company after Two Years (Rs crore)	4
Returns Expected by Round 2 Investors	25%
Case 1: Assuming only First Round of Funding	
Share of Company to be Owned by Management after Five Years (option pool)	20%
Value of Management's Share after Five Years	30.0
Value of Investors Share after Five Years = 150-30	120.0
Expected Value of Round 1 Investors after Five Years (Rs crore) = 5 x (1.4^5)	26.89
Stake Required by Round 1 Investors = 26.89/120	**22.4%**
Let Shares Purchased by Round 1 Investors	X
X/(Shares before Round 1+X)	22.4%
X = 22.4% x 1000,000/(1 – 22.4%)	288,815
Share Price for Round 1 Investors = 5,00,00,000/288,815	**173.1**
Pre-money Valuation of Company (Rs crore) = 173.1 x 1000,000/100,00,000	17.31
Post-money Valuation of Company (Rs crore) = 17.31 + 5	**22.31**
Case 2: Assuming Two Rounds of Funding	
Value Expected by Round 2 Investors by Year Five (Rs crore) = 4 x (1.25^3)	7.81
Share of Round 2 Investors	**6.5%**
Share Required by Round 1 Investors before Dilution = 22.4%/ (1-6.5%)	**24.0%**
Let Shares Purchased by Round 1 Investors	X
X/(Shares before Round 1+X)	24.0%
X = 24.0% x 1000,000/ (1-24.0%)	315,268
Share Price for Round 1 Investors	**158.6**
Pre-Money Valuation - Round 1 (Rs crore)	15.86
Post-Money Valuation - Round 1 (Rs crore)	**20.86**
Shares Issued before Round 2	1,315,268
Let Shares Purchased by Round 2 Investors	Y
Y/(Shares before Round 2 +Y)	6.5%
Y = 6.5% x 1,315,268/(1-6.5%)	91,592
Share Price for Round 2 Investors = 4 x 100,00,000/91,592	**436.7**
Pre-Money Valuation - Round 2 (Rs crore)	57.44
Post-Money Valuation - Round 2 (Rs crore)	**61.44**

Source: Prepared by authors.

b. Suppose that the co-founders anticipate that there could be a second round of funding of Rs 4.5 crore after two years. Further, the second-round investors may expect a lower return of 25% if they perceive lesser risks after seeing business revenues. What should be the price of the shares in the first and the second round of funding?
c. What will be the advantage of using two rounds of funding instead of raising the combined amount of Rs 10.5 crore upfront?

58

NIRMA'S ACQUISITION OF LAFARGE INDIA

On July 11, 2016, Swiss cement major LafargeHolcim announced that it had entered an agreement to divest its assets in Lafarge India to Nirma Ltd at an estimated enterprise value of US$ 1.4 billion (over Rs 9,000 crore).[1] The company had emerged as the successful bidder in the battle to acquire Lafarge India Ltd, which held significant cement capacities in northern and eastern regions of India, outbidding other strong contenders in the final round, including JSW Cement and the Piramal group. The acquisition would make Nirma a significant mid-size player in the Indian cement industry.

However, the company would also have to put into action the financing plan that it had stitched up with the help of three arrangers – Credit Suisse Securities, Barclays Bank, and IDFC Bank. The deal size was large compared with Nirma's total assets of Rs 7,680 crore and networth of Rs 4,853 crore on a consolidated basis at the end of March 2016. The debt required to fund the acquisition could potentially affect Nirma's creditworthiness and constrain its ability to finance its future growth.

Cement Industry Trends

India was the second-largest cement producer globally after China with an installed capacity of 415 million tonnes per annum (MTPA), production of 283 MTPA, and domestic consumption of 269 MTPA in 2015–16. India's per capita consumption of cement of 208 kg was low compared to the world average of around 520 kg but was more commensurate with its per capita income.

The growth in demand for cement was linked with India's economic growth, particularly the growth of housing and infrastructure sectors

DOI: 10.4324/9781032724478-65

EXHIBIT 58.1 Cement Industry Capacity and Production Trends

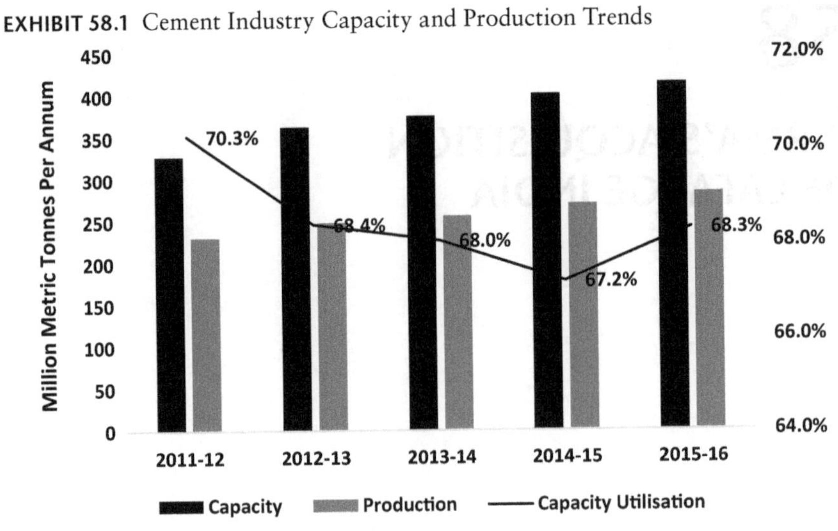

Source: Statista.

which accounted for nearly 65% and 25% of cement demand, respectively. Growth in cement demand had slowed down from 8.8% per annum during 2006–07 to 2010–11 to 5.2% per annum during 2011–12 to 2015–16. The slower demand growth resulted in a decline in capacity utilisation to around 68%. Demand growth was expected to revive over the next five years due to a recovery in economic growth and higher investments in infrastructure (Exhibit 58.1).

The demand–supply dynamics of the cement industry was region-specific due to high freight costs. In 2015–16, the demand to capacity ratio was unfavourable in the southern region but relatively better in India's eastern and western regions. More importantly, the industry was becoming more consolidated. The share of the top five players accounted for over 70% of the capacity in all the areas except the south (Exhibit 58.2).

The size, efficiency, and financial strength of the dominant players also determined competitive intensity in a region. The northern region, for instance, had a high degree of competition and had been witnessing significant pressure on prices. By comparison, despite greater fragmentation and lower capacity utilisation, the southern region provided higher price realisation and operating profit margins to the players. However, overcapacity was expected to reduce cement prices in the south in the future. In contrast, a more favourable demand–supply balance and faster demand growth would lead to firming up cement prices in the east.

On an overall basis, higher consolidation in the cement industry was expected to result in higher pricing power, including greater flexibility to pass on any increase in costs of inputs such as energy and freight. The

EXHIBIT 58.2 Regional Capacity, Consumption, and Consolidation (2015)

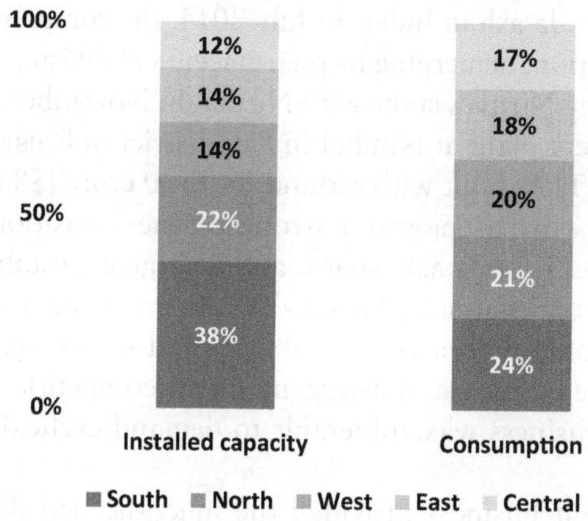

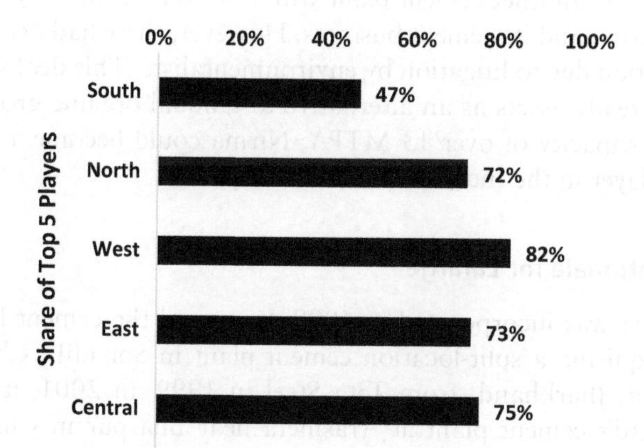

Source: Prepared by authors.

announcements in early 2016 of acquisition of Reliance Cement by Birla Corp, purchase of cement business of Jaiprakash Associates by Ultratech Cement, and the proposed divestment of Lafarge India indicated that industry consolidation would continue. Higher capacity utilisation, industry consolidation, and gradual improvement in operating efficiency of cement producers would result in an improvement in EBITDA margins of the players.

The Deal Rationale for Nirma

Nirma was established in 1980 at Ahmedabad in Gujarat by Karsanbhai Patel to manufacture detergents. It later diversified into soaps, chemicals, pharmaceuticals, and the processing of minerals. The company was the largest manufacturer of soda ash in India. In July 2014, the company announced a business reorganisation, demerging its pharmaceutical division and merging five companies holding Nirma's stake with Nirma. In November 2014, Nirma commissioned a cement plant at Nimbol in Pali district in Rajasthan, having a capacity of 2.28 MTPA, built with around Rs 1300 crore ($85 per tonne).

As of June 2016, Nirma enjoyed a strong business position due to significant market shares in soda ash, soaps, and detergents, established brand name and distribution channels, backward integrated operations, and a healthy financial profile with a comfortable capital structure. However, it had lost market share in soaps and detergents as the competition had intensified. The soda ash business was vulnerable to demand cyclicality and price fluctuations.

Though the cement business provided the much-needed diversification, the company had been a new entrant and was a relatively small player. It proposed setting up another cement plant with two MTPA capacity at Mahuva in Gujarat to expand its cement business. However, there had been delays in land acquisition due to litigation by environmentalists. This deal would provide Nirma ready assets as an alternative to gradual organic growth. With a combined capacity of over 13 MTPA, Nirma could become a significant mid-sized player in the Indian cement industry.

The Deal Rationale for Lafarge

Lafarge India was incorporated in 1999. It entered the cement business in India by acquiring a split-location cement plant in Sonadih, Chhatisgarh, and Jojobera, Jharkhand, from Tata Steel in 1999. In 2001, it took over Raymond Ltd's cement plant at Arasmeta near Bilaspur in Chhattisgarh. Subsequently, it commissioned a grinding capacity at Mejia in West Bengal and an integrated cement plant at Chittorgarh in Rajasthan with a split-blending unit at Bhiwani in Haryana. In 2008, it entered the ready-mix concrete business by acquiring Larsen and Toubro's concrete business.

By July 2016, Lafarge India had a total cement manufacturing capacity of 8.25 MTPA in the east and 2.5 MTPA in the north. It served markets in Chattisgarh, Jharkhand, Bihar, Odisha, and West Bengal in the east and Rajasthan, West MP, North Gujarat, parts of UP, Delhi/NCR, and Haryana in the north. It was also operated 72 ready-mix concrete plants across India and manufactured concrete aggregates at two plants (see Exhibit 58.3).

Lafarge manufactured blended cement by using fly ash and slag as additives which lowered production costs and environmental emissions. Its plants used a mix of fuels including coal, pet-coke, and waste materials for supply flexibility and lower costs. It also had a sourcing arrangement with several thermal power-producing companies for fly-ash, Tata Steel for sourcing slag,

EXHIBIT 58.3 Lafarge India's Cement Business Overview (FY16)

East	*North*
Plants: Jojobera (Jharkhand), Sonadih & Arasmeta (Chattisgarh), Mejia (WB) Arasmeta (Chattisgarh), Mejia (WB)	Plants: Chittorgarh (Rajasthan), Bhiwani (Haryana)
Cement Capacity: 8.3 MTPA	Cement Capacity: 2.5 MTPA
Clinker Capacity: 4.7 MTPA	Clinker Capacity: 1.6 MTPA
Sales Volume: 7.6 MTPA	Sales Volume: 2.1 MTPA
Net Sales: Rs 33.4 billion	Net Sales: Rs 7.1 billion
Operating EBITDA: Rs 7.4 billion	Operating EBITDA: Rs 0.2 billion
Top Three Markets: West Bengal, Bihar, Jharkhand	Top three markets: Rajasthan, MP, Haryana

Source: Prepared by authors.

and fertiliser companies for gypsum. The company had its captive limestone mines. Lafarge India's cement was priced at a premium and sold under various brands, including Duraguard and Duraguard MF, Infracem, Concreto, and PSC brands. The company had over 5,000 dealers spread across the East and North regions.

LafargeHolcim, headquartered in Switzerland, was the world market leader in cement and building materials with a presence in 90 countries. It had been formed based on the agreement to merge French cement manufacturer Lafarge and Swiss building materials group Holcim in 2014. The companies had to sell several of their business units worldwide under a plan to divest assets worth US$ 3.6 billion, comply with competition laws in the different regions where they operated, and complete their global merger. The divestment of Lafarge India was a part of this plan.

LafargeHolcim would continue to operate in India through its subsidiaries ACC Ltd and Ambuja Cements. With a combined capacity of 60 MTPA, it would be the second-largest cement maker in India after Ultratech Cement once it completed its acquisition of Jaiprakash Associate Ltd's cement capacity.

Execution of Lafarge India's Divestment

In April 2015, India's anti-trust authority Competition Commission of India (CCI) gave consent to the proposed merger between Lafarge and Holcim subject to the divestment of its two cement plants in the eastern region to eliminate competition concerns. CCI ascertained that while the combine would not enjoy monopoly power in the north-west region with a 37%

capacity share, it would dominate the eastern region with 79% combined capacity. CCI gave the companies six months to find a suitable buyer; else, they would have to seek a second divestment period.[2]

In August 2015, LafargeHolcim agreed to sell to Birla Corp, an MP Birla group company, two plants having a combined capacity of 5.15 MTPA to the latter at an enterprise value of Rs 5,000 crore.[3] The deal was contingent on the transfer of limestone mining rights to Birla Corp. However, the transfer of mining rights could not be completed within six months due to a clause in a January 2015 amendment to India's Mines and Minerals (Development and Regulation) Act (MMDR Act), and the deal was terminated. The clause stated that the transfer of mineral concessions would be allowed only for those concessions granted through auction.

LafargeHolcim submitted an alternative plan to CCI. It would sell the entire stake in Lafarge India to comply with CCI's April 2015 order. In February 2016, the CCI issued a revised divestment order approving the alternative plan.[4] A proposed amendment to the MMDR Act was also expected to enable the transfer of mineral reserves of the company.

The proposed sale saw aggressive bidding due to the increasing interest of players in entering or expanding in the Indian cement industry. In April 2016, LafargeHolcim received offers for Lafarge India from nine bidders, including Indian companies and multinationals, and strategic and financial players, some individually and some in consortium.

LafargeHolcim shortlisted around five bidders in May 2016, who were asked to submit their final bids after the due diligence process. In early July 2016, LafargeHolcim received the final submissions from five bidders. It evaluated the offers based on both the deal price and the conditions mentioned by the bidders. On July 11, 2016, it announced Nirma as the winning bidder and entered an agreement for sale.[5] The deal was subject to approval by the CCI. More significantly, it also envisaged payments and completion of the acquisition by the buyer in three months.

Nirma had valued the Lafarge capacities at around Rs 8,545 per tonne. The valuation compared well with recent deals (Exhibit 58.4) considering the premium pricing of Lafarge's branded cement and significant presence in the eastern region, which appeared to have better prospects.

Nirma's Acquisition Financing

The principal challenge for Nirma was financing, given the large size of the acquisition compared to its asset size (see Exhibit 58.5). The company had to arrange over Rs 8,000 crore funds to acquire the entire equity stake in Lafarge India. Since Nirma's cash accruals or group resources would not be adequate to contribute much as equity, the acquisition required significant debt funding of around Rs 7,500 crore.

EXHIBIT 58.4 Valuation of Recent Cement Deals

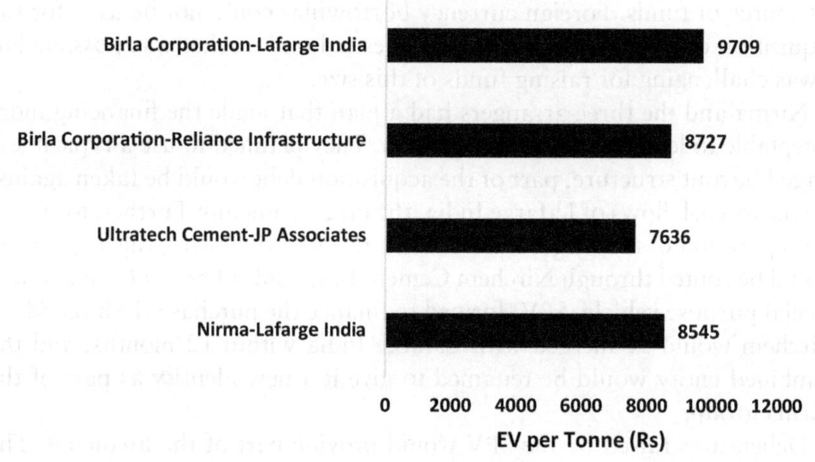

Source: Prepared by authors based on data from Bloomberg Quint (https://www.bloombergquint.com/markets/lafarge-nirma-deal-valuation-in-line-with-recent-transactions).

EXHIBIT 58.5 Financial Profile of Nirma and Lafarge India

Rs Crore	*Nirma Ltd 2015–16*	*Lafarge India Ltd 2015–16*
Revenues	7,674	5,958
EBITDA	1,538	753
EBIT	1,174	502
Finance Costs	77	88
Profit after Tax	795	231
Total Assets	7,680	6,193
Total Debt	1,259	303
Total Equity	4,853	4,205
Credit Rating (Long-Term)	CRISIL AA/ Stable	CRISIL AA/ Stable

Source: Prepared by authors based on company annual reports.

Note:

1. Financials are on a consolidated basis for both the companies.
2. In July 2016, CRISIL affirmed the AA ratings of both the companies but changed the outlook to negative.

Leveraged financing of this size would significantly stretch the debt protection indicators of Nirma, resulting in a likely credit rating downgrade by several notches. Further, there were regulatory hurdles in approaching banks for finance since the Reserve Bank of India (RBI) rules did not permit banks to provide financing for the acquisition of equity. Obtaining funding from non-banking finance companies (NBFCs) would be expensive since

NBFCs had a higher cost of funds since they depended on banks as a critical source of funds. Foreign currency borrowings could not be used for the acquisition of equity. Accessing the domestic bond market was possible but it was challenging for raising funds of this size.

Nirma and the three arrangers had a plan that made the financing more acceptable to lenders and rating agencies. They planned to use a typical leveraged buyout structure, part of the acquisition debt would be taken against the future cash flows of Lafarge India, the target company. Further, to ensure the separation of the target's assets from those of the buyer, the acquisition would be routed through Nirchem Cement Ltd, a subsidiary of Nirma, and a special purpose vehicle (SPV) formed to finance the purchase (Exhibit 58.6). Nirchem would be merged with Lafarge India within 12 months, and the combined entity would be renamed to give it a new identity as part of the Nirma group.[6]

Debentures raised by the SPV would provide part of the financing. The debentures would be serviced by the future cash flows of the target and secured by the assets and equity of the target and the SPV. Nirma would provide the rest of the funding in the form of equity and debt. As per the plans, the SPV would raise non-convertible debentures (NCDs) worth Rs 4,000 crore from the domestic market. Nirma would raise around Rs 3,500 crore of debt through term loans and long tenor subordinated debt and the rest from internal accruals and loans from promoters.

EXHIBIT 58.6 Acquisition Financing

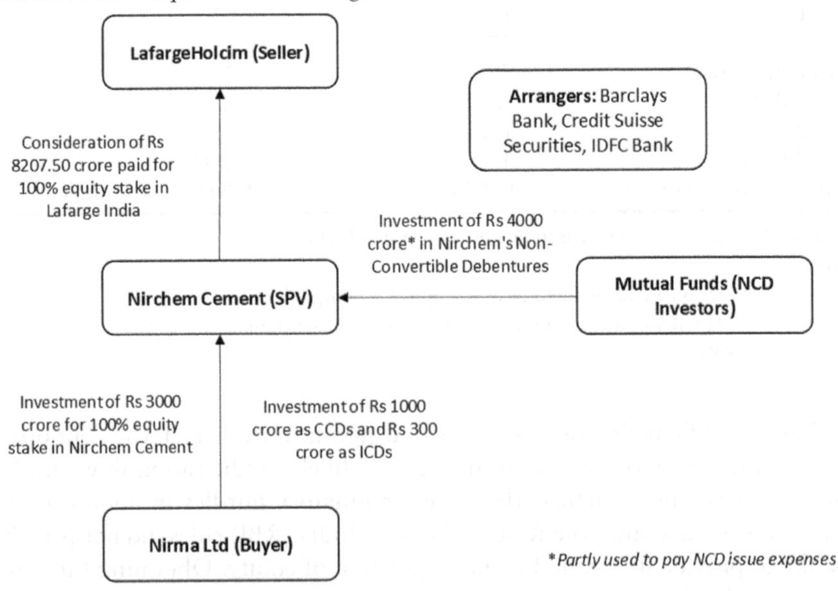

Source: Prepared by authors based on CRISIL Rating Rationales and media reports.

The financing team hoped that reducing the direct debt-servicing burden on Nirma would lessen the impact of the financing on Nirma's credit rating. The creation of the SPV meant that the funding was with no recourse to the parent company. Nirchem's debenture holders would have no claim over Nirma's assets. They would, however, have first ranking exclusive charge over the assets of Nirchem and subsequently the merged entity, and first ranking pledge over the shares of Nirchem, Lafarge India, the merged entity, and its subsidiaries. The credit-rating agency was likely to align the ratings of the Nirchem with that of the parent, given strong business and financial linkages.

On July 14, 2016, CRISIL, the credit-rating agency, affirmed the rating of Nirma as AA though it changed the rating outlook to negative from stable. As expected, the main reason for the change in outlook was the considerable debt funding of the acquisition and its impact on the consolidated profile of Nirma. However, CRISIL did recognise Nirma's business strengths as positive factors, the low existing debt obligations, the limited planned capital expenditure, and the likelihood that the company would use its consolidated cash flow for debt reduction.[7]

In August 2016, CRISIL assigned a rating of AA with a negative outlook to Nirchem Cement Ltd in line with that of Nirma. The rating agency considered the consolidated cash flows with its subsidiary Lafarge India. However, it also recognised the strategic importance and likely support by the parent company Nirma.[8] The assignment of AA rating was crucial for financing since the regulations and investment policies of most insurance companies and other institutions did not permit investments in debt instruments with credit ratings below the AA grade. A few mutual funds and smaller investors may have invested in lower-rated instruments, but the investor appetite would be limited.

On the other hand, mutual funds were showing an increasing appetite for AA and higher-rated papers. Mutual funds had become a significant source of debt financing for NBFCs and mid-size corporates since banks had tightened their lending due to their rising non-performing loans. The financing team, therefore, decided to target mutual funds for subscription to Nirchem's NCDs. Since mutual funds would prefer to invest in the paper of shorter tenor, the NCDs were divided into four tranches having two-, three-, four-, and five-year maturities (Exhibit 58.7).

The NCDs issued by Nirchem attracted significant interest from the mutual funds and were oversubscribed more than 1.6 times. They were priced at an average yield of 8.68%, which the mutual funds considered attractive in a falling interest rate environment. For Nirchem, they provided a cheaper financing alternative by around 250 basis points compared with borrowing from NBFCs.

EXHIBIT 58.7 Terms of the Non-Convertible Debentures Issued by Nirchem Cement

- Issuer: Nirchem Cement Limited.
- Instrument: Redeemable, non-convertible, listed, rated, and secured non-convertible debentures.
- Mode of Issue: Private placement with eligible institutions and companies.
- Use of proceeds: Acquisition of all the equity shares of Lafarge India Limited (including issue expenses).
- Credit rating: AA with a negative outlook by CRISIL.
- Issue tranches: Four tranches, cumulatively for issue size up to Rs 4,000 crore

	Tenor (from Sep 14, 2016)	Coupon (semi-annual payment)
Series A	2 years	8.37%
Series B	3 years	8.47%
Series C	4 years	8.57%
Series D	5 years	8.66%

- Security: first-ranking exclusive charge over the assets of Nirchem Cement and the merged entity; exclusive first-ranking pledge over shares of Nirchem Cement, Lafarge India, the merged entity, and its subsidiaries.
- Covenants: security cover of at least 1.25 times; minimm interest coverage ratio of 1.80 till FY19, 2.00 from FY20; maximum net debt to tangible networth of 1.10 till FY18, 1.00 from FY19; maximum net debt to EBITDA of 4.95 (FY17), 4.7 (FY18), 3.7 (FY19), 2.5 (from FY20); limits on capex each year.

Source: Prepared by authors.

Nirma supported the rest of the acquisition financing by providing Rs 3,000 crore of funds as equity, Rs 1,000 crore as compulsorily convertible debentures, and Rs 300 crore as inter-corporate deposits to Nirchem. To finance its funding gap, Nirma secured a term loan of Rs 1,500 crore from banks, raised NCDs worth Rs 990 crore, and planned to meet the remaining requirements from another issue of NCDs, internal resources, and loans from promoters. The successful closure of financing enabled Nirma to formally acquire Lafarge India on October 4, 2016, when the latter became a 100% subsidiary of Nirchem.

Setting a New Standard for Debt Financing in India

The Nirma-Lafarge acquisition financing set a record of being the largest acquisition-related bond in the Indian market to date. It was also the largest domestic leveraged buyout, with a large part of the funds raised against the target''s cash flows. The financing achieved not only the successful closure of a significant acquisition but was completed at attractive pricing. It was innovative in terms of customising the financing structure to the borrower's and investors' need'

The December 2016, GlobalCapital magazine recognised the Nirchem NCD issue as the best local currency bond of 2016 "for opening up a new source of funding for acquisition financing in India while overcoming a number of regulatory hurdles."[9] The International Financing Review magazine also awarded the deal in Asia Awards 2016, considering it groundbreaking and "a watershed moment in Indian acquisition financing".[10]

Questions

1. Summarise the rationale for the deal from the perspective of the buyer and the seller.
2. What was the benefit of using the SPV structure while financing the acquisition?
3. Summarise the unique features of the financing structure, which made it exceptional in the Indian context.

Notes

1 https://www.lafargeholcim.com/lafargeholcim-enters-agreement-nirma-limited-divestment-lafarge-india
2 https://economictimes.indiatimes.com/industry/indl-goods/svs/cement/lafarge-holcim-merger-gets-cci-approval-will-have-to-divest-two-cement-plants/articleshow/46775563.cms?from=mdr
3 https://www.lafargeholcim.com/lafargeholcim-enters-agreement-birla-corporation-limited-divestment-assets-india-subject-cci
4 https://www.holcim.com/media/media-releases/lafargeholcim-receives-revised-cci-divestment-order
5 https://www.holcim.com/media/media-releases/lafargeholcim-enters-agreement-nirma-limited-divestment-lafarge-india
6 https://www.globalcapital.com/asia/article/28mswlxuvybg9cbp7jim8/asia-polls-and-awards/globalcapital-asia-regional-capital-markets-awards-2016-part-iii-bonds
7 CRISIL Rating Rationale for Nirma Limited dated July 14, 2016 https://www.crisilratings.com/mnt/winshare/Ratings/RatingList/RatingDocs/Nirma_Limited_July_14_2016_RR.html
8 CRISIL Rating Rationale for Nirma Limited dated August 29, 2016 https://www.crisilratings.com/mnt/winshare/Ratings/RatingList/RatingDocs/Nirma_Limited_August_29_2016_RR.html
9 https://www.globalcapital.com/asia/article/28mswlxuvybg9cbp7jim8/asia-polls-and-awards/globalcapital-asia-regional-capital-markets-awards-2016-part-iii-bonds
10 https://www.ifre.com/download-public-attachment/e83133bb-4153-4efc-b769-e7609e063c73/ifr-asia-awards-roll-of-honour-2016
https://edition.pagesuite-professional.co.uk/html5/reader/production/default.aspx?pubname=&edid=7e584dde-7111-4b98-b833-73cbfd4f0f40

59

FINANCING DECISION AT BLACKGOLD PETROLEUM COMPANY LTD

Corporate Finance vs Project Finance

In June 2019, Ray Price and Mihir Taneja of BlackGold Petroleum Company Ltd (BPCL) were working on a note that would guide the choice between corporate finance and project finance for funding BPC's future investments. Ray was the head of Structured Finance, and Mihir was the Senior Financial Advisor working directly under him at BPCL.

BPCL was formed by the merger between Black Panther Oil Company Ltd (BPOCL) and Fossil Gold Petroleum Company Ltd (FGPCL). Post-merger, legacy shareholders of FGPC retained 47% in BPC, whereas BPOC shareholders had 53% ownership.

In 2019, BPOCL earned Rs 100 billion on revenue of Rs 1.2 trillion and assets of Rs 600 billion. During the same period, FGPCL earned Rs 60 billion on revenue of Rs 700 billion and assets of Rs 300 billion. Both firms were prominent integrated Oil and Gas business players with a significant presence in Exploration and Production (E&P), Refining and Marketing (R&M) and Petrochemicals with predominant E&P business.

While the firm decided to follow a relatively decentralised approach to managing the business, they agreed on centralised finance and HR functions. The centralised finance function would give better control over treasury management, risk management, and financial execution. Mark Ramprakash, Chief Financial Officer (CFO) of BPOCL, continued as CFO of the combined entity. Thomas Cook, then CFO of FGPCL, agreed to stay on as Treasury and Group Vice-President, Finance, in the merged entity. He was second in command in the finance group.

Besides following a typical organisation structure for the finance function (see Exhibit 59.1), BPCL allowed the Investment and Financing groups to

DOI: 10.4324/9781032724478-66

EXHIBIT 59.1 Post-Merger Organisational Chart for BPCL's Finance Function

Chief Financial Officer
Mark Ramprakash

Treasurer and Group Vice President – Finance
Thomas Cook

Business Services
- Financial Skills
- Business Insurance
- Financial Engineering
- Banking Projects
- Structured Finance – Ray Price
  - Sr. Financial Advisor – Mihir Taneja

Treasury Operations

Corporate Services
- Group Finance
- Banking Relations
- Equity Operations
- Enterprise Risk Mgmt.
- Insurance

Source: Prepared by authors.

function independently. Both BPOCL and FGPCL had maintained financing and investing as two independent functions. The job of the investment group was to evaluate and recommend capital investment proposals submitted by the firm's global subsidiaries and division based on graded project cost of the capital-based hurdle rate. The financing division had to ensure that none of the attractive investment proposals deprived funding. They would look for opportunities to raise funds at favourable terms using a mix of equity, debt, and hybrid instruments depending on financial market conditions. There were times when the financing group would have raised significant capital but were no attractive investment or acquisition opportunity to deploy it. In such times, the treasury management team would proactively manage surplus liquidity by investing them in marketable securities ensuring good yield without taking undue risk.

BPCL: Integration of Finance Function

While the integration of two firms was underway, including finance, the immediate priority was to align the financing policy of the combined entity.

Both BPOCL and FGPCL were major partners (both owned 15% each) of a large unincorporated consortium that have won the E&P mandate in an oil-rich but politically volatile region of West Africa. The total estimated investment required for the project was Rs 250 billion, spread over two phases. The first phase of initial exploration and early oil of project with investments of Rs 100 billion was over, and while BPOCL used corporate finance for its share of investments, FGPCL joined two other players to finance their share using project finance based on their share of expected cash flows from the project. Now that the next phase of Rs 150 billion of investment was due, BPCL as a combined entity required to invest Rs 45 billion, and they had to decide whether to go with project finance, corporate finance, or a mix of both.

To address this challenge Thomas Cook asked Ray Price to develop a report that would guide future financing choices at BPCL. Thomas asked Mihir to collate the information on instances when BPOCL and FGPCL used project finance and projects where project finance was a norm rather than an exception. Mihir's investigation revealed some interesting insights.

Corporate Finance vs Project Finance

Mihir proposed the following working definition for project finance.

> *Project Finance, in which lenders are dependent on assets and cash flows of the project for interest and loan repayment as opposed to corporate finance, where lenders have recourse to assets and cash flows of sponsor's assets and cash flows and are not entirely dependent on project success. Hence Project Finance is non-recourse finance.*

While this definition was not perfect, as in some cases, project lenders were secured by corporate guaranteed by the sponsor to a certain extent; such instances are few and far between. Based on the comprehensive study and internal discussions, Mihir noted that incorporated joint venture structure was typical in Power Plants and Petrochemicals. In contrast, unincorporated joint ventures were common in the E&P business, similar to the West African consortium, to which BPCL was a part. There too, lenders would fund projects with proven reserves and at the development and production stage. Most lenders would never agree to support the exploration-stage projects (Exhibits 59.2, 59.3, and 59.4 show illustrative corporate finance, project finance in incorporated JV, and project finance in unincorporated JV, respectively.)

Based on inputs from Mihir and his assessment, Thomas listed down the following costs and benefits of project finance.

EXHIBIT 59.2 Corporate Finance Model

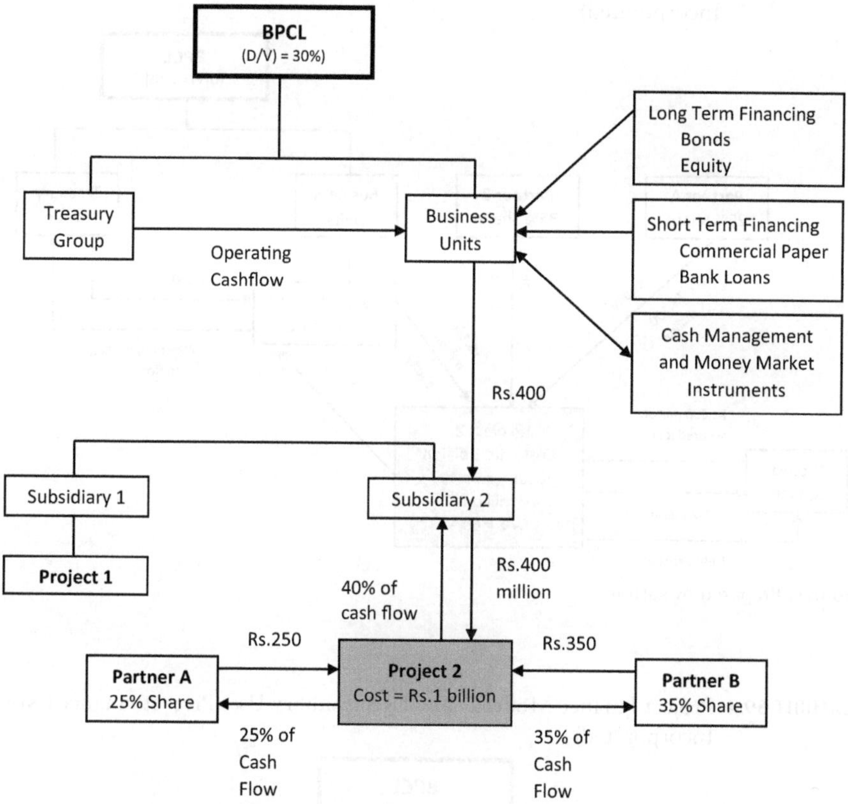

BPCL
(D/V) = 30%)
Long Term Financing
Bonds
Equity
Treasury Group
Business Units
Operating Cashflow
Short Term Financing
Commercial Paper
Bank Loans
Cash Management and Money Market Instruments
Rs.400
Subsidiary 1
Subsidiary 2
Project 1
Rs.400 million
40% of cash flow
Rs.250
Rs.350
Partner A
25% Share
Project 2
Cost = Rs.1 billion
Partner B
35% Share
25% of Cash Flow
35% of Cash Flow

Source: Prepared by authors.

The Costs of Project Finance

Higher financing cost: Given the non-recourse nature of financing, the interest cost for project finance would be consistently higher, as high as 200 to 350 bps based on available data, especially for reputed borrowers like BPCL.

Other costs: Financial advisors cost, legal fees of creating an SPV, project report costs, etc. All these would add anywhere between 50 to 100 basis points depending on the size of the project and financing required.

Structuring costs: In multiparty joint ventures, especially with heterogeneous partners, project financed deal might take longer than corporate-financed deal, and such delay might reduce the NPV of the project.

Loss of managerial flexibility: Project finance comes with a lot of restrictive covenants, and that takes away managerial flexibility of bringing new partners, changing the scope of the project, selling of assets, or making swift

EXHIBIT 59.3 Project Finance Model 1: Project Uses Project Finance (Project Incorporated)

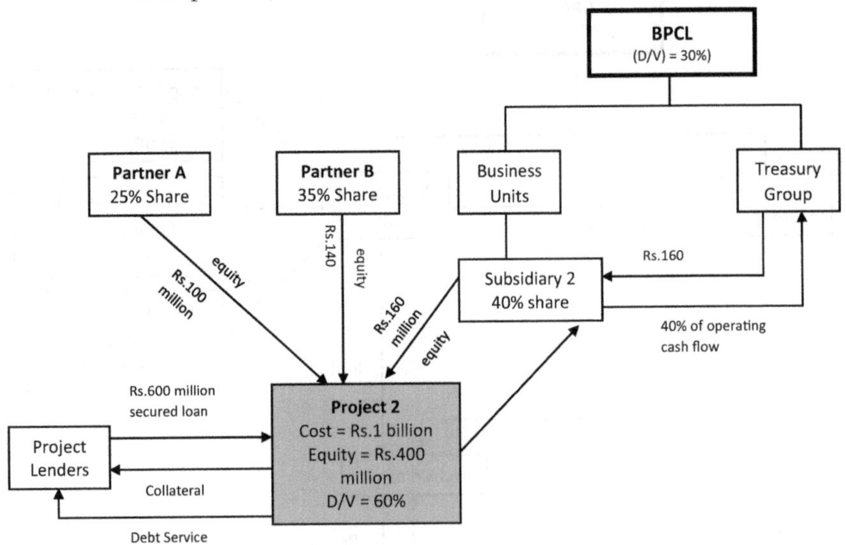

Source: Prepared by suthors.

EXHIBIT 59.4 Project Finance Model 2: BPCL's Subsidiary Uses Project Finance (Not Incorporated)

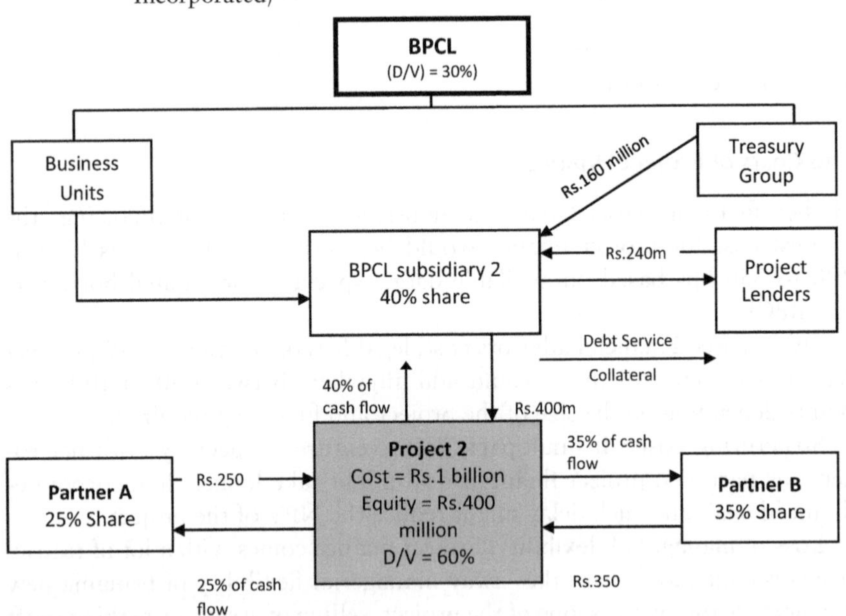

Source: Prepared by authors.

changes to respond to contingencies. Such loss of flexibility results in eventual financial implications.

Greater disclosure to lenders: Sometimes, project finance requires too much information to be shared with lenders too soon, and despite non-disclosure agreements, some confidential and strategic information might end up reaching competitors, and that might lead to loss of first-mover or competitive advantage. If the project was internally funded or used general-purpose corporate finance, project-specific detailed information might not be required to be shared.

The Benefits of Project Financing

Risk Sharing: The most significant benefit of project financing is risk-sharing. The project financing allows the firm to "walk away from the projects if projects failed. It would be handy if the firm pursued mega projects or disproportionately high-risk projects. Such projects might provide high positive NPV but carry significant tail risk. Firms have to give a pass to such projects or assume extreme tail risk. Project finance allows the firm to pursue such projects independently or with heterogeneous partners and still ring-fence the firm's assets. Such benefit is essential for a small firm with a low credit profile; whether a reputed firm like BPCL could exercise such an option hurting overall corporate image was a question mark.

Preserves firm's debt capacity: Subject to accounting regime, project finance debt might remain off balance sheet and to that extent preserves firms' debt capacity in terms of borrowing more funds without violating lenders' leverage ceiling norms. But, of course, it depends on whether rating agencies and analysts take a comprehensive look at the firm's businesses or look at the corporate balance sheet only.

Higher interest tax shields: Projects' financed structure have higher leverage than sponsoring firm. Such a difference in leverage might arise due to the firm's desire to exploit attractive investment opportunities using debt without putting the corporate balance sheet at risk. However, BPCL track leverage at the consolidated level rather than the project level and to that extent, debt at the project level or the firm level was treated in the same manner.

Reduced tax rates or tax holidays: Projects in infrastructure, healthcare, renewable energy and many other areas are on the priority list and hence offered benefits of lower taxes or tax holidays. While governments might provide such benefits to a dedicated SPV and not the firm, it might not be contingent to the way firms funded such projects.

Better risk allocation: Project financing allocates risks better among all related parties – mainly political risk and completion risk.

Flexibility to pursue high-risk projects: Many firms use project finance to pursue large-scale investment in new markets, new technology, or industry.

Project finance allows bringing in experienced partners in these domains, and it brings discipline in execution and results in swifter decision-making. While large firms can acquire or hire such expertise, it is a big advantage for smaller firms. The biggest benefit of project finance is to mitigate country risk.

Project Finance at BPCL

Thomas and Mihir concluded that while project finance might benefit many firms, the sheer size, reputation, technical expertise, financing flexibility, and experience in the oil and gas business that BPCL had, project finance costs would outweigh its benefits. Accordingly, they suggested that BPCL should use project finance as an exception rather than a rule for the projects that met the following criteria.

Mega projects: Mega projects might cause significant damage to the firm's credit profile or, in extreme cases, its survival if failed. Both BPOCL and FGPCL kept 10% of the asset size as the definition for considering the project as a mega project. Mega projects should be considered for funding using project finance, especially with co-related cash flows to the main business.

Project in politically volatile regions: Large firms like BPCL might mitigate most risks on their own; projects in politically volatile areas with high country risk might pose different challenges. Lack of developed regulatory or legal regime and contract enforcement mechanisms would always be a good idea to use project finance with the presence of a multilateral lending organisation to mitigate political risks. The presence of multiple players might put enough pressure on local authorities to take any adverse unilateral action against the project.

JV with heterogeneous partners: Many projects in politically volatile regions, including West Africa, required heterogeneous partners to mitigate non-financial risks, partners with a weak credit profile, including host governments, might find it difficult to mobilise their share of investments. For example, suppose senior partners such as BPCL opts for corporate finance. In that case, other partners with a weak credit profile or small size might not be able to mobilise their share of funds or raise funds at terms that may jeopardise the interest of the entire consortium. That, in turn, results in endless litigations. So with the projects with heterogeneous partners with a weak credit profile, senior partners should take the lead in mobilising funds for the consortium using project finance even if such a project might not meet the other specified criteria for the use of project finance.

Questions

1. What do you understand by Project Finance? How is it different from corporate finance?

2. What are the costs and benefits of project finance?
3. Do you consider project finance as one of the robust risk management tools?
4. What do you understand by the "risk sharing" and "walk away" options in project finance? Why would that be not a significant benefit for BPCL?
5. Why was BPCL averse to the use of project finance despite multiple advantages?
6. Under which exceptional situations would BPCL go for project financing?
7. How would you want BPCL to fund its share in the second phase of the West Africa E&P consortium? Internal funds/corporate finance, project finance or a combination? Explain your choice.

60

POWERGRID INVIT

What Is in It for the Issuer and Investors?

April 29, 2021, 8.00 a.m., Aarti Pradhan, Senior Analyst, Alternative Investments at GrowYourMoney (GYM) Investment advisors, saw a missed call from Prapti Sinha, a first-generation entrepreneur and one of the biggest clients of GYM. GrowYourMoney was a Mumbai-based Investment Advisory firm offering fee-only investment advice.

Before Aarti could call back, Prapti called her again at 8.30 a.m. She was a little upset that GYM did not share any advice on investing in the InvIT IPO of Power Grid Corporation Ltd. (PGCIL), opening from April 29, 2021. Aarti explained to Prapti that, given that Investors' experience from InvITs in India had been a mixed bag, GYM wanted to wait for a response to the IPO before recommending it to its clients (see Exhibit 60.1 for the Indian InvITs performance).

While Aarti promised to share GYM's IPO note on PGCIL InvIT, Prapti had several questions. She requested for telephonic conversation to understand a relatively new investment product for Indian Investors.

Prapti: What is an InvIT?

Aarti: InvITs enable investors to invest in infrastructure projects directly. InvIT is created by an infrastructure company carving out income-generating operating infrastructure assets and transferring them to a special purpose vehicle (SPV). This SPV, in turn, issues units to the investors and will get a share of income generated by these assets. The issuing company, known as the sponsor, no longer legally owns the assets. The SPV, usually incorporated as a trust, becomes the legal owner of the assets, and unitholders, just like mutual fund investors, become the beneficiary owners of

DOI: 10.4324/9781032724478-67

EXHIBIT 60.1 Performance of Listed InvITs in India

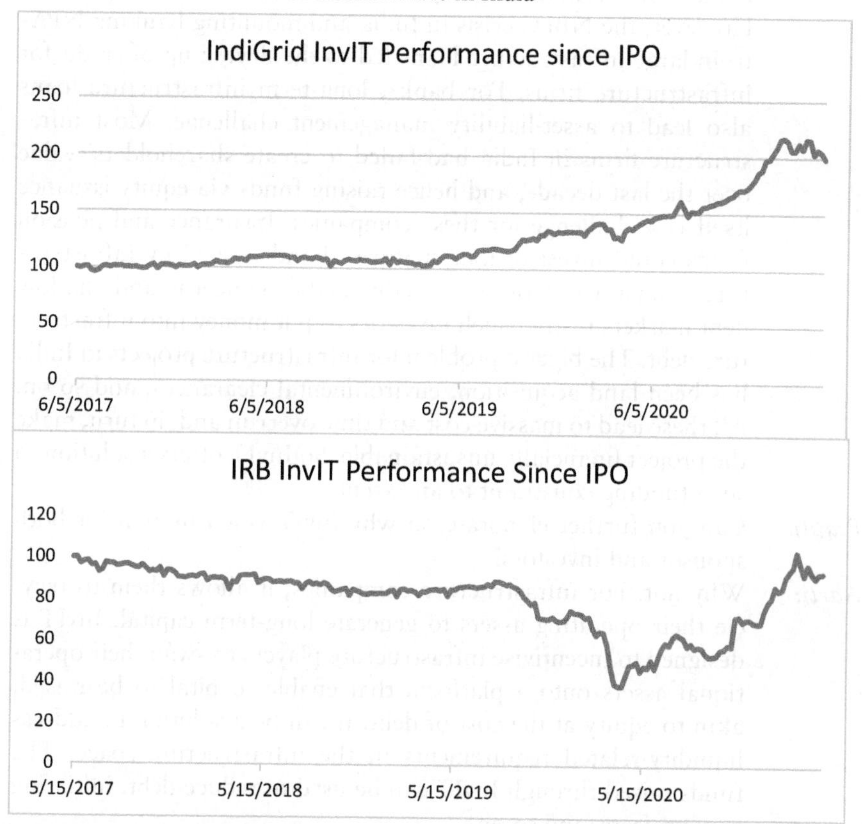

Source: Prepared by authors based on data from Yahoo Finance.

the income generated by these assets. The investors might receive cash flows in the form of dividend, interest, and capital repayment. According to Indian regulations, InvIT has to distribute income to unitholders at least once in a quarter. The InvIT will pay at least 90% of the cash available for distribution to its unitholders. It is a win–win outcome for both investors and issuers as investors can invest in a part of an infrastructure company asset.

Prapti: Why do we need InvIT in the first place?

Aarti: As you know, India needs massive capital spending on infrastructure. India has been one of the fastest-growing economies; it needs to ramp up its infrastructure spending. The Government of India has set an ambitious target of spending Rs 111 lakh crore over the next five years in 2019, which means Rs 22.2 lakh crore per annum. However, it has been able to spend only about Rs 9.5 lakh crore annually. Non-Banking Finance Companies (NBFCs) and banks offered significant debt funding for infrastructure projects. However, the NBFC crisis in India and mounting banking NPAs from large infrastructure loans led to the drying up of credit for infrastructure firms. For banks, long-term infrastructure loans also lead to asset-liability management challenge. Most infrastructure firms in India had failed to create shareholders' value over the last decade, and hence raising funds via equity issuance itself is a challenge for these companies. Insurance and pension funds could invest in long-maturity bonds issued by infrastructure companies. However, credit quality concerns and shallow debt markets restrict such investors to put money into infrastructure debt. The biggest problem for infrastructure projects in India has been land acquisition, environmental clearances, and so on. All these lead to massive cost and time overrun and, in turn, make the project financially unsustainable. So InvIT offers a solution to such funding constraint to an extent.

Prapti: Can you further elaborate on why InvIT is a win–win for both sponsor and investors?

Aarti: Why not. For infrastructure companies, it allows them to recycle their operating assets to generate long-term capital. InvIT is designed to incentivise infrastructure players to swap their operational assets onto a platform that enables capital to be raised, akin to equity at the cost of debt. It can be a solution to address liquidity-related requirements in the infrastructure space. The funds raised through InvIT can be used to reduce debt, initiating new projects, and so on.

From an investor's perspective, it allows yield-seeking institutional and individual investors an opportunity to invest in operating infrastructure assets, which are primarily free from development risk, price and demand risks. In addition, investors are also protected from capital misallocation by the firm. That is why I am saying it's a win–win for both sponsors and investors.

Prapti: Got it. Can you say something about the performance of InvITs in India?

Aarti: Well, private placement and public IPO, both routes are used for launching InvIT. We have seen a total of seven InvITs in road, power, and gas transmission and telecom towers space. Two of them are listed. IRB InvIT in road space and IndiGrid Investment trust in power transmission space. The performance of publicly traded InvITs is instead a mixed bag. While IndiGrid Investment Trust has delivered a phenomenal return to investors, inherent challenges in the road sector have led to the poor performance of IRB InvIT. So, it depends on the underlying operating assets, and it requires careful analysis before investing. But that is true for any investment.

Prapti: Ok. So good infrastructure assets and a competent, experienced sponsor is the key to InvIT's success. How do you rate PGCIL as a sponsor?

Aarti: PGCIL is the largest electric transmission company in India, backed by the Government of India. It is the third-largest power transmission company globally, engaged in bulk power transmission across different states in India. The company is also

EXHIBIT 60.2 Financial Overview of PGCIL and SPV Group

Summary Income Statements			
Annual	Mar-20	Mar-19	Mar-18
Sales	37,743	35,059	29,953
Other Income	927	602	476
Total Income	38,670	35,661	30,430
Total Expenditure	14,726	17,906	9,783
EBIT	23,944	17,754	20,646
Interest	9,509	8,736	7,324
Tax	3,530	-886	5,266
Net Profit	10,904	9,904	8,056
Summary Balance Sheets			
Share Capital	5,231	5,231	5,231
Reserves and Surplus	59,463	53,856	49,194
Current Liabilities	40,997	42,071	33,073
Other Liabilities	1,50,960	1,46,197	1,37,816
Total Liabilities	2,56,653	2,47,357	2,25,316
Assets			
Fixed Assets	2,16,289	2,10,370	1,93,866
Current Assets	28,234	25,745	23,471
Other Assets	12,128	11,241	7,977
Total Assets	2,56,653	2,47,357	2,25,316
Other Info			
Contingent Liabilities	19,993	19,742	33,954
Summary Cash Flow Statements			
Operating Activities	31,040	23,380	22,710
Investing Activities	–11,042	–18,836	–25,701
Financing Activities	–18,805	–2,430	1,284
Performance of SPV Group (IPA)			
Total Assets	6,821	7,000	6,505
Total Income	1,334	984	346
Total Expenses	847	636	217
PAT	379	248	114

Source: Prepared by authors based on company reports.

involved in consulting and telecom business. It is the third-largest public sector enterprise (PSE) in India by gross assets. The Government of India conferred Maharatna status to it in 2019. With consolidated net income of Rs 10,904 crore, total revenues of Rs 37,743 crore in FY20, and an asset base of Rs 2,56, 653 crore, PGCIL is in a great financial position except for its high financial leverage.[1]

Prapti: What are the Initial Portfolio Assets (IPA) transferred in PGCIL InvIT, and how long will it generate cash flows?

Aarti: PGCIL InvIT comprises five transmission assets transferred to the SPV group.

- Power Grid Vizag Transmission (PVTL).
- Power Grid Kala Amb Transmission (PKATL).
- Power Grid Warora Transmission (PWTL).
- Power Grid Parli Transmission (PPTL).
- Power Grid Jabalpur Transmission (PJTL).

These assets have long-term transmission contracts with an average term of 32 years and are relatively free from development, demand, or price risk.[2]

Prapti: What will be the holding structure of the InvIT post IPO?

Aarti: Power Grid Corporation of India Ltd (PGCIL) will continue holding 26% of IPA directly. The remaining 74% has been transferred to the InvIT. PGCIL will have a 15% stake, and the InvIT investors will have an 85% stake in the InvIT. The entire InvIT will be run by Power Grid Unchahar Transmission Ltd (PUTL), which will act as the Investment Manager. PGCIL will be the project manager, and IDBI Trusteeship Services (ITSL) will be the trustee to the InvIT.[3]

Prapti: How is the Power Grid InvIT a profitable investment for an investor?

Aarti: Expected contractual cash flows from InvIT IPAs will result in an 11.4% annual yield assuming InvIT distributes 90% of distributable cash flows. It can distribute cash to unitholders in the form of interest, dividends, and capital repayment.[4] However, if you do not get an allotment in IPO and the issue lists at a significant premium on stock exchanges, one might earn a lower yield.

Prapti: Oh. That is an excellent yield in today's low-interest-rate environment. Are there any risks involved in this InvIT investment?

Aarti: As such, major credit-rating agencies have assigned AAA rating to this issue. However, InvIT as a product is still new to India and is still evolving; projections might not be accurate due to a lack of historical data. The risks include faster adoption of

EXHIBIT 60.3 Post IPO Structure and InvIT Structure

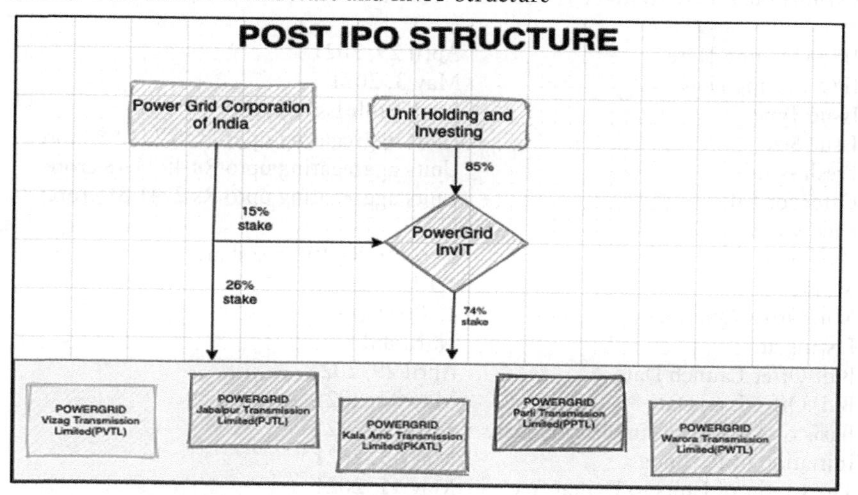

Source: Company prospectus.

EXHIBIT 60.4 Yield Calculation for the InvIT

Particulars	*Amount*
Cash flow scheduled over the next three years	1150.00
Assuming 90% distribution	1035.00
Equity stake	9100.00
Yield	11.4%

Source: IIFL Capital IPO Note.

renewal energy sources, re-negotiation of transmission charges, operational and political risks, etc. But as I mentioned earlier, the SPV group is mainly free from development, demand and price risks.

Prapti: Where are they going to invest the proceeds of this issue?

Aarti: The company will use the Offer for Sale portion to invest in other projects. It will loan out the fresh issue portion to the IPAs at a rate of 14.5% p.a. to pre-pay or repay the existing debt against them.[5] InvIT can also raise additional capital via rights issue (Just done by IndiGrid InvIT), private placement, raise debt. etc., to acquire other assets.

Prapti: Thanks, Aarti, for taking time early in the morning. Now share with me the terms of the offer and timelines of the issue. I will wait for your note before applying.

Aarti: Yes, sending it in the next five minutes.[6]

EXHIBIT 60.5 PGCIL InvIT IPO Offer Terms and Timelines

IPO Opening Date	April 29, 2021
IPO Closing Date	May 3, 2021
Issue Type	Book Built Issue InvIT
Issue Size	Units aggregating up to Rs 7734.99 crore
Fresh Issue	Units aggregating upto Rs 4993.48 crore
Offer for Sale	Units aggregating upto Rs 2741.51 crore
Face Value	NA
IPO Price	Rs 99 to Rs 100 per share
Market Lot	1,100 shares
Min Order Quantity	1,100 shares
Listing at	NSE, BSE
Bid/ Offer Launch Date	April 29, 2021
Bid/ Offer Last Date	May 03, 2021
Basis of Allotment Finalisation Date	May 10, 2021
Initiation of Refunds	May 11, 2021
The Credit of Units to Demat Acc	May 11, 2021
IPO Listing Date	May 17, 2021

Source: Company Prospectus and NSE website.

Questions

1. What do you understand about InvIT?
2. Compare InvIT as a source of fund vs. equity and debt.
3. How do you compare InvIT as an investment option compared to equity and debt for an investor looking to invest in an Infrastructure company?
4. In India, for an equity IPO minimum subscription value is Rs 15,000, but for this InvIT, it's close to Rs 1,10,000? Why? Do you think it deprives small investors of participating in this attractive investment vehicle?

Notes

1 See Exhibit 60.2 for Financial Overview of PGCIL and InvIT SPV Group.
2 Source: PGCIL InvIT Prospectus.
3 See Exhibit 60.3 for the Post IPO ownership structure of InvIT.
4 See Exhibit 60.24 for expected yield calculations.
5 Elara Capital Power Grid InvIT Note.
6 See Exhibit 60.3 for IPO offer terms and timelines.

INDEX

For Product Safety Concerns and Information please contact our EU representative GPSR@taylorandfrancis.com Taylor & Francis Verlag GmbH, Kaufingerstraße 24, 80331 München, Germany